The Youth Gang Problem

The Two-body Problem

The Youth Gang Problem

A Community Approach

IRVING A. SPERGEL

New York   Oxford
OXFORD UNIVERSITY PRESS
1995

Oxford University Press

Oxford   New York   Toronto
Delhi   Bombay   Calcutta   Madras   Karachi
Kuala Lumpur   Singapore   Hong Kong   Tokyo
Nairobi   Dar es Salaam   Cape Town
Melbourne   Auckland   Madrid

and associated companies in
Berlin   Ibadan

Copyright © 1995 by Oxford University Press, Inc.

198 Madison Avenue, New York, New York 10016-4314

Library of Congress Cataloging-in-Publication Data
Spergel, Irving A.
The youth gang problem : a community approach / Irving A. Spergel.
p. cm.
Includes bibliographical references and indexes.
ISBN 0-19-507066-6.
ISBN 0-19-509203-1 (pbk.)
1. Gangs—United States.
2. Juvenile delinquency—United States.
3. Juvenile delinquents—United States.
4. United States—Social conditions—1980–
5. United States—Social policy—1993–
I. Title.
HV6439.U5S64 1995
364.1'06'0973—dc20
94-8227

3 5 7 9 8 6 4 2

Printed in the United States of America
on acid-free paper

*This book is dedicated to the
memory of Bertha*

Preface

This book is an attempt to rethink general gang policy and program experience as well as research findings, particularly in light of my four decades of observation of gang youths and gang problems especially in Chicago, Los Angeles, New York, and elsewhere in this country and abroad. Many of the ideas in the book were developed in the course of a recent four and half year research and development program in which I was principal investigator (supported by the Office of Juvenile Justice and Delinquency Prevention, Bureau of Justice Programs, U.S. Justice Department), and a Gang Violence Reduction Program with older hard-core gang youths in Chicago, which I am currently coordinating and researching (funded by the Illinois Criminal Justice Information Authority).

I believe that while there has been much continuity over the years as to the causes and responses to the problem, gangs and gang violence have become increasingly complex, lethal, and resistant to prevention and control. A promising approach must be based on careful description and theoretically relevant understanding of gang phenomena, as well as on systematic testing of a range of interventions in particular social situations. Theory, research, and program experience must interact if we are to do a better job of dealing with gang problems. Neither social disorganization, underclass, nor poverty theory alone explains the scope and nature of delinquent or criminal gang association and gang crime. Social disorganization or lack of integration of essential elements of a local community system provides the basic stimulus for the formation of youth gangs. Lack of legitimate opportunity and the presence of alternate criminal opportunities are more likely to explain the character and scope of gang behavior.

Media reporting has also not adequately reflected the character of the problem, for example that Latino gangs are generally more violent than African-American gangs and that gang violence and gang-member drug trafficking are not necessarily closely related. Gang violence also is largely intraracial or intraethnic. There is evidence, however, that racism acts indirectly and powerfully on the creation and development of the gang problem, particularly the African-American problem. While racism can contribute directly to minority group segregation and poverty, and to conditions of social disorganization that in turn more directly precipitate development of gang behavior, desegregation or disruption of racist patterns in housing and educaiton may under conditions of inappropriate social policy and programming also lead to gang formation and gang violence.

Why one youth becomes a gang member and another, from the same family or community, does not is far from clear. What distinguishes the delinquent gang from delinquent group adaptation must be addressed. Also, not all delinquents are gang members, and not all gang members are delinquents. Of special consideration for purposes of policy and program development is the function that gangs play in satisfying social needs for structure and control and psychological needs of gang youths for personal identity and self-esteem. A coherent conceptual and policy basis must be created so that communities, their organizations, and citizen groups can better understand, prevent, and control the gang problem. Development of this basis is a central purpose of the book.

Key strategies of local community mobilization and the sufficient provision of social and economic opportunities in appropriate interactive form must be devised relevant to the nature and severity of the problem and the structure of social institutions in particular communities. However, local policy and programs are inevitably related, directly and indirectly, to larger national issues of racial segregation, immigration, illegitimate values, lack of jobs, defective educational systems, and increased access by youths to sophisticated weaponry. Furthermore, specific types of gangs, gang members, and gang incidents need to be targeted, and appropriate resources and integrated organizational arrangements created distinctively in different communities. There is no single strategy and no easy solution to the gang problem. Different strategies must be combined in meaningful ways, and they must be honestly and systematically tested.

Arrangement of Chapters

The book is divided into two parts, I. *Description and Analysis* (Chapters 1 through 9), and II. *Policy and Program* (Chapters 10 through 17). Chapter 1, *Introduction: Comparative and Historical Perspectives*, is a brief review of the problem across time, cultures, and societies. Chapter 2, *Research Limitations: Data Sources and Definitions*, is concerned with the development of a satisfactory empirical and definitional framework for the problem being described and analyzed. Chapter 3 describes the *scope and seriousness of the gang problem*. It provides best estimates, with special emphasis on violent gang activity. Chapter 4, *Gangs, Drugs, and Violence*, examines the complex relationship of gang violence and sale and use of drugs by gangs and gang members. Chapter 5 focuses on *gang member demographics and gang subcultures*. Distinctive race and ethnicity, age, and gender characteristics of gang problems are described. Chapter 6 deals with *the structure of the gang* as it appears to be evolving over time, and Chapter 7 is concerned with *the gang member experience*, that is, the character and process of gang life between the time gang members join and leave the gang. Chapter 8, *The Ecological Context*, examines the institutional environment that creates and facilitates gang development, with special attention to family, school, local politics, and prisons. Chapter 9, *Youth Gangs and Organized Crime*, points to the processes by which youth gang behavior and adult criminality become interrelated over time and sometimes interdependent in different contexts.

The second part of the book begins the analysis of what has been and what should be done about the problem. Chapter 10, *Theoretical Perspectives*, develops a bridge between the descriptive and analytical materials and policy and program issues. Chapter 11, *Planning for Youth Gang Control and Violence Reduction*, is a framework for action and analyzes five key strategies, emphasizing community mobilization and social and economic opportunities provision. Chapter 12, *Criminal Justice System: The Police*, is a discussion of traditional police suppression policy and practice, but also of evolving community policing and social outreach approaches relevant to the problem. Chapter 13, *Prosecution, Defense, and the Judiciary*, centers attention on three important units of the ciminal justice system and especially on evolving procedures and issues of effectiveness and politics. Chapter 14, *Probation, Corrections, and Parole—After Care*, continues the discussion with emphasis on the creative use of both justice system sanctions and social support or service procedures, after adjudication, required to deal with gang youths. Chapter 15, *Social Intervention*, analyzes past programs and evolving policies and procedures of social support and supervision by community-based agencies, with special attention to their effects, on the basis of evaluation research. In Chapter 16, *Social Opportunities: Education and Jobs*, emphasis is on the need to develop more appropriate educational, training, and employment contexts for socializing gang youths and young adults and thereby more effectively mainstreaming them into conventional society. Finally, Chapter 17, *Local Community Mobilization and Evolving National Policy*, summarizes policies required for a more promising approach to the gang problem, at both local community and national levels.

Chicago
March 1994

I. A. S.

Acknowledgments

I owe debts of gratitude to many persons whose ideas, research, policy suggestions, program experiences, and special moral and financial support have influenced the development of this book. My early obligations are for the thoughts and guidance of Lloyd E. Ohlin and Richard A. Cloward, as well as the ideas of Frederic M. Thrasher and Clifford R. Shaw. For many years, the empirical findings, program critiques, and policy recommendations of Malcolm W. Klein and Walter B. Miller have provided a reality test of my own observations and analyses. Some recent researchers and theorists to whom I am indebted are Joan Moore, John Hagedorn, Terry Williams, Jeffrey Fagan, Ko-Lin Chin, Martin Sánchez Jankowski, Carl S. Taylor, and James F. Short.

Dr. Candice Kane, a criminal justice policy expert and associate director, Illinois Criminal Justice Information Authority, has been an extraordinary and long-time supporter of my research and field efforts. I am indebted to James C. Howell, Pamela Swain, Douglas Donahue, Douglas Dodge, and Leonard Johnson of the Office of Juvenile Justice and Delinquency Prevention and the Bureau of Justice Assistance, U.S. Justice Department. Many of the ideas in this book stem from earlier versions of documents produced as part of the Juvenile Gang Suppression and Intervention Program sponsored by the Office of Juvenile Justice and Delinquency Prevention.

Many hard-working colleagues in our various projects have made me the beneficiary of their experiences, insights, and analyses. They include especially C. David Curry and Ron Chance. Recent mentors and colleagues in the struggle to understand and do something about the problem have included Lawrence Bobrowski, Phil Chomiak, Carolyn Block, Robert Dart, Wesley McBride, Miguel Duran, Michael Genelin, Robert Jackson, Edward Pleines, Roberto Caldero, James Rosado, Frank Perez, Alvin Delk, Angelo Torres, Roy Martinez, Javier Avila, Susan Grossman, and Josh Levy, among others.

I could not have persisted in the development of this complex and exhaustive work without excellent administrative and technical assistance from Keith Madderom, Louis Arata, Elizabeth McGiffin, Betty Bradley, Laura Anderson, and especially from Edwina Simmons, at the School of Social Service Administration, University of Chicago. Special thanks for their patience and editorial help are also owed to David Roll, Melinda Wirkus, Leslie Reindl, and Susan Hannan at Oxford University Press.

Finally, this book would not have been written without the loving support of my sons, Barry, Mark, and Danny, and my very close friend, Annot Littleton.

The projects on which this work was based were supported in part by awards from the Office of Juvenile Justice and Delinquency Prevention, Office of Justice Programs, U.S. Department of Justice. Points of view or opinions contained within this book are those of the author and do not necessarily represent the official position or policies of the U.S. Department of Justice.

Contents

I Description and Analysis

1. Introduction: Comparative and Historical Perspectives *3*

    Gang Problems in Other Countries and Times *3*
    Gangs in the United States before the 1990s *6*
    The Contemporary Gang Scene in the United States *9*

2. Research Limitations: Data Sources and Definitions *12*

    The Limits of Data *12*
    Solving the Definitional Problem *16*

3. Scope and Seriousness of the Gang Problem *26*

    Extent of the Problem *26*
    Youth Gang Violence *33*

4. Gangs, Drugs, and Violence *43*

    Gang Drug Use and Trafficking: Historical Perspectives *43*
    Increase in Gang Member Drug Trafficking *45*
    Gang Drug Trafficking and Criminal Organization *47*
    Changing Relationships of Gangs and Drug Dealing *49*
    Gang Violence, Drug Use, and Drug Trafficking *50*

5. Gang Member Demographics and Gang Subcultures *55*

    Demographics *55*
    Gang Subcultures and Social Contexts *61*

6. The Structure of the Gang *70*

    Gang Organization and Community Structure *70*
    Development of Gang Organization *71*

Patterns of Organization of the Gang   *74*
Evolving Gang Organization   *77*
Limitations of the Idea of Gang Organization   *79*
Cliques or Subgroups   *81*
Types of Gang Members   *83*
Leaders and Core Gang Members   *85*
Territory   *87*

7. The Gang Member Experience   *90*

Joining the Gang   *90*
Group Processes   *96*
Leaving the Gang   *104*

8. The Ecological Context   *110*

Local Context and Gang Development   *111*
Family   *113*
School   *116*
Politics   *120*
Prisons   *125*

9. Youth Gangs and Organized Crime   *129*

Defining Organized Crime   *129*
The Evolving Youth Gang–Organized-Crime
  Connection   *131*
Transformation of the Black Street Gang   *134*
Hispanic Youth Gang–Criminal-Organization
  Connections   *137*
Asian-American, Pacific, and Asian Gang
  Criminal-Organization Connections   *138*

II Policy and Program

10. Theoretical Perspectives   *145*

Poverty-related Theories   *145*
Social Disorganization   *152*
Racism   *161*
Personal Disorganization   *163*

11. Planning for Youth Gang Control and Violence Reduction *171*

Historical Considerations *171*
Elements of a Community Planning and
Mobilization Process *178*

12. Criminal Justice System: The Police *189*

Suppression: "Recent" Traditional Law Enforcement
Approaches *189*
Emerging Police Approach *199*

13. Prosecution, Defense, and the Judiciary *208*

The Specialized Prosecution Strategy *209*
Defense Attorneys *216*
Court Attention to the Problem *219*

14. Probation, Corrections, and Parole—After Care *229*

Probation *230*
Corrections *235*
Parole—After Care *243*

15. Social Intervention *247*

Traditional Approaches: Street-Gang Work *248*
Recent Innovative Approaches *256*

16. Social Opportunities: Education and Jobs *262*

Macro Level Educational Perspective *263*
Local School Programs *267*
Macro Level Employment Perspective *272*
Local Employment *277*

17. Local Community Mobilization and Evolving National Policy *281*

Local Citizen and Organization Mobilization *281*
State-Level Mobilization *287*
Need for National Policy *290*

*Appendix A. Community Mobilization/Planning:
Selected Structure and Process Summary* *297*

*Appendix B. Nature and Level of Youth Gang Member
    Problems to Be Addressed   299*

*Appendix C. Selected Strategic Activities/Structures
    for Particular Settings (Organizations)   301*

Glossary and Discussion of Terms   309

References   313

Index   337

I

Description and Analysis

1

Introduction: Comparative and Historical Perspectives

This chapter provides a brief set of reference points for designating gang phenomena across contemporary societies and their course in our own urban history. Gangs function as a socializing institution when other institutions fail; they are defined as problems when they engage in violent and criminal activities. The youth gang is most likely to develop into a problem in social or organizational contexts, local communities, or societies that are undergoing extensive and precipitous change, often under deteriorating (but sometimes under improving) economic conditions. During such change social institutions are weak and unstable, and organizations may be poorly integrated and in conflict with each other. Basic youth socializing functions, especially those of social control and provision of economic opportunities or social status for males, cannot be carried out. Gangs then provide a certain degree of order, solidarity, excitement, and sometimes economic gain for their members. The costs, however, usually exceed benefits for the surrounding community and society, as well as for the youth themselves.

Gang Problems in Other Countries and Times

Youth gangs have existed in Western and Eastern societies for centuries. Most recently they have been reported in England, Scotland, Germany, Italy, Russia and other republics of the former Soviet Union, Bosnia (formerly part of Yugoslavia), Albania, Kenya, Tanzania, South Africa, Mexico, El Salvador, Brazil, Peru, Taiwan, South Korea, Japan, Hong Kong, Australia, New Zealand, the People's Republic of China, and Papua New Guinea (see, for example, Oschlies 1979; Specht 1987; Burns 1993). Youth gangs are present in socialist and free-market societies, in developing and developed countries.

In the 1600s, London was "terrorized by a series of organized gangs calling themselves the Mims, Hectors, Bugles, Dead Boys . . . who found amusement in breaking windows, demolishing taverns, assaulting the watch . . . The gangs also fought pitched battles among themselves dressed with colored ribbons to distinguish the different factions" (Pearson 1983, p. 188). In the seventeenth and eighteenth centuries, English gangs wore belts and metal pins with designs of serpents, hearts pierced with arrows, animals, and stars. More recently, gangs of youths set cars and a post office ablaze

3

and stoned police in a wave of urban violence and vandalism in northeast England. The rioting, which involved 500 youths, was variously attributed to "poverty, hardened criminals, and unseasonably hot weather" (*Chicago Tribune*, 1991).

During the Russian revolution of 1917, and particularly its aftermath, bands of children and youths roamed the countryside and urban centers, foraging for food, thieving, competing and in conflict with each other for the means to survive. In the course of recent upheavals, reports indicate the presence of gangs of youths and sometimes adult criminal organizations in Russia: "Ethnic violence has left at least 35 people dead in the Republic of Kirghizia . . . on Wednesday, with gangs of youths marauding on horseback . . . Soviet media . . . blamed the violence on widespread unemployment among youths in the region and general poverty . . . " (Associated Press, 1990).

A 1992 report indicates that with the "crumbling" of law enforcement and radical change of the economic structure in the former Soviet Union, gangs are proliferating:

> There are dozens of criminal gangs in Moscow, and the most effective are highly organized and violent. . . . Gangs work in many areas, including gambling, prostitution, rackets and narcotics . . . some have acquired a stranglehold on the distribution of essential goods and services. Many police are on gang payrolls; some officers even have quit the force to work for gangs full time. (Gallagher 1992)

An observer of the radical transition of Russian society from communism toward democracy and a free market economy concludes that control has shifted to a new criminal network, replacing the old communist structure. Russian crime, he claims, is organized in three large circles:

> The first is characterized by street fighting and gangsterism. . . .
>
> The second circle . . . is made up of well-organized groups who aim higher than street robberies and burglaries. They trade in arms, narcotics and raw materials like plutonium at home and abroad. . . .
>
> A third circle . . . a network of shady high-rolling entrepreneurs—often referred to as the Russian mafia [is] in league with corrupt officials. . . . This group might sometimes employ the services of the other two. (Zlobin 1994)

The 1990s resurgence of right-wing youth gangs in Germany is associated with rapid social and political changes, weakening social institutions, and growing poverty. Nevertheless, it is important to make distinctions between a neo-Nazi movement and frustrated violent youth or street groups. Lack of a stable political structure and absence of career routes and job opportunities seem largely to account for the development of youth gangs.

> Conversations with rightist youths here suggest that while most of them are frustrated, angry, and prepared for violence, they are largely without political ideology. Many are unemployed and come from families whose lives have been thrown into upheaval by the jarring changes that have followed German unification.
>
>   But a small number of young people here, perhaps only a few dozen, have schooled themselves with neo-Nazi propaganda and emerged as leaders of amorphous gangs that harass and beat foreigners.

In the old East Germany, kids had a path clearly laid out for them. They went to school, they were given a career, they were trained and then they went to work. . . . (Kinzer 1992)

Furthermore, an attack by one group——whether of the same or a different ethnicity or race——may call for a retaliatory attack: "Berlin-Germany's tough young Turks hang out in vigilante gangs with names like 'The 20 Boys' and the '36ers,' but it's a street variant of Newton's law of physics they observe: For each and every action by neo-Nazis, there will be an equal and opposite reaction by Turkish street gangs" (Shankar 1993).

The skinheads are present in many European countries, and their development is related both to a lack of adequate employment opportunities for lower-class youth, an influx of immigrant groups, and large-scale population increase in a particular area. "The growth of skinhead movements is partly a reaction to the presence of North and West Africans, who came to peddle their wares in the summer beaches and who inspire resistance, even hatred among some Italians. . . . The region has already changed markedly since the war. From 8,000 in 1944, Anzio's permanent population has risen to 37,000" (Cowell 1994).

The Yakuza gangs of Japan may be of special relevance for governmental and community response to the future development of youth and adult gangs in countries undergoing rapid social change. The Yakuza are structured to provide an opportunity for marginal persons to participate in society. They draw youths from the lowest strata of Japanese society, including "the failures and dropouts who refuse to accommodate themselves" to the very competitive and rigid structures of Japanese life and those "who have been rejected by the broader society and who find it difficult to find jobs" (Westerman and Burfeind 1991, p. 40).

The presence or extent of gang problems may be only partially related to the scope and severity of crime in general. The level of youth and adult crime activity is much lower in Japan than in America, but gangs——both youth and adult—— in Japan probably commit a larger relative proportion of total serious crime than in the United States. The rate of violent crime in the United States is about thirty times greater than it is in Japan. The Japanese Ministry of Justice estimates that 3,197 Boryokudan groups existed in 1988 with membership totaling 86,552, or about 0.07 percent of the total population (Westerman and Burfeind 1991, p. 31).

According to Westerman and Burfeind, in 1988 this small proportion of the total population was involved in 25.3 percent of all arrests for homicide, 22.8 percent of all assault, and 64.3 percent of all arrests for intimidation. Gang members were also responsible for 45.2 percent of all arrests for violation of stimulant drug laws and 31.1 percent of all arrests for firearms and sword violations (ibid.).

Of greatest concern to Japanese society, however, are the well-established adult Yakuza gangs. For example, in 1991 the largest of these gangs, Yamaguchi-gumi, consisted of over 100 gangs with subordinate gangs to total over 750 gangs in all, with an average of twenty-five to thirty members per gang. The total income of all Yakuza gangs in 1989 was estimated by the police to be 9.6 billion yen, generated from the sale of drugs, gambling and protection, and intervention in civil disputes. "Japan may be unique in the centrality of organized crime and the extent to which the underworld plays various essential and tacitly acknowledged economic and political roles at all levels of society." Yakuza gangs have been supported by both left-wing and right-wing political organizations (Delfs 1991, p. 28).

The transition of a primitive to a modern society—for example, Papua New Guinea with its 700 separate and tiny communities or states, each with its own language, customs, and traditional practices—has been accompanied by the development of street gangs and criminal organizations (Dorney 1990, p. 288). "Rascals" was a term first used to describe Port Moresby's youth gangs, which comprised young men who moved from rural areas to the city and became frustrated with their inability to find work. These gangs have consolidated and become highly organized "with [not only] a structure of command but blood initiation ceremonies in which members cut their palms and swear allegiance to the 'King' of the gang." Gang youths are sent out nightly to break in and steal; they are heavily involved in the drug trade; they have close links to some politicians and businessmen (ibid., pp. 300–301).

In New Zealand, minority or ethnic gangs are regarded as a major problem in the prisons.

> They behave as a cohesive group . . . are in conflict among themselves . . . and present a real danger to prison staff . . . a predominant gang can virtually run a wing of a prison . . . they adopt stand-over tactics against non-gang members, which results in many inmates seeking protective segregation where there is little available . . . the active recruitment of new members in the institution is a strong impediment to reintegrating inmates into a law-abiding life on release. (Roper 1988)

The development and interrelationship of youth gangs across cultures have not yet been adequately recognized. The presence and movement of youth gangs in one society clearly has implications for their development in another where population groups are increasingly mobile across country boundaries.

> As a result of a crackdown begun by U.S. immigration authorities 18 months ago, young Salvadorans who joined street gangs while living in tough neighborhoods in the United States are being picked up and deported. On returning to El Salvador, some re-create their gangs which are now terrorizing even parts of the country that escaped the civil war. . . .
>
> Officials now estimate that the number of gang members in El Salvador has grown to several thousands, most of whom have never been to the United States but joined gangs started by deportees. (O'Connor July 1994)

Gangs in the United States before the 1990s

Youth gangs existed in urban centers of the United States before the nineteenth century (Hyman 1984). "Nearly every nationality is represented in American gang history" (Haskins 1974, p. 7). Youth gangs in the nineteenth century were often associated, as they are now, with second- and sometimes later generation male adolescent and young adult immigrant groups or in-migrant groups (groups that move to a new part of the country) clustered in low-income neighborhoods of expanding or declining industrial or postindustrial urban centers.

The Five Points district of Manhattan was a poor but relatively quiet residential area until about 1820 when the first Irish immigrants settled there. The first gangs were established in the face of poverty, squalid conditions, and great prejudice. They were mainly young adults or in their late teens. Some of the gangs numbered in the hundreds; one gang claimed 1,200 members. They had distinctive names and dress and usually fought in their undershirts. "The Roach Guards wore a blue stripe on their pantaloons, the Dead Rabbits a red stripe . . . the True Blue Americans wore . . . stovepipe hats and ankle length frock coats." The weapons used included pistols and muskets, knives, brickbats, bludgeons, brass knuckles, ice picks, and pikes (Haskins 1974, p. 31).

The early Five Points gangs expanded to, or developed in, a nearby community, the Bowery. The Irish toughs hung out in the beer gardens, out of which emerged the largest and most famous of the gangs of the period, the Bowery Boys. The chief activity of the Bowery Boys was brawling with gangs of the adjoining area, mainly the Roach Guards and the Dead Rabbits. The latter two gangs sometimes combined forces to fight the Bowery Boys. "The most bitter and longest-lasting feud was between the Dead Rabbits and the Bowery Boys. From the 1830s to the 1860s hardly a week passed that the Dead Rabbits . . . did not engage in battle. Sometimes these battles lasted two or three days [with] endless melees of beating, maiming and murder . . . regiments of soldiers in full battle dress, marching through the streets to the scene of a gang melee, were not an uncommon sight in New York" (Haskins 1974, pp. 26–29).

An urban historian surveyed a single Philadelphia newspaper from 1836 to 1878 and identified fifty-two differently named local gangs. He stated that violent gangs existed because of the concentration of poor adolescents and young adults in certain of the city's wards, and that the pre-Civil War era of Philadelphia was, therefore, one of its most "gang-plagued" (Johnson in Davis and Haller 1973, p. 79). A *New York Tribune* reporter described the northern suburbs of Philadelphia in 1848 and 1849 as swarming with "loafers who brave only gangs, herd together in squads," and write their gang names "in chalk or charcoal on every dead-wall, fence and stable-door" (Blumin in Davis and Haller 1973, pp. 43–44).

A historian of gangs in New York City wrote, "By 1855 it was estimated that the metropolis contained at least 30,000 men who owed allegiance to gang leaders and through them to the political leaders of Tammany Hall and the Know Nothing or Native American Party" (Asbury 1971, p. 105). The New York City Civil War draft riots were said to have been precipitated by young Irish youths in street gangs (ibid.).

After the Civil War, internal population movement and the influx of new waves of European immigrants brought gangs of nationalities other than Irish, not just in northern cities but in the South. White Southerners saw themselves as a "downtrodden minority, discriminated against, denied any status or identity . . . the South was in a state of extreme economic and social disorganization. There was neither money nor jobs for returning soldiers and not very much to do" (Haskins 1974, pp. 43–45). The Ku Klux Klan originated as a gang of young Civil War veterans who had returned to Pulaski, Tennessee. Six bored and discouraged soldiers formed a club with an "air of mystery and exclusiveness that might make life more exciting" (ibid.).

While the Klan was "terrorizing" the South, new immigrant gangs were forming in several of the large eastern cities, particularly in New York. German gangs formed in the Hell's Kitchen area about 1868, and a few years later the "first Mafia began operations and set up their own standards of law and order along Mulberry Street . . . there were now thousands of gangs and satellites of gangs . . . yet the gangs of the [18] 70s, 80s, and 90s were not very different from those of the [18] 20s, 30s, and 40s" (Haskins 1974, p. 47). Drug use came into being. Morphine was available in most stores and was popular among gang members, many of whom became addicts (see Asbury 1971; Haskins 1974).

Gangs, particularly from eastern and southern Europe, continued to develop in the cities of the northeast during the early part of the twentieth century (Thrasher 1936). Gangs fulfilled a range of functions for marginal youths, in addition to protecting local turf, fighting, thieving, partying, and teaching how to survive and adapt in the new urban environment. They helped politicians to get the vote out and intimidated opposition candidates. Young toughs assisted both union leaders and factory workers to protect their respective interests. Gang leaders in New York City in 1911 were on the "payroll of either a union or a company, and blackjacking, stabbing, and brawling were common fare in labor-management relations . . . " (Haskins 1974, p. 66).

By the late 1920s and 1930s, restrictive immigration had slowed the arrival of low-cost labor from Europe. New sources of cheap labor now came from the Southern United States, Mexico, and Puerto Rico, and the flow increased rapidly during World War II and immediately after. The numbers of white gangs and their criminal activities declined after the 1950s, at least at the street level. However, black and Latino gangs attracted the attention of the media, police, youth agencies, and some researchers. A great variety of gangs has again appeared and been recognized on the urban scene since the 1980s. Members comprise Central Americans and Caribbean islanders, Asians and Pacific islanders, and new immigrants from Eastern Europe (e.g., Russian, Albanian).

The gang tradition has been particularly strong and persistent in California and in America's Southwest in recent decades. Some gangs in Los Angeles date back sixty or more years—at least in terms of name and tradition (Pitchess 1979). Philibosian estimated that gangs are active in seventy of the eighty-four incorporated cities in Los Angeles County (1989, p. 7). Donovan reported that "today a Hispanic in Los Angeles may be a fourth generation gang member" (1988, p. 14). Finally, current prison gangs have evolved from or are connected to street gangs. The crimes of many prison groups are substantially similar to those practiced in an earlier period of prison gang history, including intimidation, extortion, homosexual prostitution, riots, and killings (C. Camp and Camp 1988, p. 57).

Youth gangs have also developed in a great many middle-sized and small communities and in suburban and rural areas throughout the United States and other countries, reflecting internal migrations, usually of minority populations. This "spread" of gang problems, however, does not necessarily indicate a rational and systematic or deliberately organized spread of gangs, particularly African-American and Hispanic. Rather, local gangs, sometimes similar to youth gangs in other localities, develop because similar social conditions have arisen. Curry and his associates (1992, Figure 10) indicate that the rate of increase of youth gangs, albeit from a small base, identified by law enforcement in eleven large cities of the United States between 1990 and 1991 was highest among whites and Asians.

The Contemporary Gang Scene in the United States

Differences in perception, conceptualization, and method of data collection have resulted in different views of the nature, scope, and seriousness of youth gang activities. In the earlier part of the twentieth century, the American boy gang member was sometimes regarded as spirited, venturesome, and fun loving. He was a product mainly of unsupervised lower-class youths from immigrant families situated in transitional inner-city areas (Puffer 1912; Thrasher 1936). Just before and after World War II, certain researchers (Whyte 1943; Suttles 1968) emphasized the stable, organized, and community-integrated character of youth gang members and street corner groups. The distinction between non-delinquent street groups, delinquent groups, and gangs was not usually made or observed in the earlier research. (See Chapter 2 and Glossary for a discussion of the differences.)

However, some early researchers did make close connections between youthful delinquent and adult criminal groups or gangs (Thrasher 1936; Shaw and McKay 1943). These relationships were weak or absent in much of the theory and research into gangs in the 1950s and early 1960s (A. Cohen 1955; W. Miller 1958; Short and Strodtbeck 1965; however, see Cloward and Ohlin 1960; Spergel 1964). The connections were rediscovered or reemphasized in the 1970s and 1980s (see, for example, Moore 1978; Needle and Stapleton 1983; Spergel 1984; G. Camp and Camp 1985; Maxson, Gordon, and Klein 1985; C. Camp and Camp 1988).

How much youth gangs in the United States had changed by the 1970s was a source of some controversy. The National Advisory Committee on Criminal Justice Standards and Goals (1976) stated that "youth gangs are not now or [*sic*] should not become a major object of concern. . . . Youth gang violence is not a major crime problem in the United States . . . what gang violence does exist can fairly readily be diverted into 'constructive' channels especially through the provision of services by community agencies." Walter Miller, however, after a national survey, concluded that the youth gang problem of the mid-1970s was "of the utmost seriousness" (1975, p. 75). His 1975 report, *Violence by Youth Gangs and Youth Groups as a Crime Problem in Major American Cities*, was the first nationwide study of the nature and extent of gang violence. He gathered information mainly through site visits to twelve of the nation's largest cities and from informants of eighteen types of organizations, including criminal justice, youth-based, grassroots, and planning agencies.

Miller's conclusions were handicapped by lack of reliable data on gangs and lack of a single agency "which takes a continuing responsibility for the collection of information based on explicit and uniformly-applied data collection categories which would permit comparability from city to city and between different periods of time" (ibid., p. 3). This basic methodological problem continues to handicap contemporary national estimates of the scope and seriousness of the gang problem and the effectiveness of efforts to address it. One of Miller's major contributions to conceptualization of gangs, however, was to begin to assess youth gangs and delinquent groups as separate entities and to provide rough estimates of the scope of the problem. He concluded that "Youth gang violence is more lethal today than ever before [and] . . . represents a crime problem of the first magnitude which shows little prospect of early abatement" (ibid., p. 76). Why gang problems are more serious in recent decades, how different gang structures and behavioral characteristics are today from those earlier in the century, and what accounts for these possible differences, have not been satisfactorily answered.

Since publication of Miller's 1975 study, local studies and media reports have continued to demonstrate the development and increase in severity of the gang problem in many cities. For example, Tracy's research (1982), based on findings from the Philadelphia cohort studies, indicated that youth gangs accounted for a substantial share of serious and violent crime in that city. High levels of fear of gang crime in or about schools have also been reported (Chicago Board of Education 1981; W. Miller 1982; Rosenbaum and Grant 1983; Dolan and Finney 1984; Kyle 1984). In the late 1980s, gang problems received national attention, much of it stimulated by reports from California. The executive director of the California Office of Criminal Justice Planning claimed in a newsletter that "gangs are a violent and insidious new form of organized crime. Heavily armed with sophisticated weapons, they are involved in drug trafficking, witness intimidation, extortion, and bloody territorial wars. In some cases they are travelling out of state to spread their violence and crime" (Howenstein 1988). However, the reliability of reports of the organized character of gang violence or of the close relationship of sophisticated drug trafficking and gang membership is open to serious question (see Chapter 4).

There appear also to be significant differences in the scope and character of the problem based on factors of race/ethnicity, locality, and the conditions creating the varied gang problems. White-power assaultive gang activities have been reported in various neighborhoods and the suburbs. White gangs or delinquent groups tend to be a major source of graffiti, vandalism, theft, and burglary. School desegregation brought gang problems, at least temporarily, to some communities (Hagedorn 1988). Hispanic and black gangs are largely responsible for drive-by shootings and most of the serious gang-related violence. Undocumented Latin American youths are now present in some established gangs or are forming their own gangs. Some youth from families recently arrived from Latin America, the Caribbean, and Asia have become members of gangs and a few sometimes suppliers of drugs. African-American youth gangs or gang members are now significant street-level drug dealers. Still, the drug problem within and among black, Hispanic, Asian, and white gangs appears to vary in terms of scope of sale and drug use patterns across communities and even in the same city. Some gangs had reduced outward signs of gang membership, such as colors or physical turf identity, related to increase in or more sophisticated illegal activity for profit.

Delinquent and criminal youth or street gangs and the problems they create are a periodic and enduring feature of changing urban structures across time and cultures. The 1980s and 1990s may be a time in which—in an increasing number of communities and cities—youth gangs have come to participate in a greater range of types of organizational and criminal or deviant activities and serve more social functions than in earlier periods, not only in the United States but in many other countries. We need to recognize that the youth gang or street gang has become an increasingly complex and changing social institution, much as has the family, school, and employment. The specific continuities and changes in the character and meaning of street gangs and community responses to them are covered in the chapters that follow.

Conclusion

In this chapter I have attempted to place gangs and the gang problem in historical and comparative perspective across cultures. There seem to be similarities in the behavior of antisocial gangs and probably in the conditions that give rise to them. Perceptions of the scope, character, and severity of gang problems, however, have varied considerably in recent decades. If we are to understand the nature of the complex gang problem, we must define it in some reliable and meaningful way. It is to the definition of key aspects of the problem, and the issues of quality of data sources on which these definitions depend, that I turn in the next chapter. There I describe the contemporary problem to provide a basis for understanding it, and for prescribing systematic approaches to dealing with it.

2

Research Limitations:
Data Sources and Definitions

The terms *gang* and *gang problem* are often ill-defined and amorphous. They may represent the interests and concerns of observers, from different types of organizations, professional or citizen groups, perceiving and responding to gang phenomena in terms of their expectations, organizational mission, or group experience as well as the "real" situation of gang crime. A gang problem is the antisocial or criminal behavior of a youth group, but it also includes the observer or organizational response to it. Both the objective facts of the problem and the organized perceptions of the facts must be considered in determining what will or will not be defined and/or done about gang phenomena. Sooner or later, for policy, program, theoretical, and research purposes, a common definition of the problem should be formulated. This is not to deny that gangs and gang problems differ along a variety of dimensions. But certain key dimensions must be consensually identified if we are to understand gang phenomena and take appropriate action.

This chapter describes the limits of gang data for research, policy, and program purposes. It questions research that bases conclusions on only one approach to or method of data collection. For example, ethnographic procedures have often been the exclusive means for understanding gang phenomena. The chapter discusses deficiencies of a variety of definitions. There is a tendency to regard gangs within a range of perspectives, positive and negative. Criminal justice definitions are almost exclusively based on a negative perception and result in policy that stresses suppression. Definitions by gang members, some social scientists, and some social practitioners may be positively valued. Definitions that suggest the complexity of gang phenomena and emphasize behavioral aspects are recommended. Most important is the development of a clear and consistent set of definitions of the social phenomena *gang*, *gang member*, and *gang incident*, that will contribute to national policy and program development on the basis of reliable and valid research.

The Limits of Data

Various reasons exist for the lack of "good" data on gangs. Perhaps the most important are the limitations of media reporting; the lack of interest of federal government policy, until recently; and the deficiencies and inconsistencies of local law enforcement policy and practice. Serious knowledge gaps may also result from the constraints of specific theory or disciplinary approaches as well as from the use of unitary research methods.

The news media in some cities do not consistently and carefully report gang events and tend to exaggerate or sensationalize them (Downes 1966; S. Cohen 1972; Patrick 1973; Gold and Mattick 1974). Miller suggested that the national media, centered in New York City, ignored the gang problem as it existed in other cities in the 1970s. For example, about 300 gang killings in 1979 and 350 in 1980 in Los Angeles went largely unreported nationally (W. Miller 1982; however, see Klein and Maxson 1987).

As Miller indicated almost two decades ago (1975), there still is no national center or agency for reporting gang data. Neither the U.S. Census Bureau, the U.S. Department of Justice, the Federal Bureau of Investigation, the Department of Health and Human Services, the National Institute of Mental Health, nor the U.S. Department of Education systematically collects or compiles national-level data on a range of key characteristics of youth gangs or their members. In recent years, however, the Drug Enforcement Administration and the General Accounting Office have begun to report the drug-related scope and character of the youth gang or street-gang problem nationwide. The Federal Bureau of Investigation has also become interested in tracking major criminal street gang activities across state borders (however, see Chapter 17).

Some progress has been made in the development of reliable local gang crime statistics by police in a growing number of large and medium-sized cities and county jurisdictions. Still, only gross estimates of gang crime, particularly violence, are available in most cities. Many police units gather gang crime data only on homicide and sometimes on felony assault and robbery; other index (felony or serious) and nonindex (misdemeanor or less serious) gang crime data tend to be sporadically collected (see Needle and Stapleton 1983). Data are obtained often on an incident rather than also on a gang or an individual-offender basis, which makes it difficult to target repeat offenders or to determine the extent of solo offending or non-gang companionate crime committed by gang members (Reiss 1987). Considerable interest has developed recently in the creation of information systems at city, county, and state levels and in correctional institutions (C. Camp and Camp 1988). Law enforcement officials have cited the need for a nationwide tracking and identification methodology, specifically for those gang members and criminal groups that appear to carry on illegal activities with other gangs and expand into areas outside their neighborhoods (General Accounting Office 1989, p. 57).

Local values, political considerations, statutory language, and public pressures, in addition to particular agency or organizational histories and predispositions, news media pressures, and intellectual fashions, as well as distinctive gang patterns all influence how state legislatures, law enforcement authorities, and community-based agencies establish their definitions of gangs, gang members, and gang incidents. There are differences across time, cities, and states (Overend 1988). Distinctions between delinquent or criminal gang and non-gang group crimes have not yet been clearly or consistently made.

In one study, over three-quarters of the police departments surveyed indicated that violent behavior was the key criterion for distinguishing delinquent groups as gangs (Needle and Stapleton 1983). The Los Angeles Police Department defines gang-related crime as homicide, attempted murder, assault with a deadly weapon, robbery, kidnapping, shooting at an inhabited dwelling, or arson in which the suspect or victim is identified in police files as a gang member or associate member (usually on the basis of a prior arrest or identification as a gang member). In Chicago at present, a wider range of crimes has been classified as gang related but only if the incident grows out of gang function, motivation, or distinctive gang violent circumstances. Any robbery involving a gang member is gang related in Los Angeles, but a "gang-related" robbery in Chicago must be due mainly to gang purpose or directly arises from gang process and interest. Some law enforcement agencies classify gangs in distinctive gang subcategories, for example, turf gangs, drug gangs, black, Latino, Asian, and white gangs. These categories may become the basis for establishing different operational units to deal with the different types of gang problems and related control issues.

Conceptualization and Research Method

A variety of theoretical and methodological problems have hindered the development of adequate knowledge about gangs. The approach to the study of gangs has been categorical or typological rather than in terms of variable characteristics (Kornhauser 1978). Related categories and concepts have not always been clearly defined or distinguished. There has often been a failure to distinguish between norms and behaviors, subcultures and gangs, and gangs and delinquent groups, as well as a failure to recognize differences in race and ethnic gang patterns, variability of gang phenomena in different cities, and sometimes variability within the same city over time.

Theorists and researchers have largely addressed youth gang phenomena through a variety of sociological and anthropological perspectives. Little attention has been paid to different gang social psychological or individual gang member psychological perspectives. Social scientists have tended to view the gang problem in aggregate group, subcultural, or community terms with little attention to distinctions by types and variations of gangs or delinquent groups, or of the individuals within them, within or across communities. Classic gang theory has been concerned mainly with the origins of delinquent behavior or rules of conduct (Thrasher 1936), explanations of delinquent subcultures as systems of beliefs and values (e.g., A. Cohen and Short 1958), and less often with why gang systems develop differentially usually across subcultures or neighborhoods (Cloward and Ohlin 1960).

Very little theory or research to date has assessed "both individual member and gang variation simultaneously" (Sullivan 1983). Psychological and sociological theories must be interrelated to provide a more precise explanation of highly variable gang phenomena as a basis for effective policy and program. Several efforts to introduce economic theories, including labor market explanations, of the development of the gang problem have only partially explained gang and individual behavior even in the same community (Moore 1978, 1991; Sullivan 1989). Micropsychological and macrosociological and anthropological theory must be developed interactively as a basis for explanation and policy creation.

A cluster of research methods is also required. Research on gangs has traditionally relied, and continues mainly to rely, on participant observation method to obtain data (Spergel 1992b). This has usually resulted in understanding in some depth the dynamics of gang structure on the basis of a limited sample of gangs, gang members, or gang phenomena. Overidentification by the researcher with gang member subjects often occurs. The gang member himself is not always the most reliable source of information. Gang members often have only partial knowledge of the scope of the group's activities and a biased interest in explaining those activities (Klein 1971; W. Miller 1982; Spergel 1984).

The ethnographer—usually male—provides valuable insight into the nature and process of particular gangs. He obtains data informally by going out to the streets, talking to gang youths, observing and sometimes participating in the settings and experiences of gang members. He may collect life histories, make limited use of statistical information, and even conduct a brief survey (Vigil 1988b; Taylor 1990a). The gang researcher may even have been a former, usually a peripheral, gang member or have worked in a youth agency serving gang youths. He tries to observe and understand the dynamics of the gang experience from a street perspective. Hagedorn has stated that the "only way to get a rounded picture of gang activity is to study the gang as a whole, what its members do each day, what different roles exist and how the gang functions within the neighborhood" (1988, p. 246).

The ethnographic approach, however, has a number of limitations in developing an adequate understanding of the gang problem and what to do in terms of community structure or policy to control, ameliorate, or prevent it. For example, participant-observation techniques tend to focus on what the gang member says, believes, or does. The focus is usually not systematically on the interests and reactions of the police, school, agency, neighborhood resident, or even family members to gang phenomena. There is little awareness that the agency or community response may itself be part of the problem. Such response may be a cause at various stages of the problem's development.

This is not to deny that quantitative data collection, including community and gang member surveys and use of official data from criminal justice, school, and other sources, as well as qualitative, field, or ethnographic approaches may be handicapped by problems of conceptualization and definition of key aspects of gang phenomena. Questionable research assumptions and definitions apply to quantitative studies or surveys as well as to ethnographic studies. Field studies should be combined with systematic self-reports, surveys, and official data to compare and understand a range of gang phenomena.

A common problem for surveys, official data, and field studies is how or who defines gang membership and how to control for gang member researcher and organizational response bias. Self-report surveys leave it up to the youths to define themselves as gang members. But self-definition may be suspect, since, for example, the youth may define himself as a gang member even if he is a church member who does not participate in delinquent behavior. Also, police maintain the names of persons on gang files for years, often long after these persons have ceased to be gang members. In both cases, gangs, gang membership, and the extent of the problem may be exaggerated. Nevertheless, even self-reports and official data may provide less biased or more conservative estimates at times than reports by researchers caught up in the imagery and excitement of gang member stories.

Researchers have also tended to employ availability and age-truncated samples in their studies. Often, small nonrandom samples of gangs supplied through local police, youth agencies, or correctional agencies have been studied, usually without control or comparison groups. Teenage gangs, until recently, have been the focus of research or program evaluations, often to the exclusion of preadolescent and young adult gangs. Observational studies have been time limited——usually one to three years——with no long-term systematic follow up (however, see Short and Molland 1976; Moore 1991).

Developmental histories of gangs and individual gang youths have not been carried out. Conspicuously absent have been studies of the socialization of gang youths compared with that of non-gang delinquent youths, and studies of the socialization of different roles or subgroups of youths in the gang, for example, those who are leaders or influentials and those who are fringe members, those who concentrate on using or selling drugs and those who do not, and those who are extremely violent and those who are not. Longitudinal studies that examine the stability and changing character of various types of gang structures and processes, particularly related to or interactive with characteristics of race/ethnicity, region of the country, and so on over time have also not been conducted.

Finally, I believe that the development of knowledge and effective policy and program about and for gangs must be interactive. It is essential that research and program personnel join together in quasi-experimental design, social development, and community mobilization efforts that test specific ideas or policies in regard to prevention, treatment, and control of the gang problem. Such research and development efforts are useful not only for the creation of effective approaches but for gaining new knowledge about the nature and causes of the problem in its various manifestations. Theory is thereby better related to a complex empirical reality, and policies and programs are more systematically tested. In other words, the best way to create effective programs may be through theory-oriented intervention. At the same time, significant basic knowledge is likely to be obtained in the process of trying to change or control gang phenomena. This kind of combined research and policy or program development must be carefully planned and implemented over a substantial period of years. Witte recently observes that "experiments and sophisticated analyses of longitudinal data sets are likely to be most productive. The longitudinal data will be most useful if it contains both individual information on general population groups and aggregate data on communities, institutions, and policies" (1993, p. 518).

Solving the Definitional Problem

The term *gang* can mean many things. Definitions in use have varied according to the concerns and interests of law enforcement personnel, youth agencies, schools, politicians, media, community residents, academics, and researchers, as well as the interests, and changing social reality, of the particular gang. Definitions in the 1950s and 1960s were often related to issues of etiology and based on liberal, optimistic, social-reform perspectives. Definitions in the 1970s, 1980s, and 1990s have been more descriptive and detailed, have emphasized violent and criminal characteristics of gangs, and have reflected greater community fear and more conservative social philosophy (Klein and Maxson 1987).

Gang definitions evoked intense and emotional discussions in the 1970s and 1980s (W. Miller 1977, p. 1) and more recently have become the basis for a variety of repressive laws and strategies. Definitions in different states and communities determine, in part, whether we have a large, small, or even no problem; whether more or fewer gangs and gang members exist; and which agencies will receive most of the funds to address the problem, which should be (and often thereby is) addressed one way rather than another.

The absence of a gang definition by a police department when in fact a significant gang problem exists is frequent. Denial or failure to recognize a gang problem is likely to occur during the early stages of the problem, especially when key city officials and influentials seek to protect the reputation and interests of the city as a "good place" to live, work, and do business in. The Washington, D.C. police chief not long ago acknowledged the presence of "home-grown gangs." This was a "change from a view long held by police and prosecutors that the city does not have gangs." The police chief confirmed what front-line officers and other closer and more objective observers and analysts indicated was happening (Horwitz 1991).

Positive/Neutral Perceptions. Some of the more benign conceptions of the gang— used by gang members, youth agency personnel, and a few academics——stress the gang's normal and necessary communal, clan, or family character and social support, educational, and control functions. According to one gang member, "being in a gang means if I didn't have no family, I'll think that's where I'll be. If I didn't have no job that's where I'd be. To me it's community help without all the community. They'll understand better than my mother and father" (Hagedorn 1988, p. 131).

A former gang youth, later a staff member of a local community organization stated: "A gang is what you make it. A gang is people who hang out; they don't have to be negative or positive. It's what you make them" (Allen 1981, p. 74). Sister Falaka Fattah, director and founder of the House of Umoja, a model residential and community-based program deeply committed to the social support and development of gang youths, observed: "A traditional Philadelphia black street gang was composed of friends who lived in the same neighborhood and usually had kinship links developed over generations with ties to the South. Many of these traditional gangs were founded by families, since recruitment took place at funerals where families and friends gathered in mourning" (F. Fattah 1988, p. 5).

The gang may be viewed, in this perspective, as performing significant social functions in poor, ghettoized, or rapidly changing community or organizational contexts. It is an interstitial group, integrated or organized because of a depriving and unstable social environment and defective social institutions. The gang and its members fight elements of the environment and other groups in order to survive. Recognition and reward come mainly through conflict with other groups, which may include local baseball teams, parents, storekeepers, and gangs on the next street (Thrasher 1936). The "gang is not organized to commit delinquent acts. . . . The gang is a form of collective behavior, spontaneous and unplanned in origin" (Kornhauser 1978, p. 52). Morash observed that "gang-likeness is not a necessary condition to stimulate members' delinquency" (1983; p. 335; Short 1990a; see also Savitz, Rosen, and Lalli 1980). The gang was viewed in the 1950s and 1960s, and still is viewed by some youth agencies, as essential to normal adolescent development. The New York City Youth Board titled its street-gang project with delinquent youth gangs, "The Council of Social and Athletic Clubs" (New York City Youth Board 1960). Earlier, "the Youth Board recognizes that membership in a gang is a normal thing" (New York City Youth Board 1957, p. 12). A recent national evaluation of juvenile antigang and antidrug programs reports that some youth agencies prefer that their projects supported by federal funds not be required to use the words "gang or drugs" to identify their programs (Development Services Group, Inc. 1993).

Miller observed further that there are at least two ways to perceive gang activity as constructive or benign. Some community groups, agencies, and gangs may perceive gang behaviors as "normal and expectable" so long as such behavior is relatively "unserious" or infrequent (W. Miller 1977, p. 11). Gang members may be perceived as protecting their neighborhoods or communities by preventing, attacking, and driving out "unwanted" elements, including drug dealers or members of other races or ethnic groups (ibid., pp. 13–14; see also Suttles 1968). Recently, gangs have been regarded as rational and productive organizations integrated into local communities, even bringing in local commerce and resources, for example, through drug dealing (Jankowski 1991).

Increasingly Negative Views. Definitions of *gang* by most theorists and researchers suggest that gangs are more seriously delinquent or criminal in their 1970s and 1980s behavior than in an earlier era, usually the 1940s and 1950s. Miller viewed the gang as a stable primary group, neither especially aggressive nor violent, that prepared the young lower-class male for an adult role in his society (W. Miller 1958, 1962, 1976b). Later, because of increased levels of violent or otherwise illegal behavior, Miller concluded that "contemporary youth gangs pose a greater threat to public order and a greater danger to the safety of the citizenry than at any time during the past" (1975, p. 44; see also W. Miller 1982).

Similarly, Klein initially characterized the gang as an adolescent group perceived by both themselves and others as involved in delinquencies but not of a serious or lethal nature (1968, 1971). In recent years, Klein and his associates have reported that gangs commit a large number of homicides and participate in extensive narcotics trafficking, although perhaps not as much as is commonly believed (Klein, Maxson, and Cunningham 1988; Klein 1989). Yablonsky, by contrast, has consistently portrayed gang boys—particularly leaders and core members—as lawbreakers trading in violence and primarily organized to carry out illegal acts (Yablonsky 1962; Haskell and Yablonsky 1982).

It is likely that neither set of definitions, benign or malignant, is correct for all cases. Gangs vary in their degree of commitment to antisocial behavior on a range of social, demographic, and territorial variables, to be discussed in later chapters. Further, the behavior of a particular gang and its members varies, sometimes in the period of a single day. Gang behavior is erratic and unpredictable, yet patterned over time.

Deficient Definitions

Sociologists, criminologists, and psychologists have been, until recently, slow to pay attention to the distinctive characteristics of youth gangs and gang problems. Crime and delinquency theory and research have been focused on more general patterns of delinquent behavior, particularly focused in the individual youth. It has been assumed, for example, that delinquent behavior is widely distributed throughout the social structure and not simply concentrated in low-income or socially unstable communities. Careful distinctions have not been made between the concepts of individual delinquents, co-offenders, gang members in their various roles, delinquent, groups and gangs, nor between different types or severities of gang crime or levels of gang violence. Some of these distinctions are only now beginning to appear. The dominant theoretical perspectives—labeling, social control, learning, and deterrence—have until very recently paid little attention to the group or gang level of analysis (see Erickson and Jensen 1977).

Some criminologists continue to define the gang in indefinite or neutral terms with little specification of behavioral criteria, whether law-violating or non-law violating, contrary to commonly accepted views of the negative meaning of gang. Robert Sampson reported in his research that gang membership is indexed depending on how the respondent answers (yes or no) to the question, "Do you belong to what some people might call a youth gang?" (1986, p. 880). Short defines "a *gang* as a group whose members meet together with some regularity over time, on the basis of group-defined criteria of membership and group-determined organizational structure, usually with (but not always . . .) some sense of territoriality. This definition includes neither delinquent or conventional behaviors, since these usually are what we wish to explain . . . " (1990a, p. 239). However, Moore claimed the word "gang" "can mean a group of adolescents who hang around a candy store, something like 'West Side Story,' or a highly organized Mafia family with elaborate banking connections and a tradition of clever, if shady, business deals" (1988b, pp. 3–4).

Horowitz states that the definition of gang should be kept pluralistic to broaden theory and techniques of inquiry. Gangs should be defined on the basis of particular perspectives or predispositions of researchers (Horowitz 1990). Furthermore, the definition of gang phenomena focuses more on the context that generates gangs. What is important is not the character of the gang, its delinquent or criminal behavior, but the gang as a response to a defective society, community, or organizational environment. Hagedorn saw gangs as "always formed from powerless minorities and have often become a part of the political struggle of their ethnic group to achieve quality" (1988, p. 47). Leslie Smith claimed that English female delinquent groups or gangs are not accurately defined because "law-enforcing agencies, parents and social workers tend to . . . sexualize female deviancy" (1978, pp. 74–75, 87). I believe that none of these particular definitions is accurate or sufficiently comprehensive. They are not supported by reliable data and are not useful for purposes of policy and program development. They represent the idiosyncratic views of particular researchers based on insufficient data on gang populations or specification of these populations.

On the other hand, in an attempt to stretch the definition of gang to be inclusive (perhaps too inclusive), in a recent study to "paint a fuller picture of the underground and overground experience in the urban area" and to include females and males who are in criminal as well as noncriminal gangs, Taylor states that "criminality is only one part of gang culture. . . . The fact is that organized and unorganized political, social, and criminal groups, crews, and gangs are in the city" (1993, p. 9). This definition is too broad to be useful for policy or program or even for most theoretical or field research purposes.

There are increasing efforts, however, to distinguish among the behaviors of delinquent groups, youth gangs, and other types of criminal groups or gangs. The notion of "gang member" is defined in behavioral terms. Further, the delinquent behavior of gang members may be gang or non-gang related. A report of a "New York State Task Force on Juvenile Gangs" suggests that contemporary gangs in New York may be quite different than they were in an earlier period and different from gangs as they exist in other parts of the country at the present time.

> The traditional New York City youth gang with a structured organization is becoming a thing of the past. What we generally see are small groups known as posses or crews or just disorderly groups of law-violating youths, with no real or identifiable leadership. There are no "colors," tatoos or identifiable clothing to indicate what gang or group they belong to or graffiti identifying "turf" claimed by them. Members can belong to more than one group, posse or crew. Most of the units are short-lived. (Dunston 1990)

The author of this Task Force, however, excludes from his definition "Gangs or groups that initially came together for the sole purpose of furthering a business enterprise" . . . mainly drug operations (ibid., pp. 6–7).

Most gang researchers currently define gang in delinquent or criminal behavioral terms, but not with consistency. The range of such definitions varies widely. Jankowski indicates that much of the violence of gang members is not generated by or attributable to the gang structure, but rather to individual gang members in their non-gang roles. Jankowski's gangs are organized social systems definable mainly by their rational interests in property crime or gain (Jankowski 1991, pp. 140–142). Vigil and others have claimed the opposite, viewing gangs as more concerned with fighting, and violence as one of the "strongly imbedded gang patterns requiring group effort and support." "Property-related crime is more of an individual nature" for gang members (Vigil 1988b, p. 137). Bernard Cohen believed that property crime is relatively more likely to be a pattern of younger delinquent groups and violence a pattern of older youths—sometimes the same youths (B Cohen, 1969a). Sullivan observed that younger members are more likely to engage in fighting behavior but as older youths leave the gang, they become relatively more engaged in gain-oriented crime (see Sullivan 1983).

Criminal Justice Definitions

State legislatures and criminal justice agencies have been increasingly active in the development and elaboration of definitions of gang, gang member, and gang incident, especially on behavior that address crimes of violence. Such definitions generally are the basis of suppression strategies. They are more specific but hardly more consistent than those of the social scientists and researchers already described. According to the California Penal Code, section 186.22, 1988, a "criminal street gang" is defined as "any organization, association, or group of three or more persons whether formal or informal . . . which has a common name or common identifying sign or symbol, where members individually or collectively engage in or have engaged in a pattern of criminal activity." These criminal acts are enumerated as follows: assault with a deadly weapon; robbery; unlawful homicide or manslaughter; and the sale, possession for sale, transportation, manufacture, offer for sale, or offer to manufacture controlled substances. The term pattern means the "commission, attempted commission, or solicitation of two or more" of these offenses, and "the offenses are committed on separate occasions, or by two or more persons."

Not only does the Texas legislature include arson, criminal mischief, and tampering with a witness as possible gang crimes, but some law enforcement agencies in Texas and elsewhere undoubtedly mislabel a variety of youth groups as gangs. They include a wide range of informal associations in the definition of "criminal gangs." There may be a tendency "to pin hard-to-shake labels on individuals too hastily" (Buhmann 1991, p. 27). "A city that counts every juvenile identity group or street group with a name as a gang will report a much higher number [of gang crimes] than if it only counted the gangs actually involved in serious criminal offenses" (ibid., p. 13). Buhmann, in the Texas Attorney General's Office, observes that the "criteria for gang membership vary so widely from one [Texas] city to the next that it is extremely difficult to assess the extent and seriousness of the problem" (ibid., p. i).

The attempts by some legislatures, city and state, to define a criminal gang have at times drawn the ire of civil liberties groups and special commentary by news reporters. For example, in a proposal by the Chicago City Council, a criminal gang was to be defined "as a group in which three or more members have been convicted of criminal activity. Considering the Council's history of aldermanic convictions, it is conceivable that at some future meeting of the 50 aldermen [they] might be subject to [their] proposals if adopted" (Robert Davis 1991, p. 5).

Recent work by Maxson and Klein suggests that valid comparison of gang crime prevalence and incidence rates across cities generally cannot be made because of different definitions of the gang incident. For example, the Chicago Police Department has a relatively narrow definition based on the gang-related motivations or circumstances, while the Los Angeles County Sheriff's Department has a broader definition based on the identity of the offender or victim as a gang member. It is clear that gang violence, particularly homicide, rates for Chicago would probably be half as high as for Los Angeles based on definitional differences alone. Maxson and Klein add, however, that even if prevalence rates vary, the "character" of certain gang crimes such as gang homicide would seem less vulnerable to the definitional problem (Maxson and Klein 1990, p. 91).

Typical of criminal justice definitions is the one found in Florida's Street Terrorism Enforcement and Prevention Act. It includes standards used by many police departments in determining who is and who is not a gang member. A gang member is a person who "engages in a pattern of youth street-gang activity and meets two or more of the following criteria:

(a) Admits to gang membership.

(b) Is a youth under the age of 21 years who is identified as a gang member by a parent or guardian.

(c) Is identified as a gang member by a documented reliable informant.

(d) Resides in or frequents a particular gang's area and adopts their style of dress, their use of handguns, or their tatoos, and associates with known gang members.

(e) Is identified as a gang member by an informant of previously untested reliability and such information is corroborated by independent information.

(f) Has been arrested more than once in the company of identified gang members for offenses which are consistent with usual gang activity.

(g) Is identified as a gang member by physical evidence such as photographs or other documentation.

(h) Has been stopped in the company of known gang members four or more times.
                                      (Institute for Law and Justice 1994, pp. 3–8)

Finally, we note a tendency in some criminal justice settings, for example prisons, for officials to deny that gangs, gang members, or gang incidents are present. A national advisory group of experts prefers the term "security threat group" to gang. Admission by a prison system that "it has gangs or even security threat groups, may not be viewed as politically appropriate" (Baugh 1993, p. 2).

Delinquent Group versus Gang. A key definitional question for research and policy is, what is the difference between a delinquent group and a delinquent gang? The major theorists and researchers of gangs in the 1950s and 1960s generally viewed these two as equivalent or synonymous. Reference was made to core delinquent cliques in gangs (A. Cohen 1955; Cohen and Short 1958; W. Miller 1958, 1962; Cloward and Ohlin 1960; Short and Strodtbeck 1965; Klein 1968, 1971).

Since then a number of theorists and researchers have tried to distinguish between gangs and delinquent groups (Kornhauser 1978; Morash 1983; B. Cohen 1969a, b). Juvenile gangs and delinquent groups are more likely to be viewed as equivalent than older adolescent and young adult gangs and groups. Cohen insisted that "gang and group delinquency are different forms of juvenile deviance and should be approached etiologically, as well as for purposes of treatment and prevention, from different starting points" (1969a, p. 108). On the basis of police data, he found that gang offenders were a little older and more homogeneous with respect to age, race, sex, and residence patterns than were non-gang group offenders. Violence is a distinguishing characteristic of youth gangs while property crime is most likely a salient characteristic of delinquent groups.

Suggested Definition(s)

A widely used definition developed by Klein more than twenty years ago and still commonly used today refers "to any denotable adolescent group of youngsters who (a) are generally perceived as a distinct aggregation by others in the neighborhood, (b) recognize themselves as a denotable group (almost invariably with a group name), and (c) have been involved in a sufficient number of delinquent incidents to call forth a consistent negative response from neighborhood residents and/or law enforcement agencies" (Klein 1971, p. 111).

Miller identified twenty different categories and subcategories of law-violating youth groups of which "turf gangs," "fighting gangs," and "gain-oriented gangs" were three subtypes (W. Miller 1982, chap. 1). His definition of a youth gang emphasized organization and control of turf or criminal enterprise: "A youth gang is a self-formed association of peers united by mutual interests with identifiable leadership and internal organization who act collectively or as individuals to achieve specific purposes, including the conduct of illegal activity and control of a particular territory, facility, or enterprise" (1982, p. 61).

Curry and Spergel's (1988) definition attempts to distinguish delinquent groups from gangs with attention to the variability and complexity of gang structure and patterns of criminal behavior. Group delinquency is law-violating behavior, whether minor or serious crime, committed by juveniles in relatively small groups that tend often to be ephemeral. A current variant or subcategory of such a group, particularly popular in eastern states, is the "crew" or "posse." It can be diffuse or well organized and is directed primarily to illegal gain activity, especially drug trafficking.

Gang activity is law-violating behavior committed by either juveniles or adults in, or related to, groups that are complexly organized, sometimes cohesive, and sometimes with established leadership and rules. The gang, like the delinquent group, engages in a wide range of crime—but significantly more violence—within a more articulated and structured framework of communal values with respect to mutual support; conflict relations with other gangs; and often a tradition of turf, colors, signs, and symbols. Subgroups of the gang may be differentially committed to various delinquent or criminal patterns that may or may not be gang related, such as drug trafficking, fighting, or burglary. The concepts of the delinquent group and the youth gang are not exclusive of each other but represent distinctive configurations of related social phenomena (Curry and Spergel 1988, p. 382).

Maxson and Klein, whose work focuses on gang violence, especially gang homicides, have indicated furthermore that "gang violence is substantially different in character from non-gang violence . . . the character of reported gang violence is primarily a function of the setting and participant characteristics of the violent event" (1990, p. 90). Not all violence that occurs as a group event is necessarily gang related (e.g., bar-room brawls). However, certain problem youth groups, such as racist "skinheads" and neo-Nazi groups, which engage in group-related assaultive behavior may be considered youth gangs. They can be identified distinctively by their dress and codes of behavior. They engage in violent and criminal activities for ideological—including political and religious—ends, persist over time, and are increasingly under the purview of gang units of the police and probation departments, as well as legislative commissions dealing with youth gang problems. This suggests a further extension of the reality and specification of the concept of the youth gang in behavioral terms (Reddick 1987).

Factors Affecting Policy-relevant Definitions

The principal public policy-relevant criterion currently used to define a gang has been the group's or its members' participation in illegal activity. Miller has suggested that the term can be applied broadly or narrowly by the key front-level definers of the phenomena, law enforcement officers. Police departments may apply the term quite narrowly in large cities but more broadly in small cities to cover more types of offenses (W. Miller 1980). Needle and Stapleton (1983, p. 13) indicated that the perception of youth gang activities as major, moderate, or minor problems varies with the number and size of youth gangs, the problems they are believed to cause, and the prevalence rate of youth gang criminal activity as a proportion of total crime. The media, distressed local citizens, and outreach community agencies, often seeking to "prevent" the problem, tend to use the term more broadly than do the police in order to cover more categories of youth behavior that are defined as disturbing or illegitimate but not necessarily as illegal.

Spergel and Curry (1990) found that the pattern of definitions of the gang problem and its component elements, that is, the gang, gang member, and gang incident, vary across different types of organizations, as well as by whether a city or jurisdiction has a chronic or long-term serious gang problem or a more recent and emerging, although sometimes acute problem. In a survey of 254 expert and experienced informants from criminal justice, grass-roots, schools, youth, and other organizations and agencies dealing with the gang problem in forty-five cities and six special sites, the most frequently cited elements of a definition for *gang* were certain group or organizational characteristics, symbols, and a range of specific and general criminal activities, particularly violence, drug use, and drug sales. The most frequent elements used to define a *gang member* were symbols or symbolic behavior; self-admission; identification by others, especially the police; and association with gang members. The three most frequently cited ways of identifying a *gang incident* were the *involvement of a gang member* in the activity, *function* (i.e., gang-related interest and motivation), and *modus operandi* (i.e., behavior distinctively associated with gang activity, such as drive-by shootings). In general there was more consensus on definitions according to city or location of the respondent than according to his or her professional discipline or agency affiliation.

To some extent differences in definitions could be accounted for by whether the city had a chronic or an emerging gang problem. Survey respondents from chronic gang cities emphasized the general or specific criminal or antisocial nature of the gang's activities, whereas those in the emerging problem cities focused on symbolic or organizational aspects in their definitions of a gang or gang incident. Respondents from chronic gang cities tended to use multiple factors in identifying gang members or gang incidents; the respondents in emerging problem cities usually emphasized single factors. Also, criminal justice agency respondents tended to emphasize different types of crimes in their descriptions; nonjustice organization representatives tended to emphasized symbolic behaviors in their identification of youths as gang members (Spergel and Curry 1990, pp. 206–209).

Conclusion

Serious research method and policy-relevant differences have become obstacles to the development of a common definition of the youth gang problem, or its components—the gang, gang member, and gang incident. The perceptions of the researcher or of the agency or community group responding to gang phenomena have been extremely variable, reflecting the interests and experiences of the definers as well as the social reality of the phenomena. For purposes of effective research and policy in the identification and explanation of youth gang crime, however, it is important to develop a general definition of the gang that takes account of the variability and inter-relationships of characteristics such as age, race/ethnicity, gender, organization, location of members, and community reaction, particularly focused on violent behavior that has primarily communal or solidarity and secondarily gain implications.

In the chapters that follow I will use the terms *youth* and *street gang* most frequently. However, since as shown, the meaning of these and associated or component terms has been and still is highly variable over time and place, I will also make comparisons with such phenomena labeled as delinquent groups, criminal groups, and criminal organizations, particularly in cross-cultural and older studies and reports. The key purpose, nevertheless, is to examine contemporary delinquent or criminal youth gang phenomena; for this reason it is not "gangs" in their broadest meaning, but "youth gangs" that are the focus.

3

Scope and Seriousness
of the Gang Problem

This chapter establishes the empirical basis for the proposition that youth gang activity is a social problem. Of special interest is the scope of gang-related violence in terms of the identification, number, and percent of youth in particular social settings associated with such violence. As suggested already, indicators of a gang problem are not always reliable, consistent, or valid. It is essential to determine as clearly as possible, on the basis of the best data available, whether an actual gang problem exists, and if so, what its scope and nature are and what changes have occurred in the problem over time in general and in particular communities. Adequate description of gang problem phenomena should precede understanding and diagnosis of gang problems, which in turn should come before prescriptions for prevention or remediation.

Extent of the Problem

Youth gangs today are found in almost all fifty states. In the late 1970s Miller estimated that 83 percent of the largest cities had gang problems, as did 27 percent of cities with a population of 100,000 or more and 13 percent of cities with populations of 10,000 or more (W. Miller 1982, chaps. 2, 3). Needle and Stapleton, a little later, reported a somewhat higher proportion, 39 percent, of cities with populations between 100,000 and 249,999 having gang problems (Needle and Stapleton 1983). In the early 1990s, Curry and his colleagues surveyed seventy-nine of the largest U. S. cities with populations over 200,000 and, on the basis of police information, found that 91.1 percent had a gang problem (Curry et al. 1992, p. 22). Klein recently stated that "We can estimate the number of gang-involved cities and towns in America to be at least 800, and perhaps as high as 1,000" (Klein forthcoming, pp. 38–39). He adds that "the proportion of cities with large numbers of gangs and gang members is very small. Most of the almost 800 cities . . . reported fewer than six gangs and fewer than 500 gang members" (ibid., p. 83).

In a recent small-scale survey of twelve prosecutors in rural areas of Colorado, Iowa, Michigan, Montana, New Hampshire, South Carolina, Texas, and Washington, "gangs were mentioned by one-fourth of the respondents as the prevalent criminal organization" (Justice Research and Statistics Association 1993, p. 6).

In a national study of prisons and jails, Baugh found that "the presence of STGs (Security Threat Groups, including large numbers of well-known street gangs) has significantly increased by percentage from 3 percent in 1985 to 6 percent in 1992" (Baugh 1993, p. 53).

Gangs increasingly exist in medium-sized and small cities, in towns, and in suburban communities but usually do not exhibit the same degree of organization, criminality, and violence of gangs in some of the largest cities. Gangs in certain areas have not only waxed but also sometimes waned. Some cities with youth gang problems in the 1980s and 1990s did not have, or were not aware of, such problems in the 1960s and 1970s. On the other hand, some cities that reported serious gang problems in the 1970s or early 1980s were without them or experienced less serious problems in the late 1980s and the 1990s (Spergel and Curry 1990). The terms *emerging, chronic,* and even *re-emerging,* can be used to describe the presence and changing nature of gang problems in a variety of cities and jurisdictions.

The Institute for Law and Justice conducted a nationwide survey of 368 prosecutor's offices, including all 175 counties with more than 250,000 people, and 193 prosecutors randomly selected from counties of 50,000 to 250,000 population. "Eighty percent (140) of the prosecutors in large jurisdictions responded, with 84 percent (118 respondents) reporting gang problems in their jurisdictions; and 83 percent (160) of the small jurisdictions responded, with 46 percent (74 respondents) reporting gang problems" (Institute for Law and Justice 1994, p. 1).

Gangs are increasingly present in state and federal correctional institutions and in many school systems. In a 1981 study, Caltabriano calculated that 53 percent of state prisons had gangs. A little later, G. Camp and Camp (1985) found that 67 percent of the forty-eight state prison systems they studied had gangs. Youth and young adult gangs were identified in state prisons on the West Coast as early as the 1950s and 1960s and in midwestern states in the 1960s and 1970s.

In a national study of prisons and jails, Baugh found that "the presence of STGs (Security Threat Groups, including large numbers of well-known gangs) has significantly increased by percentage from 3 percent in 1985 to 6 percent in 1992" (Baugh 1993, p. 53). In Chicago, all public and some parochial high schools and many Cook County suburban high schools reported gangs or gang members and gang problems (Chicago Board of Education 1981; Spergel 1985). Gangs or gang problems are increasingly reported in inner-city school systems in midwestern and western states. Nevertheless, the presence of youth gangs or gang members in a prison or correctional system, or in a school, does not necessarily indicate how many or few gangs or gang members there are or whether the problem is large or small in these settings.

Estimates of Numbers of Youth Gangs and Gang Members

It is not possible to devise meaningful estimates of the exact or even approximate number of youth gangs in the United States, partly because, as noted, there is no standard or national definition of "gang." Often the terms *delinquent group, criminal organization,* and sometimes a simple "aggregation of youths on a street corner" are used as equivalent to the term *gang.* Most estimates of numbers and of changes in the numbers over time are probably inaccurate (often grossly) and tend to represent an exaggeration of the scope of the problem. National estimates have sometimes been made primarily for rhetorical or organizational interest purposes. Dolan and Finney (1984, p. 12) claimed that "since the close of World War II, the number of youth gangs has grown astonishingly, with a recent study revealing that there are now far more than 100,000 in the country." There is no way to check the accuracy of this claim. Further, the implication is that these are delinquent or criminal groups. The estimate was sufficiently exciting for the U.S. Department of Justice, Office of Juvenile Justice and Delinquency Prevention, to have used it in a public request for proposals on gang research (Federal Register 1987).

The consistency or meaning of the following estimates made by Walter Miller in his national surveys of 1975 and 1982 is also difficult to determine: 760 to 2,700 gangs in the eight largest cities of the United States (1975, p. 18); 2,200 gangs in approximately 300 U.S. cities and towns (1982, chap. 4, pp. 30–31); 1,130 gangs in the ten largest gang-problem cities between 1970 and 1980 (1982). Furthermore, how would these estimates compare (or can they be compared) to Thrasher's (1936) 1,313 gangs in Chicago in the 1920s? Figures on gang membership are just as elusive. Chicago Gang Crime police commander Dart claimed there were forty-one street gangs and 36,000 "hard-core" gang members in the city in 1992 (Herman 1992). Block and Block state that the four largest street gangs in Chicago "can be identified with most of the city's gang crime." They "accounted for 69 percent of police-recorded street gang-motivated criminal incidents and 55 percent of all street gang-motivated homicides from 1987 to 1990" (Block and Block 1993, p. 8).

Figures on numbers of gangs and gang members are often unreliable and inflated. A few years earlier, Bobrowski estimated gang membership in Chicago to range from "12,000 to as many as 120,000 persons" (1988, p. 40). District Attorney Ira Reiner estimated there were 1,000 gangs and 150,000 gang members in Los Angeles County in 1991 (O'Connell 1988). However, also in 1988, Spergel and Curry surveyed cities of varying sizes with not only gang problems but multiple agency program responses to them. They obtained unduplicated police data on numbers of street gangs and street gang members from thirty-five jurisdictions. A total of only 1,439 gangs from all cities was reported. Most were from three jurisdictions: Los Angeles City (280), the rest of Los Angeles County (320), and Chicago (128). A total of 120,636 gang members was reported, among them 26,000 in Los Angeles City, 44,000 in the rest of Los Angeles County, and 12,000 in Chicago (Spergel and Curry 1990, p. 59). The estimates have probably grown considerably since then, although probably nowhere approaching Dolan and Finney's earlier figure of 100,000 gangs in the criminal sense in which we use the term youth or street gang.

Increases in the numbers of gangs, gang members, or gang incidents have been reported in many cities in recent years. In Dade County, Florida, there were four gangs in 1980, twenty-five in 1983, forty-seven in 1985, and eighty in 1988 (Reddick 1987; Silbert, Cristiano, and Nunez-Cuenca 1988). In Los Angeles County, California, there were 239 gangs in 1985, 400 to possibly 800 in 1988 (Los Angeles County Sheriff's Department 1985; Gott 1988; Knapp 1988; see also Philibosian 1986), and 1,000 in 1991, as indicated above. The Houston Police Department documented the existence of 17 criminal gangs in 1988, 56 in 1989, 83 in 1990, and 102 in early 1991 (Buhmann 1991, p. i). In Santa Ana, Orange County, California, the number of individual cases assigned to the gang detail jumped from 286 in 1986 to 396 in 1987, including eight gang-related homicides—the highest number since 1979, when there were thirteen (Schwartz 1988). In San Diego County there were three gangs and fewer than 300 street gang members in 1975, but nineteen to thirty-five gangs, if factions are included, and 2,100 street gang members in 1987 (Davidson 1987).

However, declines in gangs, membership, and gang activity have also been reported. In New York City there were 315 gangs and 20,000 members in 1974, 130 gangs and 10,300 members in 1982, and 66 gangs and 2,500 members in 1987 (New York State Assembly 1974a; Galea 1982; Kowski 1988). During the heyday of New York City's youth-gang activity in the late 1950s, "Experts at the New York City Youth Board put the total of the problem gangs at 70" (New York City Youth Board 1957, p. 10). In Fort Wayne, Indiana, the police claimed the presence of six gangs with over 2,000 members in 1985–1986, but only three gangs and 50 members in 1988 (Hinshaw 1988). In El Monte, Los Angeles County, ten to twelve gangs and 1,000 gang members were found in the mid-1970s but only four gangs and about 50 active gang members in 1988 (Hollopeter 1988). In Louisville, Kentucky, fifteen gangs and forty to fifty gang incidents per month were reported in 1985, but only five gangs and one gang incident per month were reported as recently as July 1988 (Beavers 1988): the San Antonio police claimed to have fifty-four gangs with 1,000 members in the fall of 1990 but only twenty-four gangs with 600 members in the spring of 1991 (Buhmann 1991, p. 13).

In a recent study of "expert" informants in forty-five cities and six special sites with organized cross-agency approaches to dealing with the gang problem, we asked whether "the gang situation had improved or deteriorated in the past seven or eight years" (Spergel and Curry 1990). A large majority of respondents believed that the gang situation had deteriorated. In only seventeen of the cities surveyed was there evidence of any level of improvement in the gang situation, that is, significantly lower numbers of gangs or gang members, smaller gang size, and a decline in the percent of total index crime attributed to youth gangs. Serious gang crime, including drug selling, was also reported as significantly higher. Interestingly, respondents from law enforcement agencies estimated less of an increase in the problem than respondents from non-law enforcement agencies (Spergel and Curry 1990, pp. 215–216).

Estimates from law enforcement or police agencies may be more useful than those from other organizations or sources, particularly if such figures are based on arrests or focus on clearly defined "high profile" gangs. Police prevalence figures tend to be on the conservative side compared with those of news reporters, academics, and community agency informants. For example, in the 1940s the police estimated that there were 60 to 200 gangs in New York City, but a field researcher reported that there were then at least 250 gangs in Harlem alone (Campbell 1984b). One police commander estimated that there were 127 active gangs in New York City in the 1970s, with 144 gangs that were less active (Hargrove 1981). Another police officer claimed that there were 130 "delinquent" gangs and an additional 113 gangs under investigation in New York City in the early 1980s (Galea 1982). But Campbell estimated that there were 400 gangs in New York City in 1979 (Campbell 1984b). The Chicago Police Department estimated the number of gangs to be 110 in 1985 and 135 in both 1986 and 1987, but in his 1982 report W. Miller claimed that the number of Chicago gangs was 250 between 1970 and 1980 (but see Chicago Gang Crime police commander Dart's estimate of only forty-one street gangs in 1992 mentioned earlier). Curry and his associates caution that in the majority of police jurisdictions, the gang problem may be highly exaggerated since "far more gangs and gang members are reported than gang-related incidents" (Curry et al. 1994, p. 7). They suggest that the "gang crime problem is not about young men and women forming groups with names and symbols but about groups and individuals in these groups committing crimes against persons and property" (ibid., p. 2).

Estimates of the number of prison gangs may also be meaningless unless the character and size of the gangs and the frequency and seriousness of their criminal behavior are indicated. Estimates have varied from 47 gangs in twenty-four prisons in a 1981 report by Caltabriano to 114 gangs in thirty-three prisons in a 1985 report by Camp and Camp, which also indicated that the figure could go as high as 219 gangs if gangs with the same names in different California state prisons are counted. A gang such as the CRIPS in the California prison system was counted once in reports, but in fact different unrelated CRIPS gang units probably existed in different California institutions (G. Camp and Camp 1985). A Los Angeles County district attorney's report listed 298 black gangs in the county alone, of which 213 were CRIPS and 85 were Blood gangs (Reiner 1992, pp. 108–109).

A similar problem of unclear or nonmeaningful estimates of numbers of gangs or gang members exists for school settings. A national study of school crime stated that 15 percent of an estimated 21.5 million students aged 12 to 19, claimed their schools had gangs (Bastian and Taylor 1991, p. 1). A Los Angeles County survey indicated that 50 percent of schools in the county had gang problems (Los Angeles County Office of Education 1991). Spergel estimated that there were fifty-three male and seven female gangs in sixty public high schools in Chicago in 1985. The number represented 211 male factions. These were school gangs with names of high-profile street gangs. Furthermore, on the basis of police data, nineteen male and four female major youth gang factions were also found in the city's Catholic high schools (Spergel 1985). Yet none of these figures is sufficiently meaningful unless we know how many gang-related or non-gang delinquency problems were being caused by gang members whether on school property or elsewhere. It is quite possible that schools with many gangs, but with small numbers of members in each of them, in fact may experience fewer problems of deviance or disorder, particularly if such schools are well run and have reasonably high academic standards, than poorly managed schools with one or two large gangs (Spergel 1985).

Percentage Estimates of Youth Gang Members as More Useful

The percentage rather than the number of youth gang members may be a more meaningful and useful indicator of the scope of a gang problem in a particular social context. Percentage estimates generally are quite modest and suggest the problem is capable of being circumscribed and targeted for policy and program development purposes. Ideally, both accurate numbers and estimates of different categories of gangs and gang members would be most appropriate. Historical comparisons suggest that the proportion of a youth population reported to be gang members in a particular city or locality may not vary greatly over time. Thrasher (1936, p. 412) indicated that "one tenth of Chicago's 350,000 boys between the ages of 10 and 20 are subject to the demoralizing influence of gangs." Klein (1968) estimated that the census tract with the highest known number of gang members in Los Angeles in 1960 had only 6 percent of 10- to 17-year-olds affiliated with gangs. A Pennsylvania civic commission reported that only 6.4 percent of all juvenile arrests in 1968 were of known gang members (Klein 1971, p. 115). Vigil (1988b) estimated that only 3 to 10 percent of boys in the Mexican barrios of Los Angeles were gang members. Controlling for criminal conduct, Esbensen and Huizinga estimated that less than 3 percent of a cohort sample in Denver could be classified as gang members (1993, pp. 9–10).

A variety of self-report studies have been conducted, and the proportion of youths declaring they are gang members also does not seem to have changed radically over the past two decades, with a few exceptions. Savitz, Rosen, and Lalli (1980) determined that only 12 percent of black and 14 percent of white youths in Philadelphia who claimed to be gang members had Philadelphia Police Department records. Another self-report study found that 10.3 percent of black youths in suburban Cook County reported they were gang members (Johnstone 1981). In a self-report study in Seattle, 13 percent of youths said they belonged to gangs (R. Sampson 1986). In an as yet unpublished study of several very poor inner-city neighborhoods of Chicago, the following percentages of men 18 to 45 years old reported they "had belonged" to gangs: Mexican/Mexican-Americans, 3.5 percent; Puerto Ricans, 12.7 percent; white, 10.7 percent; and blacks, 13.8 percent (Testa 1988). In another self-report study of four inner-city neighborhoods in three large cities across the country, one male in three reported gang membership; however, this sample may have been preselected for gang membership (Fagan, Piper, and Moore 1986).

Buhmann in her survey of Texas cities concludes that "urban youths are not joining gangs wholesale. . . . Less than one urban youth in ten is a gang member, even by very generous criteria applied by some law enforcement agencies" (Buhmann 1991, p. iii). Highly questionable or less meaningful for defining the actual gang problem are other estimates. For example, Ruth Horowitz in her field research of a high-gang-crime Mexican-American community in Chicago reported that "some local residents estimated that close to 70 percent of the male population, at least for a short period (a few months), joined one of the eight major gangs" (Horowitz 1987, p. 439). The *Los Angeles Times* reported "there are 25,000 CRIPS and Blood gang members or 'associates' in Los Angeles County—an estimate based on arrests and field interrogation of persons stopped but not arrested. That represents 25 percent of the county's estimated 100,000 black men between the ages of 15 and 24" (Baker 1988a). A more recent report states that "the police have identified almost half of all black men in Los Angeles [city] between the ages of 21 and 24 as gang members" (Reiner 1992, p. iv).

Issues of racist labeling are relevant, particularly in the identification of African-American youths as gang members. In addition to the nearly 50 percent of black youths listed as gang members, the following rates of gang participation were recorded on the Los Angeles County Sheriff's computer system: 0.5 percent of Anglos or white youths, 6 to 7 percent of Asian youths, and 9 to 10 percent of Latino youths. We have no evidence that a higher percentage or rate of African-American youths commit gang-related offenses, especially violent offenses, than other groups of youths, particularly Latino youths, controlling for age, gender, and location (see next section). The percentages of youths who report themselves to be gang members in public school settings seems to run about the same as indicated already, ranging between 5 and about 10 percent. Results of a large statewide self-report study of 29,000 high school and junior high school students in Arizona reveals that 6 percent of high school and 7 percent of junior high students "claim to be gang members" (Saavedia 1991). A self-report study of an "'average' large high school in Chicago reports that "10.3 percent of the students . . . had at sometime during their life joined a gang" (Knox, Tromanhauser, and Laske 1991, p. 8). Spergel estimated that 5 percent of students in elementary school, 10 percent in high school, 20 percent in special school programs, and 35 percent of school dropouts between age 16 and 19 are gang members in Chicago (Spergel 1985).

The estimated figures for gang members as a proportion of population are usually higher in criminal justice settings. This suggests that delinquent gang members are more likely to be serious, chronic, or identifiable delinquents than are non-gang offenders. A family court worker reported that 20 percent of children going before the Queens County, New York, Family Court were involved in gang-related activities (New York State Assembly 1974b). One study of Cook County juvenile court probationers indicated that 22.7 percent were gang members (Utne and McIntyre 1982). Orange County's probation department reported that it provided services to approximately 520 active gang members, or 17 percent of the total juveniles supervised by probation (Orange County 1989, pp. 7–8).

The estimates are usually higher for correctional institutions, both adult and juvenile. The proportions range from 0 to 90 percent or more, depending on location of the institution and when and on what basis the estimates were made. Forty percent of the 22,000 inmates currently in Los Angeles County jail are estimated to be gang members (Monroe 1992, p. 38). Camp and Camp (1985) stated that 34 percent, or 5,300, of Illinois prison inmates were active gang members as of January 1984 but, not quite consistently, that 90 percent of Illinois prison inmates "are, were, or will be gang members" (p. 134). "The Illinois Department of Corrections reported that 65 percent of the prison population at prisons [in Joliet] are gang members" (Koziol 1990, sect. 1, pp. 1, 20). A California Youth Authority study found that 40 to 45 percent of the wards in the system could be identified as gang members in 1979, but the estimates had increased to between 70 and 80 percent in 1982 and 1983 (Hayes 1983). However, an official in the California Youth Authority estimated that probably only a third of its 13,152 wards should be "gang identified" (Lockwood 1988).

According to a recent report of a national survey of state prison inmates carried out in 1991, 6 percent of inmates belonged to a gang before entering prison. However, the definition of "criminal gang" was defined somewhat restrictively. It had to possess at least "5 or 6" of the following characteristics: formal membership that required initiation; a recognized leader; common identifiable clothing; a group name; members from the same neighborhood or school; and turf where group activities usually take place (Beck et al. 1993, p. 20). Another survey, based on self-report responses of youths in short- and long-term juvenile correctional institutions in five states (New York, Wisconsin, Massachusetts, Tennessee, and Texas), estimated that "about half" were gang members (Knox 1991b).

In general it is important to be aware that most gang members are youths who will probably grow out of their gang involvement. Only a small percentage will go on to serious or sustained crime patterns and end up as hard-core criminals. Perhaps most significant in determining the seriousness of the problem from the perspective of gang member as well as community safety and security is the gang violence component of the problem.

Youth Gang Violence

Reasonably adequate data are available on the current nature and scope of violence by gang members. Gang-related violence has increased and gang members, at least those with arrest records, are responsible for a disproportionate amount of violent crime. The U.S. Justice Department's National Crime Survey and the Federal Bureau of Investigation's reports indicate during one recent period a continuing increase of violent crime in the United States (Associated Press 1992; Brody 1992). Much of the increase, particularly in homicides in certain cities (e.g., Los Angeles, Chicago, Milwaukee, and Minneapolis), is attributed to gang violence. Gang homicides accounted for 36 percent of total homicides in Los Angeles and 40 percent in Minneapolis in 1990 (Sahagun 1990; Worthington 1991; see also Block 1991, p. 40; and Associated Press 1992). "Gunshot wounds, almost all of them involving gang members from the inner city, recently became the leading cause of the spinal injuries treated at the Rancho Los Amigo Medical Center, a [Los Angeles] county hospital with a major rehabilitation program" (Mydans 1990b). Adolescent gunshot wounds resulting from gang violence have also become a major concern to pediatric trauma centers in Chicago (Griffin 1992).

A graphic description of the nature of gang violence is contained in the following excerpt from a *Chicago Sun-Times* editorial:

> In "one weekend under fire," this newspaper staff reported all 61 [gang] shootings between dusk Friday, August 19, and dawn August 21 in the city and surrounding suburbs.

> Of the 61 victims here, 40 were African American, 13 were Hispanic, and eight were white. Twenty-six were teenagers, the youngest was 13. All but seven victims were men. All the suspected shooters were men. Forty percent of the shootings took place between 10 p.m. and 2 a.m. (1994, p. 21)

These figures, alarming as they are, need to be placed in context of the larger crime picture. Gang violence as a proportion of total serious crime by youth or street-gang members tends to be low on a city, school, or prison system basis. Bobrowski, who uses a definition of "gang incident" based on gang function or motivation rather than individual gang membership, indicates that for Chicago, "Part I [index or very serious] street-gang offenses measured less than 0.8 percent of comparable city-wide gang crime [between January 1986 and July 1988]. . . . The seriousness of the problem lies not in the extent of street gang activity but in its violent character and relative concentration in certain of Chicago's community areas" (1988, p. 41). Property crime is still the major type of offense committed by gang members, often in a nongang capacity.

Classic research on types of offenses by juveniles, youths, or young adults in delinquent groups or gangs suggests that violent crime was less common in earlier periods than it is now (Thrasher 1936; Shaw and McKay 1943). Whyte (1943) stressed that street gangs in Boston did not typically engage in brawls or gang fights that resulted in serious injury. W. Miller's (1962, 1976a) Boston gangs in the 1950s rarely used firearms, and their gang fights seldom resulted in serious injury. Klein (1971, p. 115) noted the relative rarity of the "truly violent act" among East Los Angeles Hispanic gangs in his research project areas over a four-year period in the 1960s. At about the same time, Bernstein (1964) and Short and Strodtbeck (1965) reported that delinquency and violence by juvenile gangs were relatively mild. More fighting took place within the gang than between opposing gangs. The most common form of offense appeared to be creating a disturbance, roughhousing noisily, or impeding public passage (W. Miller 1976a). Yablonsky (1962), and to a lesser extent Spergel (1964), were in the minority of observers when they reported that New York gang conflict behavior of the 1950s frequently could be violent and result in homicides.

Gangs were "suddenly" different in the 1970s and 1980s: "the weight of evidence would seem to support the conclusion that the consequences of assaultive activities by contemporary gangs are markedly more lethal than during any previous period" (W. Miller 1975, p. 41); "the cycles of gang homicide now seem to end higher and retreat to higher plateaus before surging forward again. If homicide is any indicator, gang violence has become a far more serious problem during the most recent decade" (Klein and Maxson 1987, p. 4). W. Miller (1975, pp. 75–76) made stark claims: violent crime by gang members in some cities was as much as one-third of all violent crime by juveniles. Juvenile gang homicides were about 25 percent of all juvenile homicides in approximately sixty-five major cities in the United States. Block's study (1985, p. 5), based on police data, found that gang homicide accounted for 25 percent of teenage homicides and 50 percent of Hispanic teenage homicides in Chicago between 1965 and 1981. In the 1980s, Los Angeles City supplanted Chicago as the country's worst large gang-violence city. There were 329 gang homicides (34% of total homicides) in Los Angeles City in 1990 and 375 (36% of total) in 1991 compared with 101 gang homicides (11% of total) in Chicago in 1990 and 133 (14% of total) in 1991. The figures and percentages in Chicago have to be approximately doubled to make them comparable with those in Los Angeles because of the latter city's broader definition of a gang homicide.

I am not convinced that these statistics portend an inexorable upward spiral or trend of gang violence, even though Los Angeles and Chicago recently recorded the highest levels of gang homicides in their respective histories. There are peaks and valleys in the number of gang homicides over fairly long periods. Gang homicides averaged about 70 per year in Chicago between 1981 and 1986, 63 per year in the next highest period of 1967 to 1972, but only 25 per year in the period between 1973 and 1978. Furthermore, on the basis of official statistics, gang homicides have declined sharply in New York City and Philadelphia in the past fifteen years. Gang homicides in Chicago as a percent of total homicides have ranged from 1.71 percent in 1975 to 14 percent in 1991, with important dips, especially in the black community (see below).

Again, depending on how one reports or classifies and interprets these homicides, the *basic youth violence* situation in Los Angeles may be little different from that in Chicago or New York. Although the New York Police Department claims a very low level of gang crime, youth violence and drug violence currently "may be at an all time high" (Galea 1988). The rate of youth violence generally may be higher in Detroit than in Chicago, although Detroit police claim a very low level of youth gang activity. However, youth violence rates may actually have dropped in some city and state jurisdictions. For example, the number of youths arrested for violent crimes dropped slightly (3%) in Hawaii between 1981 and 1990, although that state claims there is a youth gang problem in a number of its cities. The most significant increase in Hawaii's youthful arrests was in the category of status offenses which increased by 17.9 percent over the decade (Chesney-Lind et al. 1992, p. 145).

The puzzles of gang-crime statistics and what they mean are not easy to resolve. The proportion of violent crime attributed to gang members is relatively higher than the proportion of violent crime attributed to non-gang members in most social contexts. Yet the relationship of gang to non-gang violent crime across seemingly similar cities is not clear. In 1987, gang homicides were 25.2 percent of the total number of homicides in Los Angeles City, but 6.9 percent of the total number of homicides in Chicago. Gang felonious assaults were 11.2 percent in Los Angeles, but 4.3 percent in Chicago. Gang-related robberies were 6.6 percent of total robberies in Los Angeles, but only 0.8 percent of total robberies in Chicago. These differences may reflect not only varying definitions but also different police practices and different local situations, as well as short-term fluctuations.

The increase in gang violence, or at least the reported problem of gang violence, in some cities has been attributed to several factors. Gangs have more weapons (W. Miller 1975; Spergel 1983) than they had in the past. Guns are used more often conjointly with moving cars (drive-by shootings). The ready availability of improved weaponry, such as.22's, .38's, .45's, .357 magnums, sawed-off shotguns, A.K. 47s, Tech-9s, Uzis, and other semiautomatic and high-powered weapons, is associated with the changing pattern of gang conflict and its more lethal consequences. Block and Block have observed an increase in the rate of gang homicides compared with "gang-motivated personal violence offenses known to the police in Chicago, from 1 street gang-motivated homicide per 44 street gang-motivated personal violence in 1987 to 1 such homicide for 20 instances of gang violence in 1990." Virtually the entire increase was attributed "to an increase in the use of high-caliber, automatic, or semi-automatic weapons" (Block and Block 1993, p. 7).

The "tradition" of intergang rumbles based on large assemblages of youths arriving for battle on foot, which may be easily interdicted, has been supplanted by the practice of mobile groups of two or three youths, usually in a vehicle, out looking for or prepared to encounter opposing gang members. Although shootings are sometimes planned, spur of the moment decisions to attack targets of sudden opportunity are common (see also Horowitz 1983).

The older ages of gang members (see below) may also be responsible for greater use of sophisticated weaponry and its attendant violence. Such weaponry may be relatively more available to older teenagers and young adults than to juveniles. The median age of the gang homicide offender in Chicago has been 19 or 20 years, with a 20- or 21-year old victim for many years (Spergel 1986). Los Angeles data (Maxson, Gordon, and Klein 1985) and San Diego police statistics (San Diego Association of Governments 1982) also indicate that mainly older male adolescents and young adult males are involved in gang homicides. This is not to deny a rise, or even possibly a greater rise, in overall juvenile or female violence in recent years, but the base figure is smaller. A recent report of the Illinois Criminal Justice Information Authority indicates that the prevalence or percentage of violent crime arrestees younger than 17 in the state actually declined between 1985 and 1991 (1994, p. 1). Moreover, we cannot accept some media reports, current estimates or so-called research reviews that conclude gang violence is more likely to occur among younger than older adolescent gang members. Such reports or "data" are unreliable or invalid, based on small observational samples or decades old data (Reiss and Roth 1993, p. 142).

The killing of innocent bystanders by gang members has received attention by community, police, and researchers. Such gang-related homicides are sometimes reported to be substantial and a growing problem. Yet the available limited data suggest that the proportion of these homicides may be relatively low. Los Angeles county and city police records suggest that such usually unintended or accidental events range from 10 percent or less to possibly 25 percent of total gang-related— broadly defined—homicides (Reiner 1992, pp. 56, 107). The Manhattan District Attorney's Office identifies a similar percentage of bystander homicides—6 to 10 percent resulting from its *drug gang* wars (Blumenthal 1992). Generally gang members know the members of opposing gangs or at least where they hang out. Gang assaults take place within a small, often well-demarcated locality or street where gang members are known to congregate. It should be noted that a significant number of "non-gang" youths also associate and hang out with gang members in these locations and are at times "accidentally" killed. They may or may not be included in the "innocent" bystander victim category.

A significant proportion of all prison homicides are estimated to result from gang activity. Some state prisons are particularly violent. Of twenty gang killings in prisons in 1983, nine occurred in the California system. Between 1975 and 1984, there were 372 gang-related homicides in California prisons, "a record unsurpassed by any other organized crime group in California" (G. Camp and Camp 1985, p. 2). The problem of prison gang assaults and homicides has grown more serious in Texas. In 1984 and 1985, the Texas Department of Criminal Justice Institutional Division . . . recorded 1,555 inmate assaults, 5,598 staff assaults, and 52 inmate homicides. In these two years, the department had more homicides than in the previous fifteen years. Eighty percent or more of inmate and staff assaults and 92 percent of the inmate homicides were attributed to gang-related activities (Buentello 1992).

On the other hand, the numbers or proportions of gang violent acts by prison inmates may not be a function of the number of gangs or STGs (Security Threat Groups) in the particular prison. There is some evidence that the "most prevalent STG tends to suppress the negative activity of other STGs" or gangs (Baugh 1993, p. 21).

Issues of Race/Ethnicity, Age, and Gender

There are important differences in patterns of gang violence over time on a racial/ethnic, age, and gender basis that must be taken into consideration in the analysis of the causes of gang problems and what to do about these factors. Street-gang violence appears to be a relatively greater problem in the Hispanic than in the African-American community in both Chicago and Los Angeles, at least on an incidence rate basis. Gang homicide victimization is probably the most reliable indicator of gang violence and is a generally accepted key indicator of the scope and seriousness of gang violence, particularly in large cities with a tradition of gang problems and reasonably good data collection procedures. The Chicago gang homicide data set of the Illinois Criminal Justice Information Authority developed by Dr. Carolyn C. Block is particularly extensive and reliable in respect to racial/ethnic, age, and gender differences over time.

Figure 3–1 shows an upward trend in overall gang-motivated homicides in Chicago between 1965 and 1992, but a decline between approximately 1971 and 1978. The data suggest a general escalation of gang homicides beginning in 1990. Estimates for 1993 are 133 gang homicides for this year), which would be the highest number of gang killings in almost thirty years in Chicago. This trend is not so clear and may not exist in the Chicago African-American community (Figure 3–2). For this community the peaks are approximately the same between 1968–1971 and 1981–1986. A sharp decline in black gang homicide victimization occurred between 1975

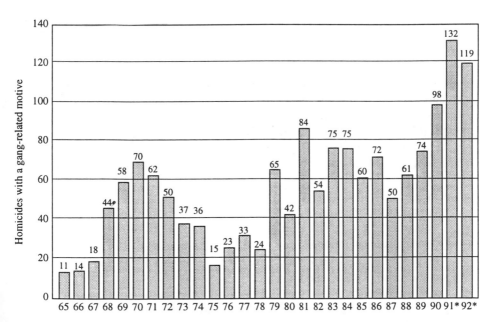

Figure 3–1.   Chicago street-gang-related homicide: Victims by year of occurrence. *Preliminary data. (Source: Chicago Homicide Project, Illinois Criminal Justice Information Authority, Dr. Carolyn C. Block.)

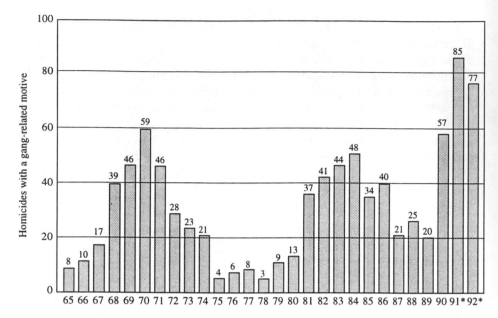

Figure 3–2. Chicago street-gang-related homicide: Non-Latino black victims, 1965 to 1990. *Preliminary data. (Source: Chicago Homicide Project, Illinois Criminal Justice Information Authority, Dr. Carolyn C. Block.)

and 1980. At this time there is no explanation why this temporary but substantial decline occurred.

The pattern for Latino gang-related homicide victims is somewhat different, representing, with fluctuation, a definite upward trend (Figure 3–3). The overall increase in gang homicide victims in the past twenty-eight or twenty-nine years is probably accounted for by the increase in the size of the Latino population.

Table 3–1 shows that rates of gang homicide victimization for different age and gender groups in Chicago are higher in the Latino than in the black community, at least between 1987 and 1989. The differences are particularly marked for Latino and black youths age 15 through 24, the years of highest incidence of membership in gangs. Gang victimization rates are systematically and very significantly higher for males than for females across all race/ethnic and age groups. In the early 1990s, whites and blacks each comprised about 39 percent of the population, with the remainder largely Latino (20%). The latter group comprised a significantly younger population than the other two groups.

The pattern for offenders is highly similar to that for victims. Block states that in Chicago "of all identified homicide offenders from 1982 through 1989, the Latino male offenders were by far the most likely to have committed the offense in a street gang confrontation. Over 40 percent of Latino male offenders, compared to only 12 percent of non-Latino white and non-Latino black male offenders were involved in a street gang-related homicide" (Block 1991, p. 33).

Block also demonstrates that Latino males are at greater risk of becoming offenders at a younger age than non-Latino black or non-Latino white males. If the Latino male "survives his teenage years in Chicago without becoming a homicide offender or victim, his risk drops sharply in his twenties and is even lower in his thirties. The risk faced by a non-Latino male, however, does not begin to diminish until his mid-twenties, and even then the drop is not as steep as for Latinos . . . " (Block 1991, pp. 18–19). Hispanic females are also at much higher risk than non-Hispanic females of becoming a gang offender or victim, at least at ages 15 through 19 years (see Table 3–1).

Black gang violence is down for a recent period of years in Los Angeles. The Los Angeles Sheriff's Department reported a 29 percent decrease in black-on-black gang killings in 1990 compared to the previous year. The Los Angeles Police Department reported that the share of killings attributed to black gangs, which was 51 percent as recently as 1988, fell to 32 percent in 1990. While black gang violence was decreasing, a sharp upward trend in Latino gang violence was detected. The Sheriff's Office reported a jump of 96 percent in Latino gang homicides for 1990 over the previous year. The biggest increases in gang crime occurred in Los Angeles' heavily Latino neighborhoods for this period.

Latino gang members were being added to the city police department's computer system files at a rate two and a half times greater than new black gang members, despite the heavier overall proportion of black youth identified as gang members. The aging of the black population and the rapid expansion of the Latino population could be factors in these pattern changes (Reiner 1992, pp. 100–102). The increase in Latino

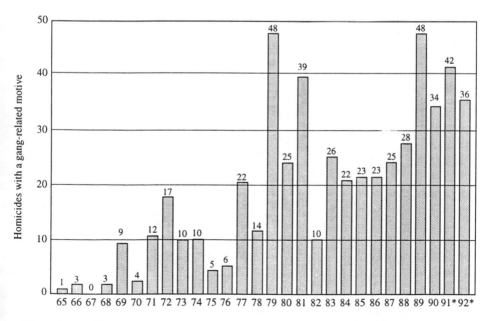

Figure 3–3.   Chicago street-gang-related homicide: Latino victims, 1965 to 1990. *Preliminary data. (Source: Chicago Homicide Project, Illinois Criminal Justice Information Authority, Dr. Carolyn C. Block.)

Table 3-1. Street-Gang-Related Homicide Rates in Chicago by Race/Ethnicity, Gender, and Age, 1988*

	Victim's Race/Ethnicity and Gender					
	Latino		Non-Latino White, Other		Non-Latino Black	
	M	F	M	F	M	F
Birth–4	.0	.0	.0	.0	.0	.0
5–9	.0	.0	.0	.0	.0	.0
10–14	11.5	a	.0	.0	3.1	.0
15–19	66.3	6.2	15.6	.0	22.1	.0
20–24	34.1	.0	2.4	.0	6.6	.0
25–29	8.5	.0	a	.0	5.5	.0
30–34	3.5	.0	.0	.0	a	.0
35–39	4.6	.0	.0	.0	a	a
40–44	.0	.0	.0	.0	.0	.0
45–49	.0	.0	.0	.0	a	.0
50–54	.0	.0	.0	.0	.0	.0
55–59	.0	.0	.0	.0	.0	.0
60–64	a	.0	.0	.0	.0	.0
65–69	.0	.0	.0	.0	.0	.0
70–74	.0	.0	.0	.0	.0	.0
75+	.0	.0	.0	.0	.0	.0
Total	11.8	.7	1.0	.0	3.8	a[+]

Source: Illinois Criminal Justice Information Authority, Dr. Carolyn C. Block.

*Annual victimization rate per 100,000 population (mean of 1987, 1988, 1989, divided by 1988 population).

[+]Number of victims is not zero, but is fewer than one a year.

population in certain communities where blacks are being displaced has resulted recently in deadly turf wars between Latino and black gangs (Dellios 1994, p. 24).

Individual Gang and Non-gang Member Studies: Violence and Serious Crime

The relationship between gangs and violence is most evident when patterns of behavior by delinquent gang members and non-gang members are compared. Gang youths engage in more violent crime than do non-gang delinquent youths. Klein and Myerhoff, almost three decades ago, (1967, pp. 1–2) observed that "the urban gang delinquent is different in kind from the urban non-gang delinquent. . . . Gang members have higher police contact rates . . . and become involved in more serious delinquencies than nonmembers." Recently the Los Angeles County District Attorney's Office reported that half of all gang members participate in violence, though minor in most cases. "This is a much higher rate (by a factor of four) than for non-gang members. There are also twice as many frequent violent offenders among gang members" (Reiner 1992, p. ii). Orange County, California, probation statistics indicate that gang-affiliated minors had significantly higher technical and new law violation rates (55.1%) than non-gang delinquent minors (26.4%) in 1987 (Orange County 1989). A Swedish researcher found that delinquents who were group or "network" related committed more frequent and serious offenses than were non-network delinquents (Sarnecki 1986).

The most consistent and impressive differences between gang and non-gang offense patterns of gang delinquents are seen in findings by different researchers in Philadelphia over a twenty-year period. Bernard Cohen (1969a, pp. 77–79), using data collected by the Philadelphia Police Department's gang unit, found that "gangs engage in more violent behavior than do delinquent non-gang groups": 66.4 percent of gang events but only 52.6 percent of delinquent group events fell into violent offense categories. Only 1.4 percent of gang events, but 13.7 percent of group events, were property crimes. Gang members' offenses were more serious and more often involved the display or use of a weapon.

Friedman, Mann, and Friedman (1975), seeking to distinguish gang, non-gang delinquents, and nondelinquents in the early 1970s, found that violent behavior differentiated street gang members from non-gang members better than all the other legal, socioeconomic, and psychological factors studied. Gang members also had more police arrests for nonviolent crime, more truancy, and more alcohol and drug abuse (pp. 599–600).

Similarly, on the basis of a sample from the 1945 Philadelphia cohort study, Rand (1987, pp. 155–156) found support for her hypothesis that "boys who join a gang are more delinquent than those who do not. The 31 boys who reported gang affiliation represented 29 percent of the total offender sample and were responsible for 50 percent of the offenses." Tracy, using the 1945 and 1958 Philadelphia birth cohort studies, also showed that juvenile gang membership was associated with significantly higher levels of delinquency, particularly for black youths. The offenses of gang members had higher average seriousness scores. For nonwhites, the rate of nonviolent offenses was about 1.7 times as high for gang members as for non-gang delinquents; the rate for violent offenses was almost twice as high; and, for aggravated assault, it was three times as high. The pattern for whites was less consistent. Analysis of the 1958 cohort, not yet completed, suggested a quite similar pattern (Tracy 1982). The self-report components of Tracy's 1945 cohort study were consistent with the official data findings.

Gang influence on criminality did not stop at the end of the juvenile period. When offense frequency and seriousness based on official and unofficial records were examined for the period 18 to 26 years of age, gang members equaled, if not exceeded, differences observed for the juvenile period. Thus, gang membership appeared "to prolong the extent and seriousness of the criminal career" (Tracy, 1982; see also Tracy 1987, p. 19). These conclusions are consistent with those of a Philadelphia researcher, who more than twenty years earlier noted that a "large portion of persistent and dangerous juvenile gang offenders becomes 'even more serious' adult offenders" (Robin 1967, p. 24).

Maxson, Klein, and Cunningham in their recent study of gang and non-gang members arrested for drug-related homicides in Los Angeles city and county, found that gang members generally had more delinquent or criminal backgrounds than non-gang drug-related homicide offenders. Whereas 63 to 75 percent of the non-gang members had arrest records, for gang members the percentages ranged from 81 to 90 percent. Gang members had more violent arrest histories, particularly for assaults, weapons violations, and robbery (Maxson, Klein, and Cunningham 1992).

Finally, a California Department of Justice study (G. Camp and Camp 1985, p. 108) found that gang members who had been released from prison committed a great many serious crimes. Two hundred and fifty gang members were randomly selected from California prison gangs (Nuestra Familia, Mexican Mafia, Black Guerilla Family, and Aryan Brotherhood gangs), and their careers were tracked. Between 1978 and 1981, 195 of the 250 gang members were arrested, often repeatedly, for: 65 misdemeanors and 350 felonies, including 24 for murder, 57 for robbery, 46 for burglary, 31 for narcotics offenses, 44 for weapons offenses, and 28 for assault with a deadly weapon. Beck and his associates in their 1991 survey of state prisons found that gang-member inmates, compared with non-gang-member inmates who were group-oriented offenders reported significantly more use and sale of drugs, more fighting with other groups, and more shoplifting, car theft, and robbery (Beck et al. 1993, p. 20).

Conclusion

It is important to adequately describe the parameters of the gang problem before I attempt to describe gang structure and dynamics, analyze its causes, and make policy or program recommendations. The problem of reliability of data affects such a description. Because of this problem, it is difficult to estimate the actual numbers of gangs or gang members, nationally or in a particular city or institutional context. Percentage estimates are probably better. Such estimates have certainly been more consistent than actual numbers for cities or parts of cities over the years, ranging from 5 to 10 percent of the youth or teenage population.

Reasonably adequate data are available on the scope of violence by gang members, especially gang homicides. Although gang homicide is on the increase in many cities, it is clear that serious gang crime accounts for only a small percentage of total serious crime, violent and not violent. Gang crime is concentrated in certain neighborhoods and ethnic groups of inner-city or socially marginal areas. Of special interest, not sufficiently recognized by the general public, is that Latinos rather than African-Americans generally account for higher rates of gang violence and for the numerical increase in gang homicides over the past quarter century, at least in Chicago and probably in Los Angeles. The data are also clear that the extreme gang violence problem is due primarily to youths between 15 and 24 years of age, particularly to those in the late adolescent years.

The evidence also consistently indicates that violent activity is more characteristic of the delinquent gang member than of the delinquent non-gang member. Gang member violence does not stop at the end of the adolescence, but continues into young adulthood. The fact that a youth is a gang member, especially if he has already committed one or more violent offenses, suggests that special attention be paid to him, for purposes of control and rehabilitation, as described later in this book.

4

Gangs, Drugs, and Violence

There is a tendency, especially by the media and law enforcement, to mix gangs, violence, and drug trafficking into one large "ball of wax." The simplistic political and policy response to these presumed interrelated problems is usually suppression. However, gangs, drugs, violence, and such characteristics as delinquency, organized crime, and minority group status are distinctive sets of variables and are not necessarily all closely related. Furthermore, their sequence and patterning may vary depending on how they are embedded in particular changing community or social contexts.

Vigil has observed that "The specific relationships between drug trafficking and gang violence contrast greatly across the broad ethnic categories, and there is diversity as well within intra-ethnic categories. . . . Such variations are also characteristic of substance abuse patterns and levels of gang violence" (Vigil 1992, p. iii).

This chapter explores the extent to which drug use, drug trafficking, and violence by different gangs have been variably interrelated in different communities in recent decades. There is some, not incontrovertible, theory and evidence that gang members may progress from gang violence to drug use to drug trafficking, which then becomes a basis for sophisticated criminal organization. There are, however, significant exceptions to this sequence. Later chapters examine why youths get into gangs and leave gangs—sometimes to pursue criminal careers. Here the focus is on issues of gang and gang member drug use, drug trafficking, and under varying conditions the interrelationship of these factors with violent gang or non-gang-related behavior.

Much speculation characterizes the heated discussions of the relation between gangs, violence, and drugs. My own view is that these problems are often distinctive and separable, and that somewhat different causes or combinations of causes create them. I believe, for example, that issues of personality disturbance contribute relatively more to drug use, particularly addiction; social status contributes more to problems of ganging and gang violence; and economic insufficiency contributes more to drug trafficking and property crime controlling for certain age categories and racial/ethnic groups in inner-city, and often rapidly changing or marginal, communities.

Gang Drug Use and Trafficking: Historical Perspectives

The relationships between gangs, drug use, and drug trafficking received only passing attention in the classic street-gang literature (however, see Short and Strodtbeck

43

1965). Alcohol and drug use were not usually differentiated (Klein 1971). The specific relationship between drug use and drug selling was not systematically explored. Chein and his associates (1964) found little drug use or selling by members of youth gangs contacted by New York City Youth Board (street-gang) workers. The existence of drug-using and-selling gangs or subcultures was not clearly demonstrated in the 1950s and 1960s, as predicted by Cloward and Ohlin (1960) (see Short and Strodtbeck 1965). Spergel (1964), however, found a close relationship between drug use and limited drug dealing by older youth gang members making a transition out of violent gang activity and gang membership. Moore, in her recent book, recalls that during the late 1940s some of the Chicano gang members of East Los Angeles were the first to use heroin. The drug became especially popular "among the older members in Hoyo Maravilla and the barrio became a center for heroin marketing." Gang members "matured" out of the gang-fighting subculture by "dropping into" the heroin subculture (Moore 1991, p. 32).

Earlier gang studies indicated a certain ambivalence or even negative reaction by gang members to drug use or sale in local gang areas. Core gang members were reported in the 1950s and 1960s, and still in the 1990s, as forcing drug-abusing members out of the gang, particularly those using or "shooting up" heroin, cocaine, and crack, and threatening neighborhood drug dealers to stop trafficking was not uncommon (see, for example, Spergel 1964; Short and Strodtbeck 1965). Many gangs have traditionally enjoyed or tolerated use of marijuana. Street workers reported that 42.5 percent of black gang members and 33.6 percent of white gang members used "pot" in the late 1950s or early 1960s. However, such drug use had relatively lower legitimacy (Short and Strodtbeck 1965, p. 82) than in recent decades.

In his more recent field studies of Mexican-American gang youths in Southern California. Vigil found that on the average the youths first began to use intoxicants at about 12.7 years of age, that polydrug use was common, but most did not "engage extensively in drug sales" (Vigil 1988b, p. 126). It is important to note, however, that there have always been drug dealers and drug users in the Mexican-American (or Puerto Rican) ghetto gang communities, but they were not necessarily gang members or affiliated with gangs. Vigil describes the process and function of drug use for the Chicano gang members (and probably for most gang members regardless of race or ethnicity):

> Drinking and drugs act as a "social lubricant" to facilitate the broadening, deepening, and solidifying of group affiliations and cohesiveness. . . . Drug and alcohol usage often facilitates gang youths' release from their felt obligations to social mores and thus increases their willingness to participate in other criminal acts, especially if such behavior seems to help them prove their loyalty and commitment to the group. . . .
>
> For those who started earliest, glue and/or paint sniffing, and sometimes the use of pills, clearly preceded the initiation of alcohol and/or marijuana consumption. Drinking beer or wine begins in earnest in at least the first year of junior high school. Liquor consumption is a decidedly group affair, and large bottles of wine (quarts, half gallons, or gallons, usually of cheaper brands) and quarts of beer are sometimes passed in almost ritualistic fashion. . . . Regular members generally move

from one set of substances to another in their teens, specialize in heroin. Peripheral and temporary members, on the likely to be marijuana users with occasional resort to other substances heroin, however. (Vigil 1988b, p. 126)

Increase in Gang Member Drug Trafficking

Changes in the structure of the economy may have been largely responsible for the entry of gang members, as individuals and cliques, into drug trafficking. Changing labor market conditions in the 1960s and 1970s, especially the decrease of low-skilled manufacturing jobs, made it difficult for older gang youths to find legitimate employment and leave the teenage gang. Economic survival and the illegal drug economy created pressures to develop the youth gang as an economic base of opportunities as well as a source of social status.

In the early 1970s, New York City officials believed that most youth gangs were not extensively involved in the sale of narcotics (Collins 1979), although gang youths could exploit or manipulate certain drug-dealing situations. A New York State Assembly report (1974a, p. 5) stated that "many gangs engage in shakedowns of area merchants, residents, and others trafficking in soft drugs, such as marijuana, amphetamines, barbiturates, cocaine." By the late 1970s there was already evidence that some black gang members in Chicago, particularly those older members with prison experience, were significantly engaged in drug dealing. The Blackstone Rangers, later the El Rukns, were a continuing target of the Chicago Police Department for drug dealing, shady property investments, and other organized criminal activities.

By the early and middle 1980s, law enforcement authorities and researchers reported extensive drug use and selling by gang and former gang members in both small and large cities. In most cities, selling was not systematic, lucrative, or "big time." Hagedorn indicates very heavy use of drugs but only some drug selling by mainly African-American leaders in Milwaukee:

> Less than 5 percent of those interviewed said that at this time they never used drugs . . . 60 percent . . . admitted they used drugs (mainly marijuana) most or all of the time. . . . Drugs are both a means of "partying" for all and a modest means of income for some of the older members. Nearly half of those we interviewed admitted they sold drugs at least "now and then" as a "hustle." Nearly one in five founders said they sold drugs regularly. Over two thirds said that members of the main group of their gang sold drugs "regularly" and nearly all said someone in the main group sold at least "now and then." (Hagedorn 1988, p. 142)

By the middle and late 1980s, it was apparent that drug use—but not drug dealing—by gang members was widespread in many localities of the country. Furthermore, it was clear that drug use and delinquency were associated with gang membership, and that drug use was higher for gang delinquent members than for adolescents generally and for non-gang delinquents in inner-city areas. A Florida legislative committee reported that 92 percent of gang members admitted experimenting with narcotics, mainly marijuana and cocaine (Reddick 1987). Fagan, Piper, and Moore (1986) reported that individual prevalence rates for different types of drug

...ency differed between gang youths and general adolescent popula-
...ons in the same inner-city area. According to Fagan,

> The prevalence of self-reported delinquency and substance use was far greater for
> gang youths compared to non-gang youths. . . . The severity of delinquent involve-
> ment was greater for both male and female gang youths . . . [however] gang and non-
> gang youths differed little in their involvement in alcohol and marijuana use. Evi-
> dently regular marijuana use is a natural social behavior among inner-city youths:
> over 32% of both gang and non-gang youths were involved in marijuana use. (Fagan
> 1990, pp. 195, 200–203)

Distinctions between the gang member as drug user and drug trafficker began
to be made. The County of Los Angeles Probation Department reported that "gang
members are now rarely addicts. Traditionally drug dealers were addicts selling to
support their own habit. . . . Typical monthly data from a specialized drug pusher/
seller intensive . . . caseload reveals that only 2 of 39 probationers had positive or
'dirty' narcotic test results. Current gang drug dealers are not habitual drug users"
(Los Angeles County Probation Department 1988, p. 2).

Furthermore, while many, if not most, gang members are heavy drug users and
even heavier drug sellers than non-gang members, this does not necessarily mean
that most gang youth are members of criminal drug organizations:

> Drugs and gangs are not two halves of the same phenomenon. Though they threaten
> many of the same neighborhoods, and involve some of the same people, gangs and
> drugs must be treated as separate evils.

- Over 70% of gang members use drugs, usually about once a week. Total incidence of
  drug use among gang members is roughly four times greater than among non-gang
  youths.
- The incidence of drug sales among gang members is seven times higher than among
  non-gang youths; but most gang members are not drug dealers in any meaningful sense
  of the word. Only one in seven sell as often as 12 times a year.
- Younger gang members (the vast majority) continue to focus primarily on ferocious
  intergang rivalries; drugs are a secondary concern, seen mainly as a source of part-
  time employment.
- The pattern is different for older members of black gangs, many of whom are disen-
  gaging from traditional activities to pursue careers in low-to-mid level drug trafficking. (Reiner 1992, p. iii)

The close relationship between gangs, drug use, and trafficking has been found
most consistently in criminal justice system populations. Of 276 documented gang
members on probation in San Diego County, 207 (75%) had drug convictions (Davidson 1987). Moore (1978) found an integral relationship between imprisoned Hispanic
gang members and drug trafficking. A close relationship between prison gangs and
drug trafficking as well as other kinds of problem or criminal behavior has been
observed by other researchers in recent decades (G. Camp and Camp 1985; C. Camp
and Camp 1988). A study of 589 property offenders from three prison intake centers
in Ohio found that drugs, unemployment, alcohol, and gangs, respectively, were the
most important factors in property crime (Dinitz and Huff 1988).

Gang Drug Trafficking and Criminal Organization

Much media or law enforcement reporting implies or states that sophisticated drug trafficking and street gangs, especially black gangs, are closely associated. For example, "Los Angeles is now the main port of entry for cocaine nationwide as well as the home of 30,000 black gang members" (Donovan 1988, p. 2). Officials in Miami claimed that the connection between gangs and drugs was now bigger than ever. A key problem was the trafficking of drugs by gang members traveling from cities of the Northeast to Miami (ibid.). All of this implied that street gangs were criminal drug organizations.

Yet the evidence has never been sufficient to indicate that all youth or street gangs are equivalent, or that they naturally progress, to drug organizations, or organizations whose primary purpose is criminal economic gain. This is not to deny that individuals or subgroups of gangs are, and traditionally have been, engaged in selling drugs, often to maintain personal drug habits, or to socialize with, share drugs with, or sell to peers in the gangs. Gangs are usually fluid and complex collectives. Their members can be simultaneously involved in gang violence and in trafficking, sometimes for drug or criminal adult organizations independent of the street gang. Some youth gang members can make a transition at various points in their careers to more organized criminal gain behavior. Drug trafficking increasingly aids in this process.

Research strongly suggests, however, that typically active conflict-oriented youth gangs are primarily concerned with issues of status, turf, and partying and are not normally engaged in organized drug dealing. Drug operations are usually conducted outside the context of the gang as a whole (Conley 1991; Klein, Maxson, and Cunningham 1991; Moore 1991).

Nevertheless, the issue of gang and drug trafficking turf may still be important. The gang member or former member drug dealer usually strongly believes that the gang's territorial or status claims are the required basis for priority in selling drugs. Thus, gang or former gang members claim they have a monopoly right to sell drugs on some streets but not necessarily on others in Chicago's West Side (Wilkerson 1991). Gang members can be recruited to sell drugs in some bars but not in others in Philadelphia (Anderson 1990, pp. 81–82). The youth gang's fluid, unstable, emotionally charged character is not suited to a rational drug organization. Hagedorn describes the short-lived experiment of one African-American street gang with drug entrepreneurship. The gang established a "drug house":

> The house was a "drive-in" where buyers drove their car up to the corner, a "waiter" or "waitress" came out and took the order and the gang filled it in a jiffy. But the house only lasted a few months and the gang discontinued organized drug sales. . . . It was too much of a hassle . . . the police did not really bother their sales, but the organization necessary to pull off an ongoing drug house was too much for this gang whose members were concerned with "making it" day by day. While many of the adult members of the gang still sell cocaine and marijuana, it is done, as in most other gangs, individually and sporadically. (Hagedorn 1988, pp. 104–105)

Taylor's experience with drug-dealing gangs in Detroit is apparently quite different from Hagedorn's in Milwaukee. For Taylor, the street gang may have graduated into sophisticated criminal corporations or corporate gangs. Both male and female drug organizations may exist independently of each other. Taylor also observes and classifies other types of street gangs into "scavengers" or turf gangs (Taylor 1990a, 1993).

"Big fights" can result if turf boundaries for selling drugs by gang or former gang members are disregarded. In fact, gangs may spring up to protect territory invaded by so-called drug gangs, primarily criminal gain organizations or cliques of other street gangs, who enter the gang's turf to sell drugs. Also, drug dealers from outside the community or out of state have been known to enter an area, for example a public housing project, to sell drugs. Local gangs may mobilize to keep the intruder gangs or cliques out. The out-of-community gangs or traffickers, however, may be sufficiently powerful or persuasive to recruit and induce local turf gang members to retail the drugs they will supply and/or they may directly "take on" the local gangs for "territorial rights" (Boston Housing Authority 1989).

The street gang fundamentally subscribes to a violent subculture. Its interests, aptitudes, and skills in the use of violence may, however, be useful not simply in the fulfillment of certain enforcement roles required to conduct a drug business. In some cases, the use of violence may be more important than drug dealing per se. Drug dealing is regarded as simply one illegitimate means for "making money," based on the violence capacity of the gang.

> Investigators said that the leaders of the C & C [gang] devised a system of collecting protection money for street corner drug sales in the area of Brook Avenue and 139th Street [Bronx], they found that extortion carried a far better risk-to-reward ratio than drug dealing. Although they and their gang did not abandon heroin trafficking, extortion became their main source of income. . . .
>
> If you wanted to deal in their area, you had to pay rent and abide by their rules. . . .
>
> They would actually designate spots, said the [federal] agent. . . .
>
> Since 1986, prosecutors charged the gang killed 14 people who tried to obstruct business. . . . (Faison 1994, B16)

Dunston draws a sharp distinction between youth gang and drug organizations, and he does not see youth gangs converting or developing into drug organizations:

> In New York City, drugs are controlled by organized crime groups. Young, weak, undermanned and poorly organized street gangs cannot compete with the older more powerful and violent groups. The fragmented street gangs do not have the network or the power to distribute or control drugs on a large scale. What we see are drug organizations employing youths in various aspects of their drug business. They are employed as steerers, lookouts, dealers, enforcers or protectors from robbers and other drug organizations. The primary difference between a drug organization and a youth gang is that in a drug organization all members are employees while youth gang membership only requires affiliation. We do not see our youth gangs become drug organizations. (Dunston 1990, p. 7)

According to Klein, Maxson, and Cunningham, while crack sales have greatly expanded in Los Angeles and elsewhere in recent years, the "purported gang connection seems in most respects to have been overstated" (Klein, Maxson, and

Cunningham 1991, pp. 646–647). They believe, along with Hagedorn and Dunston, that street gangs are insufficiently cohesive and organized and that their leadership is too ephemeral for the development of effective sales networks (ibid., p. 626). Klein, Maxson, and Cunningham provide evidence that "cocaine sales arrestees were modally in their twenties . . . 27 years for non-gang participants and 22 years for gang participants" (p. 638). The mean age of 22 years for gang members "speaks to two issues." There is, first, no support for the claim that "drug distributors have been employing juveniles in order to avoid adult prosecution of dealers" (p. 668, footnote 6). Second, drug and gang problems intersect but do not thereby become a single, comprehensive social problem (p. 647).

Klein and his associates, and others, however, may have pushed the distinction between drug gangs and street gangs too far. Klein and associates modify their position somewhat in a recent paper: "Specific 'drug gangs' have indeed emerged, but only in a minority of gang-involved cities and almost always in the company of non-drug selling gangs in the same cities" (Klein 1992, p. 8). Again, street gangs can be mobilized to protect territory of a drug dealer or organization that is associated or loosely connected with the gang from invasion by other drug gangs and cliques. Conflict between drug organizations must be distinguished from youth gang conflicts where monetary issues are not primarily at stake.

Changing Relationships of Gangs and Drug Dealing

The connection between drug and (violent) street gang is variable and a function of changing economic, cultural, racial/ethnic, and community factors. Fagan believes that "the involvement of youth gangs in volatile drug markets (such as crack) has signaled a transformation of youth gangs from transitory adolescent social networks to nascent criminal organizations" (Fagan 1990, p. 183). The General Accounting Office study and others (e.g., Chin 1990a, 1990b; Moore 1991) identify the nature of the integration or lack of integration of drug dealing and street gangs as dependent on different racial/ethnic backgrounds of gang members:

> Black street gangs first emerged in the South Central Los Angeles and Compton areas about 20 years ago. These black gangs were similar to traditional street gangs, operating only in their own neighborhoods and engaging in limited violence with rival gangs in adjoining neighborhoods. About 10 years ago, the black gangs began dealing heavily in marijuana, LSD, and PCP, and the intergang violence began to escalate for control of drug markets. In the early 1980s, the gangs began selling crack cocaine. Within a matter of years, the lucrative crack market changed the black gangs from traditional neighborhood street gangs to extremely violent groups operating from coast to coast. (General Accounting Office 1989, p. 47)

Members or subgroups of Hispanic gangs in Los Angeles, Chicago, and elsewhere seem to be increasingly involved in use and sale of PCP, marijuana, and cocaine. In New York City, Chinese youth gang leaders, connected with adult criminal organizations are reported to be highly active in the heroin trade (Chin 1990b). White motorcycle gangs reportedly "continue to produce and traffic in methamphetamine" (Philibosian 1986, p. 6). The increasing participation of street gang members in drug trafficking does not mean, however, that the relationship between drugs and gangs is interdependent or inevitable. Also, it should be observed that the drug-dealing members of street gangs, subgroups, and some drug organizations develop communal characteristics. Terry Williams described "cocaine kids" as "sophisticated cocaine distributors, wholesalers and retail sellers. . . . They have helped establish an organizational structure that sustains a regular market and outwits law enforcement authorities. These teenagers have also found a way to make money in a society that offers them few constructive alternatives. . . . In many ways, these kids and others like them simply want respect . . . " (Williams 1989, p. 8). Drug-oriented gang members may develop a certain fraternal interdependence over time.

Gang Violence, Drug Use, and Drug Trafficking

Media reports of extensive drug trafficking by gang members are often associated with the belief that drug selling by gang members is now also associated with or responsible for an increase in urban violence. The issue of the connection of gang violence, drug use, and trafficking can be approached from various perspectives. The general connection between drugs and violence has been a source of policy concern for decades. Paul Goldstein viewed violence as intrinsic to involvement with any illicit substance (Goldstein 1985, p. 497). His tripartite model distinguished psychopharmacological, economic, and systemic dimensions of the problem:

> The psychopharmacologic dimension refers to effects of substances on behavior, as when consumers become irrational, excited, agitated, or unable to control their anger and violent impulses. The economic compulsive dimension refers to violent crime committed to obtain money or other forms of currency to purchase drugs for personal use. The systemic dimension addresses violence intrinsic to the lifestyle and business methods of drug distributors and traffickers. (De La Rosa, Lambert, and Gropper 1990, p. 2)

Of special interest for our purposes is Goldstein's systemic dimension, which focuses on drug distribution as a distinctive street lifestyle. His examples of systemic violence, however, are characterized by a certain economic rationality and logic that are not typical of the violence of street gangs committed to status and turf protection:

1. Disputes over territory between rival drug dealers.
2. Assaults and homicides committed within dealing hierarchies as a means of enforcing normative codes.
3. Robberies of drug dealers and the usual retaliation by the dealer or his/her bosses.
4. Elimination of informers.
5. Punishment for selling adulterated or phony drugs.
6. Punishment for failing to pay one's debts.
7. Disputes over drugs or drug paraphernalia.
8. Robbery violence related to the social ecology of [drug] copping areas.
                                                          (P. Goldstein 1985, p. 497)

Attributing Drug-Related Violence to Street Gangs. According to law enforcement officials, gangs have become a generating force for drug-dealing activities. Black street gangs are regarded as the principal sellers of rock cocaine, and such selling is highly organized. "These gangs have a hierarchy of drug selling, with young teens at the bottom who start as lookouts or runners and later move into selling at the top of the hierarchy . . . city-wide police blame gangs for 387 homicides in 1987, almost all of it drug-related" (Washington 1988). The General Accounting Office report, less extreme, concludes that "10 percent of all gang-related murders involve narcotics . . . " (General Accounting Office 1989, pp. 3, 19).

At first, law enforcement officials in many cities, including Denver, Boston, Washington, D.C., Columbus, Fort Wayne, Seattle, Milwaukee, Minneapolis, and Jackson, Mississippi claimed that the "crack" and gang violence problems were developed during an incursion of black drug gang entrepreneurs from the central cities of New York, Chicago, and Los Angeles. Violence was associated with a deliberate plot to take over and transform local traditional turf-based black youth gangs into drug market criminal gang-related organizations. However, the "spread" of the crack gang-related problem in more recent years has been increasingly attributed more to normal market forces and migration patterns of individuals and families seeking economic opportunities in various parts of the country, than to a centralized, bureaucratic, or franchising campaign.

The National Council of Juvenile and Family Court Judges recommends that judges respond to a highly organized drug gang crisis, presumably involving juveniles:

> Beginning in the mid-1980s, some youth gangs with origins in the large urban centers of Los Angeles, Miami, Chicago, Detroit, and New York became criminal entrepreneurs in the supply of illicit drugs. In a very short time, many of the gangs have developed intrastate and interstate networks for the purpose of expanding . . . in the . . . national drug sales market . . . Ominously these gangs are even more committed to the use of violence than the most notorious old-line criminal organizations. (Metropolitan Court Judges Committee 1988, pp. 27, 30)

The systemic relationship between gang violence and drug dealing has not been demonstrated. Some analysts have argued that gang violence has increased in certain communities due to drug gangs or cliques of street gangs fighting for dominance over drug-dealing turf, while others have claimed that gang violence has declined in certain places and times due to increased trafficking and/or use of drugs by gang members (Cloward and Ohlin 1960). Moore states that gang violence escalated in East Los Angeles between 1950 and 1970, but then dropped sharply in the 1980s because drug marketing and use became important. She argues that "when heroin was introduced into the area in the late 1940s . . . gang warfare dropped sharply. Members of rival gangs crossed into each other's territories with impunity in search of heroin connections" (Moore 1991, p. 66). However, Moore is less sure about the reasons for the sharp rise in gang violence and drug dealing in East Los Angeles in the 1990s.

Available research suggests neither strong nor clear relationships between variables of street gang membership, drug use, drug selling, and violence. Fagan (1988) found both violent and nonviolent black and Hispanic youth gangs in inner-city communities of Chicago, Los Angeles, and San Diego, whether the gang engaged in drug trafficking or not. Involvement in violent gang activity is neither cause nor consequence of use of or dealing drugs: "while some incidents no doubt are precipitated by disputes over drug sales or selling territories, the majority of violent incidents do not appear to involve drug sales. Rather they continue to be part of the status, territorial, and other gang conflicts that historically have fueled gang violence" (Fagan 1988, p. 20). Fagan added that serious crime and violence seem to "occur regardless of the prevalence of drug dealing within the gang." He also stated, somewhat inconsistently, that violence seems to be "most prevalent among gangs that were involved more heavily in PCP, heroin, and cocaine . . . " (Fagan 1989, p. 660). However, Inciardi in his studies of the crack violence connection finds that "higher rates of homicide do not necessarily go hand-in-hand with higher rates of crack use and distribution" (Inciardi 1990, p. 107).

Klein, Maxson, and Cunningham (1988) explored the relationship between gangs, drug dealing, and violence in Los Angeles. Their study was based on an analysis of police records for 1984 and 1985. They found that rock cocaine dealing or its increase was principally a product of neighborhood drug-selling activity and market forces, often unattributable to gang activity. The explosion of drug homicides was more characteristic of non-gang than of gang involvement (pp. 6, 10–11). Thus they concluded that the relevance of drug involvement in gang homicides "is more limited than public reports would suggest . . . it is not often a motive of gang homicide" (pp. 645–646).

Bobrowski, an analyst in Chicago's Gang Crime unit, has provided substantial evidence for the lack of connection between gang-related drug dealing and violence. He claimed there is a strong connection between gangs and drug use in Chicago. Of sixty-two street gangs or major factions responsible for street-gang crime in Chicago between January 1987 and July 1988, 90 percent showed some involvement by gang membership in vice activity (91% of it drug related). However, the relationship between arrests for drug dealing and possession by gang members on the one hand, and gang violence on the other, is quite tenuous. On the basis of Chicago Police Department statistics, he reported that vice activity was discovered at the gang incident level in "only 2 of 82 homicides, 3 of 362 robberies, and 18 of the 4,052 street gang-related batteries and assaults" in the year-and-a-half study period. The notion that "street gangs have been enmeshed in some web of violence and contentious criminality pursuant to, or in consequence of, their interests in vice [mainly drug trafficking or use], appears to be unsupported by the available data" (Bobrowski, 1988, pp. 44–47).

Block, using another Chicago gang crime data set, confirms Bobrowski's conclusion. She says that "only about 2 percent of Chicago street gang-related homicides from 1982 to 1989 involved a drug-related motive . . . and fewer still involved an offender or victim who was high on drugs at the time of the incident. In 1989, when Latino street gang homicides increased, the proportion that were drug-related was even smaller" (Block 1991, p. 37). Sergeant McBride of the Los Angeles County Sheriff's Department agrees that there is a limited relationship between gang violence and drug possession or trafficking. He states that only 5 or 6 percent of gang homicides have been connected with drug trafficking (1994).

A report of the Institute for Law and Justice concludes that "drug trafficking does not fully explain gangs nor do gangs fully explain drug trafficking. If gangs were to disappear overnight, drugs would remain a serious problem, and if drugs were to disappear overnight, gangs would still be a serious problem. These two problems intersect and complicate each other, but there are still large areas in which they are independent of each other" (Institute for Law and Justice 1994, pp. 8–9).

Race/Ethnic Distinction. Evidence in several cities at the present time suggests a pattern in which Hispanic gangs may be relatively more involved in traditional turf gang-related activities, and black gangs or their members in relatively more drug trafficking. Between January 1987 and July 1988, there were seventy-seven Hispanic male offender suspects and sixty-six black male suspects identified by police case reports in eighty-two gang-related homicides in Chicago. In other words, the rate of gang homicides was more than twice as high for Hispanics as for blacks. The vast majority of these black and Hispanic gang homicides, 78.7 percent, were within racial or ethnic offender-victim groups.

Furthermore, while 45.2 percent of all serious gang-related assaults citywide, (N = 2,890) involved black suspects, 43.8 percent involved Hispanic suspects. However, 65.7 percent of vice (mainly drug) gang-related suspects citywide (N = 4,115) were blacks, but only 27.6 percent were Hispanics. Hispanic gang members may be less interested or entrepreneurial when it comes to drug trafficking (or less identifiable for police arrest purposes at the street level) than black gang members, at least in Chicago in that particular period (Bobrowski 1988, p. 18A).

Block and Block have demonstrated that between 1987 and 1990 the two largest black gangs were relatively more engaged in drug-related than in turf-based violent competition and confrontations than the two largest Hispanic gangs in Chicago:

Percentage of Gang Incidents Violence-Related

Vice Lords - 56.4% (N = 3,089 incidents)   Latin Kings - 80.7% (N = 2,820 incidents)

Black Gangster Disciple Nation - 43.3%   Latin Disciples - 77.4% (N = 992 incidents)

(N = 4,794 incidents)

However, the black gangs, especially the Black Gangster Disciple Nation, were still very heavily engaged in turf violence (computed from Block and Block 1993, p. 4, Exhibit 2). Block and Block were also able to compare types of gang activity on a geographic or community basis. Only one Hispanic community was ranked in the top six, where rates of street-gang turf activity (including lethal and nonlethal incidents), and gang-motivated drug activity were highest. Over all, the correlation across seventy-seven Chicago community areas "between rates of street gang-motivated drug crime and homicide was moderate (.401)" (Block and Block 1993, p. 7).

It is also important to not exaggerate the role of black gangs in the sale or spread of drugs. Black gangs, particularly the Los Angeles CRIPS, have been closely associated in the media and by law enforcement with the spread of gangs and drug problems to many areas of the country. Dan Waldorf, based on field studies, expresses strong reservations about the invasion of the CRIPS into the San Francisco drug market:

Most gangs do not have the skills or knowledge to move to other communities and establish new markets for drug sales. While it is true they can and do function on their own turf, they are often like fish out of water when they go elsewhere. Lest we forget who are the youth who make up gangs—they are nearly always young people who have few resources, who leave school early, have limited skills and are often just as unsuccessful in their illegal ventures as they are in legal ventures. (Waldorf 1993, pp. 14–15)

Finally, there is an indirect and sequential relationship between participation in gangs, violence, and drug trafficking. Johnson and colleagues (1988, pp. 63, 78), using New York City evidence, report that drug-selling organizations frequently recruit persons who have previous histories of violence. These persons may also seek out drug-selling groups. Gangs socialize members to a sense of group identification and solidarity that proves a useful qualification transferrable to a drug organization. This pattern seems to have evolved a little earlier in the African-American than in Hispanic inner-city communities. "Younger gang members are often recruited (or actively seek jobs) as street dealers. Typically, they continue to gang bang while dealing" (Reiner 1992, p. 71). The activities of gang violence and drug dealing, however, are more often parallel than interrelated. "Membership in a [black gang] can be a kind of finishing school for drug dealing . . . exposing young recruits to the trade, introducing them to the necessary local connection, etc." (ibid., p. 72).

Conclusion

The media and law enforcement have incorrectly claimed or implied a general and close connection between gangs, drug trafficking, and gang violence. The extent of each of these factors and their interrelationships have been quite variable. While there has been an increase in gang member drug use, trafficking, and participation in more lethal gang violence, relationships among these are not necessarily closely connected and are often quite distinct. The fighting gang has not traditionally been an adequate or efficient basis for drug distribution, despite the fact that individuals or subgroups, or former gang members, may engage in drug trafficking.

There is also no evidence that large increases in drug trafficking can be significantly attributed to the activities of street gangs. Increases in gang violence and in drug trafficking by non-gang members have largely proceeded independent of each other. But there may be some connections between the drug trade and particular gang members who become at some point employees of adult criminal drug organizations.

It is likely that relatively more black gangs and gang members than Hispanic gangs and gang members are currently involved in drug trafficking. At the same time, Hispanic gangs and gang members are relatively more engaged in traditional turf violence. Nevertheless, the situation may be changing in certain communities where Hispanic gang members find it increasingly difficult to make the transition to legitimate employment and easier to engage in a growing, lucrative drug market.

5

Gang Member Demographics and Gang Subcultures

This chapter continues the discussion of the gang problem, but in specific socio-demographic and related subcultural terms. The analysis of age, gender, and especially race/ethnic, gang characteristics suggests that there are distinctive gang subcultures, and therefore distinctive intervention approaches are required. These subcultures must be understood and their causes and special characteristics addressed through particular policy emphases. Large-scale social, economic, cultural, and political as well as local forces generate different patterns of poverty and social disorganization. These together, interactively, create distinctive subcultures. These forces, at both the national and the local level, must be addressed if the delinquent norms and behaviors of gang youth are to be prevented, modified, and controlled.

In the following pages I describe first the dimensions of age, gender, and race/ethnicity as correlates of different gang systems and patterns of gang behavior. Race/ethnicity or minority status is a key dimension that conditions gang patterns and the policy responses developed, but race/ethnicity per se does not generate gang subcultures. The discussion in this chapter becomes a basis for understanding the problem and for prescribing policies that are sensitive to particular communities, organizations, and cultures in later chapters.

Demographics

Age

Gang activity is still perceived as primarily or almost exclusively a teenage, if not a juvenile, phenomenon. Recent scholarly work continues to convey this incorrect perception. For example, Covey, Menard and Franzere's 1992 text is titled *Juvenile Gangs*. (Legislation and criminal justice policy has been less likely to make this mistake in recent years.) Researchers and analysts in the 1950s and 1960s often made this assumption because they largely used youth samples derived from agency street-work programs. Youth work programs then and even today do not generally address the interests and needs of older adolescents and young adults. Before the 1980s juvenile or youth units of police departments usually dealt with gang problems. Many of these units have been transformed into gang, street-gang, or organized crime units over the last decade or two.

As in pre-World War II days, there is recognition at the present time that gang membership extends well into young adulthood—certainly into the early and mid-20s, and to some extent into the 30s, 40s, and even 50s. Thrasher's (1936) gang members of the 1920s ranged in age from 6 to 50 years old, but were concentrated in two groups: "earlier adolescent," 11 to 17 years old, and "later adolescent," 16 to 25 years old. Whyte's (1943) street-gang members were in their 20s. While the gang literature of the 1950s and 1960s focused on teenage gangs, there were also young-adult street gangs and even significant numbers of young adults in so-called teenage gangs. Many case histories (New York City Youth Board 1960; Yablonsky 1962; Spergel 1964; Klein 1971) provide ample evidence of the presence and influence of young adults in street gangs of that era. There may, however, have been relatively fewer older teenagers and young adults associated with gangs in the 1950s and 1960s than appears to be the case today.

By the early 1970s, it was already clear—at least in New York City—that the age range of gang members was broader "at the top and the bottom than in the fighting gangs of the 1950s. The age range in some gangs starts at 9 years old and elevates as high as 30 years old" (Collins 1979, pp. 30–40). On the basis of New York City police data of the 1980s, Chin estimated that the age range of Chinese gang members was 13 to 37 and that their mean age was 22.7 years (Chin 1990b, p. 130). A report of San Diego's gang problem indicated that the age range of gang members was 12 to 31 years and the median age was 19 years (San Diego Association of Governments 1982). The Honolulu Police Department estimated that as of November 1991, approximately 77 percent of the 1,020 persons it suspected of being gang members were legally adults (18 years of age and over) (Chesney-Lind et al. 1992, p. 19).

Some analysts have continued to insist that the "traditional" age range of gang members in most cities was 8 to 21 or 22 years (W. Miller 1975, 1982). Miller (1982), for example, found, from a small data sample (N=121), that no gang offenders or victims in Chicago were 23 years of age or older. Spergel (1986), however, found, on the basis of 1982–1984 Chicago police data on 1,699 offenders and 1,557 victims, that the age range for offenders was 8 to 51 years, and for victims was 3 to 76 years. Miller's mean age categories were 16 and 17 years; Spergel's mean age for offenders was 17.9 years and for victims was 20.1 years. On the basis of analysis of Chicago Police Department case reports for 1987 and the first half of 1988, Bobrowski (1988) concluded that the average age of the male offender was 19.4 years and of the female offender was 15 years. For victims, the average age was 22.1 years, although the modal or most frequently arrested group was 17 years (p. 40).

The age period during which most gang homicides occur is late adolescence and young adulthood. The mean age of the gang homicide offender in Los Angeles city and county in the 1980s was 19 and 20 years, respectively (Maxson, Gordon, and Klein 1985; see also Torres 1980 and Horowitz 1983). Spergel's (1983) gang homicide offender data in Chicago for 1978–1981 indicated major age category percentages as follows: 14 years and under, 2.2 percent; 15 to 16 years, 17.6 percent; 17 to 18 years, 32.4 percent; 19 to 20 years, 21.7 percent; 21 years and older, 25.9 percent. The percentages for these age categories are approximately the same for a 1982–1985 analysis of gang homicides in Chicago (Spergel 1986; see also Klein, Maxson, and Cunningham 1991). Analysis of gang homicides in Chicago for the years 1985, 1989, and 1990 again indicates average ages identical to those in the late 1970s and early 1980s: gang homicide offenders, 19 years or 20 years; victims, 20 or 21 years.

Females and Gangs

There appears to be considerable confusion about the relation of number and proportion of females who are gang members to their participation in serious or violent crimes. An assumption is often made that increasing numbers of young females are "participating in youth gangs and [in] their violent illegal activities" (Candamil 1990, p. 1). The U.S. Department of Health and Human Services, Administration for Children and Families currently refers to evidence that there are "more adolescent females actively participating in gangs and illegal drug activities than previously estimated" [but does not cite specific data sources or evidence] (Federal Register 1992, p. 9869).

Good data on the percentage of females in gangs are difficult to obtain; data on females known to the police as gang offenders, however, are somewhat more available. In this regard it is important to distinguish the sources of data on female gang membership: arrest records, self-reports, or field observations. Bernard Cohen (1969a, p. 85) indicated that 6.3 percent of delinquent group members arrested in Philadelphia in the early 1960s were females but that only 1.4 percent of juvenile gang members arrested were females. Tracy (1982, pp. 10–11) found that 17 percent of violent delinquents in the 1958 Philadelphia cohort study were females and that most of those were arrested for non-gang-related offenses.

Focusing on females as gang members rather than as gang offenders, Collins (1979, p. 51) estimated that males outnumbered females by a margin of 20 to 1 in New York City. He also reported that half of all street gangs in New York City had female chapters or auxiliaries. Walter Miller (1975) reported that females made up 10 percent of gang members. Campbell (1984b) and Lee (1991) estimated that about 10 percent of gang members are girls. On the other hand, some analysts, using self-reports or field observations, have estimated the proportion of female gang members to be as high as 33 percent (Fagan 1990; Moore 1991). Knox found, in a 1991 survey of forty-five short- and long-term juvenile correctional facilities, that 46.4 percent of confined males and 42.2 percent of confined females "self-reported" gang membership (Knox 1991c, pp. 4–5). What the respondents referred to as gangs and what their behavior was in such gangs are not indicated.

Despite media reports, field research findings, and youth agency warnings about the large and increasing proportion of female gang members and their reported involvement in serious gang crime, police data corroboration is not available. In fact, police data suggest that a relatively small amount of serious gang crime is committed by females and that this proportion has probably not changed over the past two decades. In a study of four police districts in Chicago between 1982 and 1984, 95 to 98 percent of the offenders in 1,504 gang incidents were males (Spergel 1986). In a more recent Chicago police study that used citywide data covering a year and a half between January 1987 and July 1988, 12,602 males but only 685 females (2% of the total) were arrested for street gang crimes (Bobrowski 1988, p. 38). Of 2,984 offenders arrested for felony gang assaults over the same period, only 94 (3.2%) were females (ibid., Table 18a).

Harris claimed, on the basis of a small ethnographic sample study, that female gang members were engaged in "vandalism, narcotics, assault, battery, rape, burglary, extortion, robbery, and murder" (Harris 1988, p. 11). She reported that of the twenty-one female gang members she interviewed, two spoke of using drugs and three declared they were drug dealers (pp. 132–133). Harris provided no direct observational or police record confirmation of these statements; we also do not know how typical the gang and gang members were whom she interviewed. Again, it should be noted that self-reported gang member data are particularly suspect because of the tendency of gang youths to exaggerate their delinquent, especially gang-related, activity.

There is evidence that the number of females arrested for serious crimes has been increasing. "In New York City, the number of girls arrested for felonies increased 48 percent over four years, from 7,340 in 1986 to 10,853 last year [1990]. In New Jersey the number of girls arrested for violent crimes like robbery and aggravated assault increased 67 percent from 1980 to 1990" (Lee 1991). But as yet there is no clear evidence that female gang members are increasingly involved in serious gang violence.

The most reliable gang crime data regarding females are based on gang homicide incidents. In a study of 345 gang homicide offenders in Chicago between 1978 and 1981, only 1 was a female; of 204 gang homicide victims for this period, 6 were female (Spergel 1983). In a more recent analysis of 286 gang homicide offenders in Chicago, between 1988 and 1990, only 2 were females; of 233 gang homicide victims for this later period, 3 were females. From these data, females appear not to be significantly involved in serious criminal gang incidents as offenders or victims, nor does the situation appear to have changed over the past several decades. The youth gang problem in its violent character is essentially a male problem.

Several researchers have recently concluded that females are increasingly involved in street-gang or street-clique drug operations, either with male counterparts or on their own, as much for social and emotional support as for profit:

> It was their introduction to crack sales in the mid-1980's by gang affiliated boyfriends that precipitated the formation of this independent group. Extremely dissatisfied with the division of profits and labor from these drug ventures, they decided to enter into business themselves. . . .
>
> The importance of this association goes beyond the immediate financial benefits. Their own family ties were weak at best prior to their involvement in the gang. The group fills a void in the lives of its members. . . . This group is not merely a bunch of drug dealing deviants. For them, it is a family, a sisterhood.
>
> Many of these women made it clear, however, that, given their present circumstances, no other opportunities were available to raise their children. . . . All noted that, in time, they would prefer another lifestyle, particularly one more legitimate. (Lauderback, Hansen, and Waldorf 1992, pp. 69–70; see also Taylor 1993).

Race/Ethnicity and Class

Race/Ethnicity. Race and ethnicity have played a role in the development of the urban gang problem, especially since World War II, but in more complex ways than is ordinarily indicated. Blacks and Hispanics have constituted the largest numbers of youths arrested for gang offenses. In his first national survey, Walter Miller (1975) estimated that 47.6 percent of gang members in the six largest cities were black, 36.1 percent Hispanic, 8.8 percent white, and 7.5 percent Asian. A few years later (1982), Miller found, in a more extensive survey of all gang members in nine of the largest cities, that 44.4 percent were Hispanic, 42.9 percent black, 9% white, and 4.0 percent Asian. He speculated that illegal Hispanic immigrants, especially from Mexico, may have played a large role in the increasing numbers of gangs in California and in their spread to smaller cities and communities in that state (ibid., chap. 9).

In their 1989 and 1990 survey of the gang problem and organized programs to deal with it in forty-five cities and six special jurisdictions, Spergel and Curry found a similarly high proportion of African-Americans and Hispanics as gang members. The race/ethnic composition of gang members was also, to a considerable extent, dependent on who was doing the defining or perceiving. The majority of gang members contacted (or arrested) by law enforcement agencies were blacks (53%), considerably more than Hispanics (28%). On the other hand, grass-roots organizations and social agencies in the same cities reported contact with relatively fewer black (46%) and relatively more Hispanic (30%) gang members. Law enforcement agencies were defining and contacting blacks more often as gang members than were other justice agencies (Spergel and Curry 1990, p. 64).

The dominant proportions of blacks and Hispanics identified as gang members based on police reporting seem hardly to have changed, although the numbers have significantly increased in the past twenty years. The analysis by Curry et al. of the ethnic composition of gang members remains predominantly black (48 percent) and Hispanic (43 percent). The black groups comprised primarily African Americans but also included some blacks from other countries, particularly the Caribbean area. There was, however, some evidence of a relative increase of Hispanic gang members compared to black gang members from 1990 to 1991 (1994, p. 9).

Whites and Asians comprised a very small proportion of youth gang members reported by either law enforcement (2.2% and 1.6%, respectively) or non-law enforcement organizations (4.2% and 2.2%, respectively) (Spergel and Curry 1990, p. 65). Whites were the most numerous racial group in most of the cities surveyed. Why contacts with or arrests of white gang members were so much smaller is not entirely clear. Part of the answer is the relatively smaller numbers of risk-age youths in the white population. Part of the answer also may be matters of perception and definition. Youthful white delinquents or nondelinquents are simply less likely to be stereotyped, labeled, or feared as gang members. Also, what one racial or ethnic community or group of youths considers a gang may not necessarily be what another racial or ethnic community or group of youths considers a gang. Nevertheless, Curry, Ball, and Fox's recent survey of 79 large city police departments between 1990 and 1991 reported a greater rate of increase of white and Asian gang members than of blacks and Hispanics, although from a much smaller base (1994, p. 9).

The largest variety of youth gang types by race/ethnicity probably occurs on the West Coast, particularly in Southern California, and increasingly in Texas, New Mexico, Colorado, Utah, and Florida, based on recent population settlements or migrations. Asian and Pacific Island youth gangs are reported in many states and communities, but particularly in Los Angeles, Denver, and Salt Lake City. American Indian gangs have been active in Minneapolis and in several southwestern states. Mixed-race and ethnic gang membership patterns are not uncommon in many localities, although black gangs tend to be all black. The relation of black American gangs to Jamaican gangs ("posses") is unclear; ethnicity may be both a stronger basis for bonding and gang conflict than race.

Hispanic gangs tend to be predominantly Mexican-American or Puerto Rican, with increasing numbers of Central and South Americans. Asian and Pacific Island youth gangs include Korean, Thai, Cambodian, Hmong, Japanese, Samoan, Tongan, Filipino, and Chinese with origins in Hong Kong, Taiwan, and Vietnam. White gangs can be predominantly second and third generation or of mixed Italian, Irish, Polish, or middle-European origin, situated in inner-city "defensive" enclaves, suburban areas, or small towns. Recent first-generation Russian, Jewish, and Albanian youth gangs have been identified in certain neighborhoods of New York City. The more entrepreneurial gangs, regardless of race or ethnicity, tend to travel more often and have weak territorial identifications. Jamaican posses, some black drug gangs, and white motorcycle gangs roam widely.

In general, gang violence tends to be intraracial or intraethnic. Exceptions occur during periods of competition and conflict by different ethnic groups over local resources (Thrasher 1936) and rapid community race/ethnic population change. Local gangs, often acting out the anxiety of adults in the neighborhood, become organized to defend against newcomers, who in turn establish themselves—protectively at first—as gangs to ward off the hostility and aggression of the established low-income youth population. The most serious and long-term gang conflicts, however, arise and are sustained within and across adjacent neighborhoods with quite similar racial/ethnic populations.

Class. Contemporary youth gangs are located primarily in lower-class, slum, ghetto, barrio, or working-class changing communities, but it is not clear that either class, poverty, culture, race or ethnicity, or social change per se primarily accounts for gang problems. A variety of social and economic factors mainly must interact with each other.

The gangs of the early part of the century in urban areas like Chicago were usually first-generation youths born of Irish and German, and later Polish, Russian, and Italian, parents who lived in areas of transition or first settlement (Thrasher 1936). Gang neighborhoods more often than not represent lower-class population concentrations in the city. Nevertheless, delinquent and somewhat violent youth gangs do occasionally arise in middle-class neighborhoods but are less prevalent; they are also of different character from lower-class gangs (Myerhoff and Myerhoff 1976; see also Muehlbauer and Dodder 1983). At the same time, the most serious gang problems, at least in their violent manifestations, are not necessarily concentrated or most prevalent in the poorest urban neighborhoods (Spergel 1984). Furthermore, gang members do not necessarily come from the poorest families in these low-income communities. Although delinquency and crime rates are generally associated with poverty or class, this relationship is less strong for gang-related than for non-gang-related crime (Curry and Spergel 1988).

The assumption that poverty, low socioeconomic status, or lower-class lifestyle are highly or singularly related to the prevalence of violent youth gangs has been questioned in various studies. The communities in which black gangs flourished in the early 1960s were generally below city averages in housing standards and employment rates, but not below city average unemployment rates (Cartwright and Howard 1966). Gang members often came from low median family-income census tracts in Philadelphia, but not from the lowest (B. Cohen 1969a). The members of conflict groups in New York City were not drawn necessarily from the poorest families of the slum town areas (Spergel 1964). Many of the street gangs of New York City in the 1970s "emerged from a lower-middle-class lifestyle" (Collins 1979). Hispanic fighting gangs in East Los Angeles were not limited to the lowest-income areas of the city (Klein 1971).

Also, the spread of gangs in Los Angeles County and other suburban areas around the country reportedly is due in part to the movement of upwardly mobile families with gang youths to middle-class suburban areas (Los Angeles County Sheriff's Department 1985). Violent and criminal motorcycle gangs are reportedly composed of mainly lower-middle-class, white, older adolescents and young adults (Roger Davis 1982a, b). White youth gangs in suburban communities, "Punks," "Stoners," "White Supremacists," "Satanics," and others, seem to come from lower-middle-class and middle-class communities (Deukmajian 1981; Dolan and Finney 1984). The class identity of the newly developing Asian gangs is not clearly established: gang members may come from two working parent families, where there is inadequate supervision of the youth rather than insufficient access to income (Sung 1977; Chin 1990b). Issues of family and neighborhood disorganization as well as class must be considered as variables in the explanation of the development of the gang problem (see Chapter 10).

Gang Subcultures and Social Contexts

Gangs are quasi-organized component elements of communities, in which youths and young adults are only partially integrated with the general or dominant interests, resources, needs, and customs of local residents. Gang structures and activities, especially violence, vary by race and ethnicity conditioned by class, access to legitimate and illegitimate opportunities, social isolation, and community stability or instability, as well as particular history of gang culture or subculture. These factors can be interrelated and analyzed for policy purposes, using two general causal dimensions— *poverty,* or limited access to social opportunities, and *social disorganization,* or the lack of integration of key social institutions including youth and youth groups, family, school, and employment in a local community.

Violent youth gang subcultures or social subsystems have persisted in inner-city African-American and Hispanic communities at least since World War II. More recently these subcultures and systems have developed not only in central cities but in smaller cities and suburban areas where social, family, economic, and educational supports are increasingly inadequate. Furthermore, in inner-city African-American communities, limited criminal opportunity systems have evolved as gangs partially change from status-oriented conflict groups to more rational but predatory organizations, with special interests in drug trafficking and other criminal gain. Violent gang subcultures may develop when poor immigrants arrive in urban communities. Some blue-collar, white, low- or middle-class communities, subjected to severe economic pressures and consequent social or cultural changes, may also spawn youth gangs or deviant youth groups, such as Satanic, Stoner, punk rocker, hate, neo-Nazi, or racist Skinhead groups, characterized by perverse, negative, or violent behaviors including vandalism, drug use, homosexual assaults, and sometimes homicides (Spergel 1992a, pp. 3-5). This section describes particular gang subcultures and systems in somewhat greater detail.

Black Gangs

In no other community are legitimate opportunities more thoroughly blocked than in the urban African-American community. More limited systems of illegitimate opportunity have evolved, based pervasively on street-gang structures, than is the case for any other racial or ethnic group. Black youths in these communities tend to maintain gang connections longer than nonblack youths in other communities. Because of persistent poverty associated with racism, black male youths also become overidentified as gang members. Anderson, in his study of the black ghetto in Philadelphia, states

> Many disadvantaged young blacks living in the ghetto of Northton find themselves surrounded by a complex world that seems arbitrary and unforgiving. Major changes in the regular economy . . . combined with the massive influx of drugs into the local community—have exacerbated social breakdown . . . All of this has undermined traditional social networks that once brought youths into the world of legitimate work and family life. . . . (Anderson 1990, pp. 109–111)

Sullivan, in his study of a public housing project in Brooklyn's black ghetto, observes

> Projectville youths had the fewest family and neighborhood connections to jobs . . . Projectville youths left school early because they were about to become fathers and wanted to find full-time jobs to support their new families . . . [compared to Hispanic and white neighborhoods] Projectville youths suffered from the most joblessness. . . . Their neighborhood's physical isolation from centers of employment limited the work opportunities of residents. . . . (Sullivan 1989, pp. 43, 55, 104)

Distrust, estrangement, segmentation, and social distance characterize many inner-city impoverished black communities. Gangs and crime touch a great many households. Everyone seems vulnerable to "assault and incivilities" almost any time of the day or night. The perpetrator of a crime—whether a drive-by shooting, burglary, or drug deal—might be a nephew, a best friend, or the young man down the block. Anderson observes that "new role models are being created." The currently respected gang member or gang-related drug dealer who is out to make fast money does not look forward to an unskilled or semiskilled job that may not be available to him, anyway. "He is out to beat the next fellow" (Anderson 1990, pp. 78, 103).

A process of destructive socialization occurs: youths who have insufficient social support at home from separated, alienated, or unemployed parents receive inadequate and uncaring attention at school, where they consequently fail or are inadequately educated. Furthermore, youth or community agencies no longer have the resources or capabilities to reach out to these now more socially detached and disorganized young people. Youths must learn to survive on the streets through attachment to a variety of semi-organized illegitimate structures and criminal and status-providing activities. Unsupervised black youths in inner-city areas are reported to become, in sequence, "scavenger" groups, turf gangs, and even corporate drug gangs (Anderson 1990; Taylor 1990a). Access to earlier socially compensatory legitimate routes (e.g., Job Corps, the Army, special education and training programs) has been increasingly closed off. A few roles and systems, for example drug trafficking, more and more offer some social status and personal satisfaction necessary to achieve even limited economic and social success. Taylor observes that "cocaine and crack cocaine have provided goals, jobs, and economic realities that African-American communities in Detroit had never seen before" (1990a, p. 98).

Taylor claims also that America's drug habit

> has created the economic boom needed to trigger gang imperialism. . . . African-Americans have moved into the mainstream of major crime. Corporate gangs . . . are part of organized crime in America. Drugs, as a commodity, have become the same unifying economic force for gangs today (adult and juvenile) as alcohol during prohibition. . . . Detroit gangs are using drugs as this vehicle for social mobility. . . . (Taylor 1990a, pp. 97, 103, 112)

Taylor has probably exaggerated the success of black gang members moving into corporate crime.

Hispanic Gangs

Parallels—within limits—can be made between the emergence of Latino (Hispanic) and black street gangs. Some observers claim there are similarities, for example, in Southern California between the

> origins of Cholo gangs in the mid-to-late forties and the rise of the CRIPS and Bloods a generation later. . . . Both were products of communities only recently arrived in Los Angeles. Neither group was truly new, of course. Just as there had been a significant Mexican-American community in Los Angeles long before the 20s, so the black presence long predated the population surge around World War II. But like the great Mexican migration which preceded it, the wave of black migrants during and after the war, all but submerged the older community. . . . (Reiner 1992, pp. 4–5)

Much of the writing on Latino or Hispanic gangs in the past several decades has focused on Mexican-American groups in Southern California and the Southwest. However, Hispanic gangs, including Mexican-American, Puerto Rican, Dominican, and Salvadoran groups, have been a major problem also in the Midwest, on the East Coast, and in Texas. Nevertheless, the longest continuous Mexican-American or Chicano gang tradition has probably developed in the Los Angeles area. Some Latino street gangs in Southern California have existed within particular localities as extended families or clans for three or more generations, although the families of gang members often arrived in the area at different times. "Parents and in some cases even grandparents were members of the same gang. There is a sense of continuity of family identity" (Jackson and McBride 1985, p. 42).

Each new wave of Mexican-American immigrants and more recently low-income Nicaraguans, Salvadorans, and other Central Americans provides a new generation of poorly schooled and partially acculturated youths around which gangs seem to organize or perpetuate themselves. Vigil and Long claim, particularly in reference to Mexican-Americans, "the gang subculture is embedded in and representative of the larger cholo (marginalized) subculture to which large numbers of Chicano youths (especially urban youths) subscribe . . . " (Vigil and Long 1990, p. 56). *Cholo* refers to the poorest of the poor marginalized immigrants. These are persons who were marginal to Spanish culture and are now marginal to "the more recent European culture" in America (Vigil 1990, p. 116). Vigil believes the cholozation process becomes "more intensified in the third generation, within which a subculture of the streets has become institutionalized . . . youths with particularly problematic, traumatic family and personal experiences . . . are forced into the streets" (ibid., p. 124).

However, not all or even a significant minority of poor Mexican-American youths become gang members in East Los Angeles or elsewhere. First- and second-generation Mexican-Americans in substantial numbers move out of barrios and become integrated into the larger society. Many rise from the lower economic stratum (see Moore 1978, 1991). This is not to deny that Hispanic gangs, particularly Chicano gangs, are probably the most turf oriented and most expressive of gangs in terms of "street styles of dress, speech, gestures, tatoos, and graffiti" (see Vigil 1988b, p. 2). But such patterns also vary considerably among Mexican-American gangs in different parts of the country, and within particular localities over time (Hutcheson 1993). Bobrowski (1988) noted differences between Hispanic, white, and black gangs in Chicago. Symbolic property crime (graffiti) is more common among Hispanic than black gangs (p. 19). The ratios of personal crime to property crime (mainly graffiti) for Hispanics and whites are 3 to 1 and 4 to 1, respectively, while for blacks it is 8 to 1 (Bobrowski 1988, p. 21).

Mexican-Americans and other Hispanic youths are also more likely than African-Americans to be integrated into multiethnic/racial gangs, in large measure, because they more often reside in less racially or ethnically segregated communities. Further, not all low-income and/or recently settled Hispanic or black communities necessarily or consistently produce violent gangs in a particular city. For example, although there was a tradition of gang formation and gang violence in Philadelphia's inner-city neighborhoods in the 1970s, that did not happen in Puerto Rican enclaves or in Mexican-American low-income enclaves in a number of other cities. Nevertheless, Duran (1987, p. 2) observed that while Chicano gangs in certain parts of East Los Angeles have declined in membership, immigrant gangs from Mexico and Central and South America are on the increase; the tradition of Hispanic gangs that fight, kill, and risk their lives for turf and "respect" remains dominant.

White Gangs

White lower-class youths have the longest (recorded) history of street gang activity in the United States, as indicated in Chapter 1. They have been far less visible and in fact considerably less violent than black and Hispanic gangs in recent decades. There were more white than black gangs in Boston in the 1950s and 1960s, and there was more violence among white gangs than among black gangs (however, the level of violence among Boston gangs may have been lower than among black or white gangs in other cities (W. Miller 1976b). In Chicago, white gangs, comprising youths of a somewhat higher class origin than black gangs, were reported in the late 1950s and early 1960s to be rowdier, more rebellious, more openly at odds with adults, and more into drinking, drug use, and sexual delinquency than black gangs (Short and Strodtbeck 1965). White gangs in Philadelphia in the middle 1970s were less territorially bound, less structured, and therefore more difficult to identify and consequently to label than black gangs (Friedman, Mann, and Adelman 1976).

White gangs come in many varieties. Not unlike black and Hispanic gangs, some are concerned with protecting turf or territory, less often with expanding it. They may be in coalition with certain Hispanic or black gangs. White gangs have at times been suppliers of weapons (often stolen in home burglaries) and certain types of drugs to black and Hispanic gangs, or in turn have sought out dealers in black and Hispanic gang territories in order to buy drugs. White gangs or deviant groups have been identified as Stoners, freaks, heavy-metal groups, satanic worshipers, bikers, Skinheads, and copy-cat gangs, involved in a greater range of delinquent activities, but generally of a less violent character, than have black or Hispanic gangs in recent years.

White gangs have been generally better integrated into the life of their particular communities than black or Hispanic gangs, and thereby have better access both to legal and illegal opportunities. They have probably been more exposed to adult social constraints (Sullivan 1989, p. 46). To the extent that white communities are fearful and insecure about interacting with "invading" minority (especially low-income) newcomers to the local culture, youth gangs assist directly and indirectly in the defense and protection of their neighborhoods, often by aggressive or violent means (Suttles 1968). White gangs also do not have to resort to violent or street level criminal acts as extensively to achieve status or income. For younger adolescents, "illegal sources of income often . . . supplement rather than substitute for wages, but these sources were drug selling and drug errands for local adult organized crime figures rather than the high-risk, low-return thefts so prevalent among minority youths" (Sullivan 1989, p. 179; see also Cloward and Ohlin 1960; Spergel 1964).

In certain communities, whites—at least those recently arrived from certain European countries—become the newcomers. In a series of violent gang attacks on other youths, police in the Bronx, New York, reported:

> Some of the [Albanian] cliques . . . also include black, Hispanic and other white teenagers as well, often friends they met in elementary school.
> Albanian immigration began with political refugees during the 1960s, followed by a record wave from Kosovo in the early 1970s. Estimates of their numbers in the region range from 75,000 to 150,000, with about a fifth of those in the Williamsbridge neighborhood of the Bronx. Many of them started in blue-collar jobs, with a sizable number attaining a measure of success in residential real estate and small businesses. (Gonzalez 1992)

The Albanian Boys or Albanian Bad Boys were described as loosely knit groups of teenagers who often gathered near a mural that took up an entire wall of a building. It contained an epitaph to a youth killed in a gang fight. "'Rest in peace' is written flamboyantly on one side and a blood-red Albanian flag flank[s] the other" (ibid.). The area is considered turf for the group of perhaps several dozen youths who hang out, "raising cain and eagerly taking on all they perceive as interlopers. . . . Sometimes an odd look or a casual remark would trigger a confrontation" (ibid.). Much of the fighting was to earn or maintain a reputation.

Increasing numbers of white youths who become gang or pseudo gang members seem to come from disorganized and disrupted or recently unemployed, working, and middle-class families. Many no longer live at home and are regarded as throwaways. To survive, they turn to ephemeral forms of antisocial gang activity, sometimes closely identified with a particular neighborhood, sometimes not (see Dunston 1990, p. 20). Stoners originally were groups made up of persistent drug or alcohol abusers, sometimes with heavy-metal rock music as a common bond. One of the special early traits of Stoner groups in Southern California was satanism, including grave robbing and the desecration of churches and human remains. Stoner groups have been known to mark off territory with graffiti. They may adopt particular dress styles (Jackson and McBride 1985, pp. 42–55). Stoner youth gangs ("taggers," graffiti groups, or "tag bangers") have been present in Hispanic communities, such as Los Angeles, alongside and sometimes interacting with or converting to violent gangs (Ayres 1994). Taggers may interact with and/or become gang bangers.

Various middle- and upper-income communities, particularly on the West Coast, have reported white youth gangs forming in imitation of certain Hispanic and black gangs. Justice agencies have reported these groups, sometimes ephemeral, as a kind of "dalliance" or flirtation that may be "as innocent as a fashion statement or as deadly as hard-core drug dealing and violence. . . . [Certain white youths] are joining established black . . . gangs like the CRIPS or Bloods; others are forming what are sometimes called copy-cat or mutant yuppie gangs" (Office of Criminal Justice Planning 1990, p. 11).

Some Skinhead groups are neo-Nazi youth gangs, originally modeling themselves after punk rockers and Skinheads in England. They may have ties to racist or Nazi adult groups, such as the Ku Klux Klan, the American Nazi Party, and the National Socialist White Workers Party. The SWP (Supreme White Pride) young adult gang has recently spread from the prisons to the streets. Racist and violent Skinheads have been identified in major cities on the West Coast, in the Midwest, and in the South. Some law enforcement officials of Southern California believe the Skinhead movement may be a reaction by white youths in certain middle-class neighborhoods to a sudden increase in the number of black, Hispanic, and Asian residents. Skinhead group structure and style fit the gang pattern: a gang name, colors, tattooing, distinctive dress, drug use, and criminal behavior (Coplon 1988, p. 56; see also Jackson and McBride 1985; Anti-Defamation League 1986, 1987; and Donovan 1988).

A report of the Florida state legislature (Reddick 1987) noted that the Skinheads in Florida started in Jacksonville and are now uniformly found in major urban areas all over the state. They profess to being "anti-black, anti-Jew, and anti-homosexual, while promoting their pro-God, pro-white American ideology." Their activities in Florida have been "primarily harassment, violence, fighting, and provoking riots and racial incidents." Often, parents of these youths are either unaware of their activities or support them (Reddick 1987, p. 9). Some of these loosely knit groups and their members drift from one city to another. Coplon (1988, p. 56) claimed that Skinhead ranks swelled throughout the United States from 300 in 1986 to 3,500 in 1988. The Anti-Defamation League has noted that Skinhead membership has stabilized at about 3,000 to 3,500 nationally (Anti-Defamation League 1990, p. 3; Applebome 1993). The League observed in 1993 that the number of Skinhead anti-Semitic homicide incidents had risen in recent years. Attacks on "blacks, Jews, homosexuals, immigrants, and members of other minority groups . . . have resulted in 28 deaths since 1987, 22 of them since 1990" (Applebome 1993).

Another type of white gang is the criminal biker or motorcycle gang. Some Hispanic and black motorcycle gangs and groups also exist. They may have elaborate rituals, signs, symbols, and tattoos and complex organizational structures—including written constitutions—with chapters of the larger gangs in Canada and Europe, as well as in many states. Some are white supremacists. They consist mostly of working-class young adults, sometimes from rural areas, with limited education. They have engaged in a wide range of illegal activity, including the sale and use of drugs, extortion, disorderly conduct, vandalism, theft, prostitution, white slavery, and hijacking (Commission de Police du Quebec 1980). They have been, in some cases, connected to major criminal organizations and syndicates, particularly in the transport or sale of drugs. In 1986 the Drug Enforcement Administration estimated that "outlaw" motorcycle gangs were responsible for manufacturing over 40 percent of the methamphetamine sold on the streets (Lyman 1989, p. 70).

Asian and Pacific Island Gangs

Increasing numbers of criminal and violent Asian youth gangs were reported in the 1970s, 1980s, and early 1990s. In the 1970s, Walter Miller (1982) estimated that the number of Asian youth gangs almost equaled the number of white gangs on the West Coast. In the 1980s, Duran believed that Asian youth gangs were almost twice as numerous as white gangs (Duran 1987). The gangs have "spread" from the West and East coasts to inland American cities. Several factors have especially contributed to the current development of Asian and Pacific Island gangs in the United States. First, the expansion of immigration quotas during the Kennedy and Johnson administrations provided an influx of immigrants from various countries, particularly from Southeast Asia. Large pools of immigrant youths began to collect in various parts of the country, especially in the West Coast, but also in several cities on the East Coast. In some cases they found existing gangs of the same or a related ethnicity; in other cases they formed their own distinctive ethnic gangs or later became integrated into older established gangs, particularly Chinese.

Second, the communities in which these groups settled, mainly white but also black and Hispanic, have sometimes failed to accept the new Asian immigrants and have either isolated or attacked them. The communities were not prepared to provide for the special cultural, social, and legal learning needs of the new immigrants. Asian immigrants also have been viewed by resident minority black or Hispanic communities as competitors for limited existing resources. A great deal of tension and animosity may develop, which leads to or encourages the creation of youth gangs as defensive groups to protect against the hostility of the established youth groups or gangs.

Asian youth gang members tend to be more secretive than non-Asian members. They are also less apparently interested in status, honor, or reputation, and more involved in criminal-gain activities such as extortion, burglary, and narcotics selling. Asian youth gang members are sometimes used by adult criminal organizations as "enforcers" (Breen and Allen 1983). They are difficult to detect because most police units lack Asian language facility or the confidence of Asian communities. However, significant numbers of Vietnamese, Cambodian, and other Asian youth gangs are reported to be typical street gangs: they protect turf, are involved in street violence, dress alike, take gang names, use graffiti, and have affiliate girl groups.

Third, each type of ethnic Asian or Pacific Island gang may have distinctive characteristics. Japanese, Taiwanese, and Hong Kong youth gangs are reported to be the better organized, and perhaps more secretive. Vietnamese street gangs may be particularly mobile. Some Samoan gang youths manifest tattoos and particular gang dress, use graffiti, have reputations for violence, and are reported to have become assimilated into black gangs. Violent acts are said to be relatively more likely among Vietnamese, Chinese, Cambodian, and Laotian compared with Khmer or Hmong youth gangs. Filipino gang members in California are reported to be older, ranging in age from 20 to 40 years. While they may adopt black or Hispanic gang violent behavioral characteristics, they engage mainly in property crime activities (auto theft, extortion, burglary, drug trafficking) (Donovan 1988).

Some of the Asian youth gangs are found in expanding business communities. For example, Chinese youth or street gangs may be found in communities that are economically robust. They may be connected to Tongs—certain businessmen's associations—which may in turn be closely related to Triad criminal societies. Tongs may recruit or enjoy the allegiance of particular youth gangs. "The fear that gangs inspire in merchants is enormously useful to the Tongs which govern the community through intimidation" (Dannen 1992, p. 77). Chinese youth gangs in New York City were reported engaged in economically rewarding criminal ventures, especially heroin trafficking. With the new waves of Chinese immigrants, however, established street-gang and criminal or legitimate adult business relationships have been disrupted. Violence by competing street gangs, Tongs, and Triad groups has periodically escalated (see Chin 1990b). Dannen notes also that Chinese youth gangs in New York's Chinatown have a distinctive subculture: "a bizarre mixture of traits borrowed from the Hong Kong Triads (secret criminal societies) and the clichés of American and Chinese gangster movies. Gang members dress all in black and have their chests and arms tattooed with dragons, serpents, tigers, and sharp-taloned eagles" (Dannen 1992, p. 77).

Conclusion

Age, gender, and culture as well as economics and community structure affect the character and development of the youth gang problem. Youth gangs—as they concern the larger community—comprise mainly male adolescents and young adults.

The gang problem, however, is distinctive in particular racial, ethnic, and cultural, often lower-class, contexts. Not only poverty but social disorganization, especially population change and movement, are key conditions or pressures for the development of gang systems and subcultures. The way the factors of poverty and criminal opportunity, family, and neighborhood disorganization interact and combine with racial and ethnic cultural traditions creates the basis for certain patterns of gang crime behavior. Certain gang subcultures, for example, Hispanic tend to be characterized by greater identification with turf and violence; black gang systems appear to be shifting toward an emphasis on economic survival and development of criminal opportunities, especially through street-level drug trafficking. Asian groups tend to be more interested in property crime, and in some cases are more integrated into adult crime and/or business organizations. White youth gangs are less violent but more varied in their structures and patterns of criminal behavior.

6

The Structure of the Gang

This chapter discusses the organizational character of the gang and the social contexts in which different types of gang organization seem to develop. Major dimensions of gang structure have been identified as "age, size, subgrouping, level of involvement, leadership and role differentiation, and sex" (Klein 1971, pp. 64–65). But it is important also to add the sociocultural and community structural dimensions, especially as they affect race/ethnicity and gender. Political interests, location, and particular time period also condition and provide meaning to gang organization. More specifically, this chapter deals with how gang structures develop, the characteristics of different gang organizations, their component parts, and the functions these organizations or their subunits play in particular social, political, and cultural as well as economic contexts.

Gang Organization and Community Structure

The literature on gangs is rich in description of the nature of gang organization but has paid little attention to its function. It is the function of gang organization, however, that is most relevant for understanding why gangs arise and what patterns of delinquent or criminal behavior develop, and especially for determining what strategies of intervention are required to deal with, prevent, or control the particular gang problem that occurs.

Gangs are created when established institutional and organizational arrangements in a community are weak or break down. Gangs are collectives, quasi-institutions, and are somewhat tribal or clanlike, with long-term viability, to the extent that normal communal and economic arrangements for the social and job development of youths are unsatisfactory or unavailable. Gang organization, it can be argued, substitutes in distinctive ways for a particular pattern of inadequacy of existing community institutions and organizational interrelationships.

More than two decades ago, Klein questioned whether the type of gang structure relates to patterns of delinquent or criminal behavior. He suggested that the "paucity of data available on gang structure and behavior [indicated possibly] that structural differences between gangs may be greater than differences in delinquent patterns . . . and that the relationship is somewhat ephemeral" (Klein 1971, p. 80). More recently Sampson suggested that "membership in a gang may have no independent influence on police contact" (Sampson 1986, p. 821) and therefore implicitly on gang behavior. He concluded that "while gang membership and delinquent peers are positively related ($r = .20$), it appears that it is the extent of peer delinquency rather than gang membership per se that influences official reaction". In other words, it is not merely adolescent peers hanging or flocking together, or the contours or shape of their associations, but rather the characteristics of the youths in the particular groups that make the difference in peer delinquency and police contact. Sampson did not substantially address the relation of differential community structure or network of organizational relationships to delinquency rates or the shaping of peer groups.

Fagan only hints at the relation of gang patterns to sociocultural contexts. He suggests that:

> gangs are only one of several deviant peer groups in inner cities. Among male gang members [he finds] several types of gangs with varying involvement in substance abuse, drug selling, and other delinquency. Evidently, there are qualitatively different peer networks that exert parallel but independent influences on peer relationships and problems associated with delinquency and substance abuse. To understand why gangs differ from other youths in their participation in delinquency and substance use while reflecting natural adolescent social processes and influences, we must look to the social and historic context of the gang itself. (Fagan 1990, pp. 209–210)

Development of Gang Organization

How the gang develops as a social entity has been a principal source of interest for gang researchers. The current focus is on gang organization mainly at a particular point in time (however, see Moore 1991). Nevertheless, there is an older tradition of viewing the gang developmentally, or over time (Thrasher 1927; Shaw and McKay 1943), although not in terms of distinctive sociocultural contexts, especially not those of race or ethnicity (however, see Cloward and Ohlin 1960; Sullivan 1989). Thrasher spoke generally of "the beginnings of the gang," which can best be observed in the

> slums of the city where an inordinately large number of children are crowded into a limited area . . . spontaneous play groups are forming everywhere—gangs in embryo. Such a crowded environment is full of opportunities for conflict . . . the conflict arises on the one hand with groups of its own class in disputes over the valued prerogatives of gangland—territory, loot, play space, patronage in illicit business privileges to exploit . . . [and] on the other, through opposition on the part of the conventional social order to the gang's unsupervised activities. (Thrasher 1927, p. 26)

Thrasher emphasized the genesis of the gang in opportunities for conflict rather than in the needs of youths for social boundaries and structure as they contribute to personal and social development in particular institutional and organizational contexts in the community. Thrasher went on to say that with the juvenile "play group," a

> real organization . . . natural leaders emerge, a relative standing is assigned to various members and traditions develop. It does not become a gang, however, until it begins to excite disapproval and opposition and thus acquires a more definite group-consciousness. It discovers a rival or an enemy in the gang in the next block. . . .

... the gang has its beginning in acquaintanceship and intimate relations which have already developed on the basis of some common interest. These preliminary bonds may serve to unite pairs or trios among the boys rather than the group as a whole. . . . The gang may grow by additions of twos and threes as well as single individuals. . . . (Thrasher 1927, pp. 30–31)

What is critical is the need for structure that provides the social support, controls, and opportunities for development that the youth requires. Conflict and opposition are means to establish boundaries, turf ownership, or social status. They are thus one important process for achieving meaningful structure or organization. The gang forms in various ways. It can be a small group or clique within an established conventional setting, such as a school or youth agency. It may be based in common interest or fate—such as reprimand or expulsion. The clique can serve—when there is no supervision—as the basis for a group in opposition to established norms and recognized as a hostile force. An individual on his own may form a gang, recruiting others to an association of individuals who will perform unapproved and unsupervised activities, often in some covert fashion. More usual today is not the formation but the extension and development of the gang spatially, in size, and in terms of function and specialization.

The gang at first is "nonconventional and unreflective." It forms through the "mechanism of interaction in social situations" and "represents a social order which is natural . . . rather than enacted" (Thrasher 1927, pp. 56–57). "If conditions are favorable to its continued existence, the gang tends to undergo a sort of natural evolution from a diffuse and loosely organized group into the solidified unit which represents the matured gang . . . which may take one of several forms. It sometimes becomes a specialized delinquent type such as a criminal gang . . ." (ibid., p. 58).

Thrasher did not foresee the varied patterns of gang development as they occur today. He believed that the juvenile gang "usually . . . becomes conventionalized and seeks incorporation into the structure of the community" (ibid.). Whether this process in fact occurs when the community itself is or remains fragmented and substantially divorced from the resources, social controls, and norms of the larger society is open to question. This is not to deny that the gang substantially "reflects in its activities the adult life and the customs of the particular community where it is found" (Thrasher 1927, p. 251).

Each local community seems to provide a somewhat different context for the development of the gang, particularly when race/ethnicity, class, and cultural traditions vary. Moore describes the development of the gang structure in the Mexican-American community of East Los Angeles in a particular time period. She writes that in the 1930s and 1940s male groups were defined as "the boys from the barrio. . . . It was just a meeting of youngsters in the street" (Moore 1991, pp. 25–26).

The gangs started out as friendship groups of adolescents who shared common interests, with more or less clearly defined territory in which most of the members lived. They were committed to defending one another, the barrio, the families, and the gang name in the status-setting fights that occurred in schools and on the streets. They were bound by a norm of loyalty. (Moore 1991, p. 31)

Much depends on the larger community structure and its system of opportunities, adult-youth relations, and legitimate or illegitimate traditions for survival, social status, and economic gain. The genesis of the gang also depends on specific immigration wave characteristics, culture, race/ethnicity, racism, and class factors. Chin describes the history of the development of one youth gang that emanated from the Chinese community when other gangs were already present. This pattern is quite different from that described by Moore, although there are significant similarities. Chinese street gangs often develop within a cohesive youth-adult integrated community structure but one that is somewhat disengaged from larger societal values and norms. Street-gang youths in the Chinese community early on may learn to perform functions useful to the maintenance of an existing illegal enterprise system:

> Chinese street gangs [most recently] appeared in San Francisco in the late 1950s. The first juvenile gang was known as the 'Bugs' and was formed by American-born Chinese. Members were heavily involved in burglary and were easily identified by their mode of dress, which included high-heeled 'Beatle'-type boots.
>
> In 1964, young immigrants organized the first foreign-born Chinese gang, which was known as the Wah Ching (Youth of China). The main goal of the gang was to protect members from American-born Chinese. . . . Before the gang became a predatory group, Wah Ching leaders sought help from San Francisco's Human Rights Commission and the Chinese Benevolent Association. . . . [But] the coffee house where they gathered was forced to shut down.
>
> Following the closing of the coffee house, certain community associations hired Wah Ching members as look-outs for their gambling establishments. . . .
>
> Later, Wah Ching members became part of the Hop Sing Tong, and the gang converted itself from an ordinary street gang into the Youth Branch of the well-established adult organization. . . . [The gangs] started to prey upon Asian people. . . . Most store owners paid the gangs regularly to avoid being disturbed. . . . (Chin 1990, p. 68)

While black gang organization is similar, in many respects, to that of the Mexican-American gang formation (in East Los Angeles) and to that of Chinese-American gang formation (in San Francisco), it is also affected by factors distinctive to the black community. Furthermore, it represents an innovative movement into the larger American system of criminal opportunities. Carl Taylor describes the changing developmental structure of black gangs in Detroit.

> Groups of black males ranging from ages 11 to 17 were constantly changing in size and leadership (. . . near groups . . .). The uniqueness of these neighborhood groups is that they would join a "confederacy" of a sort with other neighborhood groups and grow into a new type of urban gang, the scavengers. . . . Despite the fact that scavengers had no set goals or purposes, they all had one bonding point. They all knew about corporate gangs. (Taylor 1990a, p. 41)

Taylor's initial-stage Detroit gangs are different from the Mexican-American gangs in East Los Angeles in the 1940s and at later times described by Moore. Taylor depicts African-American "scavenger" gangs in Detroit as "having no common bond . . . no particular goals, no purpose, no substantial camaraderie . . . (p. 4). Moore's gangs in East Los Angeles, however, "started out as a friendship group of adolescents who shared common interests, with more or less clearly defined territory . . . " (Moore 1991, p. 31). She also notes the similarity of the patterns of formation of black gangs in Milwaukee and those in East Los Angeles.

. . . In Milwaukee as in Los Angeles, the emergence of some of the gangs was associated with a youth fad. . . . Break dancing and drill teams swept the black communities. In some cases, the transition from dance groups to gangs came about as fights broke out after dance competitions. But there were also a number of traditional corner boy groups already in existence at the time. As fighting between groups became more common, the corner boys like the dance groups, began to define themselves as gangs. (Moore 1988b, p. 6; see also Hagedorn, Macon, and Moore 1986, p. 3)

Taylor indicates further that the "scavenger" gang may be transformed or integrated into the "territorial" gang and the "territorial gang" into the "corporate" gang over time. The major opportunity connection among these three kinds of gangs in the black neighborhoods of Detroit, according to Taylor, was narcotics. While gangs define and defend territory at an early stage, it is soon mainly "to protect their narcotics business" (Taylor 1990a, p. 6). Furthermore, the connection between "scavenger" and "corporate" narcotics-dealing groups was quite close. "Some of the scavengers auditioned for [Corporate] Gang C-1 acceptance by performing various illegal or criminal acts" (pp. 33–34). Many scavengers also belonged to more than one gang.

All of these data are drawn from field observations. While they may reflect the particularistic views of different researchers, they also indicate both similarities and differences in gang formation and development across different cities, and even within the same race/ethnic group, depending on local social and economic structures of opportunities and local traditions at different points in time. In other words, developmental patterns or careers of gangs may differ as social or organizational entities depending on the community context.

Patterns of Organization of the Gang

A great deal of attention has been paid by policymakers and practitioners, as well as by researchers, to the organization of the gang per se, usually in cross-sectional terms, that is, at particular points or over limited time durations. Gangs have been viewed as either or both loosely knit and well organized. It is likely that the loosely knit characterization refers to the gang member's diffuse and seemingly erratic pattern of interaction with other gang members, while the well-organized characterization refers to the large membership size of certain gangs, their location in different streets or sections of the neighborhood or city, their supposed hierarchical organization, or simply gang longevity. The notion of well-organized gang may also refer to the more business-oriented, usually drug-dealing, clique or gang. These notions may be, in fact, complementary or overlapping rather than contradictory. Thrasher (1936, p. 35) originally conceived of the early street ganging process "as a continuous flux and flow, and there is little permanence in most of the groups. New nuclei are constantly appearing, and the business of coalescing and recoalescing is going on everywhere in the congested area." Yablonsky (1962, p. 286) called the gang of the 1950s and early 1960s a "near-group" characterized by (1) diffuse role definition, (2) limited cohesion, (3) impermanence, (4) minimal consensus of norms, (5) shifting membership, (6) disturbed leadership, and (7) limited definitions of membership expectations.

It is possible that gang analysts have failed to distinguish between the concepts of gang member position and role in their descriptions of gang structure. Yablonsky (1962) may address more often the characteristics of gang member role and Jankowski (1991) those of position. Gang member role indicates activities and the dynamics of the individual in a particular position, which suggests a more stable and functional aspect of gang structure. The distinction is elaborated later in the discussion on gang leadership.

The "traditional" gang of the same period, according to Klein (1968), was an amorphous mass; group goals were usually minimal and membership was unstable; group norms were not distinguishable from those of the surrounding neighborhood. Short and Strodtbeck noted, in their research of gangs in the same period, the difficulty, if not impossibility, of creating lists of gangs from which probability samples could be drawn in their research, "so shifting in membership and identity are these groups" (1965, p. 10). Gold and Mattick also concluded that gangs in Chicago were "loosely structured sets of companions" (1974, p. 335), less stable than other groups of adolescents (p. 37). Torres observed that Hispanic gangs in the barrios of East Los Angeles were "always in a state of flux" (1980, p. 1).

At the same time, analysts of the New York City Youth Board street-work program indicated the complexity of gang structures in New York City in the 1950s in their typology of gang organizations: vertical, horizontal, and autonomous or self-contained. The vertical gang was structured along age lines among youngsters living on the same block or in the same immediate neighborhood. There may be a younger "tots" group, 11 to 13 years old; a "junior" division, 13 to 15 years old; a group of "tims," 15 to 17 years old; and the seniors," 17 to 20 years old and older. The age lines were not viewed as hard and fast. This type of structure occurred when there was a long history of group existence and activity dating back ten or more years. Group morale and fighting traditions were informally handed down. This kind of group tended to be ingrown, with cousins and brothers belonging in the respective divisions (New York City Youth Board 1960, p. 20).

A later description of the vertical gang structure in New York City in the 1970s suggested an even wider spread of age-based subunits, with Baby Spades, 9 to 12 years old; Young Spades, 12 to 15 years old; and Black Spades, 16 to 30 years old (Collins 1979). Later, in Philadelphia, the police department described three general age-related gang divisions: bottom-level "midgets," 12 to 14 years old; middle-level "young boys," 14 to 17 years old; and upper-level "old-heads," 18 to 23 years old (Philadelphia Police Department 1987). On the West Coast and elsewhere the aspirants to gang membership, usually 8 to 12 years old but sometimes considerably older, are presently labeled "wannabes."

The New York City Youth Board (1960) described horizontal gangs as follows: "The horizontally organized group is more likely to include divisions or groupings from different blocks or neighborhoods comprising youngsters of middle or late teens with little differentiation as to age. The horizontal group may, and usually does, develop out of the vertical or self-contained group structure" (pp. 23–24). It is a later form of gang structural development. The horizontally organized youth gang has currently become the most common type of structure when gangs with the same name spread across neighborhoods, cities, states, and countries. These horizontal structures have evolved into coalitions, confederations, "supergangs," and nations—presumably creating or developing even more sophisticated structures on the basis of prison experience. They developed primarily out of the black and Hispanic gang experience in Chicago and Los Angeles after the 1960s.

The *self-contained* gang, according to the New York City Youth Board streetworker experience,

> may pre-exist or grow out of a horizontal or vertical structure. It may be a newly organized group of neighborhood youngsters. It may have splintered off from a horizontal organization. It may comprise several members who, unable to get along in an age division of a vertical nature, have banded together to form a new grouping. The self-contained group is often an older gang in a state of equilibrium. . . . (New York City Youth Board 1960, p. 25)

Klein, building on the seminal New York City Youth Board typology, and focusing more on the internal dynamics of gang structural change, suggested

> two modal patterns of structure, and several variations deriving from the . . . *spontaneous* or *self-contained* group . . . from 10 to 30 members within a two or three-year age range, was and is more likely to appear in areas of transition. It is not a permanent grouping, seldom lasting more than a year or two. Sometimes it is a splinter group, having broken off from a larger gang cluster to pursue a particular interest pattern (social or criminal). Members know each other on a personal basis, although core and fringe levels can be distinguished. (Klein 1971, pp. 64–65)

Klein suggested or implied that the degree of stability of community structure may influence these varying gang organizational patterns. He referred to a more complex organizational arrangement of gangs that he termed *traditional*, which implies more stable and established institutional arrangements in the community:

> The second pattern variously termed vertical, area, traditional, or cluster is far more complex. . . . The essential feature of this pattern is the inclusion of from two to five age grade subgroups within an overall cluster. . . . Each subgroup has a sense of self-identity and a specific name as well as a strong identification with the overall cluster as a superordinate structure.
>   Such a structure may include as many as 100 or 200 boys over a period of only two years. . . . Core members comprise the majority of clique membership, although some fringe members also fall into cliques. (Klein 1971, pp. 64–65)

Recently Klein stated that the "old turf-oriented, vertically organized cluster of groups . . . is now far less prevalent, being one form of many and occurring principally in Hispanic enclaves, especially in the Southwest. More gangs are relatively age-integrated, autonomous units" (Klein 1992, p. 6). I do not believe this is entirely correct. Gangs with the same name are now "spread" or developed across many communities. Gang members and units or sections increasingly identify themselves as part of "nations." Population movements of minority groups, local community structural changes, and the greater economic survival concerns of gang youths may be responsible for these changing gang organizational patterns.

Fagan, who studied gangs in Los Angeles, San Diego, and Chicago, identified four types of gangs based less on structure and more on frequencies of certain patterns of deviant and criminal behaviors: "social gangs," involved only in a few delinquent activities and little drug use; "party gangs," involved in drug use and drug sales; "serious delinquent gangs," engaging extensively in both violent and property offenses; and those "drug" gangs extensively involved in serious drug use and sales, and who appear at risk of becoming formal criminal organizations. Fagan also suggested that cities vary according to their mix of gang types (Fagan 1989). Fagan did not explicitly elaborate how or whether patterns or distributions of gang behavior are related to gang or local community structural characteristics.

With the increased prevalence of drug gangs, and especially the involvement of gang members, cliques, and former gang members in drug trafficking, has come the notion that the gang is or can become a primarily rational, bureaucratic, entrepreneurial, corporate, or business organization. Knox notes that different levels of gang organization exist: level 1—emergent gang; level 2—crystallized or more formalized gang; and level 3—highly formalized gang with satellite units, organizational goals, stable leadership, and diverse sources of criminal income (Knox 1991a, pp. 158–159).

Evolving Gang Organization

More implicit than explicit in these analyses of gang organization is the proposition that gang organization, as it becomes better developed and rational, functions to provide increasing sources of criminal economic opportunity. The rapid movement and quasi-integration of minority populations into these criminal systems across local communities and the systematization of gang relationships facilitate this process, particularly as local community institutional structures weaken and legitimate economic means to social status become more limited. In these descriptions of different levels or types of gang organization, variation is based largely on race or ethnicity.

An example of an increasingly formalized criminal street-gang structure could be that of African-American street gangs such as the CRIPS, originating in Los Angeles, or the Vice Lords or Gangster Disciples in Chicago. According to law enforcement authorities (probably with some exaggeration and overgeneralization) CRIPS in a few cities have established the following "marketing" plan:

> Before moving their operation into a given area, the gang will first send a scout (usually a peewee) to test the market in that city. If it appears that the demand is right as well as other factors panning out, a large group of members will then proceed to the city and establish residency in an inner-city apartment or house.
>
> The apartment or house will then be established as a "crack house" for cocaine conversion, packaging, and sales. Although it is the members who establish the operation, CRIPS will usually recruit local-level youths to actually conduct the street transactions. (Lyman 1989, pp. 105–106)

Taylor, also probably with some exaggeration and overgeneralization, describes the rational structure of the African-American street gang—now a corporate gang— as follows:

> These well-organized groups have a very strong leader or manager. The main focus of their organization is participation in illegal money-making ventures. Membership

is based on the worth of the individual to the organization. Each member understands his or her role and works as a team member. Criminal actions are motivated by profit. Unlike scavenger gangs, crimes are committed for purpose, not for fun. Although they have members from lower classes and the under-class, middle-class and upper middle-class youths are also attracted to this type of gang. (Taylor 1990a; see also Skolnick 1988)

Jankowski has developed the most sophisticated, and probably also most exaggerated, claims for the highly organized or formal character of gang structure. He states gangs are generally integrated into local community institutional structures. There exist basic and explicit components of gang structure as well as models of gang organization:

> The first has to do with formal leadership structures, in which leadership categories are labeled and assigned a degree of authority. The second has to do with the definition of roles and duties for both leadership and the rank and file. The third involves the codes that each collective creates and enforces in an effort to engineer order. (Jankowski 1991, p. 64)

The first organizational model, according to Jankowski, is the "vertical/hierarchical" divided into three or four categories or offices—president, vice president, warlord, and treasurer. The second model he identifies as the "horizontal/commission type," where officers share roughly equal authority. It takes much longer to arrive at a decision in this model. The third form of organization is the "influential model. In this model, the formal leadership operated under the guise of informality." These leaders usually have special skills, talents, or "special qualities." Jankowski also suggests that there is some relationship between ethnicity and the types of organizations that gangs adopt, with Chicano and Irish gangs relatively more likely to employ the influential and horizontal/commission types of leadership structure in order to "fit better into the cultural environment of many Chicano and Irish neighborhoods" (Jankowski 1991, pp. 63–100). Moreover, it is possible that socioeconomic and community organizational differences may be more important than culture or ethnicity in the determination of gang structure.

Moore also suggests a relationship between type of gang organization and ethnicity of gangs: "The [Mexican-American] East Los Angeles groups are informally organized, without acknowledged leadership. Black gangs studied in both Los Angeles and Milwaukee are more formally organized, with pre-planned meetings, dues, and officers" (Moore 1990, p. 168). She adds that these gang variations point to "the need for an empirically based taxonomy of gangs that is related to community variations. What is true of one gang is not necessarily true of another.

Spergel and Curry in their survey of responses of law enforcement officials in forty-five cities found there was a perceived relationship among the variables of race/ethnicity of gangs, criminal organization, and to some extent drug criminal behavior, particularly drug trafficking. This is contrary to Klein's comment quoted earlier in the chapter (1971, p. 80) in which he suggests there may be little relationship between gang organization and delinquent patterns.

> In regard to more organized forms of gang criminality, we found that there is a negative or inverse relationship between the percentage of Hispanic gang members in a

community or jurisdiction and the involvement of gangs with criminal organizations. Affiliation with criminal organizations is related to a high level of serious or index crime by gang youths. The relationship between selling drugs as a primary purpose of the gang, and ethnicity, is characteristic of black gangs, but not of Hispanic gangs. The greater the percent of black gang members in an area, the greater the likelihood that drugs are being sold by gangs. However, the greater the percent of Hispanic gang members in an area, the less the likelihood of drug selling. When drug distribution is a primary purpose of the gang, there is a significantly higher percent of the total of all index crime attributed to gangs. (Spergel and Curry 1990, p. 88)

Gang typologies and classifications suggest a bewildering array, complexity, and variability of structures, purposes, and behavioral characteristics of gangs, with these dimensions not clearly identified or interrelated. Gangs, or more precisely the inter-relationship of member roles, may be cohesive, loosely knit, or bureaucratic, or part of a small or large network across neighborhoods, cities, states, and even countries (Collins 1979), or they may specialize in different kinds of criminal behavior. Many current classifications[1] of gang organization are of an ad hoc, cross-sectional, or nondevelopmental nature. The classifications usually represent the particular interests of the practitioner or researcher without reference to how the particular organization has evolved or how it relates to community or economic structure. How important particular organizational arrangements are for explaining different patterns of gang behavior and what implications can be drawn for policy or practice have not been developed.

Limitations of the Idea of Gang Organization

Despite the sophisticated organizational analyses or attributions of gang researchers and law enforcement officials, street gangs must still be regarded as more like "amoebic" social movements than rational business organizations. The idea of sophisticated gang organizations is still largely a product of the self- or organizational-interested

---

[1] A great variety of gang dimensions for classifying or typing youth gangs has emerged in recent years. They include (1) age; (2) race/ethnicity; (3) gender [all male, all female, or mixed]; (4) setting [street, prison, or motorcycle (G. Camp and Camp 1985; C. Camp and Camp 1988)]; (5) type of activity [social, delinquent, or violent (Yablonsky 1962; Haskell and Yablonsky 1982; Jackson and McBride 1985)]; (6) purpose of gang activity [defensive or aggressive (New York City Youth Board 1960; Collins 1979), turf, retaliation, prestige, or representation (Bobrowski 1988)]; (7) degree of criminality [serious, minor, or mixed (Pleines 1987)]; (8) level of organization [scavenger, territorial, corporate (Taylor 1988), vertical or horizontal, spontaneous specialty clique, horizontal alliance, or violent gang (Klein and Maxson 1987), vertical/hierarchical, horizontal/commission, influential (Jankowski 1991), levels of formal organization (Jankowski 1991)]; (9) stage of group formation or development [early, marginal, or well-established (Collins 1979; New York State Assembly 1974b)]; (10) degree of activity [active, sporadic, or inactive (Philadelphia Police Department 1987)]; (11) nature or level of personality development or disturbance of group members (Scott 1956; Klein 1971; Jackson and McBride 1985); (12) level of member involvement [regular, peripheral, temporary, situational (Vigil 1988b)]; (13) group function [socioemotive, expressive, or cultural and instrumental (Berntsen 1979; Huff 1988; Skolnick 1992)]; (14) drug use/selling (Fagan 1988); (15) cultural development (traditional, nontraditional, or transitional (Vigil 1983; McBride 1988)]; (16) new types [heavy metal, punk rock, satanic, or skinhead (Baca 1988; Coplon 1988; Buhmann 1991)].

musings of gang leaders, certain police officials, academic researchers, and media reporters based on very limited hard data. Thrasher (1936, p. 323) noted a long time ago the possibility of complex, affiliated, but ephemeral gang structures: "In some cases federations of friendly gangs are formed for the promotion of common interests or protection against common enemies. These may be nothing more than loose alliances." In several cities, gangs or sets of gangs have been paired as enemies with "enmity brief, sometimes lasting" (W. Miller 1975). The terms *nation* and later *supergang* were coined in Chicago in the late 1960s to describe one particular large gang reportedly numbering in the thousands with units spread throughout the city. "Nation" is still commonly used. Several of the now older, established gangs have claimed the existence of hierarchies, board structures, elders, and elites (Sherman 1970).

Two major multiethnic gang coalitions (somewhat distinct from the idea of a specific gang nation or supergang), "the People" and "the Folks," developed in Chicago and Illinois prisons in the middle 1970s. These various nations, supergangs, or gang alliances contained older as well as younger members, and supposedly were more criminalized, more sophisticated, and better organized than the gangs of the 1950s and early 1960s (Short 1976). The origins of the People and the Folks as alliances of other named gangs took place in prison, according to Chicago Police Department information, when the predominantly white Simon City Royals agreed to provide narcotics in exchange for protection from inmates belonging to the Black Disciples, a loose constellation of street gangs ("Folks"). Shortly thereafter, and in response to this alliance, members of the Latin Kings, a constellation of gangs of mainly Hispanic ethnic origin (Mexican-American and Puerto Rican), aligned with the Vice Lords, a "nation" of black gangs or factions, to form a counteralliance ("People"). These superalliances spread to the streets of Chicago and other midwestern and southern cities.

According to a fairly recent report, there are currently about thirty-one street gangs in Chicago that identify with the Folks and about twenty-seven that identify with the People. A few particular gangs in certain neighborhoods are known only as Folks or People with no other identifiers. About nineteen street gangs remain independent. In addition, there are factions of gangs and gangs with unknown affiliations. Membership is about evenly divided between Folks and People. Seventy percent of the gangs identifying with the Folks are Hispanic, 19 percent are black, and 10 percent are white; 56 percent of the gangs identifying with the People are Hispanic, 22 percent are black, and 19 percent are white (Bobrowski 1988). It is not clear how meaningfully or firmly these gangs, or gang members, outside of prison are related to the prison gangs or to the larger gang entities with similar names across the country. Most individual gang members are closely identified with particular gangs or gang factions in a particular location, street, school, or correctional institution. There is "no centralized organization and chain of command . . . and no clear leadership has emerged. . . . In fact, local disputes, power struggles, or ignorance often result in conflict among . . . affiliates" (Bobrowski 1988, pp. 30–31). The development of drug enterprises by gang cliques or personal animosities by leaders of "renegade" groups or sections frequently may result in more violence within gang sections of the same gang rather than between gangs or supergang or coalition formations at particular places and times.

Gang coalitions were reported to be common in the Los Angeles area, throughout California, in adjoining states, and increasingly in correctional institutions across the country. Black gangs, for example, were divided into two main aggregations in California: CRIPS and Bloods, with the CRIPS containing more units or sets and members. Coalitions of black gangs with Hispanic, Asian, Pacific Island, and white gangs also apparently existed on the West Coast. Different gang coalitions were said to develop somewhat different characteristics. CRIPS were reportedly more aggressive in their dealings with each other; Blood sets rarely fought each other. Fights between CRIPS gangs were reported to have accounted for one-third to one-half of all gang-versus-gang incidents in various Los Angeles jurisdictions (Baker 1988b). Hispanic gangs in the same coalition in Chicago may fight each other for a variety of economic, individual member personality, or situational reasons. On occasion members of the same gang, whether black or Hispanic, may clash, and these fights can result in serious injuries or fatalities.

Some of the older, well-established street gangs, black, Hispanic, or motorcycle, have developed extensive written histories, organizational charts, and rules and regulations, including detailed codes of punishments that are followed, however, more often in the breech than in reality. They are formulated and used by gang leaders in prison with much time on their hands or by older gang members to impress younger recruits. These documents indicate a strong need to establish a sense of solidarity with a larger subcultural and social supportive identity and also to bring protection and especially order to comrades in a chaotic and hostile environment both in prison and on the streets. They do suggest, however, a greater sense of structure or organization among gangs in recent than in earlier decades.

Again, how well internally organized and integrated any and all of these street gang coalitions, alliances, corporate structures, nations, or supergangs actually is is not reliably known. Gangs are probably less rather than more organized, and none certainly approaches the degree of integration and efficiency of most large organizations or legitimate corporations in society. To what extent the gang as a total structure is integrated into established major criminal adult organizations, such as the Mafia, Triads, or Yakuza, is highly questionable (however, see Chapter 10), although there is probably integration of particular cliques or subgroups into these and other criminal organizations.

Cliques or Subgroups

The clique is the basic building block of the gang. It is a relatively cohesive subunit that often gives the larger group its special and persistent character. Thrasher (1936, pp. 320–321) defined the gang clique as a "spontaneous interest group usually of the conflict type which forms itself within some larger social structure such as a gang. . . . In a certain sense a well-developed clique is an embryonic gang." The idea of "delinquent group" is often congruent with that of gang clique. Shaw and McKay (1931) noted that the most common type of delinquent group in which juvenile offenses are committed is the small companionship group, consisting of two or three boys. Downes (1966), a British researcher, observed that small cliques were responsible for the bulk of delinquency. However, he made a distinction between them and more "organized," differentiated and larger gangs. Klein (1971) referred to a "specialty clique" that may be part of the larger gang structure, but sometimes exists as an independent unit. It consists of three to a dozen boys. It can maintain or stimulate distinctive patterned behavior, criminal gain, conflict activity, and drug use.

Harris noted that "whenever a male Latino gang is active, there almost always appears to be a female component or auxiliary," at least in Los Angeles County. These female cliques as a rule do not participate in all activities of the main group or clique (Harris 1988, p. 4; see also Taylor 1990a, pp. 8–9). This is not exactly true for Chicago's Latino gangs, where the existence of female auxiliaries and the extent of their involvement in gang activities are highly variable. Moore states that researchers have generally paid little attention to the characteristics of female cliques associated with male gangs. Contrary to Harris, she estimates that "only about half of the [East Los Angeles Latino] male cliques had female cliques affiliated with them" (Moore 1991, pp. 139–140).

The clique and the gang may be viewed as parts of a large, loosely knit network. Cliques may operate outside gang structures and even across opposing gang structures. Theft or robbery subgroups or cliques—and more recently, drug-trafficking cliques—may identify with a particular gang for socialization and conflict purposes but may recruit members from outside that gang for special "jobs," or ally themselves with similar interest cliques, even in so-called opposition gangs. Gangs that are ordinarily opposed to each other may also join together temporarily to deal with larger issues such as riots, interethnic or racial conflicts, police pressures, support for a social movement, or a major community development program. The pattern of activity of the specific gang is usually determined by an influential clique. The particular clique activity, for example a gang fight or intergang hostility, furthermore, may cause the membership of the gang to expand rapidly (Gold and Mattick 1974).

Clique/Gang Size

Clique and gang size are important for identifying the scope and character of the gang problem, and for the development of appropriate gang control or prevention strategies. We know that in a gang incident more offenders or suspects are usually involved than in non-gang incidents. In one Chicago study of reported violent gang incidents, Spergel (1986) found that approximately three offenders were arrested per gang incident. In an earlier Chicago study, he found that slightly less than two offenders were arrested per gang homicide incident (Spergel 1983). In a more inclusive Los Angeles gang and non-gang homicide study, Klein, Maxson, and Gordon (1987) found approximately four suspects per gang homicide incident, about twice as many suspects as for non-gang homicide incidents (1987).

Some researchers have emphasized that gangs are generally small—hardly larger than a clique—ranging from four or five to twenty-five members—eight to twelve being most common (Gold and Mattick 1974). Others, including police specialists, youth agency informants, and researchers, have viewed the size of the gang as ranging from 25 to 75 members (Thrasher 1927, p. 318; New York City Youth Board 1957, p. 10; Collins 1979; Chin 1990, p. 122), from 25 to 200 (Philadelphia Preventive Patrol Unit 1987; Vigil 1988b, p. 87), and from about 30 to 500 (Torres 1980). Since the late 1960s, some analysts have believed that the size of some gangs—

whether supergangs or coalitions of gangs—may range into t
1972; W. Miller 1975, 1982; Short 1976), or even tens of tho
law enforcement estimates. These numbers may include peri
well as core members, both active and inactive, and also wai
estimates are often based on sightings of large groups of yout
such as a dance, or during "declarations" by gang members t
housing project, or prison is "theirs." Law enforcement estima̲ₒₒ ᵤ̲ₒ ᵤₗₒₒ ᵤ̲ₓₓ ₓₓₓₒ
gerated, based on arrest or contact data over a multiyear period—sometimes eight or
more years—whether gang members on the rosters are active or not. Prison officials
use estimates from guards, self-reports of inmates, and/or police information. Beck
and colleagues (1993) suggest that the more a gang is structured or the greater the
gang's formal characteristics as a gang, at least on the basis of a survey of inmates in
state prisons, the larger the gang membership. Most of these estimates are probably
unreliable or have to be highly qualified to particular context or time.

As a rule, gangs tend to be smaller in newly established than in older settled inner-
city communities (Vigil 1988b, pp. 94–95). In Chicago, Latino gangs generally are
smaller than African-American gangs, although differences in the size of cliques or
subgroups in these various gangs are not reliably known. There may be more African-
American gang members, but more discrete Latino gangs in Chicago. The presence
of many factions, cliques, or gangs of smaller size in a particular area may lead to
more intergroup conflict than if fewer large gangs are present.

There is some evidence that gang size grows during crisis—especially with threats
of gang attacks, retaliations, or periodic competition for drug markets—and decreases
in the absence of conflict and during periods of gang "peace" or truces. Gang size
may also vary during different school seasons or academic transition periods—larger
in the fall when school starts, during school holidays, and especially at the start of
the spring or summer break. Recruitment efforts in the fall of the first year of high
school also may produce an increase in gang ranks (see Klein 1971).

Many questions can be raised about the relationship of variables of numbers of
gangs, gang members, and gang problems to community structure. Is the number of
gangs in an area or organizational setting related to the number of gang members?
Are there more gangs, but not necessarily more gang members, in newly settled communities, compared with settled areas? We know, for example, that there are more
Hispanic than black gangs in Chicago but not necessarily more Hispanic gang members (Bobrowski 1988). There may be more gangs, but fewer gang members, represented in a magnet or citywide high school than in a low-income neighborhood high
school, but does this mean there are more gang problems present in the magnet school
(Spergel 1985)? Probably not. Similarly, size of gang membership and gang problems may or may not vary with the number of gangs in a particular prison (G. Camp
and Camp 1985).

Types of Gang Members

The youth or street-gang is not composed simply of members of common or equal
rank. From the perspective of understanding gang structure and dynamics, especially
for purposes of gang control, it is important to know what different positions and

ng members are required to carry out gang activities and functions. Spe-
ng policy and program necessitate that relatively more attention be paid to
m types of gang members than to others.

The structure of the gang is substantially based on the need for group maintenance or development. A variety of types of members are needed—core members,
including leaders and regulars; peripheral, or fringe, members; associates; wannabes,
or recruits; veterans, or old gangsters (OGs). The core may be regarded as an inner
clique that is actively engaged in everyday functioning. Core members interact frequently and usually relate easily to each other. They have been described as "those
few who need and thrive on the totality of the gang's activity. The gang's level of
violence is determined by the hardcore" (Pitchess 1979, p. 2). Core members may
make key decisions, set standards, and support and sanction the action of leaders.
They are also the key recruiters (Sarnecki 1986; Reiss 1987). Vigil and Long suggest that in East Los Angeles core members are least attached to legitimate roles of
the American or Mexican-American culture (1990, p. 57).

Associate and peripheral members are those associated with or adjunct to the
gang but not recognized by others or themselves as important or full members of the
gang as core members. They may be irregular in attendance at particular gang events
or gatherings. Their relationships may be primarily to particular core members. Their
status tends to be lower.

"Floaters" may exist in and across gangs. They are special kinds of associates
and have high status, although they are not clearly identified as gang members. They
are often brokers across gangs, with access to special resources or having special
talents needed by the gang. For example, they may possess information about the
activities of other gangs and serve as communication links and negotiators in times
of tension or intergang conflict. They may arrange deals for weapons, drugs, or stolen property between gangs and with others outside the gang. They tend to be entrepreneurial, well respected, and articulate, with many community connections, legitimate and illegitimate.

Wannabes or recruits are usually younger, aspiring or potential gang members.
They are the targets of efforts by core or associate members to maintain or increase
the size and status of the gang. Recruitment drives may be especially heavy during
times of crisis or threat, or when the need exists for individuals with special talents
or qualities to assist the group. Wannabes and recruits are usually younger teens but
may be almost of any age.

Veterans or old gangsters are usually older youths, young adults, or those who
have spent years committed to the gang. They are no longer active or regular in their
gang involvement, particularly in violent or criminal gang activities. They may or
may not be known or respected by younger members in the gang. However, some
older gang leaders, still in jail, serve as very important symbolic reference persons.
They may be considerably more influential in relation to organized criminal gain than
to street conflict activities.

Law enforcement agencies have strategic and tactical reasons for identifying
different types of gang members. Most police departments want to arrest or neutralize gang leadership. They may sometimes be concerned with not exaggerating estimates of the numbers of gang members, as much because of limited department

operational manpower as for city administration or political purposes. Law enforcement agencies also may not always indicate whether gang members are "verified" or "alleged" members (New York State Assembly 1974b, p. 3). The verified hard-core members are often viewed as making up about 10 percent of the gang and are the targets for most law enforcement intervention (Collins 1979).

Social agencies and school officials are generally more concerned with wannabe's and issues of prevention than with hard-core gang members. They are prone to conducting educational awareness campaigns directed to younger youths and parents to "ward off" the gang problem before it becomes serious. Prevention strategies are also employed to attract resources to maintain or broaden existing social or educational programs.

Whether and under what circumstances gangs/members develop particular positions and roles is unclear. Gang membership criteria and gang roles are vague and shifting. Most youths who hang around or associate with gangs are usually regarded as gang members. Some members join for a short time—days or weeks. Gang members may "graduate" from lower- to higher-status gang positions, particularly as they grow older. However, they may also shift from core to peripheral or associate positions and back again. A youth may switch membership from one friendly gang to another and even to a formerly hostile gang, as when gang membership requires little in the way of formal identification or involvement or, more often, when the gang member's family moves to a different gang-controlled neighborhood, or the youth decides to join a different dominant gang at a new school or in a correctional setting. Gang members themselves may not know who is a member of another gang or even their own gang, although higher status or core gang members are readily recognized. Leadership and core-member positions and roles assume greater stability, function, and articulation in certain stable social contexts, particularly low-income, black ghetto communities and in prison (Jacobs 1977).

Leaders and Core Gang Members

The status or designation of leadership or core gang membership is not often clearly or consistently identified across race/ethnic groups, particular communities, or regions of the country. Some gangs have formal leadership positions such as a president and vice president. Black gangs in inner cities, black and Hispanic gangs in prisons, and older more established gangs have referred to their leaders variously as king, prince, prime minister, general, ambassador, don, chief, president, governor, lieutenant governor, or chairman. Some highly violent gang leaders or influentials may have no formal designation or title and are simply referred to as "shot callers" or "shooters" by gang members or police. There is a tendency for leaders in black gangs to be more clearly or "officially" identified than in Hispanic gangs.

There is some agreement that core members are more involved in delinquent or criminal activities than peripheral or fringe members, based mainly on official police records. Klein (1968, p. 74) reported that during the four years of the Los Angeles Group Guidance Project, "core members were charged with 70 percent more offenses than fringe members." Core members committed their first offenses at an earlier age, committed subsequent offenses at a more rapid rate, and their last juvenile offenses at a later age than fringe members (p. 274). Sarnecki's (1986) findings in Sweden are similar. The more central the positions and the more active the roles played by the juveniles, the greater the likelihood of their continuing in a delinquent career. Those who were accomplices of the central characters in the networks also ran greater risks of arrest than the average participant (Sarnecki 1986, p. 128; see also Vigil 1988b, p. 137). Conversely, Fagan (1988, p. 22) found no significant differences between leaders and other kinds of members indicated in drug and delinquent activities, on the basis of self-reports. Esbensen and Huizinga, also using self-report data, conclude there is no difference between core and peripheral members in levels of gang involvement as well as in self-reported delinquency in Denver, an emerging gang problem city (1993, p. 16).

Finally, a debate has raged, mainly in terms of whether core or fringe members are more or less socially adjusted or psychologically troubled. Yablonsky (1962) claimed that core members were psychologically disturbed or sociopathic, and fringe members were more likely to be "normal." Short and Strodtbeck (1965), Klein (1971), and Gold and Mattick (1974) took an opposing position: leadership and core members were likely to be more socially capable, perhaps more intelligent. Fringe members or "crazies" were likely to have low status or to be ostracized by the group, except when used for certain aggressive purposes (Horowitz 1983). The extensive case vignettes in the descriptive and program reports of the New York City Youth Board (1960) suggested that core and fringe members come with all sorts of personality makeups, capabilities, and disabilities and that it is extremely difficult to relate gang role to personality type.

Vigil and Long suggest that individual personality and motivation not only determine the roles that gang members play, but that their distribution in particular gangs determines the different character of gangs. Some gangs may have more troubled or disturbed individual members or cliques and are thus more committed to violence, gang fights, robberies, larcenies, and so on . Vigil and Long suggest further that social context, social condition, and social policy influence the size of Hispanic gangs, the nature of cliques, and the nature of the involvement of disturbed members: "Higher unemployment and fewer intervention programs, for example, will exacerbate the stress and strain that shapes those marginal youths who tend to become the most 'loco' regulars in the gang" (1990, p. 63).

A thorough analysis of gang leadership positions and roles, and their distinctions, is important for policy, programmatic, and theoretical reasons. Leadership functions and positions are essential to the purpose and character of gang structure and experience. Gang position and role signify interrelated but not the same social phenomena. The role of the gang leader may be more volatile and unstable. In more violent gangs, change in leadership and competition for leadership may be more frequent and arrest more likely than in less violent gangs.

Furthermore, the more disorganized the community, the more likely is the violent, volatile character of the gang and its leadership. Policies and programs need to attend to characteristics of community and related gang leadership structure. The law enforcement officer or social worker may hitch his or her professional role to the wrong star if he or she assumes either that elimination of a particular gang leader automatically leads to disintegration of the gang or that development of a positive relationship with a given gang leader necessarily changes gang structure and reduces gang violence.

Territory

The traditional youth gang is defined and organized in terms of the territory in which it is located or which it claims as its own. Territory may be regarded as an essential component of gang identity as well as a basis for gang dynamics and behavior. The notion of territory, or turf, is integral to the rationale for the gang's existence. The gang is organized in such a way as to protect and develop turf. The territorial and communal nature of the traditional gang is nowhere better illustrated than in many Hispanic areas of Los Angeles where the terms *gang* and *barrio* are usually synonymous with the concept of neighborhood and the two terms may be used interchangeably (Moore 1978). Further, the notion of gang turf is part of a larger conception of community ecology in which the gang problem develops (see Chapter 8). The degree of commitment to turf by the gang and its members varies by particular cultural tradition, community stability and socioeconomic pressures, age of the gang's members, and the changing interests or purposes of the gang.

Thrasher long ago observed that "gang warfare is usually organized on a territorial basis. Each group becomes attached to a local area which it regards as peculiarly its own and through which it is dangerous for members from another group to pass" (1936, p. 175; see also Suttles 1968; Anderson 1990). Territorial proximity among gangs has always been a critical factor in determination of the purpose, structure, motivation, and frequency of gang conflict. Of 188 gang incidents among thirty-two gangs in Philadelphia between 1966 and 1970 (homicides, stabbings, shootings, and gang fights), 60 percent occurred between gangs who shared a common boundary, and another 23 percent between gangs whose territories were two blocks or less apart. Only two incidents occurred between groups whose turfs were separated by more than ten blocks (Ley 1975, pp. 262–263).

Certain inner-city groups experience not only an economic but a social and cultural marginality. Their marginalization provides the mandate for a "territorial imperative . . . for the establishment of a small secure area where group control can be maximized against the flux and uncertainty of . . . the city" (Ley 1975, pp. 252–253). Graffiti become the visible manifestation of a gang's control of social space. Gang graffiti become denser with increasing proximity to the core of a territory. Graffiti are a clue to both the extent and intensity of "ownership" of a territory by a gang, which often varies inversely with the strength of adult involvement or community organization in the exercise of control over the particular area.

The "territorial imperative" pattern may have been modified somewhat in recent years as gangs have become more mobile and new gang sections have been established in adjoining and suburban communities through population growth and migration. Gang member partying and gang retaliations may now occur in different parts of a city or jurisdiction, causing a spread of actual and potential gang conflicts based on control of particular social situations at particular times as well as territory. The traditional concept of turf or territory has now been elaborated. Physical, social, and economic dimensions of turf have been added. A gang may now hang out, socialize, or do business in different parts of the neighborhood, city, or county. It may no longer need—as much—a specific location or the same center or building as a point of identification or control for each of these purposes.

Conflict over gang turf most often results from tensions and competition over who "owns" or controls schools, parks, jails, prison areas, illegitimate enterprises or rackets, and even social or political institutions of neighborhoods (Thrasher 1936; Asbury 1971; Spergel 1972; Kornblum 1974; Kotlowitz 1988). At the heart of the concept of territoriality or turf are two ideas: control and symbolic identification. Control, often by intimidation, is the stronger imperative or driving force for gangs. Collins (1979, pp. 68–69) observed that "street gangs have been known to actually control the activity and events of certain streets and blocks. They attempt to control playgrounds, parks, recreation centers . . . to the exclusion of all other gangsters. . . . Other gangs have been known to march in front of a witness' residence, exhibiting guns and weapons, inferring 'keep your mouth shut.'"

W. Miller (1977, pp. 23–25) carried the notion of territory or turf beyond simple geographic and status concerns. He suggested three categories of turf rights: (1) ownership rights, where gangs "own" the entire area or property and control all access, departure, and activities within it; (2) occupancy rights, where gangs share or tolerate each other's use and control of a site under certain conditions (for example, respect or deference, time, and the nature and the amount of usage of the space); and (3) enterprise monopoly, where gangs claim exclusive right to commit certain kinds of crimes. Miller gave as an example of "enterprise monopoly rights" a Boston gang that claimed the exclusive right to steal from stores in a marked-off territory and forcefully thwarted others who attempted a store robbery in the area. Also, Chinese gangs in a few cities, especially in San Francisco and New York, have a tradition of violence resulting from challenges to exclusive extortion rights of certain businesses.

In recent years, much of the violence among black gangs or their subgroups apparently results from competition over drug markets. Gang entrepreneurs or former gang members may seek to develop or expand their business operations by recruiting or converting existing street groups—often in different neighborhoods or cities—to sell, deliver, store, protect, or aid in the marketing of drugs. Conflicts develop when these new entrepreneurs enter an area already controlled by another clique, gang, or criminal organization engaged in drug trafficking.

Miller (1977) noted that certain cities do not have a well-developed tradition of locality-based gangs. Youth gangs in these cities are more sophisticated and criminalized and less identified with physical location. Increasingly important is the availability of criminal opportunities or markets as gangs have become highly mobile. A law enforcement officer in New York City observed that criminal youths no longer hang out; now they move from corner to corner and neighborhood to neighborhood to join with others for a burglary, robbery, drug deal, or whatever criminal opportunity arises that day (Galea 1988). Under such circumstances, the notion of "gang" changes or becomes more closely associated with that of delinquent or crime group; gang turf, colors, symbols, jackets, caps, signs, names, and traditions become less important. The purpose and structure of the gang change, in the direction of more rational and differentiated organization and probably smaller unit size.

With this changed organization, the gang can become more integrally a part of the social, economic, and cultural environment in which it is located. A symbiosis is more fully established. The gang becomes careful not to randomly antagonize the local citizenry. It increasingly claims that a major purpose of its presence and activities is not only to protect the area but to cooperate with legitimate organizations, including the police—at times—to maintain order and provide services and income—legitimate and illegitimate—to the community (see Suttles 1968, Campbell 1984b; Horowitz 1987; Jankowski 1991).

Conclusion

Gangs form in communities when established institutional and organizational arrangements are weak or break down. The gang becomes a vehicle for organizing the interests and needs of alienated youths. Violence or gang fighting is one means for defining organizational boundaries essential to obtaining social meaning and important status and, in due course, criminal resources. Over time, the gang develops in increasingly complex and specialized ways, yet it always resembles more a collectivity, clan, or social movement with strong symbolic concerns than a typical bureaucratic or business organization. Each local community seems to provide a somewhat different context for the development of the gang, particularly with regard to race/ethnicity, class, community organization, and cultural traditions.

Gang organization, as it becomes better developed and rational, is a function of increasing criminal and decreasing legitimate sources of economic opportunity and social status. There seems to be greater pressures on African-American gangs to evolve from turf to more criminally oriented gang organizations. In newly settled Hispanic communities, gangs generally appear to be closely associated with turf and violence to protect and extend their "ownership" of territory for status or symbolic purposes.

Gangs can be small and self-contained or large, and extended across localities, cities, and states. Gang alliances are fairly common, but do not necessarily represent increased elaboration or rationalization of gangs engaged in conflict or systematic criminal-gain activities. The gang structure contains cliques and various types of member positions, often informally constructed and labeled. Core gang members are most influential in the determination of the nature of gang activity and usually have more extensive juvenile and criminal records than peripheral or associate members. Gang leadership positions and roles need to be carefully distinguished and assessed, since they have implications for the value of suppression or social intervention policies and programmatic relationships with particular gang leaders of highly violent gangs.

The idea of gang territory and social control by the gang, whether for status or income-producing purposes, is at the heart of the purpose and organization of the gang. As the gang shifts toward more criminal-gain activities, its integration with community institutions appears to strengthen. Less violence characterizes relationships between such gangs. As gang members get older they generally move out of the traditional fighting gang structure to a more conventional life or into a more criminal-gang adaptation.

7

The Gang Member Experience

The gang is an important life experience for a growing number of youths in low-income, changing, and unstable minority communities. Gangs serve the interests and needs of certain vulnerable youths, particularly during the adolescent and young adult period, when existing social, economic, and even religious institutions do not function properly. Gangs provide a certain degree of physical protection, social support, solidarity, cultural identification, and moral education as well as opportunities for self-esteem, honor, and sometimes economic gain.

This chapter describes why youths join gangs, what satisfactions they obtain from the gang, and why in due course they leave it. It deals with the role of members and the meaning of the gang to the youth, and focuses on group processes that contribute to his antisocial, especially gang-related violent, behavior. Analysis of these social facts is particularly important for community agencies and organizations seeking to intervene meaningfully at critical periods in the youth's gang life cycle.

The emphasis of the chapter is on the male gang member. We know considerably less about female gang members, despite the fact that females have been known to be an integral part of the gang experience since the 1800s (Campbell 1990, p. 166). The picture constructed of the female gang member is fragmented. The notion seems to be that female gangs and their members are "pale imitations" of male gangs (Campbell 1984b). Despite claims about a recent relative increase both in female gang members and female gang-related violence, "hard" police-based statistical data suggest little change in the traditional role of females in gangs. However, there is some evidence for increased drug-related activity by females in gangs.

Joining the Gang

There has been much theory and case description but little systematic empirical or quantitative research on why, how, and especially under what particular circumstances a youth joins or leaves a gang. Presently, efforts are being made to specify the risk factors that predispose a child or youth for entry into a gang. These include: known association with gang members; presence of neighborhood gangs; having a relative in a gang; failure at school; delinquency record, particularly for aggressive acts; and drug abuse (see Nidorf 1988; Curry and Spergel 1992). Probation officers in Orange County, California, identify minors "at-risk for gang involvement" also if they display one or more of the following characteristics: self-identification with a gang, wearing colors, and writing about a gang (such as *placas*, or graffiti) (Orange County Probation 1989).

Most often the process of joining a gang simply occurs as a youth hangs around and comes to be accepted by certain key members: "You come to the square, you belonged to the group" (Berntsen 1979, p. 92). Forcible recruitment is not common and intimidation is more indirect than direct. The threats of violence are seldom carried out, although on occasion a youth who refuses to join can be severely beaten. Initiation requirements have also become part of the tradition or folklore of gang life (New York City Youth Board 1960; Yablonsky 1962; Jansyn 1966; Patrick 1973), but they may be inconsistently observed. According to gang lore, gang initiations have ranged from drinking a large quantity of alcohol to using or selling drugs, fighting other members or running a gauntlet, stealing from a store, and doing a "hit" (e.g., shooting a member of an opposing gang). Females may be required to have sex with a male core gang member, or fight a leader or core member of the female gang.

Potential members, male or female, usually join through friendship networks or family ties. Some females join gangs because brothers, other relatives, or boyfriends are already in the gang, sometimes even to protect them or provide a source of social control on deviant or dangerous behavior. One researcher stated that a female may be socialized to the gang even before she joins. "She selects the clique as her reference group sometimes as early as age six" (Harris 1988, p. 108). The usual age of females entering a gang appears to be slightly younger than for males, between 12 and 13 years.

Individual Motivation

A great many reasons for joining a gang have been identified. Some youths join because of needs or wishes for recognition, status, safety or security, power, money, excitement, and/or new experiences—particularly under conditions of social deprivation, including inadequate adult supervision (see Thomas and Znaniecki 1918; Ley 1975). The youths seek identity and self-esteem they cannot find elsewhere (Cartwright, Tomson, and Schwartz 1975). Joining can be a means of rebellion against parents, a way out of a hostile, conflictual, or unbearable home life. It meets the social and psychological needs of some troubled youths. It can provide an opportunity for the exercise of power and control of turf, schools, parks, and prisons.

Jankowski believes that youths in low-income areas join gangs because of their "defiant" *individualist character,* which is based on or results from certain personality attributes or social circumstances: *competitiveness* (i.e., the struggle for scarce resources in the low-income community), *mistrust or wariness,* the need for *self-reliance,* the *survival instinct,* a *social Darwinist world view,* and a confrontational or *defiant air* (Jankowski 1991, pp. 23–29). However, many youths in low-income or marginal areas share many of these traits but do not become gang members. We have no systematic data on the so-called defiant characteristics of gang members. Many members can in fact be mild mannered, "cool" or placid, hot or angry, impulsive or calculating, and many other things, depending on particular circumstances. For example, we know that a gang youth can be defiant in a gang context but quite compliant when in a different setting or alone. Gang members, regardless of temperament, probably most often join gangs out of a need for personal identity, social status, and the search for social or moral boundaries.

A number of analysts have recently argued that despite, or in addition to, certain predisposing factors, whether of a personality, environmental, or social nature, gang members probably make rational decisions, "just like a businessman," to join the gang and participate in certain types of activities. Being a gang member is best for them under certain circumstances (see Horowitz 1990; Short 1990a; Jankowski 1991). However, what is not explained is why a youth decides to join a gang to participate in particular criminal or violent activities. Why do some youths, whether in or out of a gang, take certain risks at times while others of similar background and circumstances or personality do not? Why are certain youths more interested in the instrumental or material gain-oriented possibilities of the gang experience, while others are more committed to the symbolic or expressive aspects of gang life, such as fighting, or become actively and fully engaged in both types of activities?

Fagan suggests that individual decisions and actions to join a gang and participate in certain types of activities may not be calculated or planned: "In studies of initiation into gang life, it was apparent that participants did not carefully calculate the rewards and risks of participation, nor were they pressured by subcultural values. Rather gang members drifted into gang life, taking advantage of opportunities presented for money, status, protection, and social life" (Fagan 1990, p. 212).

Personal Safety. Joining a gang may result from a rational calculation to achieve personal security, particularly by males new to a particular community, school, or prison. The youth may be harassed or attacked if he is unaffiliated, belongs to the wrong gang, or comes from the wrong neighborhood. Ironically, although the youth may feel safer as a gang member, there is evidence that he or she is more likely than a non-gang member to be attacked, at least by a member of another gang (Savitz, Rosen, and Lalli 1980). On the other hand, there are a variety of ways for youths to avoid pressure to join a gang or attacks from gang members. Protection may not, in fact, be the simple, main, or true reason a youth joins a gang.

Pressures to avoid attacks from other gangs may take on an interethnic or interracial character. Youths from Hispanic, Asian, white, or black populations new to a school or community or residing in a community dominated by a different ethnic or racial group may be constrained or persuaded to join a gang for the purpose of protection, often during a period of neighborhood change. Chin observed that Chinese gangs most recently emerged in New York City between 1960 and 1968 when youths "found out that neither their parents nor school officials could protect them. . . . They bonded together to protect themselves. The first Chinese street gang, the Continentals, was formed in 1961 by native-born Chinese high school students. The gang had as many as one hundred members. It fought against not only the Puerto Ricans and the blacks but the Italians and whites as well" (Chin 1990b, pp. 76, 106–107).

Chin also noted that when more established Chinese youths from the Wah Ching gang moved from San Francisco to Los Angeles, they recruited recently arrived immigrant Chinese youths into the gang by persuading them that they needed protection from the Mexican gangs (Chin 1990b, p. 70). Many of these Chinese youths may have been coerced. "Some youths join the gangs voluntarily, while others are coerced. If potential recruits are unimpressed by what the gang offers, gang members send street soldiers to beat them up, a crude way of convincing them their lives are more secure if they are gang members than if they are alone" (Chin 1990a, p. 134).

Mydans reports a similar situation involving Cambodian youths. They "complained that they were tormented by groups of Hispanic youngsters who beat them or waved pistols as they waited at bus stops. . . . Cambodian youths first called on Asian gangs in other cities for help in defending themselves against harassment [but later formed their own gangs]" (Mydans 1991). Recent accounts of reasons for joining a gang or for the formation of black or Hispanic gangs, however, seem less often to stress the need for protection but rather emphasize a constellation of other reasons for joining the gang: (1) jobs that make big money, (2) status or a sense of belonging, (3) a sense of camaraderie among peers, and (4) adventure (see Taylor 1990a, p. 111).

Fun. Much of the attraction of ganging for adolescents or for any age group, social or antisocial, is simply "partying" and enjoying the company of, and interaction with, others like themselves. Joining a gang may be viewed as normal and respectable, even when the inevitable consequence can be a series of delinquent and violent acts. The idea of partying may mean just hanging around. Stealing, aggression, and vandalism, furthermore, may be secondary to the anticipated excitement and satisfaction of interacting with peers of similar background, interest, need, and persuasion (Sarnecki 1986). The negative consequences of joining a gang for fun or adventure are often not recognized by adolescents or even by young adults (Deukmajian 1981; Rosenbaum and Grant 1983).

"Fun and thrills" characterize much delinquent gang behavior and can yield a positive sensual reaction (Katz 1988). Certain pleasures can be derived from acts of vandalism, intimidation, or even violence of the most brutal kind by gang youths. The violent gang experience is viewed as fun not only during the act and its immediate aftermath, but in the recollection and exaggeration of particular events long afterward. The interpretations of acts—whether they actually occurred or not—can be especially important for youths who are socially and emotionally deprived or disorganized:

> Street talk also highlights the glory days: the spontaneous parties, the pranks, the drinking and the drugs . . . these events stand as a bulwark against the loneliness and drudgery of their future lives. They also were the day-to-day reality of gang life. The lack of recreational opportunities, the long days unfilled by work or school, and the absence of money mean that hours . . . are whiled away on street corners. . . . (Campbell 1990, p. 176).

The gang context provides opportunities for fun, which at the same time contribute to learning certain attitudes and skills useful to criminal purposes. Not only is fun experienced but certain skills of risk-taking, daring, and intimidation are learned (Vigil 1988a, pp. 52–53). The youth learns the importance of backing up his friends or other members of the gang. Bonds of friendship or collaboration are tightened in the course of fun activities. Nevertheless, it should be noted that heavy drug use and serious violence, more likely among older than younger youths, are dysfunctional. Heavy use of heroin or cocaine and gang homicides take on less and less a spontaneous or fun character and become, in due course, a response to extreme frustration, anger, and desperation when the excitement of gang life begins to diminish, but some-how needs to be rekindled (see Moore 1990).

Money. Some youths say they join and stay in gangs for financial reasons. The gang provides sanction or street "rep," and contacts in preparation for a criminal gain ca-reer. The gang member is able to attract the attention of criminal adults through his street-gang leadership, daring, or fighting (Spergel 1964; Ianni 1974). The gang in recent decades has become a place to make contacts and prepare for a career as a street dealer, enforcer, or hit man (W. Miller 1975). Some observers have especially emphasized the primary need or desire for money or material goods in the youth's entry into the gang. Making money seems to be of more interest to Chinese youth gangs (Chin 1990a,b) and black street gangs (Taylor 1990a) than to Hispanic youth gangs (Vigil 1988b, p. 141). What is not clear is under what social or personal con-ditions different youths join gangs for different reasons.

Jankowski claims, without sufficient evidence, that "the entrepreneurial spirit . . . was a driving force in the world view and behavior of gang members. . . . Nearly all the gang members . . . possessed certain entrepreneurial characteristics: 'com-petitiveness,' 'the desire and drive to accumulate money and material possessions,' 'status-seeking,' 'the ability to plan,' and 'the ability to undertake risks.'" Jankowski claims that leaders of gangs encourage "defiant" individual members to invest in the development of collective gang resources. He adds that gangs in the different cities vary in their commitment to organizational planning and investment. New York City gangs, he suggests, are particularly interested in supporting the entrepreneurial spirit of their members for making money (Jankowski 1991, pp. 101–122).

Substitute Family. The gang serves as a basic personal development, social identity, and morality-providing system. It recruits youths without a background of adequate family caring and social instruction and becomes a basic support system for mem-bers. The social, emotional, and moral support the gang provides is not often explic-itly identified or expressed, yet observations by researchers and comments by gang youths suggest that relationships among gang members may indeed have a familial, social, and moral developmental character. Vigil noted:

> The gang has become a "spontaneous" street social unit that fills a void left by fami-lies under stress. Parents and other family members are preoccupied with their own problems, and thus the street group has arisen as a source of familial compensation. . . . Feeling like a homeboy, backing someone up, and gaining acceptance are all personal motivations, but they are interwoven with the sense of familism. (Vigil 1988b, pp. 90–91).

The idea of the gang as family pervades many discussions of gang life. The spe-cific nature of the family function varies by the cultural and social background of gang youths and the community in which the gang is located. Distinctive historical, political, and immigration conditions that contribute to the defects of family social-ization and the rise of the gang problem need to be identified. Ima and Nidorf ob-serve that the traditional Chinese criminal society, the Triad, was a means of provid-ing a substitute family support system. Also, Japanese single males in their early days of migration to the American frontier engaged in a lot of drinking, gambling, and illegitimate behavior, but such behavior diminished as women arrived and families were established and became functional. The establishment of Chinese and Japanese communities in the United States was associated with the development of normal family life and consequent community pressures to prevent and control delinquency (Ima and Nidorf 1990, pp. 1–2).

The gang continues to have special familial value among recent Asian immigrants. Older youths in the street gangs may play older brother or parental roles for younger youths. Some Asian youths have been deprived or cut off from family life during wars and revolutionary upheavals, before their arrival in the United States. Furthermore, the transition across cultures is facilitated by the gang in the absence of a family structure. "For many [Cambodian] youngsters, the gangs more importantly offer a structure that is absent in some families broken by the Pol Pot years and bewildered by the United States" (Mydans 1991; see also Chin 1990b).

Gangs in certain Hispanic communities can be viewed not only as substitutes for families, but families can be viewed as the means for socialization to gangs. Many Mexican-American youths, male and female, were "raised into the gang . . . through relatives and close friendships" (Moore 1991, pp. 47–48). Of those interviewed by Moore, 44 percent of the men and 59 percent of the women gang members had a relative in a gang. Some came from "gang families," with three or more relatives in a gang. These families were steeped in gang traditions. Gang influence and continuity seem to come more directly through brothers, cousins, and uncles than from parents. Women were more likely than men to mention problems at home when they talked about joining the gang. Further, parents who were gang members often did not want their children to join gangs (Moore 1991, p. 49).

Even when youths engage in drug dealing and have developed a primary interest in making money, the gang or "posse" structure can serve family support functions. In his case study of a Dominican drug-dealing "posse," an organization of adolescents and young adults in New York, Williams wrote: "Over the last few years, most [drug] dealing has moved from individuals acting alone to institutional arrangements like the houses and to vertically organized groups or crews. They often include members of one family, but even when that is not the case, they maintain family-like structures" (Williams 1989, p. 54).

The gang as family in the low-income black community may perform even more basic identity and self-esteem functions. The basic family nurturing process has been progressively weakened, if not destroyed, in these areas, particularly through the rapidly changing socioeconomic, especially job, structure in recent decades. The gang serves in perverse ways, particularly in the black community, to destroy the value of family life:

> The sexual conduct of poor Northton adolescents is creating numbers of unwed parents. Yet, many young fathers remain strongly committed to peer groups. They congregate on street corners, boasting about their sexual exploits and deriding conventional family life. These interconnected realities are born of the difficult socioeconomic situations in the local community. The lack of family sustaining jobs denies many young men this possibility of forming an economically self-reliant family, the traditional American mark of manhood. . . . " (Anderson 1990, p. 112)

This is not to say that the gang should be viewed as a benign idealized model of a family. In fact, significant feelings of distrust and conflict behaviors are common among gang members. Conflict between members of the same gang can lead to physical attack and even death. Gang members do not necessarily look on each other as brothers or sisters, but often as rivals for attention, status, and various benefits. Such internal gang disruptions and fractures may not, however, be much different from family conflicts, separations, and parental divorces (Jankowski 1991, pp. 86–87; see also W. Miller 1962; Chin 1990b, p. 116).

Female Role

 Females have been perceived as secondary or accessary to males in the development of the youth or street gang. Much of the meaning or function of females in the gang has been conceived around the issue of sex, rather normal patterns of dating, and partying for adolescents in lower-income communities. Jankowski states that in "every gang I studied, women were considered a form of property" (Jankowski 1991, p. 146; see also Sung 1977, pp. 40–41; Moore 1991, pp. 54–55, 57). At the same time, there is evidence that female gangs, or more often groups of females affiliated with male gangs, meet a variety of personal and social needs, independent of the sex drive, in the gang—the same as the males (Bowker, Gross, and Klein 1980; Quicker 1983).

The pattern of female entry into the gang or auxiliary differs somewhat from that of males. Females are less likely to be pressured or coerced into joining. However, like the male, she is simply "likely to hang out and attach herself to a group which participates in gang behavior" (Harris 1988, p. 112). Where a formal initiation ceremony exists, it may take the form of a prearranged fist fight between the prospect and an established member. She also needs to demonstrate her "heart" or "courage" (Campbell 1990, p. 178). At a psychological level, at least one analyst judges that females who join gangs come from more troubled family backgrounds than males (Moore 1991, p. 29). The female gang member (relative to non-gang females) is reported to have particularly low self-esteem, to do poorly in school, to be rebellious, and to use her affiliation with auxiliary gangs or with gang members to shock parents or other peers (Campbell 1984a; Harris 1988).

Nevertheless, we have little longitudinal or comparative data to indicate why or how females join gangs or what kind, or more important what range, of roles they perform within the female affiliate group with or for the male gangs. There has been little discussion in the literature about the various leadership, core, peripheral, or associate female gang member roles. Female gang members are more likely to be peripheral or associate members both in the female group as well as in their relationship to the male gang, simply by their shorter duration as a gang member.

Group Processes

A variety of status-related group factors must be present and interact with each other to produce gangs and gang problems. These are manifested in processes that uniquely characterize the gang experience and directly contribute to violent behavior. The motivations of individual youths are insufficient for the creation of the violent gang problem. It is possible for a youth to be caught up in a set of inexorable gang processes that make him either victim or offender in a gang incident (Sanders 1994). A persistent and all-encompassing search for excitement, fun, and friendship; protection; and especially honor or status, which can be attained in a certain social situation, street group context, or in certain neighborhoods, can sweep both potential offenders and victims into unanticipated deadly confrontations.

Recruitment and Gang Symbolism

Joining a gang is viewed in certain communities as expected and desirable. At a certain age, honor, loyalty, and fellowship are reasons youths give for joining gangs, particularly in lower-class Hispanic, black, or white communities. The gang is seen as a vehicle for "preserving the barrio and protecting its honor" (Torres 1980; Horowitz 1983) or its integrity (Suttles 1968). Jankowski observes that joining a gang is "never an individual decision alone . . . gangs are . . . ultimately both the initiators of membership and the gatekeepers, deciding who will join and who will not" (Jankowski 1991, p. 47). He identifies, perhaps with some tendency to excess categorization, three types of recruitment processes, based on persuasion or coercion, that meet the need for the development of status and honor both of the group and the individual in the gang organization:

> In the fraternity type of recruitment, the gang adopts the posture of an organization that is "cool," "hip," the social thing to be in . . . the individual will need to be assessed in terms of his ability to fight, his courage, and his commitment to help others in the gang . . . assessing the potential member's ability to fight is not done simply to strengthen the gang's reputation as the meanest fighters, but rather to strengthen the confidence of other gang members that the new member adds to the organization's general ability to protect and defend the collective's interests. . . .
>
> The second recruiting technique is . . . the "obligation type" . . . "You know what the whole deal is, but I want you to know that your barrio [community] needs you just like they needed us and we delivered. We all get some battle scars [he shows them a scar from a bullet wound], but that's the price you pay to keep some honor for you and your barrio. We all have to give something back to our community. . . ."
>
> A third type of recruitment involves various forms of coercion. Coercion is used as a recruitment method when gangs are confronted with the need to increase their membership quickly. . . . The coercive method . . . is used most by gangs that find their existence threatened by competitive gangs . . . two types of coercive tactics are used: physical intimidation and psychological intimidation. (Jankowski 1991, pp. 47–59)

A gang member may seek challenges to achieve or maintain honor in a public or a group-defined manner. He must find ways to command deference. This is often done through the only means available—a demonstration of his toughness through violent behavior. Violence is not, in most situations, the rational or efficient way to obtain status or respect. But it is a key distinctive expression of gang functioning. Violence in the name of honor, "rep," or "machismo" may serve as a way of expressing extreme frustration and anger over personal and social situations unrelated to gang functioning. It serves as a means both to meet the identity and personality needs of gang members and the development and maintenance of the "gang subculture" (Vigil 1990, pp. 125–126; see also Horowitz 1987).

Honor is designated through a range of street-oriented symbols and dress codes. Youth or street gangs, motorcycle, prison, or even more organized criminal associations, use street monikers, nicknames, or placas to distinguish the individual and his specific contribution to the reputation of the gang. Horrific, provocative, or family, as well as descriptive terms such as Mad Bear, Killer, Little Wolf, Cato Junior, Joker, or Tiny, may be used (Lyman 1989, p. 102). The symbolic street-gang names of individual youths are often ascribed by senior gang members to younger members. The birth and family names and other social characteristics of the individual are often not known to other members of the gang. The symbolic names are more important and enduring for gang function and tradition. They are inscribed along with gang names on the walls of the ghetto or barrio, particularly as a form of threat to other gangs, as acknowledgment of deference, as representative of the gang's ownership or dominance over a particular territory, or in commemoration of those members fallen in battle (see Harris 1988, pp. 147–148).

Special items of clothing or dress, whether a jacket, a baseball cap, colors, earrings, or hairstyle, as well as gang signs and mannerisms, are often—but also variably in terms of time and place—identifiers of the particular gang and youth in the search and struggle for status and "rep," preferably in a particular gang domain. The bandanas worn by the Bloods and the CRIPS are referred to not only as "rags" but as "flags of a nation." Disrespect for the "rag" or "flag" is not only an attack on the particular individual but on the gang as a whole, and generally warrants a physical confrontation.

Defacing the opposing gang's graffiti, inverting a hand signal, or a drive-by shooting is not merely a way to attack and degrade the other gang. It is a way for an individual gang member to maintain or augment both his and the gang's status. Graffiti and criminal activities are not only distinctive to particular gangs, ethnic or racial cultures, and communities, but evolve over time and reflect the changing character and interests of gangs and their members to prove they are different, that they are better than a previous generation or a competitive gang, and that they are "the greatest" (see Hutcheson 1993).

Status Seeking and Gang Cohesion

The need for recognition, reputation, or status is the common denominator in why individuals, whether or not personally troubled or socially disadvantaged, participate in gangs. This recognition is achieved through delinquent or violent activity that must be based on gang norms, involve group support, and contribute to or grow out of group cohesion. The violent act also can create a further need by the individual to maintain or augment his status in the gang over time. The need for interaction with the group can therefore stimulate even more delinquent and violent activity. These relationships may be nonrecursive (see Figure 7-1).

Status seeking is a central concept in the explanation of the violent behavior of the youth gang (see Cloward and Ohlin 1960; Spergel 1964; Short and Strodtbeck

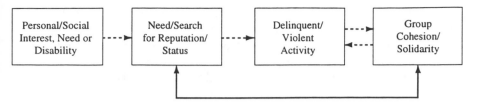

Figure 7-1. Gang behavior paradigm.

1965; Klein 1969, 1971; Moore 1978; Horowitz 1983). The process of achieving social status is sometimes interpreted by psychologically oriented analysts as simply a way of resolving a variety of personal and social problems. However, gang violence is not always precipitated by individual gang members. It often develops situationally and for purposes primarily related to group processes. Certain gang processes, such as role or leadership development and needs for group cohesion, are essential to the expression of gang crime, especially violence, although the exact mix, sequence, or causal direction of specific individual motivations or acts in relation to group dynamics in the creation of gang violence is not always clear.

Relationships among gang members may be viewed as a continuing struggle to manage status as defined and redefined by the gang (Thrasher 1936, pp. 275–276). Each gang member seeks status through types of behavior that must be meaningful to members of his gang and members of opposing gangs, but is less often so to non-gang peers and adults in the community (Cartwright, Tomson, and Schwartz 1975). The achievement of traditional gang status signifies primarily power and influence and only secondarily access to illegal opportunities and the criminal market. The drive for status can be an all-compelling motivation of the younger gang member. It constitutes the key basis for the behavior required to achieve it, and sometimes a resulting arrest and imprisonment become a further means to elevated status. Group process and the gang's status system create special problems for law enforcement officers; they must therefore acquire special group process related knowledge to curb the violent behavior of individual gang members.

Short and Strodtbeck observed that the "existence of the gang is crucial to an understanding of the manner in which status management is carried out by gang boys regardless of whether the threat originated from within or outside the group. The gang provides the audience for much of the acting out which occurs. . . . It's the most immediate system of rewards and punishments to which members are responsive much of the time" (1965, p. 215). Gang leaders, youths striving for recognition or higher status, are most directly involved in these group status-related mechanisms. Short identifies them as: "(1) the reactions of gang leaders to status threats, (2) the reactions of gangs (or segments of gangs) to status threats, and (3) a utility-risk paradigm of individual decision making in situations involving the group" (Short 1990a, p. 196).

For example, a situation may "arise when a gang leader acts to reduce threats to his status by instigating outgroup aggression . . . leaders resort to this action because of the limited resources they have for internal control of their group—particularly when their status is attacked" (Short and Strodtbeck 1965, p. 185). Short notes also that one gang leader was able to deal with status threats without violence because of his negotiating skills: "Duke was a very cool leader of a tough conflict-oriented gang of black teenagers. More socially skilled than the others, he maintained his position by cultivating nurturant relationships with other members of the gang and by negotiating with other leaders in intergang councils . . . " (Short 1990a, p. 196). The strong need for status comes fundamentally from the lack of resources and the weakness of controls internal and external to the group. The constant competition for honor and reputation, the precarious ranking system, and a hierarchical structure that "depends on continuous confirmation by others of one's placement" results in a constant state of flux, highly unstable relationships, and a continual forming and reforming of the group (Horowitz 1983, p. 89; see also Patrick 1973). Unstable and frustrating as the gang status system is to individual gang members, it is often the only "game" in town for a youth to achieve some form of social identity. It assumes special importance in poor minority or changing neighborhoods, in schools with extremely high failure rates, and increasingly for youth and gang adults in prisons where other meaningful social alternatives do not exist.

The competition for status and resources is often mediated by considerations of ideology, particularly as gangs containing older youths and young adults go through a transition from gang fighting to drug dealing, at least by key subgroups. Such transition may occur, for example, when older, former gang leaders return from prison and attempt to recapture leadership, either by moving the gang back to a central traditional focus of gang reputation and individual member status through turf control and symbolic violence, or by shifting goals and objectives to making money through drug trafficking. Factions of the gang may subsequently engage in a lethal battle to either maintain dominance of traditional gang fighting values or develop a more rational, structured money economy.

Gang Cohesion and Delinquency

Two sets of arguments have arisen regarding the relation between cohesion and delinquency, including violence. The first has to do with whether gangs are normally cohesive or not. Are gangs loosely or closely knit, stable or unstable? Most researchers and some youth agency workers claim that youth gangs are more disorganized than media and some police reports suggest. Many gang-type groups, particularly in eastern cities (e.g., New York City in the 1980s), have been regarded as so loosely knit that they are essentially "pick-up groups" (Galea 1988). The members or participants may hardly know each other and may associate for only a few hours or days. These groupings, at one extreme, are not classified as gangs but rather as delinquent groups that participate either spontaneously or with ephemeral purpose and limited plan in violent and/or nonviolent crimes.

The so-called more established gangs have also often been regarded as loosely knit across social and ethnic groups in different parts of the country across time. Short states that:

> The Chicago gangs [of the 1960s] were characterized by loose criteria of membership, frequently changing membership, and low-cohesion except under circumstances that drew members together. Members of the gangs came and went for days or weeks

at a time, and unless they occupied particularly strong leadership or other roles central to the group were hardly missed. (Short 1990a, p. 198)

Chin in his description of Chinese gangs in New York City in the 1970s and 1980s states that they were loosely knit or weakly organized. There were a variety of factors both internal and external to the gang that contributed to the group's weak cohesion:

> Group cohesion appears to be weak. Intragang conflicts erupt frequently, and members sometimes transfer from one gang to another. . . . A Chinese gang leader is more likely to be killed by his associates than by a rival. . . . (Chin 1990a, p. 135)
>
> Another indicator of group cohesiveness or lack of it is gang members' behavior toward their fellow members when they are arrested or prosecuted. Normally, convicted members are not very supportive of one another, especially when they find themselves abandoned by their gang or Tong. (Chin 1990b, pp. 126)
>
> Some intragang conflicts are instigated by Tong elders who are associated with a particular clique. These mentors prefer to have a divided rather than a united gang; therefore, they intervene to ensure that no particular clique gains enough power to challenge the supremacy of the Tong. (Chin 1990a, p. 135)

In regard to female gangs or affiliate groups, some evidence suggests that they tend to be smaller and more diffuse than male gangs. Female members move in and out of gangs more rapidly. Like their counterparts, particularly in Hispanic communities, they can be organized, albeit less formally, into senior and junior cliques (Harris 1988; Moore 1991). Some recent reporting suggests that the female gang or clique is becoming better organized and more cohesive (Taylor 1990a). However, there is no substantial evidence for a shift in degree of organization or a greater commitment to gang-related criminal or violent behavior currently than in an earlier period.

The counter view for this first argument that gangs are diffuse and weakly organized is that gangs may be more cohesive and stable than is traditionally recognized. In some communities, particular gangs persist over time, members interact as friends, and mutual support develops and continues. Gang members trust and depend on each other and create strong bonds that last for years. "There are few culturally accepted forms of affiliation in which they can maintain close relationships and remain tough warriors—an identity for which there are few alternatives" (Horowitz 1983, p. 179). Young adult gangs involved in a good deal of criminal activity may also require bonds of trust and mutual dependence. Jacobs has emphasized the important attitudinal dimension of gang attractiveness in prison:

> By far the most important function the gang provides their members at Stateville is psychological support . . . the organizations give to the members a sense of identification, a feeling of belonging, an air of importance. According to the Chief of the Vice Lords, "It's just like a religion. Once a Lord, always a Lord. People would die for it. . . . The Lords allows you to feel like a man . . . it is a family with which you can identify." (Jacobs 1977, pp. 152–153; see also Moore 1978)

Jankowski in his participation-observation study of thirty-seven gangs over a ten-year period in the 1970s and 1980s claims that all but one of the gangs had "a great deal of cohesiveness, brought about through a conscious organizational effort" to "regulate the behavior of their members." Both formal and informal codes played e in gang life. He claims that gangs subscribe to certain ideologies explaining world about them and what distinctively characterizes the particular gang. Conflict, whether internal or external to the gang, is also used to establish control of the gang and further cohere its organization (Jankowski 1991, pp. 78–88).

In the argument over whether gangs are cohesive, it is likely that somewhat different criteria of group cohesion are being used by the various theorists and researchers, policymakers and practitioners. A further view in respect to the argument and the one that we share is that gangs can be both cohesive and loosely knit, stable and unstable in the same settings or communities at different times. Gangs do not have to be either organized or well organized to survive over time. The same gang may go through various phases or cycles. In his study of an Italian gang in a stable community, Jansyn (1966) observed that gangs go through periods of high and low cohesion, and when the threat of disorganization is strong, there may be a push or dynamic for increased gang solidarity. The key policy-relevant issue is what external conditions or pressures exist to precipitate and maintain or weaken gang structure and processes.

The second set of cohesion arguments has to do with the relationship between gang cohesion and delinquent or criminal behavior. In question is the sequence of the connection between the gang member's need for status, group member interactions, and cohesion in respect to frequency and pattern of delinquency. Jansyn (1966) argued that when gangs go through a phase of disorganization (i.e., less interaction among members), a burst of criminal activity—often violent—occurs to mobilize and cohere the group again. Klein and Crawford (1967), by contrast, argued that group cohesion first has to be present, preceding delinquent or violent behavior, and that the highly cohesive gang is likelier to engage in gang activity than is the diffuse or weakly organized gang. Klein (1971) later modified this view and proposed that delinquent behavior and gang cohesiveness were interactive, although the predominant direction was from cohesion to delinquent activity. The argument is particularly important for purposes of policy and program development. An important issue addressed later in this book is whether the direction of policy should be to accept the gang structure and attempt to redirect it, or to diffuse or destroy the structure to control or reduce gang criminal behavior.

Klein's (1971) Ladino Hills experiment in Los Angeles was an effort to test the proposition that gang cohesion causes delinquency and that a reduction in group cohesion would be followed by a reduction in delinquent behavior. This first, theoretically conceptualized quasi-experiment in gang intervention was partially successful. Attempts at decohering the gang were somewhat successful. Gang size and group delinquency rates were reduced. However, the rate of mutual interactions of those who remained, or were part of the gang system, was not reduced. Fewer delinquent gang events occurred, but individual delinquency rates did not significantly change during the two-year test period (one and one-half years of program and a subsequent six-month follow-up period). Klein (1971) claimed he was most successful in limiting the recruitment of new members, which delayed development of a new Klika, or cohort of youths of approximately the same age, to the gang.

A more fundamental consideration, I believe, is to what extent can we affect not only the gang directly but the community environment, especially its key institutions of social support, social opportunity, and social control, and do so interactively, in order to reduce the need for the gang in the first place or to modify its development later.

Character of the Violent Gang Act

The most distinctive aspect of the gang experience is gang-related violence. The range of violent gang acts seems almost boundless. Gang violence often appears to the observer to be senseless, sadistic, and bizarre. Violent acts have included: drive-by shootings in which innocent bystanders or neighborhood residents are killed; deliberate invasion of a funeral parlor to remove the body of an opposing gang member from a casket, shoot it again, and dump it in the street; licking the blood of the victim off one's fingers (T. Wilson 1992, p. 10); or the situation of two female gang members who "celebrated the[ir] shootings [of two rival male gang members] by buying an ounce of marijuana and two cases of beer" (*Chicago Sun-Times* 1992).

> There are few limits to what may be done to an "enemy" or his people, from brutal assault and rape to torture and murder. And the rule of retaliation is that every member of the offender's gang is fair game—a virtual guarantee that hostilities will escalate. One of the most infamous gang wars in Los Angeles has raged for a dozen years between two factions of CRIPS—the Rollin' 60's and the Eight Tray Gangsters. It supposedly began with insults hurled over a junior high-school romance. More than two dozen people have since been killed. (Reiner 1992, p. 54)

Many kinds of violence cannot be classified under the rubric of gang related. The act of gang violence is not simply motivated by personal hostility or even prior direct acquaintanceship with the victim (see Farrington, Berkowitz, and West 1982, p. 323). Gang homicides can be distinguished from non-gang homicides, robbery homicides, and family and contract violence (see Block 1991; Klein and Maxson 1987). Violent gang acts are not restricted to the early and less well-developed and possibly more volatile adolescent period, as some analysts suggest (Vigil 1988b, p. 172; Sullivan 1989, pp. 109–110, 179). In fact, serious gang violence is concentrated among older adolescents and young adults. Gang-related violent acts are more typical of Hispanic than of African-American gang members at the present time, although they can be perpetrated as well by white and Asian gang members.

Moore notes that the character of violence typically varies among Hispanic gangs and over time:

> . . . there are many reasons for gang fights: invasion of territory, rivalry over dating, fights in conjunction with sports events and personal matters in which the gang is brought in to back up an individual. But even during the most violent epoch, there was considerable variation in the levels of violence from one clique to another . . . and even within the same gang . . . men who had been active in the 1970s were significantly more likely to emphasize violence in their self descriptions [than those in the 1950s]. . . . Respondents from the more [recent] violent cliques were significantly more likely to believe that their clique was more violent than its immediate predecessors. (Moore 1991, pp. 45–46, 57–60)

Vigil and Vigil and Long claim that machismo or male aggressiveness as well as "locura," craziness, or wildness represents core values of Chicano gangs, at least in Los Angeles (Vigil 1988a, p. 166; Vigil and Long 1990, p. 61). Harris has emphasized the enduring group and subcultural motivations for engaging in gang violence. "Honor, local turf-defense, control and gain—operate within the gang subculture. Machismo, even for girls, is involved in the value system . . . this subculture of violence appears to be across generations—the parents of many of the girls are or had been gang members. . . . 'Being bad,' 'being crazy,' and 'acting wild' earn respect and status" (Harris 1988, p. 174).

On the other hand, Jankowski claims that violence is often "committed by gang members acting as agents of the organization . . . undertaken as a result of an organizational directive, almost never as a result of an instinctive response" (Jankowski 1991, p. 160). Jankowski also states that gang violence can be accounted for by the defiant character of gang members and in particular by certain traits or needs of gang members: "fear, ambition, frustration, and personal group testing of skills" (p. 140). Jankowski argues for a rational utility of gang violence for its members: "In substance, violence is understood to be the instrument to achieve objectives that are not achievable in other ways" (p. 177).

I am in partial agreement with these analyses, and with Short and Strodtbeck (1965), who stated that acts of gang violence are aleatory, that is they occur mainly by chance. But these explanations are insufficient. Gang violence can be predicted on the basis of knowledge about a complex of interacting factors, for example, territorial boundaries of gangs, gang history and character, availability of weapons, anniversaries of prior gang killings, certain holidays, particular day, time of day, and weather, in addition to other factors cited earlier. However, neither the presence of a violent gang, a gang leader with a reputation for violence, a gang retaliatory situation, gang members vying for leadership, a gang decision to commit a violent act, hot weather, a particular time of day or night, nor any other single event or situation is sufficient to produce a violent gang incident. Comprehensive understanding of these factors in relation to one another in a particular community is required as the basis for predicting the occurrence of gang incidents. Furthermore, interactive strategies by organizations to prevent, intervene, and suppress gang violence are necessary, related to these factors.

Leaving the Gang

There is very little research on why a gang ceases to exist or why a particular youth leaves a gang at a particular time. This may be due in part to the limits of research methodology. Most research on gangs either is cross-sectional or covers a relatively limited period of a particular youth's active and street-based participation in gangs. Few analysts have attempted to look at what happens to gang members after, say, ten to fifteen years. Most studies suggest that gang members simply "mature-out through a process of gradual disaffiliation and breaking away from the gang" (Vigil 1988b, pp. 106–107), at least in terms of commitment to and participation in violent gang activities. This normally occurs by the time the male youth is in his late teens or early twenties, although there are variations based on particular factors of the local community economy, culture/race/ethnicity, and the degree of integration of the youth or street gang with the criminal structure.

Members leave the gang for a variety of reasons. Probably more members leave for positive reasons, related to desire to conform with dominant societal expectations, than negative reasons, (e.g., fear of getting caught or imprisonment). Most members probably leave for a combination of reasons: marriage, fatherhood, steady and satisfying employment, religious conversion, fear of imprisonment or return to prison, or simply "battle fatigue." Frequent arrests and incarcerations take a toll on the gang youth physically, emotionally, and economically. The youth's family finances may be severely taxed in the course of many court cases and having to pay high lawyer's fees. Not all gang members come from poor or the poorest families in a low-income or working-class community. Some families of gang members have substantial assets or access to them.

The youth reaches a certain point in his social learning or "growing up" when he realizes there are long-term negative consequences for being a gang member and that he can find an alternative, less stressful way to meet his social and economic needs. As the youth reaches the end of adolescence, he may feel that he is ready for a job and settling down, especially if alternate roles are available to give him status and income (New York City Youth Board 1960; Spergel 1966). This realization materializes as the youth and sometimes his family decide to move out of a neighborhood to escape the gang experience. Better job and housing opportunities elsewhere may also be available. The gang may naturally splinter or dissipate. Law enforcement or school officials sometimes successfully break up a gang, mainly through suppression and harassment and/or counseling, mentoring, or rehabilitation activities.

In weakly organized or loosely knit gangs, youths may not be strongly attached and may move in or out of the gang, or change from one gang status to another. Many members are in the gang for periods averaging a year or less. They may also be spasmodic or partial in their participation in gang activities or functions. Chin notes that "intragang conflicts erupt frequently, and members sometimes transfer from one gang to another. . . . Attachment to the gang is not absolute [even in the Chinese community with close integration of street gang and adult Triad units] (Chin 1990b, p. 125). Peripheral or fringe members may be at some advantage in leaving the gang or "maturing-out" earlier and more readily (Vigil 1988b, p. 98).

On the other hand, a youth may wish to leave a particular gang, or at least not participate in its violent or criminal activities, but be unable to do so, particularly if he is a core member and has established close relationships with other important members. If the youth remains in the community and is visible and recognizable, pressures of various kinds are often brought to bear for him to remain in the gang. Also, the threat of violence from other gangs in the neighborhood may induce him to maintain his membership and carry a weapon simply for reasons of protection. Core members in gangs that are well organized and highly criminalized may have special difficulty in leaving the gang. The murder of core members or leaders planning to leave the gang has been reported (Collins 1979, p. 5). The imprisonment of a gang member where fellow members are present also makes it difficult for him to sever relations.

Considerable and growing evidence suggests that more and more gang members may for a variety of reasons continue to better meet their social and economic or survival needs in the gang than outside of it. Horowitz concluded that "older gang members' sense of self-worth remained partly dependent on interaction with peers who remained in the streets, and they continued to act to maintain the respect of street peers" (Horowitz 1987, p. 446).

> Only a few core members turn away from street status once they reach 18. Some become politically conscious, others turn to families, and a few become drug addicts. . . . Once a reputation has been publicly confirmed, it does not fade away overnight. It becomes difficult for a former gang member to refrain from fights when a breach of etiquette against him was meant as a challenge to his claim to precedence. . . . Many gangs on 32nd Street have senior organizations or previous members now in their twenties, thirties and even forties. . . . If asked, they still identify themselves as gang members and claim other members as their best friends. (pp. 181, 183, 184)

Horowitz, however, did not sufficiently portray the differential capacities and commitments of older, now mainly former gang members—who simply do not participate in violent gang-related activity, although they may participate in non-gang violent or criminal roles or activities. In many gangs there are specific exit points for gang members: marriage, jobs, family crises. Former gang members can play special albeit limited roles as "old heads," "veteranos," coaches, job finders, and so on.

Hagedorn, Macon, and Moore, referring mainly to black gangs in Milwaukee, stated that "More than 70 percent of the 260 who founded the gangs were reported as still being involved with the gang today, more than five years after the gang was founded" (1986, p. 5). Some observers have come to view gang membership in recent years as "permanent and lifelong" (Moore, Vigil, and Garcia 1983) and as "a way of life, a cause" (Daley 1985). Again, perhaps because gang researchers usually do not sustain their observations for long periods, they tend to underestimate the socialization of most gang youths to conventional careers as they reach their adult years. Esbensen and Huizinga observe in their cohort study of delinquent youths that "when asked what role they expect to have in the gang some day, over 60 percent of year 4 gang members indicated they would like to *not* be a member and expected *not* to be a member" (1993, p. 11). This fact has important implications for social policy and for targeting gang youths who can be assisted to either leave the gang or change their pattern of gang member behavior as they get older.

Walter Miller, emphasizes that for many, gang membership is a passing phase and that gang youths "become law-abiding citizens. Pressures to leave or not join gangs are in many cases supported by community antigang pressures. . . . Crime by gang members is largely a product of social and cultural learning; it lacks the element of physiological addiction that makes the rehabilitation of drug addicts and alcoholics so difficult" (W. Miller 1990, pp. 265–266). This is not to deny, as other analysts have suggested, that the matter may be far more complex, involving significant changes in national policy and local economic conditions:

> Economic restructuring has taken "good" jobs away from East Los Angeles, and replaced them with exploitational jobs—unstable, low wage and unsheltered. . . . One consequence, of course, is that young adult gang members have to find non-job means

of survival—and our data indicate that this means more dependence on transfer payments and illicit income. Increased job instability leads to changes in behavior. It prolongs the involvement with the home boys and home girls. . . . (Moore 1991, p. 133).

Moore also indicates that the process of leaving the gang is largely an individual one. Some youths have a more difficult time leaving and settling down to a stable adult working-class existence than others. Many men who become "squares" may have been only "peripherally involved in the gang" to begin with. They did not go "for the more extreme gang violence or drug use. For some, this was because concerned parents restricted them. Others saw the gang simply as a neighborhood friendship group rather than as a place to play out scenes of teenaged bravado. They were square kids at heart, for whom gang membership was something of an aberration" (Moore 1991, p. 127).

Religious Conversion

Rarely if at all, mentioned in social science studies is the influence of religious conversion in a youth's ability to leave the gang. Conversion is usually associated with a period of extreme crisis or trauma, such as the youth's near-death in a gang fight, his killing of another person, or the death of a parent directly or indirectly attributable to his gang activities. The youth simply, dramatically, and inexorably forswears gang involvement, or at least violent gang involvement. He may not give up contacts with gang peers, particularly on social occasions. He may even become an agent of a minister, the church, or a gang program in prevention or social intervention activities.

Evangelical protestant ministers may be particularly influential in the process of conversion of gang members, through their missions in jails or prisons, or in their church or outreach programs. Such conversions often involve a close and positive relationship by the youth with his mother. While we have no statistical evidence of the frequency or success of such conversion, there is anecdotal evidence that it occurs.

Females Leaving the Gang

Most females cease their gang membership between the ages of 16 and 18 years, an earlier age than that for males. By 16 or 18 years, female members' interests are directed beyond the gang. Some female members "become pregnant, some get married, some go 'straight,' some are institutionalized, others graduate to heroin use; also 'getting a fix' overrides all other interests and considerations" (Harris 1988, p. 172). The predominant reason for leaving seems to be pregnancy. Hagedorn in his study of thirty-five female African-American founders of gangs in Milwaukee found that "more than half (18) already had a family. None of the women were married, and those with children were all reported to be on AFDC" (Hagedorn 1988, p. 125).

Harris noted that females are not as "firmly enmeshed in the gang milieu" as males and have commensurately less difficulty in leaving the gang (Harris 1988, p. 149). When the female gang member leaves, she may have regrets, not so much at leaving as at having been so "dumb, stupid" as to have joined in the first place (Harris 1988, pp. 151–152). A variety of reasons have been set forth as to why females are less committed to gang life than males. Thrasher suggested that females traditionally are less aggressive and violent. They are "more closely supervised and guarded than boys and are usually well incorporated into the family group or some other social structure" (Thrasher 1936, p. 222). Brown suggested that "lower class black females have more exposure to mainstream ideals. . . . [They] move [more] freely between the ghetto . . . and mainstream lifestyles than do black males" (Brown 1977, pp. 222–223).

Influence of the Female on the Male to Leave the Gang
—The Next Generation

Women have been viewed traditionally as both cause and cure of much male gang member delinquency. Evidence for these contrary assertions has not been systematically gathered. The general assumption is that women achieve status and excitement through provocation of fights between members of rival gangs, carrying messages, spying, sexually setting them up, and carrying concealed weapons (Giordano 1978; Quicker 1983; Campbell 1984a). There is some evidence, however, that men will avoid gang delinquencies in the presence of women, and also that women, whether gang or non-gang members, can persuade boyfriends to leave the gang and settle down (Klein 1971; Bowker, Gross, and Klein 1980).

Moore states in her important 1991 study that prior gang member patterns and problems not only characterize different ways of leaving the gang, but may account for the various ex-gang-member adult social adjustments and that of succeeding generations:

> Marriages did not last, this was particularly true for the men who used heroin early in their lives. Most of these men began to go in and out of prison when they were in their teens. . . . Hanging around with the homeboys, down in the barrio—if only on weekends—often leads to problems for the family. First of all it means that the emotional focus remains strongly on the gang. This weakens marriages. . . .
>
> Another gang-related source of marital instability that is especially important for women is the tendency to marry other gang members. Slightly more than a third of the men, but 55 percent of the women had been married to a gang member. . . .
>
> Women [however] were more likely to report that their children had joined gangs (22% of the women compared with 5% of the men). This is not surprising. Male gang members were less likely than women to marry gang members in the first place, and even less likely to live with their children. Thus, most of the men's children were brought up by square mothers, whereas the gang tradition, if there is such a thing, was more likely to be present in a women's household. (pp. 111–114)

Conclusion

Youths join gangs for many reasons: status, security, money, power, excitement, and/ or new experiences—particularly under conditions of social deprivation or community instability. The idea of the gang as a family pervades discussions of the function of gang life.

The strong need for status and its expression in a group context comes mainly from the lack of resources and the weakness of controls internal and external to the group. Gang violence functions both as a cause of gang cohesion and a consequence of it. There is some evidence that a decrease in gang cohesion or membership results in less gang-related crime and perhaps slows down gang development.

Machismo or male aggressiveness as well as craziness or wildness represents a core value of the violent gang subculture. Although acts of gang violence can be only partially predicted, certain factors—such as influence of core gang members, availability of weapons, certain border locations between gangs, and particular seasons or days of the week and times of day—are conducive to violent gang confrontations. Knowledge of these factors can help in planning policy and program to control or prevent gang violence.

There is little research to indicate why particular gangs die out or why a particular youth leaves a gang. Most studies suggest that gang members simply mature out. They reach a certain point in their social learning or growing up when they realize they can find an alternative, less stressful, way to meet social and economic needs. A religious conversion sometimes facilitates such departure from gang affiliation, especially from violent gang activity. The female, less firmly enmeshed in the gang world, more readily leaves the gang than the male. Women appear to play a key role in getting gang members to cut down on gang violence or leave the gang.

8

The Ecological Context

This chapter examines the local social institutions and contexts that contribute to the development of gangs and that in turn are affected by gang problems. It focuses on the defective character of family, school, politics, and prison relationships, particularly as they create and interact with gangs. These local institutions or contexts are in significant measure products of the external environment—population movements, changing social and economic conditions, unemployment, racism, lack of resources, and ineffective governmental policies. However, the problem is most directly produced by defective local institutions and their fragmented interrelationships.

Insight into the development of gangs has often been sought through theories of ecology and social disorganization. Ecological theories attempt to interrelate characteristics of a population and its institutions to surrounding space and material conditions through processes of cooperation, competition, or conflict (Park and Burgess 1921; Bursik and Grasmick 1993). Social disorganization, more specifically, refers to the disarray of norms, values, and social and organizational relationships or the lack of their integration at system rather than subsystem levels. Sometimes families, groups or gangs, and particular social organizations seem to function with some adequacy on their own terms but not as part of a coherent overall system committed to dominant cultural norms and values. No pejorative connotation or value judgment is necessarily inherent in the term *social disorganization. However, I believe this lack of sufficient social integration and social control, particularly at the local community level, initiates a distinctive community gang problem.*

In the perspective of the present chapter, the youth develops as a gang member largely in response to his interactions with local social institutions over time. For example, youths from certain disorganized families are vulnerable to becoming gang members. These youths are induced through failure in school, defective local community socializing agencies, and especially peer pressures, to seek alternate means for achieving status in the context of the gang. Gangs and gang youths subsequently can become sources of organizational and political influence in these weakly organized or malintegrated communities. The gang on the streets, in prison, and across neighborhoods and communities becomes part of a significant but malfunctioning adaptation and network. Together the family, school, politics, prison, and the youth gang contribute in a complex, rapidly changing, and increasingly fragmented local community and society to the further development and sustenance of the gang problem.

Local Context and Gang Development

More than sixty years ago, Thrasher wrote that "gangland" occupies the "poverty belt," and "interstitial areas" of the city and is characterized by "deteriorating neighborhoods, shifting populations, and the mobility and disorganization of the slum. . . . It is to a large extent isolated from the wider culture of the larger community by the processes of competition and conflict which have resulted in the selection of its population. Gangland is a phenomenon of human ecology" (Thrasher 1936 [also 1927 edition], pp. 22–23; see also Shaw and McKay 1943).

Urban ecologists and criminologists have speculated that different kinds or degrees of social organization may exist in low-income communities. The disorganized community is characterized by more extensive deterioration, more pronounced social disorder, and greater violence than other communities (Kobrin 1951; Gold 1987). However, gangs arise and develop in both more stable and less stable slum areas, but assume a differential character when social institutions fail to function as agencies of social control (Shaw and McKay 1931, pp. 107–108).

The growth and development of cities in the United States have been characterized historically by a succession of different racial, ethnic, and income groups, with "a corresponding succession of gangs, although gang names and traditions may persist in spite of changes in nationalities" (Thrasher 1936, p. 198). This process may occur in small or large, inner-city or suburban areas where poor immigrant populations are settling. Gangs also develop in poor or working-class communities where social institutions are in the process of rapid change and where community organization has weakened.

The 1960s through the 1980s saw the exodus of higher-status whites and nonwhites from many central city areas, a consequent increase in the proportions of lower-status minorities in these areas, and the development of segregated barrios or ghettoes, often through low-income public housing projects. The recruitment pool from which members of youth gangs and law-violating youth groups are drawn increased (W. Miller 1975). Some analysts noted that in the newer ghetto areas, children, adolescents, clubs, developing gangs, and established gangs teem and engage in conflict with each other because groups of many different backgrounds and orientations come together at schools, community centers, and on the streets (New York City Youth Board 1960; Breen and Allen 1983; Hagedorn 1988).

Short observed that the most unstable or disorganized local communities produced violent gangs in Chicago in the early 1960s: "Areas which have undergone very rapid transition from white to Negro, such as the West Side. . . . Here was found the fullest development of the conflict subculture . . . and areas on the fringe of expansion of the 'Black Belt' . . . in such areas, conflict most often occurred for the purpose of 'keeping the niggers out'" (Short 1963, p. 32).

Gang violence may be less virulent in the stabilized low-income ghetto. Internecine conflict may subside as smaller gangs are integrated into larger, better-organized gangs and then later into the local community or across communities. Competition and conflict may be rationalized and focused on criminal gain, not simply on control of turf and social status. Some very poor but more stable areas in due course may achieve lower rates of gang conflict but higher overall rates of delinquency and crime, as well as of gain-oriented gang crime such as drug-dealing, than high-gang-crime areas.

The gang is thus an important organizational form for obtaining a competitive advantage in poor and/or unstable communities. In this process it may meet the needs, directly and indirectly, of local residents and the representatives of various institutions in the area. In turn, it may acquire tolerance or resources from them. On the other hand, the gang can become alien to the community, especially when it engages in violent activities injurious to its members.

Systematic tests of these ideas have only begun to be carried out. Cartwright and Howard (1966) performed an ecological analysis of the prevalence of gangs in Chicago in the 1960s using community area data. They did not find support for Thrasher's (1936) notion that delinquent gangs were concentrated in Chicago's "poverty belt"; gangs in the 1960s were found in all parts of Chicago. In the 1980s, gang incidents were reported in all of the Chicago Police Department's twenty-five districts, although violent gang incidents were concentrated only in certain districts. Cartwright and Howard (1966, pp. 357–358) found that high-crime rate gang areas were coterminous with only about half of the high-crime-rate delinquency areas. In other words, high rates of gangs and gang activity were also found in lower delinquency-rate areas.

Bernard Cohen (1969a, b) found that gangs, mainly black, in Philadelphia in the 1960s were located not simply in poor communities but in those segregated sections of the city that were culturally and socially isolated. He reasoned that certain populations—whether first-generation European immigrants in the 1920s and 1930s; blacks in the post-World War II era; or most recently Hispanic groups—may be "set apart, stereotyped and placed in a ghetto culture." The entire life experience of youths may be confined to a particular area or social context and result in intense identification with the territory (ibid.). Social and cultural isolation may interact with social disorganization, poverty, and low income to produce not only different gang problem rates but different types of gang problems.

Curry and Spergel (1988) performed an ecological analysis of the relation of gang homicide, robbery, and burglary to poverty level, unemployment rate, and mortgage investment on a community-area basis in Chicago in the 1970s and early 1980s. Gang homicide and serious delinquency rates were differentially distributed in Chicago's seventy-seven largely racially segregated community areas. The best predictors of delinquency rate were economic variables; the best predictors of gang homicides, however, were a combination of social disorganization factors that in turn were identified with percent of recently settled Hispanics and income variations in certain communities.

The presence of these ecological forces, and more specifically the interaction of factors of social disorganization and lack of legitimate and/or availability of alternate illegitimate resources, may largely account for the development of deviant gang subcultural phenomena in certain communities and institutional contexts. The family, school, politics, organized crime, and prison—as critical components of community and its failures—contribute in special ways to the formation and development of gang patterns and individual gang-member behavior. Very limited direct attention has been paid to the relation of gangs to these institutional contexts. What we do know about the influence of these relationships is usually a product of studies designed for other purposes—such as the relation between family and delinquency, between school and delinquent peer group, the assessment of safe schools, the nature of participation in grass-roots or "machine" politics, the patterns of recruitment to organized crime, or the problems of correctional system change. Some exceptions exist: Thrasher's (1936) chapter on "The Gang in Politics," Cloward and Ohlin's (1960) formulation of the "criminal subculture," Spergel's (1964) discussions of "Racketville" and "Haulburg," Jacobs' (1977) description of the development of the gang problem in a correctional institution, Sullivan's (1989) discussion of different patterns of work opportunity and youth crime in three Brooklyn neighborhoods, and most recently Bursik and Grasmick's (1993) expansion of social disorganization theory.

Family

Criminological theory and research find the origins of delinquency; youth affiliation with delinquent groups, including gangs; and related individual personal and social disorders primarily in defects of family relationships, parental character, and early child-rearing practices (Rutter and Giller 1983; Sampson and Laub 1993). In addition, certain societal conditions, mainly economic, are believed to create strain and community disorganization, which contributes to a weakening of family structure and ineffective relationships both within and external to the family. The youth's needs are not met because of deficient parenting, supervision, and support; and he or she turns to delinquent activity.

However, while some evidence suggests that many youth or children, in gangs have records of delinquency before entry into the gang (B. Cohen 1969a, b), other research indicates that some do not, and do not develop such records (Curry and Spergel 1992). Theory and research on delinquency are not sufficient to provide an explanation of the gang problem and specifically the links between early delinquency experiences and predisposition to gang membership. Moore states furthermore that "large segments of the Mexican-origin population suffered from economic and ecological marginality and from culture conflict as well" (Moore 1991, p. 81) but did not become delinquent, criminal, or gang members. She says that the existence of poverty in the family is insufficient, per se, to explain the gang problem:

> In most of these aspects, these families differed very little from their neighbors. They were Mexican, they were large, they were working, they were poor. Occasionally, the fathers departed, but the overall profile is not desperately poor, and there is a lot of variation. *There is really very little support in these data for the notion that gang membership is generated by the strains of poverty and immigrant life* [italics added]. It is when we turn to the emotional climate of the family during childhood that problems begin to be evident. (Moore 1991, p. 89)

Moore documents that many of these families from which gang youths derive

> were not particularly happy, and in some cases, they were acutely unhappy, at least in the reminiscence of these former gang members. . . . Much of the paternal violence—towards the kids as well as towards the mothers—appears to have been asso-

ciated with heavy drinking. . . . More than half of these gang members were clearly afraid of their fathers. . . . In a quarter of the men's homes and in 46 percent of the women's homes somebody was physically handicapped or chronically ill. Most often this was a parent. In 47 percent of the men's homes and 69 percent of the women's homes, some member died when the respondent was growing up . . . 20 percent of the men and 45 percent of the women grew up with a heroin addict in the home . . . And finally, 57 percent of the men and 82 percent of the women saw somebody in their home arrested when they were children. . . . In 17 percent of the cases, respondents reported their own arrests during early adolescence. Even though most of these families seem reasonably conventional and hardworking, there seem to be a large number of families with troubles. (Moore 1991, pp. 89, 92, 100, 101)

The Schwendingers suggested further that family relations can be troubled or strained "but not necessarily destroyed by unemployment, because mutual aid and reciprocity compensate somewhat for economic insecurity [however] . . . when economic insecurity increases and supportive communal relationships decrease, families fall apart and crime and delinquency increase rapidly" (Schwendinger and Schwendinger 1985, pp. 22–23). A great many types of families and variations in family customs and relationships can contribute to youth delinquency and predispose him or her to joining a gang.

A sizable proportion of gang youths come from apparently stable and adequately functioning families. Also a significant proportion of youths who come from dysfunctional families avoid gang involvement, even where siblings may be gang members. Not all well-intentioned parents with good parenting skills can ensure that their children will not become involved in gangs, particularly in low-income, social-problem-ridden neighborhoods. Sometimes both immigrant parents in a family work, and children are insufficiently supervised. Power may shift to children who have greater command of English and learn to control communication channels between parents and outside American institutional representatives. Parents may not be aware of or understand the "pull" of the gang for the child, who may not be performing particularly well at school. Family tolerance, lack of contact with or failure to understand local institutions, negligence in supervision of adolescent behavior as youths begin to engage in delinquency or gang-related behaviors, may all contribute to the youths' participation in and commitment to later gang activities (see Sung 1977; Ianni 1989; Vigil and Yun 1990; Moore 1991).

Insufficiency of the Family Disorganization Argument

Defects of family structure and social relationships are not necessarily related to gang membership. For example, as just indicated, not all male offspring of the same family will join a gang or join the same gang (Horowitz 1983). Why one brother joins and another does not, is not clear. Equal numbers of non-gang boys and gang boys seem to come from the same types of family structure and low socioeconomic backgrounds (Tennyson 1967; see also Shaw and McKay 1931). Gang and non-gang delinquents do not vary significantly in such characteristics as broken homes, having parents with criminal histories, level of intelligence, or the highest school grade achieved (Friedman, Mann, and Friedmann 1975). The educational levels of the parents of gang members may not be especially low (Cartwright and Howard 1966; Klein 1968).

Distinctive cultural or race/ethnic factors in particular communities may be more important than the contribution of family structure to ganging phenomena. In a recent cohort study of sixth through eighth graders in four inner-city schools in Chicago, Curry and Spergel (1992) found that the absence of a father was a fairly strong predictor of arrests for Hispanic youths, but was a weak predictor of arrests for black youths. More important, family structure did not enter into a second series of regression equations to explain gang-related activities. Instead, the presence of a gang member sibling or parent in the home was the best predictor of gang activity, particularly for Hispanic youths (ibid.).

There seems to be some agreement that variables other than family structure and defective patterns of family relationship may be critical to produce gang problem youths (Rutter and Giller 1983). While Thrasher (1936) saw the lack of adequate parental or family supervision as contributing to the likelihood that a youth would become a gang member, this occurred mainly in a poor, disorganized community. Also, the defects of family relationships and family-related pressures (Joe and Robinson 1980) may not lead to gang membership, except where gangs are developing or already exist. On the basis of a series of studies, Reiss concluded that "it is the territorial concentration of young males who lack firm controls of parental authority that leads them into a peer control system that supports co-offending and simplifies the search for accomplices" (1987, p. 251).

W. Miller (1976b) suggested that the family and the gang may play complementary socialization roles for gang members, teaching them different survival skills. Sager (1988) saw the gang as complementary to the family in the lower-class Mexican-American barrio culture in Los Angeles: the women perform dominant roles in the home and the men perform their warrior roles on the street. Fagan and Wexler claimed that the "role of families in explaining self-reported delinquency among adolescent violent delinquents may be overstated" (1987, p. 662). The contributions of peer groups and school experience may be relatively more important. Fagan and his associates, as well as others favoring social control theory as a primary explanation of delinquent behavior, have suggested that "the strength of the association to delinquent peers is mediated by several factors, especially conventional bonds to family, peers, norms, and institutions . . . " (Fagan, Piper, and Moore 1986, p. 443; see also Hirschi 1969).

Dr Feys, chief psychologist at the Juvenile Division of the Cook County Circuit Court, said recently of youth who enter the juvenile justice system, "Most of the minority kids come from families that are in complete chaos. They have no support system at home to guide them. They know right and wrong but it's not incorporated in the traditional sense. Rather, it fits what they do on the streets" (Hickey 1993, p. 7).

Importance of Community-level Factors Other Than Family Disorganization

Sampson and Groves in their research on delinquency in Great Britain found that the level of unsupervised teenage peer groups had the largest independent effect on the three forms of victimization they studied: mugging/street robbery, stranger violence, and total victimization. "[The indicator of] unsupervised peer groups transmits 47 percent of the variance on total victimization rates" (1987, pp. 788–789). From these findings, Sampson and Groves concluded that community disorganization, as indicated by "poor heterogeneous communities with pronounced family disruption, foster street-corner teenage groups, which in turn leads to increased delinquency and ultimately to a pattern of adult crime" (p. 797).

In a more recent paper, Sampson and Wilson suggest that community disorganization is a response to external forces, as well:

> These structural dimensions of community social disorganization also transmitted in larger part the effects of community socioeconomic status, residential mobility, ethnic heterogeneity, and family disruption in a theoretically consistent manner. For example, mobility had significant inverse effects on friendship networks, family disruption was the largest predictor of unsupervised peer groups, and socioeconomic status had the largest inverse effects on organizational participation. (Sampson and Wilson 1991, p. 15)

While such encompassing analyses emphasize the importance of community disorganization and socioeconomic status in the development of conditions contributing to delinquent and criminal adaptations, they do not establish the differential importance of social conditions producing different types of community disorganization and consequently different kinds and levels of youth gang problems. Furthermore, they tend to emphasize the importance of sociological and often overlook personality variables in the creation of delinquent or gang adaptations. The interactive failures of personality, organization, and social structure together provide a more precise explanation of why, under certain family, social, and peer group conditions, particular youths join and become committed to delinquent gangs (see Ianni 1989, and Chapter 9).

School

While there has been considerable attention to the relation between a youth's delinquency and his school adaptation (Elliott and Voss 1974; Rutter et al. 1979; Rutter and Giller 1983; Toby 1983; Elliott, Huizinga, and Ageton 1985; and Gottfredson and Gottfredson 1985), there has been limited research on the relation of gangs to school adaptation. Thrasher (1936), for example, paid scant attention to youth gangs in schools. However, Albert Cohen (1955) noted that delinquent subcultures were often in opposition to the norms of the school's middle-class culture. Hargreaves (1967) and Rutter and colleagues (1979) described delinquent groups and subcultures in public schools in Great Britain that developed not so much in opposition to the school's system of norms and values, but as alternatives to it.

Special concern with the impact of schools on the delinquency problem and vice versa arose in the mid-1970s. National school crime surveys at the time, however, scarcely addressed gang or group-related delinquency in or around the school or differentiated between delinquent group and gang-related problems (National Institute of Education 1978; Gottfredson and Gottfredson 1985), although they did analyze organizational and community structural factors contributing to individual delinquency. A few studies in the 1970s and 1980s specifically addressed the school gang problem but were based on unreliable informant samples. Although questions about research methods could be raised, the results of these particular studies nevertheless showed a certain consistency. Gangs clearly were obstacles to the formal educational process.

Agency and community informants in a study of six large cities reported "the presence of identified gangs operating in the schools, stabbings, beatings, and other kinds of assaults on teachers." The study claimed that the schools in Philadelphia were "citadels of fear" with "gang fighting in the halls" (W. Miller 1975, p. 46). In a Chicago Board of Education study, 50 percent of schools surveyed reported that students believe "identifiable gangs are operating in and around the majority of public schools, both elementary and secondary." One in ten students reported that street-gang members made them afraid when they were in school, had either attacked or threatened them, and had solicited them for membership—although mainly when they were not at school. Gangs were reported as present in all twenty districts of the Chicago school system (Chicago Board of Education 1981, pp. 182–184, 189).

Kyle (1984) reported that 45 percent of the boys and 22 percent of the girls in two public high schools in probably the most gang-ridden communities of Chicago were asked to join gangs in or around the school (p. 10). Twenty-five percent of the dropouts interviewed said that their major reason for dropping out of school was "fear of gangs" (Kyle 1984, p. 10). Kyle also claimed that "the authority within the schools ultimately belonged to the gangs, rather than the school administrators" (p. 10).

A report concerning the Evanston, Illinois, school system provides a similar picture. Ninety-one percent of the high school students "personally know one or more students who are gang members" and "almost half (47%) of the students describe the gang problem as a big problem" (Rosenbaum and Grant 1983), p. 16). In an evaluation of alternative education programs in fifty schools around the country in 1982, 13 percent of boys and 5.2 percent of girls reported they had been involved in a gang fight (Gottfredson, Gottfredson, and Cook 1983). In a recent national study of gangs and schools, a higher percentage of black students (20%) than white students (14%) said their school had gangs. A relatively higher proportion of Hispanic students (32%) compared with non-Hispanic students (14%) said they attended schools with gangs. While students reported some gang fighting at school, this did not seem to be a frequent occurrence (Bastian and Taylor 1991, p. 8).

Relation between School and the Street Gang Problem

The school-related gang problem appears different in character from the street-level gang problem. It is generally less serious and involves younger youths. Self-report and police arrest data appear to tap different dimensions of the gang problem. The Chicago Board of Education study reports that students aged 12 or 13 are as likely as students aged 18 or older to be solicited for gang membership (1981, pp. 184–187). However, a substantial majority of youths arrested for gang-related crimes are over 17 years of age (Spergel 1986). Teachers and principals perceive gangs to be considerably less of a problem in and around schools than do students (Chicago Board of Education 1981, p. 189).

Police data generally indicate a more limited school gang problem than do other reports. Chicago Police Department statistics show that 10 to 11 percent of reported gang incidents in 1985 and 1986 occurred on school property generally. Only 3.3 percent of the reported gang incidents took place on public high school property in 1985. Chicago public school discipline reports for the same period showed that only 2 percent of discipline code violations were gang related, but that gang incidents were disproportionately serious—accounting for 12 percent of weapons violations, 26 percent of robberies, and 20 percent of aggravated batteries (Spergel 1985).

Yet it is difficult at times to separate out school-based gang problems and community gang problems. A variety of youth agency- and community-based programs are increasingly using school facilities for recreation, such as "midnight basketball" and special remedial training. Older youths and young adults are more and more part of the school milieu. With the spread of weaponry, both older and younger youths are now more likely not only to plan but to carry out gang violent activities on school grounds which are no longer regarded as safe, neutral, or sacrosanct territory. Some of the violence can also take on an interracial or interethnic conflict character.

> Chicago police closed Farragut High School on Wednesday after a series of fights between rival gangs erupted in the school, then spilled into the streets, where hundreds of students took part in the melee, some of them brandishing guns.
>
> One teacher was treated at a nearby hospital after being hit in the head with a chain, and some students were treated by paramedics at the scene.
>
> At least 30 students were arrested in the day-long series of skirmishes. Most of the students were charged with disorderly conduct or mob action. . . .
>
> Members of at least four gangs took part in the skirmishes. . . .
>
> The school is located on the border between a predominantly black neighborhood and a predominantly Hispanic neighborhood. Dozens of gangs compete for status in the area.
>
> "What we have are kids from several neighborhoods coming into an area claimed by another gang," De Lopez [district police commander] said, "and they don't want them there. They claim that school as part of their territory, and whether you are white, black, or Hispanic, if you are crossing gang territory you become fair game."
>
> "It transcends racial boundaries," De Lopez said, "the underlying problem is more gang related than racial." (Recktenwald 1991)

Gangs and School Dropout

Participant observation and informant studies over three decades consistently indicate that gang members are typically behind in their studies or are school dropouts (Klein 1968). All of the forty-seven gang "founders" interviewed in Milwaukee had dropped out or been kicked out of school; most had been suspended (Hagedorn, Macon, and Moore 1986). In a later Milwaukee study, less than a third of gang members graduated from high school or later returned for a general equivalency diploma (Hagedorn 1988). In one Florida study, 80 percent of gang members were estimated to be high school dropouts (Reddick 1987). In another study, "the director of Aspira of Florida, an Hispanic youth services organization with a gang program component, estimated . . . between 50% to 60% of the gang members in the program are dropouts" (Conley 1991, p. 21).

The school is regarded as alien ground by many gang members, and they seek to leave as quickly as possible (Horowitz 1983); in school gang members' weaknesses and inadequacies are made public (New York City Youth Board 1960). All forty African-American students identified as gang members in a Detroit study said, "they disliked school and viewed it primarily as a place to hang out" (Taylor 1988, p. 27). Chin associates the frustration that Chinese immigrant students have at school as a basis for ganging: "Going to school can be a frustrating experience for Chinese immigrants who find themselves unable to compete with younger students, belittled by other ethnic groups, and held in contempt by native-born Chinese. As a result they tend to congregate with others who share their problems" (Chin 1990b, p. 95).

However, gang members do not necessarily devalue school and do not criticize others for doing well (Short and Strodtbeck 1965; Horowitz 1983). Gang members tend to believe that formal public education has little to offer them: "In an environment where education is meaningless, the gang barrio fulfills the young man's needs. . . . It is not the school . . . but in the neighborhood gang is the stuff of living as he knows it" (Pineda 1974, p. 15).

It should also be noted that many gang youths and others who drop out of school often return to school later through special or alternative programs to obtain their diplomas, often a G.E.D. "Despite their doubts, they did not totally discount the value of a high school diploma. Many of those who admitted irregular attendance also claimed that they would eventually return to school and finish" (Sullivan 1989, p. 35). After a year or more out of school, gang youths often reconsider their earlier skepticism, they seek out programs in alternative schools in public school systems and in human service agencies that prepare them to re-enroll in regular high schools and classes. More often they seek to obtain a high school equivalency diploma.

Researchers have observed that gang behavior may result as much from school defects as from problems and pressures at home (Short and Strodtbeck 1965; Joe and Robinson 1978). School variables, attendance, achievement, student satisfaction, and educational climate are apparently predictive of later criminal adaptations and careers of delinquent group or gang youths (Gold and Mattick 1974; Sarnecki 1986). The Gottfredsons suggest that there are several kinds of organizational characteristics important in explaining school disorder, and that these characteristics are probably also relevant, although not sufficient, in explaining why gangs are created and why gang-related violence occurs both within schools and outside in the vicinity of schools. Not only the characteristics of the community and the youth populations served but the "make-up of the body of teachers," the "sizes of the schools and the resources available to them," the way the school is run," and the "schools' psychosocial climates" may be important in accounting for variable rates of gang problems (Gottfredson and Gottfredson 1985, p. 16).

Delinquency and antisocial gang behavior may be responses to school failure and the alienation of youths. These responses are probably causally involved in school drop out; and drop out, in turn, contributes to increased delinquency and gang behavior. Alienation from school and association with gang peers, along with antisocial appear to be mutually reinforcing, and require a kind of attention from authorities and teachers that does not lead to further isolation of youths from conventional school activities and increased delinquent or gang associations (see Elliott and Voss 1974, p. 199).

Politics

Institutional contexts other than schools also play key roles in gang development, and in turn are affected by gang problems, especially after the initial stages of gang formation. Youth gangs have been a source of stability for local urban political systems and established community organizations as well as a source of potential power for aspiring politicians, especially in times of rapid change and social turmoil. In some cities, for example New York, Chicago, and Philadelphia, gangs traditionally have provided a means of communication between elites and unorganized low-income or isolated populations. At times of crisis, gangs act out many of the aspirations, feelings, and legitimate and illegitimate interests of populations in communities that are weakly organized, and they can be sources of control of such populations. According to one analyst, in the middle of the nineteenth century,

> gangs were the medium through which the grass-roots and City Hall communicated. Politicians relied on the gangs for contact and stability, while residents used the gangs to acquire and distribute services and jobs. The gang imposed a social conscience on local businessmen by policing the neighborhoods; periodically sacking the homes, hotels, warehouses, and factories of the rich; and instantly redistributing scarce goods to the needy. From the 1850s through the dismemberment of the Tweed Ring in the 1870s, New York's political machine was largely run from below. (Stark 1981, p. 441)

In Philadelphia in the middle of the nineteenth century, gangs assisted in political change and in the development of new ethnic power groups. Volunteer fire companies were the primary instigators of such changes but also involved local street gangs in the process. Fire companies were:

> barometers of demographic, political, and social change. They proliferated with the rapid population increase in the late 1840s. They became social centers for property-less wage earners . . . and most of them were held together by political allegiances and ethnic identities. [Fire] companies formed in the 1840s drew their members from the surrounding neighborhood [including] gangs and neighborhood sympathizers. . . .
>
> . . . Turf and neighborhood loyalties of the gangs coincided with those of the fire companies. . . . Gangs 'ran' with the fire companies, and the gangs shifted in and out of them, blurring the distinction between the two institutions. (Laurie in Davis and Haller 1973, pp. 78, 82)

During times of social unrest and political crisis, the gang was recognized as an instrument of power and influence and could facilitate either the development of resources by new political leadership or continuing control by established political organizational or community leadership. A symbiotic relationship often developed between urban politicians and gangs. In Chicago in the first third of this century, Thrasher (1936) observed:

the political boss finds gangs . . . ingratiates himself by means of money for camping, uniforms, . . . children's picnics . . . to "get him in good" with potential voters . . . parents and friends. . . . . To repay the politician for putting gang members on official pay-rolls, and providing subsidies, protection, and immunities from official interference, the gang often splits . . . the proceeds of its illegitimate activities; controls for him the votes of its members . . . and performs for him various types of "work" at the polls, such as slugging, intimidation, . . . vandalism (tearing down signs), ballot fixing, repeating, stealing ballot boxes. (p. 452, 477)

Kornblum gave evidence of the continuity of these patterns in Chicago in the early 1970s:

A second group of neighborhood influentials which joined the opposing 10th ward faction was a small group of superannuated Mexican street fighters. Men with nicknames such as "The Rat" and "The Hawk" with reputations in the Mexican precincts to match . . . were in ward politics. . . . When a campaign becomes heated . . . a challenging faction may see fit to call upon its 'heavies' for various strategies for intimidation—including the systematic removal of the opposition's street signs and lamp posters. (1974, p. 166)

Street gangs in the 1960s were not precipitants or primary components of the civil rights movement or urban disturbances that followed. They did not start the urban disorders, but individual gang members were at times opportunistic participants (Knopf 1969; Skolnick 1969), as they were again in the riots of Los Angeles in 1992. Gangs are ordinarily not committed to or participants in social or political causes (however, see Anti-Defamation League 1986, 1987). Gangs seek to be influential. They can be used and can use others for legitimate as well as illegitimate purposes. They were enlisted in Chicago and elsewhere during the 1960s to "cool" out and control disorderly local residents. They were used by the police as an auxiliary force to maintain order; sometimes they were organized into youth patrols with identifying hard hats and arm bands to patrol riot-torn streets. Some gangs also protected storekeepers against riot damage for a fee.

In the 1960s, gangs—mainly African-American—were solicited by frightened representatives of government, private foundations, social agencies, and local community organizations as partners and became recipients of funds in a variety of community development and social service projects. Gangs were viewed as one of the few viable organizations that could stabilize the disordered ghettoes (Dawley 1992). The fact that gangs could represent criminal interests and were often alienated and not necessarily competent to perform dependably a variety of conventional control functions was usually overlooked or misunderstood. Major controversies arose between politicians, community organizations, police, and units of government over the participation of gangs in community and political affairs (see Spergel 1964, 1972; Spergel et al. 1969; Poston 1971; Short 1976; Jankowski 1991). Such politicized gang involvement in community affairs subsided in the 1970s.

There continue to be periodic efforts by African-American gangs in Chicago's West and South sides, not only to sponsor or take leadership in community social and development activities, but to charter nonprofit organizations and even to establish separate political parties. Members of the Black Gangster Disciples attempted to organize as "The Young Voters of Illinois." The El Rukns formed the "Young

Grassroots Independent Voters." Gang members ran for aldermanic and other political offices or tried to influence elections in Chicago even after the 1960s. Gangs put forward members as candidates for election of a local school council in the black community, but the candidates dropped out (Rudel 1991, September 1, p. 1).

Gang members continue to be useful in both Chicago's Hispanic and black politics. The primary elections in the twenty-sixth ward in 1986—containing mainly newcomer, low-income Puerto Ricans—involved fierce competition between Hispanic Alderman Torres, supported by the Democratic machine, and his challenger Gutierrez, preferred by reform Mayor Harold Washington. Both candidates used gang members to perform a variety of tasks—getting the vote out, putting up election posters, and persuading voters whom to vote for. The different gangs supported different candidates. One candidate's coordinator of precinct captains was formerly the leader of a major Hispanic gang renowned for its violence and drug-dealing activities.

Testimony at a recent series of trials of El Rukns for racketeering, drug selling, assaults, and intimidations indicated some effort to become legitimate or develop a legitimate facade through financial contributions to white and black officials' election campaigns. Contributions were said to have been made to Chicago "Alderman Edward Vrdolyak and then-State Representative Larry Bullock . . . called . . . our 'link to the city power structure.'" The El Rukns "campaigned for Mayor Jane Byrne, Alderman Bobby Rush . . . and then Alderman Timothy Evans. . . . El Rukns also had plans to run one gang member . . . for alderman" (O'Connor 1991c, p. 1).

The weakness of the black political machine in Chicago and the growing strength of black street-gang organizations may be making for a complex and volatile alliance in certain urban areas. Local black politicians and civil rights organizations may be aggressively campaigning to legitimize and win the support of street gangs for their own purposes. The current Chicago situation is similar in many respects to the former political scene in New York and Philadelphia more than a century ago. For example:

> From his prison cell in southern Illinois, Chicago's most powerful street gang leader is forging new alliances aimed at influencing elections from the state legislature to City Hall.
>
> Larry Hoover, the man who runs the Black Gangster Disciples, is being hailed as a community leader and visionary by former Chicago Mayor Eugene Sawyer, Chicago Aldermen Virgil Jones (15th) and Allan Streeter (17th), community groups and the local chapter of the NAACP.
>
> They are asking state officials for Hoover's early release from prison, 20 years after he was sentenced to a 150–200 year term for murder. . . .
>
> G.D., which is street shorthand for Gangster Disciples, now stands for Growth and Development; they say. . . .
>
> Hoover's gang members, meanwhile, are flocking to join a new organization, 21st Century V.O.T.E., a political action committee.
>
> Its goals are to influence and to change the way the Prisoner Review Board works. . . .
>
> There has been a vacuum of political power in the city's black wards for years. It was disguised by Harold Washington's election as the first black mayor of Chicago and only grew following his death. The decaying black ward organizations have been running low on morale, patronage and discipline.

"These young street leaders have more influence over larger numbers of young people than anyone else," said Joe Gardner, a county sewer commissioner who ran the late Mayor Washington's political apparatus and may run against Mayor Richard M. Daley in 1995. (Papajohn and Kass, 1993)

V.O.T.E. is in fact a registered political organization and was at the center of a controversy involving the mayor and city councilmen over the allocation of public funds to conduct a small job development program on a subcontract with the Chicago Urban League. The allocation was cancelled. V.O.T.E., containing gang and nongang members but clearly representing the interest of both older gang members and a particular gang organization, made rapid political progress.

Last July, 21st Century V.O.T.E. members were outside City Hall, many dressed in gang colors of blue and black, chanting slogans on LaSalle Street.

Since then, they've run political campaigns, raised money, registered voters, formed alliances with other mainstream groups in the African-American community. . . . (Kass and Papajohn 1994, p. 5)

Gangs, Social or Political Movements, and Community Development

Evidence of the gang's occasional ideological interests in this country may be observed in the involvement of some Chicano street gangs in the LaRaza Movement in East Los Angeles and Chicago during the 1960s (see Moore 1978); the support of the Young Lords in the Free Puerto Rico Movement in Chicago, and the civil rights marches of the Blackstone Rangers, Vice Lords, and Young Lords gangs organized by Jesse Jackson to desegregate Chicago Trade Unions also in the 1960s. More recently, Irish gangs assisted the Irish social clubs in Boston and New York to move guns to the Catholics in their fight against the Protestants in Northern Ireland (Jankowski 1991, p. 121). Neo-Nazi Skinheads celebrated the anniversary of the birthday of Adolph Hitler in Colorado not long ago. All of these political statements by gangs in this country, however, have been quite fragmentary. They certainly are less significant than the widespread political demonstrations of Skinheads in Germany and other European countries supported by substantial segments of the "good" citizens of various communities (see Hamm 1993).

Gangs have become complex organizations or collectivities combining community organizational, social support, political, and criminal business functions in socially isolated low-income public housing projects of Chicago. The gangs cannot be defined simply in terms of control of street turf or development of patterns of illegal behavior. They contribute community resources, sociopolitical control, and a certain degree of stability in some communities.

The gangs . . . buy food for the elderly and sneakers for kids, making allies of both. They sponsor picnics where they put up huge banners flaunting their names and colors. . . . The gangs are the only formal structure out there that's effective. They control the social and economic environment of people in public housing. . . .

In mid-July, residents of Robert Taylor Homes, which is Chicago's largest public housing complex, received invitations to a picnic. Fliers promised free food and drink and softball for the children and a car show and wet T-shirt contest for adults.

> The sponsors of the third annual Players Picnic [were] some of the city's top drug dealers and gang leaders. . . . On the last Sunday in July, about 2,000 Chicagoans convened in Dan Ryan Woods on the far South side. They danced to the funk rock of a live band and grilled hot dogs and ribs. Cars were so backed up going into the park that the police had to assign extra traffic details. . . . (Kotlowitz 1988)

A group of anthropologists described the community influence role of a well-known violent Hispanic gang as follows:

> Northwestern University professors and researchers "expected to do a scholarly study of the great ethnic integration taking place in the neighborhood on Chicago's Northwest Side. . . . They watched gang leaders negotiate a truce after a black family accused a Vietnamese family of eating their pet dog. They helped dig a hole to turn on the water in an apartment building after the city shut it off. They tried to volunteer at the 39th Ward Democratic headquarters." (Dold 1990, p. 1)

Cross-cultural Considerations

Youth gangs have played a variety of important political and economic roles in developing and developed societies in modern as well as earlier times. After Chiang Kai-shek fled to Taiwan and his regime was challenged by liberal candidates at local elections, members of secret societies, including youth gangs, were used to intimidate local liberal opponents. Gangs in China in recent years have been used to neutralize the influence of social movements (Chin 1990b, pp. 23–24). In the 1950s, the Yakuza were recruited by the Liberal Democratic Party (LDP) an ultrarightist organization, to counter left-wing groups planning to disrupt U.S. President Eisenhower's visit to Japan. The result was the development of a new generation of ultra-right-wing and paramilitary organizations and a further blurring of the lines among Yakuza, rightist groups, and politicians (Delfs 1991, p. 29).

The Japanese gangs were until recently not treated as crime organizations as they are in most of the world. There were no antiracketeering laws in Japan. The police could on occasion negotiate with Yakuza organizations or gangs to induce to exercise restraint, especially in regard to limiting the effects of intergang warfare on the public, and in eliminating certain free-lance criminal activity and violent street crime (Delfs 1991, pp. 34–35). However, with the increase of drug trafficking and related violence, Yakuza racketeering activities reached into the highest echelons of business and government. Recent law allows authorities to designate certain groups as crime organizations, on the basis of the proportion of convicted criminals among their membership. Members of designated organizations were also "prohibited from practicing extortion and the use of coercion or enticement to juveniles, and may also be barred from assembly at their headquarters during periods of intergang warfare" (ibid., p. 34).

There are limits to which any legitimate society can tolerate criminal activities that threaten the basic cultural, economic, political, and social life of the community. While the patterns of ganging are significantly different across the United States, Japan, and other countries, the dynamics of gang formation and the basic tendency of gangs to relate symbiotically to the political structure are remarkably similar.

Prisons

The contemporary prison gang has been defined as a "close-knit and disruptive group of inmates organized around common affiliation for the purpose of mutual caretaking, solidarity, and profit-making criminal activity" (C. Camp and Camp 1988, p. 71). The gang's tangible goals may be the acquisition of money, drugs, and property, while the less tangible goals are prestige, respect of its members, and fear from inmates who are nonmembers (Lyman 1989, p. 53). Prison gangs today, just like their counterpart street gangs, may be quite varied in their degree of commitment to criminal economic gain behavior and status-related or symbolic activities. Variations may be related to racial/ethnic, regional, historical, and particular correctional facility factors.

Of thirty-three state correctional systems reporting the presence of gangs, twenty-one indicated counterpart organizations in the streets of cities within the same states in 1985 (G. Camp and Camp 1985). Increasingly, the leaders of the inmate gangs are individuals who held high street-gang rank and still have influence on the streets. The number of gangs and gang members rapidly increased not only as state antigang crime laws have been passed, but as gang members have been transferred within and across state and federal prison systems. Gang codes, traditions, and structures are developed in the process. Sometimes families of gang members may settle in cities close to the prisons, and are joined by ex-gang inmates upon their release.

The National Institute of Corrections describes one prison gang in California currently as follows: " . . . By the mid-1960s, the gang [Mexican Mafia] regulated heroin traffic and controlled much of the inmates' activities. Later it successfully infiltrated several cultural groups supported and sponsored by the correctional staff. Intelligence indicates that the Mexican Mafia has continued to be a dominant force in California Institutions" (National Institute of Corrections 1991, p. 3).

Sergeant McBride of the Los Angeles Sheriff's Department claims that the Mexican Mafia has ordered Hispanic street gangs in the Los Angeles area to reduce the incidence of drive-by shootings that have resulted not only in killings of innocent victims but in interference with the prison gang's drug trafficking activities on the outside. Street-gang homicides among Hispanic street gangs coincidentally dropped significantly in 1993 (McBride 1994).

The prison gangs of the 1970s may not be like the prison gangs of an earlier period that were unique to prison life. Many of the current prison gangs exist as a response, not only to the prison but to the streets. The power of prison gangs in recent decades appears to result from urban social and economic breakdown, changes in the prison control system (Jacobs 1977), and the situational need to establish control, social support, and economic opportunity systems within particular prisons, based on related community street-gang interests and needs. For example, with the mass jailing of their gang leaders and members, Chicago gangs gained a foothold in the Illinois prisons in the early 1970s. Some observers have attributed contemporary problems in the Illinois prisons to the 1970s when certain prison administrators accepted the gangs as organizations with positive potential and tried to work with them to maintain inmate control. Gang leaders were expected to keep order, and in return were rewarded with special privileges and prestige. The result was "increasing gang power and control, as well as gang rivalries and violence" (C. Camp and Camp 1988, pp. 57–58).

When prison officials recognize, legitimize, and collaborate formally with gangs, they may gain a short-term improvement in housekeeping routines but a long-term struggle among staff, administration, and gang leaders for power (G. Camp and Camp 1985). The gang can serve as a source of control and stability, but with negative consequences for legitimate order and the long-term conventional adaptation of gang members to the institution as well as later in the community upon release. Further, with the sharp increase of gang members in a number of state prisons and especially with overcrowding, prisons are volatile settings; explosions frequently occur. The instigators of prison disorder may be gang members with strong ties to street gangs:

> Sunday's uprising at Stateville Correctional Center, the second violent incident at the prison in two days, was instigated by inmates from a Chicago-based gang who were angry that a member of their gang had been killed Saturday by a guard, the state's prison chief said Monday. . . .
> Critics of the prison system have charged that gangs enjoy free rein in some facilities and, in some cases, are so powerful that officials must negotiate policy and procedures with them. (Tijerina and Karwath 1991)

The special violence-related gang problems that confront prison administrators and staff include intimidation of weaker inmates; extortion resulting from strongarming; requests for protective custody; occasional conflict (usually racial) between gangs that creates general prison disturbance; and contract inmate murders (G. Camp and Camp 1985, pp. 46–55; see also W. Smith 1987). Discipline problems are far more severe among gang members than non-gang members. Jacobs observed that disciplinary tickets were considerably higher for gang members, whether in segregated cells or not. Most depredations of gangs generally are not directed against prison officials but are related to "taking care of gang business" (1977, pp. 138–174).

Gangs are apparently much less a serious problem in juvenile than adult correctional institutions. Knox recently sampled administrators of 274 short- and long-term juvenile correctional facilities and found that 20.8 percent of boys and 4.9 percent of girls were gang members. However, he also found that only 8 percent of the administrators indicated the particular institution had a gang problem, which included gang assaults on staff (Knox 1991c, pp. 13, 15). It is possible that juvenile institutions are less a source of gang problems, because they have more adequate correctional controls and individualized services and supports for inmates. Older more difficult gang juveniles are often referred to and concentrated in special sections of adult institutions.

Nevertheless, juvenile as well as adult institutions can provide opportunities for the development of gangs. Insulation and isolation from the outside world promote the creation of networks in both types of institutions that reinforce gang identification, and with it strengthened antisocial and illegitimate value systems. This may result in large measure from the "lack of clear alternative structures of socially sanctioned and prolegal values" among inmates in both juvenile and adult correctional facilities (Ianni 1989, p. 215).

Prisons as Functional to Gang Development

It is not at all clear that prisons serve a significant deterrent or incapacitation function for inmates, especially gang members. Gang members who lead a somewhat irregular, if not chaotic, life on the outside may find a certain stability in prison routine and gang peers.

> Prisons provide housing that is often far better than the tenements or homeless shelters where the inmates had been living. They furnish three meals a day; decent medical care, especially for victims of AIDS; drug and alcohol detoxification programs; remedial education and job training.
>
> Moreover, inmates soon find that many of their friends and relatives are in prison, too, giving them a large social network on the inside. (Butterfield 1992b, p. 4)

This is not to deny that incarceration, in general, is still a highly undesirable experience for gang youths, especially young-adult leaders. Thousands of dollars for bond are sometimes raised through gang membership dues, special taxes, and fundraising affairs to keep core members and leaders out of jail pending trial, conviction, or sentencing.

The sense of ganghood, derived from the street, is further developed and reflected in macho images, tatoos, special attire (G. Camp and Camp 1985), official titles, and sometimes even religious symbolism. "Gangs infiltrate strategic prison work assignments; bribe weak officers; and abuse visitation privileges, money and drugs" (C. Camp and Camp 1988, p. 57). There is also evidence that as gangs become better organized behind bars and as they influence street-gang operations—particularly criminal gain operations—they become more secretive and "have gone to the extent of eliminating . . . outward symbols that were once used" (Riley undated). Gang leadership and influence have thereby become more difficult to detect.

The gang experience in prison and on the streets has now become almost a seamless web. With the aid of beepers and cellular phones and the increased movement of gang members into prison and in due course out of prison, communication and control in respect to gain-oriented criminal activity are easily maintained. What is particularly troublesome is the greater sense of solidarity and organization that has resulted. Senior gang members in prisons are recognized as heroes and mythologized as leaders, not simply by younger, aspiring members in the streets but by older gang members and local citizens now acculturated to gang life and themselves more and more isolated from the conventional norms and legitimate opportunities of a society that is segmented by race, ethnicity, and an increasingly pervasive criminal justice system.

Conclusion

Gangs develop in the context of local communities that are often socially disorganized and/or impoverished. The process of becoming a gang member occurs through the interaction of defective parenting as well as certain community forces. But even parents with good parenting skills are unable to ensure that their children do not become involved in gangs, particularly in low-income, social problem-ridden neighborhoods.

Gang members are typically behind in their studies or are school dropouts. Researchers have suggested that gang behavior results as much from school defects as from problems and pressures at home. The school variables that contribute to the gang problem include the make-up of the body of teachers, the size of the schools and the resources available to them, the way the school is run, and the school's psychosocial climate.

A systematic relationship sometimes develops between urban politicians and gangs in certain cities, particularly during periods of social unrest and political crisis. The gang may come to be recognized as an instrument of influence and power. Gangs may obtain resources or benefits from politicians in exchange for gang influence in getting out the vote, intimidating opponents or voters, or otherwise maintaining them in office. Gangs may be more likely to serve conservative than liberal interests.

The street gang, in recent decades, has immigrated to the prison and become further organized and criminalized. The prison gang today maintains ongoing communication with its counterpart on the streets. Furthermore, it is not clear that prisons serve significant deterrent or incapacitation functions. Rather, prisons have become extensions of disorganized communities. Prisons serve to solidify gang structure and criminal processes, particularly when alternative social structures and legitimate opportunities are not sufficiently available in or outside the prison.

9

Youth Gangs and Organized Crime

An important institution for the development of youth gangs is the organization of crime opportunities in particular communities. Variable cultural and population settlement patterns influence gang connections to organized crime. Access to criminal opportunities—or to legitimate labor market opportunities—depends largely on factors of race or ethnic status and location. These variations in opportunities must be addressed in policies and programs that try to stop older gang youths from turning to crime as a career. Cultural sensitivity and structural understanding therefore provide an important basis for developing appropriate community-oriented intervention strategies that control the link between youth gang and adult crime activities.

This chapter emphasizes the economic and organizational characteristics that connect youth gangs to and transform them into elements of organized crime. Gang life on the streets often involves gang members in adult-directed criminal gain activities. Jankowski suggests, with some overgeneralization, that the youth gang can no longer be regarded—if it ever should have been—simply as a preparatory school for membership in crime syndicates. It should be viewed as an important component of "the broad structure by which contemporary crime has been organized" (Jankowski 1991, pp. 131–132).

Defining Organized Crime

Some case studies (Spergel 1964; Ianni 1974) and theoretical speculations (Cloward and Ohlin 1960) portray certain youth gangs as stepping stones to roles in adult organized crime. Although a significant number of gang youths become adult criminals, it is unclear what proportion move into organized crime. Much depends on how one defines organized crime. A narrow definition is offered by the President's Commission on Organized Crime: "Groups that engage in a variety of criminal activities are [classified as] organized crime when they have the capacity to corrupt governments" (1985, p. 181). Ianni stated, more broadly, that "any gang or group of criminals organized formally or informally to extort money, shoplift, steal automobiles, or rob banks is part of organized crime—regardless of its size or whether it operates locally or nationally" (1974, pp. 14–15). If burglary, the selling of weapons, and drug trafficking are added, most criminally oriented youth gangs, individual gang youths employed by criminal gangs, or youth segments of adult-controlled criminal gangs should be considered as components of organized crime under the broader, more inclusive definition.

A more appropriate middle-range definition is perhaps the following: "All organized crime is any crime committed by a person occupying a position in an established division of labor designed for the commission of crime" (A. Block 1991, p. 8, quoting Cressey 1972). A criminal organization is one that has been "rationally designed to maximize profits by performing illegal services . . . " (ibid.). By this definition, most street gangs are not ordinarily components of organized crime, except perhaps particular cliques or groups affiliated with or outgrowths of street gangs.

Furthermore, not all crime organizations are large and well integrated or rational in pursuit of economic gain. The members of the largest or most successful criminal organizations can engage in violence for a combination of group profit, personal, and social status reasons. The distinction between organized crime and youth gang criminal activities, particularly in relation to use of violence, should then be considered as one of degree rather than kind. The distinction between organized crime and youth gang activity is particularly difficult to make in certain inner-city communities where the level of criminal organization may be well developed.

The question of definition of organized crime in relation to the youth gang is further complicated depending on the legitimacy of the actions of key organizations in the community. The definition can hinge not only on the issue of direct or indirect corruption of government and legitimate business by crime organizations or street gangs, but also on the sometimes unintended spread of the gang problem and its connection to adult crime by public or nonprofit agencies, churches, and legitimate businesses. Corruption of values exists when community agencies accept funds or community support to prevent or control the gang problem, when in fact the primary objective is to expand existing programs or social agendas that do not address and may have a negative impact on the problem. Further complication exists in defining the activities of youth or street gangs as organized crime. For example, when a conflicting or double standard prevails in a community, schools, police, and city government may attack the symbols and consequences of criminal youth gang activity but the media, movies, music industries, and clothes manufacturers encourage youths to find excitement in gang symbols and adopt gang attitudes and behaviors:

> Many young people today are wearing fashions inspired by the streets, spurred in part by mass marketing of what once was considered purely gang symbolism. Yesterday's gang emblem becomes today's mainstream fashion statement, thanks to television, movies and music videos.
>
> A problem, anti-gang activists say, is that at a time when schools, towns, and even some malls are outlawing gang-linked clothing in an effort to halt the spread of gangs, youths are seeing the same clothing promoted everywhere: on rock, rap and sports idols, at the movies and even in the malls they frequent and advertising circulars they read. (Goering and McRoberts 1992)

American society, through its basic institutions, can on the one hand severely condemn and punish gang activity, and on the other contribute significantly to its development. Gang activity can be a source of profit to a variety of entrepreneurs. According to a recent report, small unlicensed telephone companies in Chicago are apparently installing telephones in locations that facilitate the business of drug dealers and are thereby a convenience to gang members:

> A City Council committee took . . . the ordinance under consideration [that] would immediately halt the installation of new telephones. . . . Aldermen complained that an influx of pay phones [by 40 or more companies] brings in drug dealers and gang members.
>
> . . . [Mayor] Daley said last month that there are too many smaller companies that continue to install pay phones without any city control [or payment of licensing fees]. (Robert Davis 1992)

The issue of the development of links between gangs and adult criminal organizations should be looked at in systemic terms to determine who and what practices contribute to the sustenance and criminal development of the gang problem. The gang problem is a result not only of the nefarious activities of gang members but of significant actors in the legitimate society, including government, business, industry, and criminal justice and social agencies, that may create the conditions for and in fact encourage, directly or indirectly through their response, the increasingly sophisticated development of the gang.

The Evolving Youth Gang–Organized Crime Connection

Thrasher noted more than fifty years ago, in a period similar to the contemporary one of mass immigration, rapid social change, and variable definitions of crime, that there is "no hard and fast dividing line between predatory gang boys and criminal groups of younger and older adults. They merge into each other by imperceptible gradations, and the latter have their real explanations for the most part in the former. Many delinquent gangs contain both adolescents and adults" (1936, p. 406). Scholars and researchers in the 1950s and 1960s probably exaggerated the distinction between youth gangs or delinquent subcultures and adult criminal organizations in different lower-class neighborhoods (Cloward and Ohlin 1960; but see Short and Strodtbeck 1965). Minority groups, including African-Americans, in lower-class communities across the country may no longer be blocked from significant access to street-level criminal opportunity systems, particularly drug trafficking.

Youth gang and adult criminal subcultures are more integrated since the 1970s than they were in the 1950s and 1960s. The changing nature of organized crime includes the entry of newer minority groups, greater competition among nascent criminal organizations, an increased number of older youths and adults in street gangs, and the expansion of street-level drug markets. Jankowski claims that street gangs have become more and more involved in traditional adult crime activities such as protection, illegal demolition (i.e., arson) and "indirect participation in prostitution." He states that "nearly all the gangs [he observed] had developed a fee schedule according to types of protection [for prostitutes] desired" (Jankowski 1991, p. 122). Noteworthy and alarming, according to some analysts, is that gangs are learning how to "specialize in marketing and distributing illegal drugs such as heroin, crack, and cocaine. . . . Gang migration and franchising [were beginning to occur]" (Federal Register 1992, p. 9867; see also Taylor 1990a).

It is also no longer possible to claim a sharp distinction between conflict and criminal gang subcultures, if indeed such a typological distinction ever existed (see Cloward and Ohlin 1960; Short and Strodtbeck 1965). Gangs, drug trafficking, and violence are related, but in contradictory and unclear ways. A recent increase of gang violence and homicide in some black communities in Los Angeles and on the south side of Chicago has been attributed to competition for control over drug markets. By contrast, the decline of gang problems in other cities—such as New York and Detroit—has been attributed to increased opportunities for drug trafficking and the ready transfer of street gang knowledge and skills to street-level drug distribution networks, in other words, to the better integration of youth gangs or their equivalent into organized crime.

Cities and neighborhoods also differ in the degree to which the youth or street gang is being transformed, on the basis of factors of culture and ecology. Youth gangs that engage more or less in violent and/or criminal gain activity can be explained only partially in terms of available legal and illegal opportunities, criminal and conventional values systems (Sullivan 1989, pp. 201–202). Both economic and ecological factors are important. For example, the increasing concentration of unemployed males in certain Hispanic communities may be hastening the transformation of traditionally violent youth gangs to organized drug dealing. The links between street gangs and organized crime exist across race/ethnicity and culture and national boundaries:

> When Mexico's Arellano drug lords needed new gunmen, they looked across the border to the impoverished Logan Heights barrio, where opportunities for youths are as scarce as shade from the searing sun.
>
> The drug traffickers found what they were looking for in the Calle Treinta (30th Street) street gang, whose angry young members are known across San Diego for their eagerness to settle even petty turf battles at the point of a gun.
>
> U.S. and Mexican officials believe the San Diego gang members were responsible for gunning down a popular Roman Catholic cardinal, perhaps by mistake, and six others, May 24 at the airport at Guadalajara. . . .
>
> There have been other examples of American street gangs hooking up with international organized crime operations. U.S. officials cite Chicago's El Rukn gang conspiracy with Libyan terrorists in the 1980s and links between the Mafia and outlaw motorcycle gangs. (Dellios 1993)

Planning and Organization

Planning and organization increasingly characterize the actions of some street gangs and their subgroups, particularly those whose members are engaged in significant drug trafficking. The penetration by some of them into legitimate businesses (albeit under somewhat unclear circumstances), such as store owner and slum manager, has occurred in Chicago (Pleines 1987). Law enforcement officials state that some of the older and more successful black street gang members in the Los Angeles County area "purchased legitimate businesses in order to launder money. Some of the businesses are car washes, auto-painting and fender shops, motels, auto dealerships, and liquor stores. The next step could be the added respectability for these subjects in the community as business leaders or through politics" (National Law Enforcement Institute 1990, p. 24).

Ianni (1974) claimed a close relationship between youth gangs and adult organized crime for purposes of recruitment, criminal socialization, and organizational development. He stated that in New York City, "black and Hispanic crime activists follow the street 'rep' of youngsters just as carefully as the Italians did, and use the same process of gradual involvement to draw youngsters into the networks" (p. 124). He suggested that the youth gang and the prison are the two major institutions that prepare youths for participation in criminal networks. Ianni predicted the transformation of "what is now a scattered and loosely organized pattern of emerging black control [and Hispanic participation] in organized crime" into a "Black Mafia" and into a future "Hispanic Mafia" (1974, p. 11). Youth gangs and organized crime serve, in interrelated fashion, institutional functions of integrating deprived minority and low-income groups into the larger American culture—in effect serving as early and middle stages of America's complex social mobility system (Ianni 1974, p. 15; see also Bell 1953).

Our own observations of gangs in several Hispanic communities in Chicago suggest that a variety of pressures and opportunities exist for youths in violent gangs to participate in organized criminal behaviors. Gang youths 14 or 15 years of age or younger engage in part-time drug peddling—often to augment (public aid) family income. One gang leader led younger gang members in violent intergang rivalries and shootings while also engaging in burglary, receiving stolen goods, and selling cocaine. In another instance, a local drug dealer employed a gang leader on a contract of $4,000 to kill a rival drug dealer. The youth shot and killed the wrong person, however.

Gang members and drug dealers have developed symbiotic relationships in some inner-city slum neighborhoods, particularly in the poorest areas, where drug selling is rampant. Gang members provide protection for drug dealers and in return are paid for running errands, sometimes selling drugs, and performing other favors. Antagonisms between drug dealers and youth gang members may no longer be as serious as reported in the earlier literature; youth gangs no longer chase dealers out of the neighborhood (New York City Youth Board 1960; Spergel 1964; see also Moore 1978; Skolnick 1992). Street-gang members and leaders can be both turf or status-oriented shooters and drug-trafficking entrepreneurs. Sometimes the two roles interrelate, sometimes they are quite incompatible. Established street gangs increasingly have taken over from traditional neighborhood drug dealers, particularly in African-American communities, to develop their own drug distribution systems.

A variety of competitive business strategies and techniques have been adopted in enhancing profit margins in the gang experience. The reputed corporate drug trade in Detroit did not evolve with the "crack" epidemic, but was initially based on lucrative heroin sales. By the mid-1980s, better products—cocaine and "crack"—further expanded the market through the development of a variety of marketing practices, including "price slashing," targeting of various consumer groups, and use of "physical intimidation and deadly force to sell their product" (Taylor 1990b, pp. 106, 112).

However, there is evidence in some Hispanic working-class communities in Chicago that gang members who have made the transition to systematic drug dealing often have family connections. They may come from higher socioeconomic status families than members of other Hispanic gangs in the same community who are more oriented to turf violence and status and even keeping drug dealers out of the community. Different kinds and levels of integration of criminal organization and youth gang activities are present among gangs and gang members in the same community.

Irish youth gangs, for example, have a very old and settled tradition of integration with a variety of established adult groups representing both legitimate and illegitimate interests. In the early part of the twentieth century on the lower west side of Manhattan, they "burglarized shops along the gaslit streets at night, ruled the saloons and pool halls, and staged frequent raids on the docks and the Hudson River Railroad, later named the New York Central Railroad" (English 1990, pp. 38–39). Jankowski observes that Irish gangs in Boston and New York more recently have been closely connected to the Irish social clubs in stealing and running guns to the Catholics of Northern Ireland, probably for a price. The Irish social clubs also assisted youths in gangs to obtain legitimate jobs later in life (Jankowski 1991, p. 75–76, 121).

The Gang Member as Racketeer

The gangster, robber baron, or bandit has always played a significant part in American cultural and economic development. Now more than ever, the youth gang leader— grown up as a racketeer—becomes not only a culture hero or antihero, but a model of American success, especially in inner-city areas.

> On Monday, federal authorities announced Sims, the alleged leader of a street gang, was indicted on charges that he has headed a major narcotics operation on Chicago's West Side since 1985. . . .
>
> He bought luxury houses in suburban Westchester and Lisle and spent another $65,000 renovating the Lisle home with gold faucets, a marble staircase and other improvements.
>
> He paid almost $130,000 in cash and traded in a luxury car to buy a champaign-colored Rolls-Royce Corniche convertible.
>
> The Internal Revenue Service estimated the jewelry's value at $250,000.
>
> . . . Forman [Federal Northern District prosecutor] also charged that Donald Moore, Sims chief lieutenant, had responsibility for maintaining large quantities of machine guns, automatic weapons and grenades for providing security for the narcotics operation. . . .
>
> . . . Sims' organization sold $6.4 million in narcotics in one 2½ year period. (O'Connor 1992)

Transformation of the Black Street Gang

Taylor, in his study of black gangs in Detroit, states that "drugs, as a commodity, have become the same unifying economic force for gangs today (adult and juvenile) as alcohol was during prohibition" (Taylor 1990b, p. 103). He believes that drug trafficking has permitted African-Americans for the first time in modern U.S. history" to move into the mainstream of major crime and have become a "vehicle for social mobility." America's drug appetite has triggered an economic boom that has moved black gang youths beyond the street gang or turf conflict stage. The Detroit drug business has meant "a new life for many individuals who no longer have the Job Corps or special education programs available" (Taylor 1990b, p. 111).

Youths in gangs with an evolving criminal corporate structure have been recruited from "various places, such as playgrounds, recreation centers, video arcades, schools, and neighborhoods, friends, and associates" (Taylor 1990a, p. 34). The range of jobs available to gang youths can be from "being lookouts to couriers, messengers to distributors, sales persons to crew chiefs and enforcers." There are clear rewards to be obtained in identifying and serving gang crime interests, at least for some youths, especially in lifestyle terms: "large amounts of cash, trips to Las Vegas and New York, and exotic, expensive automobiles. . . . " (ibid.). Professional and legal advice is available in the development of the criminal structure.

The employees of these drug organizations represent a symbiosis between youth gangs and drug dealers that has grown stronger, more pervasive, and may not be confined simply to inner-city or ghetto area low-income residents. Taylor speaks of a small sophisticated group of "organized corporate gang members" 13 to 19 years of age (1988, p. 27). He estimates that 30 percent of gang youths come from middle-class and 2 percent from upper-class African-American homes. Some attend school regularly, a few may do better than average academic work (p. 27). The predominant majority (80%) said they did not use drugs, but all said their main objective in joining gangs was money through drug sales (ibid.).

El Rukns

The media reports of the trials of leaders of the El Rukns in Federal District court in Chicago in 1991 and 1992 illustrate the transformation of a major African-American street gang in the mid-1960s into a criminal business. A local street gang, the Blackstone Rangers, later the Black P Stone Nation, evolved into the El Rukns, a coherent criminal business organization with links to drug dealers in various parts of the country and with a brief connection to a foreign government soliciting terrorist activities. Much of the twenty-five-year history of the gang revolved around the leadership of Jeff Fort.

> Born in 1947 in a small Mississippi town, Fort stopped his formal education in 4th grade. He dropped out. As a teenager living in Woodlawn [Chicago], Fort was classified as 'retarded' with an I.Q. of 60, in a Cook County Court Service Evaluation. The finding was grossly inaccurate. Fort could not read or write at the time.
>
> Fort's philosophy took on its religious bent in 1976, upon his release from prison for defrauding a federal anti-poverty grant. He founded the Moorish Science Temple of America, El Rukn tribe . . .
>
> Within three years [1981], according to extensive court testimony, Fort and the El Rukns were running one of the largest heroin and cocaine operations in the city. . . . (Blau and O'Brien 1991)

Fort showed organizational talent, if not genius, in his late teens and early 20s when, during his gang fighting days, he organized a network of Blackstone Ranger and Black P Stone Nation units on street corners throughout the south side of Chicago. The major opposition gang to the Blackstone Rangers in the 1960s was the Devil's Disciples. Fort and Gene Hairston, another major leader at the time, organized a kind of corporate structure for the gang in which a "mains 21," or a board structure, was responsible for a great deal of decision-making. Fort was able to develop some of his organizing skills with the aid of unwitting community organizations, including the First Presbyterian Church where the Blackstone Rangers' weapons cache was stored for a time, and The Woodlawn Organization, which obtained a large federal antipoverty grant to conduct a manpower training and gang violence control program. Fort manipulated church staff and defrauded the manpower program (Spergel et al. 1969).

After a set of nationally televised Senate subcommittee hearings and federal trials of key Blackstone Ranger leaders in the late 1960s, Fort and others were sentenced to moderately long prison terms. On release, Fort and his gang colleagues became engaged in distribution and sale of marijuana and amphetamines as well as reported intimidation and extortion of local businesses. According to news reports, however, it was not until his contacts with a "respected" Southside Chicago businessman did his career as a major local criminal organizer and entrepreneur take off:

> Robinson offered to set up the El Rukns with major [heroin and] cocaine suppliers if they wanted to make some quick money. . . .
> Fort approved the idea, and in the summer of 1983, Robinson introduced El Rukns to Garfield Hall . . . who operated out of New York and South Carolina. . . .
> . . . Robinson arranged an introduction to . . . a New York dealer who then supplied the El Rukns with several ounces of China White heroin. . . .
> Prosecutors have alleged that the gang made $1 million in its first month of dealing heroin, and that one-third of the take went to Robinson.
> The El Rukns' heroin selling led Fort to form a subgroup within the El Rukns that he code-named the "Guerilla Family" [which] teamed up with drug dealer, Alexander Cooper, and in a turf battle with another gang, four people, including two bystanders were killed in April 1985. . . .
> Prosecutors have charged the El Rukn members on trial used murder and intimidation to put a stranglehold on illicit activities on the Southside for 25 years. (O'Connor 1991b)

The Chicago businessman Noah Robinson was a key instrument for the El Rukns in contacts with legitimate business and public officials. If the restricted definition of organized crime is used, which is based on the "capacity to corrupt governments" (President's Commission on Organized Crime 1985, p. 181), then El Rukns must be placed in the same general category of crime organizations as the Mafia and Yakuza, albeit with less developed organization and success:

> Noah Robinson . . . helped El Rukn street gang form a security-guard agency in the mid-1980s in part to allow the gang to legally carry weapons, a former Rukn leader testified Tuesday. . . .
> The government contends Robinson helped organize Security Maintenance in an effort to aid the El Rukns in establishing legitimate businesses with proceeds from the gang's distribution of cocaine and heroin. (O'Connor 1991b)
> Noah Robinson offered El Rukn leader, Jeff Fort, a silent partnership in a Chicago City Colleges contract so the gang could use the business to launder its illegal drug profits, an El Rukn general testified. . . . (Rossi 1991a)

Robinson is charged with hiring El Rukns to kill a former employee in South Carolina . . . to kill a witness to that murder and also to kill a former partner in Texas. . . . The gang also operated a restaurant with the help of Robinson who owned several fast-food restaurants himself." (O'Connor 1991c)

The fifth El Rukn racketeering trial of the year started Tuesday with a prosecutor charging that two of the defendants were involved in the "ultimate fix"—an attempt to rig a murder case.

Assistant U.S. Attorney Theodore Paulos said in opening statements that El Rukn generals Bernard Green and Roland Lewis were tape-recorded while discussing efforts to fix the 1986 murder trial of El Rukn general Earl Hawkins.

The case was pending before then—Criminal Court Judge Thomas J. Maloney, who has been charged with taking money to fix Hawkins' and other trials. (Rossi 1991b)

At a recent count of members tried in federal court over a year and a half period in 1991 and 1992, thirty-six El Rukns were convicted and sixteen others pleaded guilty. Prosecutors declared the gang had been decimated. However, there was some evidence of "prosecutorial misconduct," and the possibility of retrial for several members was being considered (O'Connor 1992). In a series of more recent court rehearings, several El Rukn case convictions have been overturned, retrials ordered and prosecutor misconduct established (O'Connor 1993; Lehmann 1993). Convictions of former Chicago businessman, Noah Robinson and at least nine reported El Rukn "generals" have been overturned and retrials ordered (O'Connor 1994).

With the apparent demise, or at least highly reduced criminal activities, of the El Rukn gang, other street gangs, mainly African-American but also increasingly Hispanic and especially Puerto Rican, continue to develop as criminal organizations in Chicago and environs. The street gangs or former street-gangs are primarily engaged in drug trafficking in cooperative relationships with other selected former street-gang cliques across the country. Rational distribution and selling arrangements have been established, at least according to news media and police reports (Recktenwald 1991).

Hispanic Youth Gang–Criminal-Organization Connections

In Hispanic communities, youth or street gangs are usually not the primary basis or vehicle for the development of criminal organization. Where organized adult-based criminal opportunities already exist in some measure, the need for development of violent street gangs may be less or shorter-lived in the first place, particularly if access to adult opportunities exists for older gang youths. Gangs or gang youths in the same community may have differential access to drug-dealing opportunities.

Terry Williams in a study of cocaine criminal youth organizations noted that as quality entry-level jobs were disappearing in the legitimate or above-ground economy, "illegal opportunities were emerging with considerable force because of the growth of a powerful and profitable multi-national drug industry" (Williams 1989, p. IX). An underground economy was established based not only on similar organizational considerations but similar values and rewards as in the above-ground economy. Williams observed that:

Dealers start out in lowly positions, then move up through hard work, skill, intelligence and a little luck. A kid who can routinely handle money, control personal use of cocaine, deal with buyers, and control a weapon, may make it out of the street [of drug selling and hustling] and into the elite world of the superdealers. Getting behind the [weighing] scale is the first real step—indeed, the major move up in the cocaine business. . . .

Max runs part of his operation in a loosely organized way, hiring workers as needed to sell cocaine and crack in a variety of locations. He can draw from a sizable pool of teenagers who have dropped out of high school and are unemployed. Like workers in the above-ground economy, the kids have a chance to be promoted and make more money; many can look to an eventual move up behind the scale. (Williams 1989, p. 45)

The weakness and disarray of aging adults in criminal syndicates, for example the Mafia, in certain American cities have provided opportunities for many newcomer immigrant gangs. One such gang is the JHERI Kurls, a Dominican gang in uptown Manhattan:

Dominicans have emerged as New York's preeminent retail distributors of crack and powder cocaine—the foot soldiers of the Colombians. Manhattan District Attorney Robert M. Morgan . . . estimates that the JHERI Kurls are but one of about 40 Dominican drug gangs of comparable size and clout that have turned the long neck of upper Manhattan, where most New York's half-million Dominicans live, into the "crack capital of America."

Mostly illiterate and unable to speak English, these immigrants . . . receive bogus immigration papers, an appropriate permed hairdo and a plane ticket here. The aspiring traffickers start out under conditions akin to indentured servitude. . . .

Next up [in court] was 17-year-old Andre Gomez—accused of being a $750-a-week armed enforcer for the Martinez brothers. Mr. Gomez was until recently, a student at George Washington High School in Washington Heights. . . . Police say the school, now predominantly Dominican, is a major labor pool for the drug gangs. (Berkeley 1992)

Asian-American, Pacific, and Asian Gang Criminal-Organization Connections

Asian-American, Pacific, and Asian youth gangs comprise a broad range of youth or street gangs who generally are often better integrated into adult criminal societies than gangs of other racial or ethnic background, except white gangs. Certain historical, cultural, and community factors appear to account for these differences. Our discussion proceeds from relatively less-to-well-organized or integrated Asian youth and adult gangs.

Vietnamese, Korean, and Taiwanese Youth Gangs in the United States

Chin comments that Vietnamese, Taiwanese, and Korean youthful gang members are prone to use excessive violence in their criminal activities. They are involved primarily in extortion, robbery, and burglary. They are unlike Chinese-American gangs, at least those known to Chin, which are closely associated with well-established adult groups and controlled to a considerable degree by them. Vietnamese gangs tend to be loosely knit. They are not tied to a particular community that they can call their own turf. Because they are not embedded in Vietnamese communities, they are often extremely mobile, engaging in regional or nationwide crime sprees, committing a series of robberies from city to city. Chin states that Vietnamese youths from one city "team up with local Vietnamese criminal elements who provide them with information about victims and logistical support" (Chin 1990a, p. 74).

Although some Vietnamese youths have ties to individual adults in the adult crime groups, these "relationships tend to be sporadic and distant" (Vigil and Yun 1990, pp. 155–156). Peer pressures, supports, and controls are especially important. The peer groups provide "money, recreation, autonomy, and a sense of family." As yet they have neither the organizational nor value system of the Yakuza and Triad to depend on and guide them in the development of organized crime careers (ibid., pp. 155–156).

Vigil and Yun elaborate the social context in which Vietnamese gang youths are able to commit their crimes, mainly house burglaries, robberies, and assaults against Vietnamese families, recently arrived in the United States:

> Vietnamese . . . do keep cash at home and also tend to be leery of police and courts. Indeed, some law enforcement officials estimate that as many as 50 percent of the residential robberies go unreported as victims may be intimidated by the legal system, fearful of retaliation, or even unwilling to expose their own crimes, such as welfare fraud. . . . In addition, the simple fact that both the criminal and the victim often do not speak fluent English is another factor behind the intra-ethnic nature of the phenomena. (Vigil and Yun 1990, pp. 158–159)

Vietnamese and some Taiwanese youth gangs have no adult criminal organizations and businessmen's groups to emulate. They do not have connections with local community organizations. They do not have access to the stable protection and extortion operations of established crime organizations as is the case in many Chinese-American communities. Thus they are outside the established illegitimate opportunity structure and lack supervision and control by adult criminal elements (Chin 1990b, p. 139). Vietnamese youths must subsist on residential robberies as they bide their time until the development of and their integration into adult crime groups (Vigil and Yun 1990, pp. 157–158).

Chinese-American Gangs

Finally, we consider those Asian-American and Asian-born youth gangs most directly linked to organized crime. Chin states that the emergence of Chinese street gangs is closely related to the Tongs [i.e., certain businessmen's or community benevolent associations]. Street gangs were formed in the mid-1960s by newcomer Chinese students to protect themselves from other students, including more fully Americanized Chinese youths. When members dropped out of schools and began to hang around street corners in the community, Tong leaders hired them to run errands for gamblers and to protect the gambling places from outsiders and the police (1990b). Chin traces the historical socialization sequence as follows:

> In 1964, the first foreign-born Chinese gang known as Wah Ching (Youth of China) was organized by young immigrants to protect themselves from American-born Chinese. . . . A year later, when the immigration laws were changed, the Wah Ching rapidly evolved into a powerful gang by recruiting members from the influx of new arrivals. . . . Later, Wah Ching members became the soldiers of the Hip Sing Tong. The gang converted itself from an ordinary street gang into the youth branch of a well-established adult organization. (1990b, p. 68)

Chin emphasizes that Chinese gangs are different from Italian, black, and Hispanic crime groups, mainly because of the influence of the values and norms of the traditional criminal subculture of the Triad associations or traditional adult criminal societies. Chinese youth gangs may be less interested in status and protection of turf per se, in "ego trips" and "being the boss of their blocks" than youth gangs of other ethnic or cultural backgrounds. They are more interested in making money (Sung 1977, p. 72; see also Chin 1990b). They are far more involved in racket-type activities such as protection, extortion, robbery, prostitution and drug trafficking than most other youth gangs. Some are also involved in legitimate business dealings (Chin 1990a, p. 149).

Chinese youth gangs are said to be more closely connected to (Chinese) organized crime than almost any other recently arrived ethnic youth groups. They are more likely to be controlled by powerful local community organizations; they also invest their money in legitimate business; they sometimes become part of a national or international crime network; they go through various stages to qualify and become integrated into organized crime. New members are assigned to carry out the most serious assaults in systematically victimizing the businesses in their communities (Chin 1990a, pp. 136–139).

> In order to solidify the youth groups' connections to the Tongs, leaders of the youth groups are recruited into the Tongs through a Triad initiating ceremony. This way Tong officials can control the gang. . . . The gang leaders serve as middlemen between the Tong elders and the street soldiers. For this service, they receive from the Tong money that they distribute to their members. In addition, the leaders relay the elders' messages to other members. (Chin 1990b, pp. 98–99)

On the other hand, there is evidence that Chinese youth or street gangs vary across cities over time. Joe and Robinson (1980) observed that Chinese gangs in Vancouver were like other American gangs, fighting each other for status and turf. Although Chin reports that a youth gang leader can be extremely well paid, for example $3,400 for protection of a gambling parlor in New York's Chinatown (Chin 1990b, p. 62), Sung claimed that the amount of money made by Chinese gang youths in the same New York's Chinatown was exaggerated, ranging from $10 to $15 to a couple of hundred a week (Sung 1977, pp. 37–38). Chin also observes that emerging Chinese youth gangs in certain American communities can be engaged in street mugging and household robbery—patterns different from those of traditional Triad-inspired gangs (Chin 1990b, pp. 130–131).

Conclusion

Variable community structures, the specific nature of integration of criminal and conventional opportunities, and distinctive race/ethnic cultural traditions in particular locations at certain time periods, affect the linkage between youth or street gangs and organized crime. Adult crime groups are both a context and a spur to the development of youth-gang crime.

Gang members and drug dealers have developed symbiotic relationships in some inner-city slum neighborhoods. Established gangs in certain black inner-city communities have taken over from traditional neighborhood drug dealers. The distribution of narcotics is increasingly rationalized in these neighborhoods, but the threat of violence is also present in the control of gang narcotics turf. Traditional turf gang violence may continue to occur in many of these neighborhoods.

Certain African-American and possibly some Hispanic youth gangs are increasingly integrated with adult organizations, as Chinese youth gangs are now and Irish and Italian youth gangs were in the past. Prevention and control of youth gang crime must address the pattern of linkage between adult organized crime and specific youth gangs and their activity in particular communities. This linkage depends on both culture and ethnicity and on ecology, especially physical proximity or access to legitimate and illegitimate opportunities. These factors create distinctive problems for policy and practice at local and national levels.

II

Policy and Program

10

Theoretical Perspectives

This chapter elaborates and integrates a variety of theoretical and policy-relevant perspectives already touched on—societal, community, organizational, subcultural, and personality—to explain the gang problem. I will present a more systematic analysis of the ideas presented in earlier chapters, to set the stage for a discussion of institutional social planning and the development of a variety of organizational strategies for dealing with the youth-gang problem. The theoretical framework presented in Figure 10-1 seeks to explain primarily violent gang crime rather than economic gang crime. It offers some analysis of the interrelationships of these two types of crime.

The failure of structure or connectedness—a key concept—is addressed at various levels of analysis. A principal proposition of my analysis is that the cause of the youth gang problem, particularly its inception, is failure of societal, community, interorganizational, and organizational structures and processes as they relate to youths prone to become gang members. A major concern is the critical analysis and especially reinterpretation of existing theory of the gang problem in a way that is useful for planning policy, community, and organizational levels of action.

Poverty-related Theories

Most recent analysts assume that poverty straight and simple is the root cause of gangs and the violence they produce. Poverty creates problems. People who have low levels of income, whether on an absolute or relative basis in particular communities, are predisposed to more problems than people with high incomes. Poor families, particularly as they are concentrated in poor communities, have higher rates of personal and social problems. Yet there is no straight-line relationship between poverty and the production of gang problems. Furthermore, gang membership in interaction with, or as a response to, poverty is not necessarily a social problem. Many gang youths from poor families manage to leave gangs in due course and complete high school or its equivalent (some even go to college) and settle down to working- or middle-class lives. The notion of delinquent or criminal youth or street gangs is itself a variable.

A series of theories have developed since the mid-1950s to explain youth gangs and subcultures. These are macrostructural theories that focus on the social and economic environment as a primary source of *strain* or pressure on youths, including

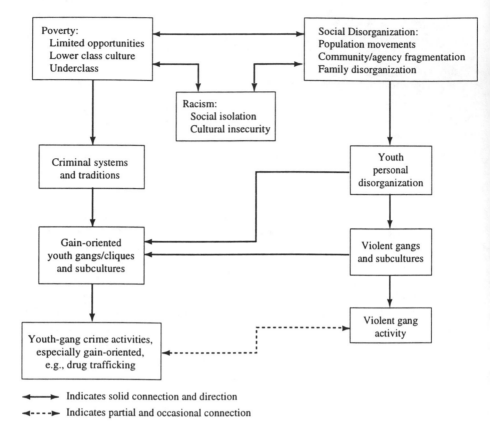

```
┌─────────────────────────┐              ┌──────────────────────────────────┐
│ Poverty:                │◄────────────►│ Social Disorganization:          │
│   Limited opportunities │              │   Population movements           │
│   Lower class culture   │◄────────────►│   Community/agency fragmentation │
│   Underclass            │              │   Family disorganization         │
└─────────────────────────┘              └──────────────────────────────────┘
```

Poverty:
  Limited opportunities
  Lower class culture
  Underclass

Social Disorganization:
  Population movements
  Community/agency fragmentation
  Family disorganization

Racism:
  Social isolation
  Cultural insecurity

Criminal systems and traditions

Youth personal disorganization

Gain-oriented youth gangs/cliques and subcultures

Violent gangs and subcultures

Violent gang activity

Youth-gang crime activities, especially gain-oriented, e.g., drug trafficking

◄────► Indicates solid connection and direction
◄----► Indicates partial and occasional connection

Figure 10.–1.   Youth gang crime: A theoretical framework.

those in gangs, which leads them to actions regarded as deviant by society or the local community. The theories seek to explain the formation of different types of delinquent or gang subcultures as a result of larger structural or cultural systems and forces. The discussion that follows briefly refers to classic opportunity and lower-class theories and also to more recently developed underclass theory. In general, I believe that strain theories better explain the nature, process, and development of gang adaptations than they do their cause, origin, or inception, which social disorganization theory perhaps explains better. Both sets of theories must be integrated to provide a satisfactory explanation of the problem, particularly as a basis for specific policy and social planning.

Strain Theories

Opportunity.   Cloward and Ohlin (1960) integrated certain notions of anomie or strain theory of Merton (1957) and a series of propositions derived from Chicago School sociologists (Shaw and McKay 1943; Sutherland and Cressey 1978) concerned with explaining delinquent behavior on the basis of availability and importance of neighborhood, peer, and adult learning environments. Cloward and Ohlin believed, with Merton, that Americans internalize certain cultural and economic success goals, but that not all are provided with adequate access to legitimate opportunities for achieving these goals. Young people then find alternate routes to success goals that depend on the extent and nature of opportunities, legitimate and illegitimate, available to them. In some communities, alternate significant criminal means are integrated with enough legitimate means to facilitate achievement of success. In other communities such routes are closed off. Conflict gang subcultures develop in these communities. They are alternate systems devised to achieve success under social and economic conditions where both good criminal and legitimate opportunities are in short supply.

Cloward and Ohlin's ideas were the basis for policies and programs sponsored by the President's Committee on Juvenile Delinquency and Youth Crime in the early 1960s (see W. Miller 1990), which assumed that structural conditions rather than individual personality defects accounted for high rates of delinquent behavior in certain sectors of society. Local social institutions, especially schools, had to be given more resources and induced to more effectively reach out to low-income minority youth. The emphasis on increased opportunities for young people in inner-city areas became a major component of the "War on Poverty." However, the distinction between delinquent and nondelinquent youths, whether or not gang related, may not have been sufficiently made in these policies and programs. The gang problem was often bypassed. Emphasis shifted away from individual delinquents or gang members to more general issues of local community economic development and political empowerment.

The ideas of Merton, Cloward, and Ohlin, without sufficient research support (Kornhauser 1978), continue to reverberate in many explanations of gang, delinquent group, or criminal behavior of lower-class youths. The distinctions among these are not made, however. Hagan notes, for example, that African-American youths who expected higher earnings in the street were more likely to participate in crime than those who did not. There was also evidence that the number of African-American males who perceived there were higher earnings to be made in crime relative to legitimate work rose in the booming '80s (Hagan 1992, p. 2). Sullivan, building on opportunity theory, added notions from segmented labor market theory (i.e., the differential availability and values of human capital) to explain the development of several kinds of delinquent subcultures in Brooklyn neighborhoods in the 1980s: "The young men we studied spoke of their criminal opportunities as 'getting over' and 'getting paid' [and] . . . reflect the perception of a social structure of restricted opportunity . . . 'Getting over' means beating the system, a rigged system in which one is unlikely to succeed by competing according to the rules" (Sullivan 1989, p. 2).

Labor market theory, according to Sullivan, states that there are "at least two labor markets: a 'primary' one in which steady employment at relatively high wages can support families, and a 'secondary' one in which low wage jobs, welfare, employment and training programs, informal economic activities, and crime must be alternated and combined because none of the economic activities alone can provide a steady living" (p. 11; see also Moore 1978). Variable age-role and conventional-criminal networks based on available opportunities apparently contribute to the development of different crime and youth gang patterns in the different neighborhoods.

Because of acquired poor motivation, limited education, and inadequate social relationships and job skills, youths are socialized to the lowest paying jobs, the welfare system, and street crime. This is not to deny that a few opportunities for high income and success may be accessible, particularly in the expanding drug trade. Many gang youths, as they grow up, also migrate back and forth across the different components of the segmented or tripartite market system (Moore 1978) from dependence on the family and its access to welfare, to marginal jobs, to various forms of individual and group supported crime that provide both status and income. Race/ethnic factors are regarded as especially important across both legitimate and illegitimate opportunity systems. School drop-out rates, for example, seem to handicap African-Americans and Hispanics most in terms of access to the primary labor market jobs.

Lower-class Theory

While Cloward and Ohlin saw delinquent subcultures and gangs as deviant phenomena, W. Miller, in his early formulation of lower-class theory and discussions of gang behavior (1958), did not view gang behavior as seriously aberrant but rather as preparatory to adult roles in lower-class communities. He stated that the lower-class culture emphasizes certain focal concerns, particularly for male youths: "trouble," "toughness," "smartness," "excitement," "fate," "autonomy." Female-based households also create a need for male youths to assert masculinity outside the home. The gang is a context for developing these traits that will be useful to youths in their adaptation often to dull and meaningless adult jobs and the uncertainties of life in lower-class communities. Gang members were not engaged in serious intergang violence and relatively more violent behavior occurred among members in the same group than between members of opposing gangs. Lower-class delinquency was a normal response to sociostructural and cultural demands. The gang served normal socialization functions, and gang members were not regarded as particularly troubled psychologically.

In his writings after the mid-1970s, however, Miller emphasized the extremely violent behavior of gang members (see W. Miller 1975). He believes that the contemporary lower class is not a "new social class created by a new set of demographic, technological, and economic conditions" in which lower-class youth are increasingly locked out of the labor market. The idea of "'underclass' represents a logical historical development of a traditional population category" and the "underclass notion has little relevance to the newcomer gang phenomenon" (W. Miller 1990, pp. 279–282). Miller essentially adopts a "culture of poverty" view to explain the self-perpetuation of gang life, a view that emphasizes the adaptational aspects of the gang. Other analysts share this view, for example:

> Street life in the ghetto is exhilarating—at least in the short run. In a world where jobs are dull, arduous, or difficult to obtain and hold, it is more fun to hang out, make love, listen to and tell exaggerated stories of love and danger, plan parties and escapades, and exhibit one's latest purchases or conquests. Gangs provide young people thrills, protection, mutual support, friendship, prestige, and enough income to allow them to buy fashionable clothes, alcohol, and drugs. (Peterson 1991, p. 42)

We do not believe that lower-class cultural or subculture theory is sufficient to explain the development of youth gangs, let alone its inception. A culture or a subculture is a "system of widely shared beliefs and values and a set of characteristic behaviors used in organizing social process." The culture includes an ideology, a cognitive map or framework within which people explain their own characteristics and their relations to others of different cultures [subcultures or gangs] (Whyte and Whyte 1991, pp. 270–271). However, a subculture arises out of efforts of people to solve social, economic, psychological, developmental, and even political problems. Furthermore, the existence of a culture, subculture, or gang does not mean that it offers optimal solutions to these problems.

Underclass Theory

The most popular and influential theory currently to explain a whole range of socially disordered or deviant behaviors, particularly in African-American inner-city communities, is Wilson's underclass theory. It rejects a simple "culture of poverty" thesis "on the right . . . or a racist explanation on the left" (W. Wilson 1991, p. 462). Wilson's version of the underclass attempts to integrate social structural, social-psychological, and cultural variables in a systematic formulation. Wilson suggests that those groups in socially isolated neighborhoods that have "few legitimate employment opportunities, inadequate job information networks and poor schools not only give rise to weak labor force attachment but also raise the likelihood that people will turn to illegal or deviant activities for income" (ibid., p. 472). Wilson does not primarily address the problem of gang formation but indicates it is one of several problems, particularly in the inner cities of the Northeast and Midwest, that can be theoretically explained by underclass theory, as he has formulated it.

The specific factors or clusters of variables that comprise his theory are both "exogenous" and "endogenous":

> The exogenous factors, representing the sources of the racial concentration of urban poverty, include racial discrimination, changes in the economy that relocated industries and restructured occupations, and political processes (anti-bias legislation and affirmative action programs) that have had the unanticipated consequence of widening class divisions among urban blacks. The endogenous determinants created by these exogenous factors include such demographic variables as urban migration, age structures, and the pool of marriageable men, and economic factors such as the distribution of employment and income. These variables are important for understanding the experiences of all low-income urban groups not just the ghetto underclass.
>
> The endogenous determinants further include social isolation which is unique to the social environment of the underclass. Social isolation deprives residents of inner-city neighborhoods not only of resources and conventional role models whose former presence buffered the effects of neighborhood joblessness, but also of cultural learning from mainstream social networks that facilitates social and economic advancement in modern industrial society. The lack of neighborhood material resources, the relative absence of conventional role models, and the circumscribed cultural learning produce outcomes, or concentration effects that restrict social mobility. Some of these

outcomes are structural (lack of labor force attachment and access to informal job networks) and some are social-psychological (negative social disposition, limited aspirations, and casual work habits). (W. Wilson 1987, pp. 462– 463)

There are limits to an all-encompassing theory of underclass to explain a large range of social problems, including gangs and violent crime, particularly in the African-American and the Hispanic communities. Jencks and Peterson observe that the education levels of African-American youths, in fact, have been rising in recent decades as measured by high-school graduation and achievement level. But standards of the job market as well as aspirations of low-income youths may be rising at a faster pace (Jencks and Peterson 1991). A recent article in *The New York Times*, based on an analysis of census data, indicates that the white-black disparity in income narrowed in the 1980s. The median household income of blacks and Hispanics is certainly higher in those states, and probably in those cities, where the gang problem is most severe than in states where household income is relatively and absolutely lower. Relative poverty appears to be more explanatory of the gang problem than absolute poverty. But even relative poverty or prosperity may be insufficient to explain current high gang crime rates (Barringer 1992).

Wilson's formulation does not explain the development of specific types of gang problems. He does not identify the factors that contribute to varying youth gang adaptations in different cultures and communities. His formulation, in addition, insufficiently recognizes the different importance of public policy, local community, and agency program responses, which serves to elaborate and intensify the development of youth gang subcultures and systems. Nevertheless, the underclass formulation, or variations of it, has been a useful basis for explaining gang development and its sustenance by gang researchers and scholars, particularly in African-American inner-city communities. Hagedorn "looks at the minority gangs of the 1980s as including both juveniles and young adults and as a fraction of a forming underclass" (Hagedorn 1988, p. X1; 1990). More recently Hagedorn has stated that underclass theory is insufficient to explain the presence of gangs and violence in lower-class communities where significant proportions of working class African Americans continue to live. Such communities, he indicates, lack sufficient development of local institutions of social control and citizen mobilization (Hagedorn 1991).

Anderson finds underclass theory a powerful explanation of why African-American youths "join the criminal underground":

> With rising unemployment, brought on in part by increasing deindustrialization and the exodus of major corporations, the local black community suffered. The employment lives of its members are further complicated by continuing racial prejudice and discrimination, which often frustrate efforts to make effective adjustments to these changes and the emerging reality. Many who have difficulty finding work in the regular economy become even poorer and may join the criminal underground. (Anderson 1990, p. x)

Gangs and gang violence are assumed to be directly proportional to the development of an underclass or the degree of limitation on available social and economic resources according to a number of analysts:

The theme of survival is an important one to young men. . . . Few have experienced anything but severe economic deprivation throughout most of their lives. They were not accorded the comfort of material security during formative years, and they find themselves at the brink of adulthood without requisite education or training to compete successfully in the labor market. . . . (Krisberg 1974, p. 116)

The "War on Poverty" is a perpetual state of conflict for those who are socially and economically trapped in the underclass. The welfare rolls are the "Selective Service" for potential gang members of both the scavenger and territorial groups with final graduation to the corporate stage. (Taylor 1990a, p. 107)

Vigil made use of a variety of concepts—poverty, racism, segregation, segmented labor markets, also Mexican lower-class [cholo] culture—in a metatheoretical framework, similar to William Wilson's underclass, to explain the gang problem. Vigil developed the idea of "multiple marginality" and applied it to Mexican-American gang youths in the Los Angeles area:

Multiple marginality encompasses the consequences of barrio life, low socioeconomic status, street socialization and enculturation, and problematic development for self-identity. The gang features arise in a web of ecological, socioeconomic, cultural, and psychological factors. . . .

The small percentage of barrio youth who become affiliated with a gang are generally members of the underclass. They are affected by the economic hardships of this life before entering the streets. Such socioeconomic difficulties are related to troubled families, problems with schooling, limited job opportunity and even dress styles.(Vigil 1988, pp. 9, 53)

Vigil applied his concept of multiple marginality as an all-purpose explanation of gang formation to other cultural and ethnic groups, including Vietnamese gangs:

The effects of the Vietnam War, low socioeconomic status, governmental neglect, culture conflict, and racism have manifested themselves in multiple interrelated stresses and pressures. This marginality complex, in turn, prevents many youths from attaining their version of the American dream via the traditional pathways of education and hard work. Unable to adopt the dominant culture, they turn to gangs as a means of acquisition without assimilation. (Vigil and Yun 1990, p. 147)

Poverty is at the heart of the underclass formulation—and the absence of economic resources leads to distress and compensatory efforts to achieve some form of economic and successful social adjustment. T. Williams observed that those youths, mainly African-American and Latino boys and girls, involved in posses engaged in distributing or selling cocaine in New York City, came from families whose incomes:

are below the poverty line, and from neighborhoods where there is little chance to rise above that line. . . .

Many teenagers are drawn to work in the cocaine trade simply because they want jobs, full time or even as, casual labor—the drug business is a safety net of sorts, a place where it is always possible to make a few dollars. Teens are also pulled by the flash and dazzle, and by the chance to make big money, and pushed by the desire to be somebody. . . .

Money and drugs are the immediate rewards for kids in the cocaine trade. But there is another strong motivating force, and that is the desire to show family and friends that they can succeed at something. Moving up a career ladder and making money is especially important where there are few visible opportunities. (T. Williams 1989, pp. 8, 10)

As indicated above, Joan Moore in her recent research seriously questions the proposition that poverty or segmented labor markets is sufficient to explain Mexican-American gang phenomena and specifically violent behavior among males and especially females. Many of the families generating gang youths are "acutely unhappy" with highly conflictual relations between parents and problems of alcoholism, drug addiction, mental illness, and incest prevalent. Furthermore, she questions whether gang members come from "desperately poor families." Most respondents (61%) in her survey of former or older gang members felt "they were no poorer than most other people in the barrio . . . slightly more than a third owned their own homes. . . . In only a handful of male members' households was nobody working" (Moore 1991, pp. 88–89).

Social Disorganization

Another set of major theories explaining the gang problem revolves around the notion of social disorganization. These theories are independent of poverty-related theories, including underclass. I believe that social disorganization better and more specifically explains the origin of youth gangs at different levels of analysis. Both types of theories are interactive and necessary to fully explain gang problems and formulate public policy. Nevertheless, there is evidence that the conditions of social and personal disorganization may be a more direct and powerful precipitant of the gang problem than is poverty or underclass per se.

Social disorganization refers to the ineffective articulation of elements of social structure, and even the personality system, at various levels of value, action, and relationship. At societal and community levels, social disorganization is often associated with, or a consequence of, large and rapid population movements of minority low-income or working-class groups; social, political, economic changes or political disruption, for example, the influx of a minority population from another country, or from central city to smaller cities, towns, or the suburbs; war or revolution; rapid industrialization or urbanization; a radical shift in the labor market; or the failure of key socializing and control institutions, such as schools, law enforcement, employers, and youth agencies to understand and develop policy and programs to appropriately meet the needs of a different, new, or changing population. These social structural elements may be distinct yet interacting.

The concept of social disorganization may also signify a failure by individual youths to effectively mesh personal motivations, norms, values, and activities with those of their family; by parents or family units to mesh with organizations such as the school; or by organizations to mesh within or across each other in a community over a significant period of time. This is not to deny that individual personalities, gangs, organizations, communities, and even the society may be successfully organized for particular and limited purposes. In many social contexts, gangs partially meet their own social, economic, and cultural or subcultural needs as well as sometimes those of people in their community, and even of the general society under certain conditions for a particular—usually short—period of time.

The variables of social disorganization can be conceptualized as independent of poverty, racism, culture conflict, or acculturation, as well as created or modifiable by these factors. Poverty creates conditions of social disorganization, but social disorganization in turn can create conditions leading to poverty. Social disorganization can provide the basic stimulus for the formation of youth gangs, usually (but not always) in interaction with the effects of poverty. The youth gang arises under circumstances in which the social relatedness—usually the structural or connectedness—needs of its members have not been adequately satisfied by local community institutional capacities and arrangements. Vulnerable youths find each other and create, or join already established, peer groups to meet these needs.

The extent of the disorganization, as conditioned especially by limited opportunities and cultural factors in a particular organizational or community context, determines the distinctive character of the youth gang problem. While members of youth or street gangs may have a similar range of psychological or social psychological characteristics, they may yet have distinctive features by virtue of such factors as community socioeconomic level; age distribution; type of available opportunities (criminal or conventional); race/ethnicity, institutional racism, or particular cultural tradition; and degree of social isolation. Thus, vulnerable African-American, Asian (or particular ethnic Asian), Pacific Island, Hispanic (especially Mexican-American or Puerto Rican), and white youth gangs (e.g., Irish, Italian, Albanian), share certain traits, yet they may develop different organizational arrangements and patterns of criminal and noncriminal behaviors. Social policy and programming must be related to the configuration of these causal factors in particular communities.

Classic, or even currently modified, conceptions of social disorganization, like poverty-related theories thus may be too general and ultimately too simplistic to explain the formation of different kinds of youth gangs. Shaw and McKay and other theorists have focused on delinquency or crime rates rather than on the differential character of delinquency or crime on a particular community basis. They proposed that three structural factors—low economic status, ethnic heterogeneity, and residential mobility—lead to community disruption or social disorganization, which in turn accounts for variations in crime and delinquency rates (see Shaw and McKay 1943; Bursik 1988; Sampson and Groves 1989). However, Shaw and McKay and the other authors do not specify distributions of types of delinquency and crime or gang behaviors by these structural factors.

Classic social disorganization theory focused on the ability of local communities to realize the common values of local residents in solving their commonly experienced problems (see Thomas and Znaniecki 1918; Kornhauser 1978). Emphasis was on the weakness of local citizen-group self-regulation, that is, the inability of neighborhood groups to supervise the behavior of fellow residents, especially youths. Effective social controls were viewed as absent in disorganized communities. Social control was not necessarily equated with social repression but with the collective pursuit of shared values and the ability of its sectors to mutually regulate each other. Emphasis, however, particularly by Shaw and McKay (1943), was primarily on informal social networks, rather than also on interorganizational networks or the meshing of individual and institutional norms and values (however, see Bursik and Grasmick 1993).

The relationship of high gang-crime rates and social or citizen participation rates may not have been adequately specified by poverty-related and social disorganization theorists. Both peer friendship and adult citizen groups may abound in a particular neighborhood, but they may not be adequately interrelated to become sources of legitimate opportunities or role modeling for gang youths. Gang youths may be in conflict with each other and often with other community groups in high gang-crime areas. The presence of a large number of local community adult organizations that are poorly integrated with each other does not necessarily signify a high degree of integration with, or control of, local community youth or street gangs. High gang-crime rate areas are not necessarily areas with low organizational or citizen participation. Rather the reverse can be argued (see New York City Youth Board 1960; Spergel 1976; Williams 1989; Chin 1990b).

Also, communities with the highest rates of crime and delinquency are not necessarily communities with the highest rates of gang problems. The problems of gangs and of delinquency or crime are overlapping but not the same. Different formulations are required to explain the development of different kinds of gangs and the increase in the gang problem in particular places, organizations, and communities over time. Poverty-related variables may be relatively more important in explaining crime generally than in explaining the formation of gangs. Poverty per se, however, may not be a critically important condition in gang formation. Serious gang problems may arise during periods of rapid social and economic development or economic boom, as well as during times of sudden economic decline.

Population Movement

A principal factor and indicator of social disorganization across culture, race/ethnicity, and community, (but controlling for socio-economic status) appears to be significant or mass population movements. This is not to deny that immigrant populations can arrive and settle in many communities without the development of gang problems. This is particularly true when forces for family and cultural cohesion are strong. Bursik and Grasmick state that "rapid population turnover and heterogeneity can decrease the ability of a neighborhood to control itself in order to provide an environment relatively free of crime" (1993, pp. 33–34). This can occur because institutions that contribute to effective social controls are difficult to establish when residents are planning to leave at the first opportunity. Informal structures of neighborhood resident controls are less likely when "local networks are in a continual state of flux," and when the local populations are heterogeneous, communication among the different groups is poor, and common local problems and goals and means to solve them are not present" (ibid.).

Pitchess described the formation and development of gangs resulting from major population movements in the Los Angeles area, including migration and population displacements of Mexicans and Mexican-Americans, during three historical periods:

Between 1910 and 1925, great influxes of immigrants [came] from Mexico due to the revolution and political instability. . . . Rivalries developed between the different areas which eventually evolved into our first gangs. Gangs such as Bunker Hill, North Broadway, Boyle Heights, Maravilla, and San Fernando became well-known.

The depression of the 1930s and the pre-World War II era attracted families from Arizona, New Mexico, and Texas. These new-comers, as well as those in the geographical areas already mentioned, fragmented into several groups, each claiming its own territory or turf. This brought about gangs with names like . . . Happy Valley, Hoyo Soto, Alpine, Hazard, El Hoyo Mara, Little Valley, White Fence.

Freeway displacement in the 1960s created a movement of families from the central city areas. Most moved eastward into the eastern area of Los Angeles County. This created more new gangs, such as Lomas and Bassett. Urban renewal, the ethnic migration eastward, and the urge of some parents to escape this type of environment in the 60s and early 70s created new gang territories in the so-called suburbs. Gangs formed with names like El Monte, Flores, Barrio, Norwalk, Peaceful Valley, Dog Patch, etc. (Pitchess 1979, pp. 1–2)

Several gang researchers do not sufficiently recognize the importance of these population movements. Moore, despite her emphasis on poverty or underclass as the prime causal factor of gangs, admits that "After World War II, when the two gangs [she studied in her recent research] became established, Los Angeles enjoyed a *spectacular post-war boom* [italics added]" (1991, p. 13). She observes that "the 1970s and 1980s saw a dramatic increase in immigration from Mexico to Los Angeles County . . . as always Boyle Heights and East Los Angeles were ports of entry for many immigrants. . . . New waves of Mexican immigrants have continued to settle in poor Mexican barrios, as those barrios were vacated by upwardly mobile residents" (pp. 17–18). These are the areas, especially East Los Angeles, that have again experienced major and record increases in gang violence in recent years.

Vigil, despite his metatheoretical notion of "multiple marginality" including "choloization" and racism, also refers to immigration and the cultural transition process as creating social disorganization that, in turn leads to or solidifies gang culture:

It is this cultural transition process that creates the confusion and ambiguity that affect youths' sense of cultural identity and loyalty. When ethnic boundaries are weakened by cultural change, as happens in the cultural transition process between the first and second generations, there is a change in the ethnic group's ability to command and retain the involvement, attention, and identity of its members. In such circumstances, a [gang] subculture based on new boundaries evolves and becomes a cohesive cultural system . . . .

These newcomers . . . have learned to "gang" together to protect and defend themselves from aggression and threats posed by established gangs. In recent years, there has been a proliferation of such new Latino gangs throughout the area, some of which, have even replaced the older gangs. (Vigil 1990, pp. 122, 127)

Vigil also states that gangs can arise as a consequence of a major war when no positive role models or adequate learning environments are available and existing institutional arrangements have been disrupted:

As these events unfolded, World War II took many positive Mexican male role models away from the barrios (neighborhoods) to fight the war; ironically, this occurred soon after segments of the population had been repatriated. The males that were left in the community for the younger cohort to look up to were those rejected from service, with criminal records, and usually the poorest of the poor cholos. Thus "model absence" was a major turning point in transforming the boy gang into a gang. (Vigil 1990, p. 118)

Population movement has been a key (but not sufficient) component of social disorganization, not only in changing Hispanic but also African-American communities throughout the United States. As white and middle-class African-American populations have left inner cities and retreated to the suburbs, as African-American populations have moved across neighborhoods in large cities, back South, and to smaller cities and also to the suburbs, both older segregated neighborhoods and communities from which they have come and the newer resegregating neighborhoods and communities to which they have moved have become arenas for gang development. Short writes:

It is notable that Chicago's supergangs of the 1960s emerged in communities characterized by recent and rapid population turnover. Chicago's most notorious supergang, the "Black P. Stone Nation," began in the community of Woodlawn, which like Lawndale, had recently and rapidly undergone racial transition. Other supergangs arose in communities of recently arrived immigrants from Puerto Rico and Mexico.

These communities lacked stable populations and institutions. . . . The supergangs emerged as multi-purpose institutions. (Short 1990a, p. 219)

Immigration or emigration, rapidly expanding or contracting populations, and/or the incursion of different racial/ethnic groups or even different segments or generations of the same racial/ethnic population, can create fragmented communities and gang problems. This is again illustrated in recent accounts of Asian, particularly Chinese and Vietnamese, immigration to cities on the East and West Coast:

As waves of Chinese and Southeast Asian immigrants flood New York in search of better lives, their expanding neighborhoods are being plagued by increasingly violent street gangs and new criminal enterprises that law enforcement officials say may come to rival the Mafia in its heyday.

The crimes, concentrated almost entirely in the hardworking Chinese community itself, are likely to mount even more as three forces separately challenge the traditional order of the Tongs, the fraternal order that ruled Chinatown for generations.

One is the growth of street gangs fighting for control of burgeoning Asian communities in Queens and Brooklyn. Another is an effort by the Hong Kong Criminal Triad Societies to establish a foothold in New York in anticipation of the 1997 Communist takeover of the Colony. The third is the emergence of a ruthlessly violent young generation of Vietnamese. (Kifner 1991)

Ko-Lin Chin has elaborated the idea of social disorganization into three components: structural, cultural, and political. He observes that with liberalizing changes in U.S. immigration policy,

the increasing number of Chinese immigrating to the United States has affected the stability of the Chinese communities in unprecedented ways. Traditional groups such as the family and district associations were ill prepared to cope with the influx. . . . The breakdown in support coupled with the growth of the Chinese population in isolated and fragmented communities brought a corresponding increase in criminal activities among the Chinese. (Chin 1990a, pp. 129–130)

Chin notes that many organizations—benevolent societies, social agencies, and district associations—exist in the Chinatown community, but they are often inward-looking or have limited resources. "They frequently vie for control in the community, are plagued by high staff turnover, and have little support from community residents. Businesses within the community show little interest in the community's affairs, perhaps because they are often victimized by local crime groups and distrustful of people with whom they could not identify" (Chin 1990b, p. 51). Chin observes there may also be cultural clashes among the different Chinese now settled in New York's Chinatown. Youth gangs arise to defend the ethnic enclaves from the incursions of other ethnic Chinese youth gangs. This pattern of fragmentation within a particular ethnic or racial group is fundamentally the same in many newly settled Mexican-American, Puerto Rican, and even established African-American inner-city communities that have developed their own ethnic, generational, or subcultural enclaves and identities that have to be defended (see also Suttles 1968):

> Cultural values are weakened and become obsolete. The values of each subgroup of the community are not compatible with those of other subgroups or with those of the mainstream society. The norms and values of the Fook Chow, Chui Chao, Cantonese, and Hakka coexist within the community and are followed closely in intra-group interactions. However, when people of diverse groups come into contact, there are no communal norms to follow. As a result, social interactions among residents of different ethnic origins are often filled with misunderstanding and tension. In addition, the isolation of Chinatown from the rest of the society makes American values and norms irrelevant within the community. (Chin 1990b, p. 51)

Finally, Chin observes that New York's Chinatown is politically fragmented: "The associations are divided according to their political orientation in the conflict between the Kuomin-Tang and the Chinese Communists. The associations themselves are fragmented internally. Within each organization, many factions are involved in power struggles" (Chin 1990b, p. 52).

The notion of political fragmentation or community disorganization, as suggested in an earlier discussion of gangs and process, is relevant in many newcomer Latino or Hispanic communities. Recently in Chicago, aldermanic candidates vied with each other for elective office, and each was supported by different gang as well as community organization factions.

Agency/Community Group Fragmentation and Its Consequences

Population change—the "incursion" of a new ethnic group and the exodus of the "old" or established population groups—may result in disruption of existing institutional contact and service patterns, both at formal and informal levels. The new population may be of a different racial or ethnic and/or class origin and class composition— usually lower-income. The established population group tends to comprise solid leadership or middle-class elements. In the process of large-scale, rapid, social mobility or population change, patterns of relationship between the newcomer and established or residual groups are often strained. There is a failure to understand the other population's norms and values. Youth gangs are sensitive to these differences and act out parental and community fears, threats, and hostile intentions through attacking or defending against newcomer groups at school, on the streets, and in other public places.

With the arrival of new racial/ethnic groups in the community, local agencies and established institutions may fail to understand the degree of suspicion and tension that arises among the new competing or mutually suspicious groups. Churches, schools, youth agencies, and local community organizations begin to lose their old constituencies. The community's churches increasingly draw their congregations from elsewhere in the cities or suburbs where the "old" population now resides. The established organizations may suffer a loss of funding from local sources and do not feel comfortable educating or serving new clientele and parishioners. Local organizations may not understand or have the communication abilities to develop sensitive relationships and serve newcomer youths and their often unresponsive families.

The problem of social distance is particularly severe in school and law enforcement situations. The staff of these institutions and the newcomer population or clientele to be served are in frequent contact with each other, but mutually acceptable and co-productive relationships are not easily developed. The white teacher or even the middle-class minority group teacher or police officer has difficulty identifying with and meeting the needs of the newcomer population or lower-class population that now is concentrated in the area. The gang arises to provide the missing socialization, social support, and control functions. There seem to be only limited ways these different populations, groups, and organizations can work together.

Social distance or disruption of local agency or organizational patterns is often a response to larger political, cultural, economic, and social forces, particularly radical change in government policy and social movements. Youth gangs develop and thrive during times of institutional crisis and rapid change. Youth gangs entered a period of rapid growth as well as innovative corporate development in Los Angeles, New York, Chicago, and Philadelphia in the 1960s. The change in the character of gangs and the increased severity of criminal gang behavior occurred during the height of the antipoverty programs and in the midst of the civil rights movement. Economic conditions were improving for low-income groups, and additional civil and political rights were accorded to minority groups, yet youth gangs grew larger, better organized, and more criminalized (Spergel 1969, 1972; Poston 1971; Short 1976).

Hagedorn observes that Milwaukee's and Columbus's school desegregation process "shattered black neighborhoods" and scattered black children all over the city. "This weakened social controls in the neighborhoods, and the black gangs developed in part to fill some of this social control vacuum" (Hagedorn 1990, p. 4):

Desegregation in Milwaukee was not the "forward step" hoped for by the Civil Rights Movement. Instead it increased the alienation of black youths . . . the scattering of black students in schools throughout the city reduced the ability of black parents and neighbors to participate in the schools and help control the emerging gang problem. . . . The public schools no longer community institutions of training and control had no relationship to the neighborhoods and were ineffective for both education and social control. (ibid., pp. 137–138).

Schools, police and youth agencies in changing communities may also not coordinate their internal or external organizational efforts in dealing with gang or gang-prone youths. The police gang unit may fail to collect and share information about gang youths with the narcotics or youth division as well as with other units of the justice system, such as prosecution, judges, probation, or correction, or vice versa, as well as with community groups. Many organizations may be in conflict with each other for ideological reasons or simply as they compete for scarce resources. It is common knowledge that the criminal justice system is "not characterized by a smoothly functioning system, but rather by a fragmented amalgam of agencies which lack central coordination" (Manikas et al. 1990, p. 100). Manikas and his associates in their analysis of the Cook County juvenile justice system conclude that juvenile justice and community-based organizations, including mental health agencies, "share few relationships." Agencies become self-contained subsystems, and as a result policy is not effectively coordinated and "children are suspended between warring agencies, and the minors often languish in the Juvenile Temporary Detention Center" (ibid., p. 104).

There is also a history of exploitation of gang problems in disorganized communities, particularly when consensus among key organizations, basic rules of discourse, and civil relationships break down. In the 1960s, some antigang programs were used by agencies or community organizations to fight City Hall (Spergel 1969, 1972). Some civil rights organizations attempted to co-opt gangs to their cause. Some foundations, federal agencies, churches, and community groups viewed gangs, and still view them, as a source of influence to support or justify their social causes. They may see the function of gangs as that of stabilizing communities that may be on the verge of riot and disorder (see Bursik and Grasmick 1993). Some politicians see gangs as suppliers of manpower to turn out the vote in their favor and intimidate opposition candidates. Youth gangs, however, are usually not sufficiently well organized or competent to meet or sustain the expectations of these would-be sponsors or manipulators (see Poston 1971; Spergel 1972).

Family Disorganization

Family disorganization is also viewed as a key social and psychosocial dynamic contributing to gang development. Coleman observes that, at the end of the twentieth century, the family as an original building block of social organization moved "from the center to the periphery of society. Into its place has moved constructed social organization exemplified by the modern bureaucracy. This is organization by design, organization constructed for a purpose, and organization intended to be functionally rational" (Coleman 1990, p. 101). The gang is a primordial organization functional in those communities where both family and modern organization are insufficient and ineffective in their relationships with each other to meet the needs of support, control, and socialization of certain youths.

The presence of social and economic opportunities, or human capital, is not sufficient to generate useful social adaptations for youths. The opportunities must be organized or structured in appropriate fashion (social capital), especially but not exclusively at the family level, for the youth to develop into a conforming adult. The availability of social and economic resources through parents does not guarantee positive achievement for the child. Chin observes that Asian immigrants, particularly Chinese families, although intact do not perform appropriate social functions. Both parents may be present and working long hours without sufficient time to supervise youths (Chin 1990b, pp. 95–96). Parents may not understand the importance of education for the youth's future social and economic development. A communications barrier may exist between the family and important institutions in the community, preventing parents from accessing and making use of resources to socialize their offspring. Gang youths—who usually speak English quite well— often participate in a subtle process of manipulation, cutting off communication between parents who do not speak English and school officials (see Vigil and Yun 1990, pp. 152–153).

A variety of analysts indicate that the strong sense of social isolation and personal stress begins with the child's or youth's problematic relationship in the family:

> The great majority of gang members interviewed for this study report family histories full of stress, and many of them explicitly maintain that they become involved with a gang (at least in part) to seek the kind of support they felt was lacking from family sources. . . . [after a youth's father's death] "My mother could not take care of the house, her children. . . . I began to feel lonely and started a complex that my mother didn't love me because she didn't take care of me the way she used to. . . . As I got older . . . I was not able to communicate with anyone, not even the teacher or the rest of the people at school." (Vigil 1988b, pp. 44–45)

Joan Moore reports that a surprisingly large proportion of gang members—even in notorious gangs—were able to conceal their membership from their parents because "parents are working, are preoccupied with a large family, and often just believe that their child is out playing with one of the numerous other adolescent groups in the neighborhood." (Moore 1990, p. 73). Parental rejection is often associated with peer group selection by the youth gang member. Upwardly mobile as well as personally troubled parents may not be sufficiently committed to a traditional family support system and too preoccupied with their own problems to sufficiently attend to the needs of their children.

At the same time, gang youths do not appear to verbalize a great deal of anger or resentment against parents, and may indeed be quite attached to and respectful of parents. They feel mainly alienated.

> "I was full of hot blood. I had all sorts of energy. I found that my parents were like anchors, trying to hold me down from all the glory I could obtain. There was no animosity toward them. It was stand back and let me do my own thing". . . .

"Yeah. My mother always said that my heart was restless. She used to tell me to cut it out, but I couldn't. I was intoxicated by the streets. I couldn't stay home. . . . I think my parents were pretty cool." (Sung 1977, pp. 30, 41)

Racism

There is some controvertible evidence that racism acts indirectly and powerfully on the creation and development of the gang problem as well as a variety of other human problems. Racism may contribute directly to minority group segregation and poverty and to conditions of social disorganization that in turn more directly precipitate gang formation of criminal or violent gang behavior. Racism is also likely to be characteristic of a community agency's response to gangs once identified as a problem. Racism has been defined by some analysts in rather broad terms—perhaps too broad for specific understanding and purposes of dealing with the gang problem. In a recent New York State report on the youth gang problem, the concept of racism, from a social psychological perspective, is divided into two components: Personal and Institutional:

> *Personal racism* involves those attitudes that individuals hold, and subsequent behaviors that they perform which are prejudicial and discriminatory. Personal racism involves the name calling, bias-related violence, overt physical oppression, sexual harassment and a plethora of other activities they impart to certain classes or categories of people. The effects of personal racism upon those who are its victims include the development of low self-esteem, feelings of hopelessness and helplessness as well as the acquisition of those aggressive behaviors which often characterize living within a hostile environment.
>
> *Institutional racism* is the systematic denial of a group of people to the power, privilege, and prestige that is available within an existing culture or society. The effects of institutional racism include issues of access to power (social and economic), resources, as well as affiliation. Such limited access to power is a direct result of the fear of those who are in power to relinquish their position. Indirectly people who are in power fear becoming victims themselves. The fact that certain classes of people are denied access to the "in-group" and its resources, often leads those very same individuals to form groups of their own, often anti-establishment in nature, which are then characterized by the established groups as "antisocial," such as gangs, posses, or clubs. (Dunston 1990, pp. 16–17)

Racism represents a deep sense of both personal and system insecurity, fear, and hatred of the stranger or the person who is regarded as very different from oneself and the established or dominant community. There is some consensus that racism seriously handicaps minority youths, particularly African-Americans, in the job market (Sullivan 1989). Racism has been included as one of the key factors concentrating "urban black poverty family disruption in the inner city" (Sampson and Wilson 1991, p. 9). Street youths in the inner city are seen as "demoralized by racism" and "lack an outlook and sensibility that would allow them to negotiate the wider system of employment and society in general" (Anderson 1990, p. 66).

Vigil claims that racism transformed the relatively benign Mexican-American boy gang, not very different from the *palomilla*, a traditional male cohorting cultural pattern, into a serious, enduring, violent gang phenomenon. He asks what "led to this transformation and acceleration of boy gang to gang?" His answer is that "racist practices in schools, public facilities, and the like . . . added insult to injury" and that one reaction was "an increase by some Mexicans in challenging and somewhat antisocial behavior, especially among the second generation youths" (Vigil 1990, pp. 118–119).

The Zoot Suit Riots were regarded by Vigil and others as a watershed in the development of Mexican-American youth gangs. Second generation Mexican youths:

> liked to consider themselves Americans but . . . realized they were being rejected . . . the response of such individuals often was aimed at proving that they were Americans, by frequenting restricted movie theaters, swimming pools and restaurants, with the understanding and expectation that they might be turned away. Approximating a mild form of antisocial behavior, such incidents became even more inflamed during World War II, when the Zoot Suit Riots erupted. Preceded by a steady increase in Anglo-American friction, these 1943 riots culminated with servicemen and Anglo citizens hunting down and beating up Mexican youths dressed in "zoot-suits". . . . The events of this period mark the beginning of the "labeling" of the youths as gang members; the labeling in turn led to an intensification of gang participation. (Vigil 1990, pp. 118–119)

At the same time, Vigil and Long are aware that gang problems have increased as racism and discrimination have declined over the past four or five decades, but claim that " . . . although many of the more overt forms of racial discrimination against Mexican-Americans have lessened dramatically since the 1960s, opportunities for unskilled workers to find permanent productive roles in the local economy also have decreased dramatically" (Vigil and Long 1990, p. 66). The assumption is that change in the local economy contributes to racism in some complex and undefinable fashion.

These explanations generally fail to explain the direct, or even indirect, connection between racism and gang phenomena, especially violent gang behavior against other gang members of the same racial or ethnic background. Racism better explains the occurrence in this country of attacks by neo-Nazi Skinhead or Ku Klux Klan gangs against minority groups, including blacks, Hispanics, Jews, and gays. Racism may also explain the aggressive and "retaliatory" behavior of some white ethnic gangs when minority groups are regarded as "invading their neighborhoods." Youth gangs identify with and protect turf or community against competitor gangs. Usually in these latter cases, the situation of one gang versus another gang of a different background is not fundamentally at issue. Interestingly, there is ample evidence that gang coalitions frequently form across racial and ethnic lines; also certain gangs are multiethnic and/or multiracial.

This is not to deny that in certain situations, sometimes in high schools, the community, or prisons, rival gangs of the same race or ethnicity can be aligned against other rival gangs of a different race or ethnicity. However, the racism hypothesis is not sufficient to explain: why many youths from the same environment subjected to similar patterns of personal or systemic racism do not join gangs and/or participate in antisocial behavior; why certain populations, particularly African-Americans, most discriminated against on the basis of color are not necessarily more prone to gang-motivated violence than Hispanics; why gang violence by minority groups of the same class level varies greatly across communities, and over time in the same community, regardless of level of racism or discrimination, and sometimes regardless of conditions of economic boom or depression.

Miller notes furthermore that the issue of racism may be used for purposes in addressing the gang problem that in fact have little to do with the gang problem:

> Programs aimed at controlling gangs in minority communities may face opposition from one community faction for unfairly stigmatizing minorities or violating their civil liberties while supported by another faction as a necessary measure for protecting the safety of law-abiding citizens. For some the explanation that minority gang problems are a product of racism is so compelling and complete as to override the need for further research into causes. (W. Miller 1990, pp. 282–283)

Personal Disorganization

In this final part of the chapter, it is important to focus on the individual motivations of youth for becoming and remaining a gang member. Considerations of individual motivation or personality predisposition are generally overlooked by gang theorists. Why one youth becomes a gang member, and another from the same family or community does not, is far from clear. What distinguishes the gang from the delinquent adaptation must be addressed in psychological or cognitive as well as social and cultural terms. Not all delinquents are gang members and not all gang members are delinquents (Curry and Spergel 1992). Most important, some basis for preventing, intervening with, and controlling individual gang-prone as well as core gang members is essential for social planning and program development.

While defects of social structure may account for differences in rates of the problem, they do not account for why certain youths subjected to these same conditions become gang members and others do not. Two factors of individual personality may induce youths to become and remain gang members. The first is a deficiency of personality organization. The second, probably related to the first, is the tendency toward defiance and aggression in certain youths under certain social conditions (see Kotulak 1993, pp. 1, 8). In the following, aspects of intelligence or cognition that distinguish the gang youth from the non-gang youth are discussed. Certain social and psychological, but not biological, factors related to personality organization are emphasized.

Intellectual Development

We know little about the intellectual or cognitive abilities or disabilities of gang youths as they may be distinguished from those of delinquent non-gang youths or non-delinquents. We have paid scant attention to differences among different types of gang youths by personality or intellectual development (however, see Yablonsky 1962; Klein 1971). We have little systematic knowledge about gang member's intelligence in relation to physical or mental health.

Expert opinion appears to be that gang members' intelligence is in general somewhat below normal (Klein 1971), despite occasional expert and popular claims and some evidence that certain gang members seem to have extraordinary street intelligence, leadership, or organizational ability, and indeed that a few gang members with notoriously delinquent histories have gone on to graduate and professional school and then to outstanding professional or business achievement in the legitimate world. On purportedly culture-bias-free measures of arithmetic, vocabulary, and information, gang members have tested lower than other lower-class non-gang boys. "Gang boys made the lowest scores on six measures of intelligence, below the scores of lower-class non-gang and middle-class non-gang boys, in that order. In each category, black youngsters scored lower than did their white counterparts" (Short 1990a, pp. 203–204; see also Short and Strodtbeck 1965). Klein reported that in a sample of 243 gang members, the median IQ was 84, and only eight youths tested above 100. "One-third of the boys have scores that would dictate their placement in special education classes" (Klein 1971, p. 85). Farrington, Berkowitz, and West (1982, p. 331) indicated that "frequent group fighters" tended to have low vocabulary scores at ages 10 and 14.

Gang boys are reported to have cognitive difficulties in perception and understanding as well as low self-esteem. They are "inferior in their general powers of concentration and in their perceptual ability to integrate meaningful wholes out of partial information" (Cartwright, Tomson, and Schwartz 1975, p. 11). They are more self-critical and self-questioning. They tend to daydream. "They had poor immediate memory, were slower in making judgments and they were less effective in performance tests" (Short 1990a, p. 204).

Harris observed that no core members in the group she studied in the Los Angeles area had finished high school. She noted that "For the girls . . . the stronger the attachment to the gang, the less the attachment to societal institutions . . . especially schools" (Harris 1988, p. 156). Thus, it may not be possible to obtain an adequate assessment of the intelligence of gang youths if they are extremely alienated from school and cannot handle testing procedures well. However, in a recent survey of prison gangs, officials estimated that gang members were of average intelligence. In fact, they were perceived to have achieved higher levels of education than non-gang youths (G. Camp and Camp 1985). Taylor (1988) stated that, among corporate drug-dealing gangs in Detroit, several members did well in school and some came from middle-class families. Sung (1977) and Chin (1990b) observed that some of the Chinese gang youths were attending college.

We have no comparative data on intelligence, school achievement, family, or personality factors within or across gangs from the same or different cultural communities, and how these factors might be related to gang participation and especially criminal behavior. Sullivan suggested there may be more variation in these cognitive and school achievement factors within gangs than across gangs or communities. He also observed that "individual age, family background and school experience are certainly important correlates of delinquency and youth crime, but these factors cannot be neatly separated from social factors" (Sullivan 1989, p. 222). To what extent the gang youth's developmental history in the family relates to his intellectual or school achievement is not known.We do know, however, that different youths in the same family are variably prone—for as yet unknown reasons—to gang and delinquency. Children in a family with a gang youth frequently attend and complete college and graduate school and go on to legitimate professional careers.

Personality Development

More attention has been paid to the socioemotional than to the intellectual limitations or disabilities of gang youths in understanding the gang problem. One view is that gang youths are reasonably normal. They simply adapt to extremely disadvantaged or socially disorganized contexts in ways that maximize personal survival and preparation for marginal adult working careers. An opposing view is that gang youths are personally isolated, seriously disturbed, or maladjusted. All of these perspectives recognize explicitly or implicitly that gang youths are mainly adolescents, passing through a stage of development that is normally filled with crises. Peer group relationships are particularly important in their passage from childhood to adulthood. Adolescence is a "transitional, marginal period where experimentation with new roles is expected and usually enacted. Biological and physical changes underway usher in the question of social maturity, for a bodily change must somehow be accompanied by a psychological behavior change" (Vigil 1988b, p. 152).

There is a general awareness that males in gangs are more likely to engage in serious and persistent violent behavior than females in gangs. While these differences can be attributed to cultural, social, and even economic opportunity and/or lack of personal or community control factors, there are also obvious biological and physiological differences that may drive males to more aggressive behavior. Vigil, using a cultural perspective, claimed that the drive to gang membership is based on a "personal need to prove oneself" and that the drive is "central to ritual and most members do so . . . by exhibiting courage, bravery, and daring in accepted street affairs, such as fighting (either friendly encounters among peers or more serious aggression against rival barrio members" (Vigil 1988b, p. 163). The inherent and/or socially conditioned drive to aggression seems to be considerably stronger in males than females, particularly during the adolescent years.

The Environmental Perspective

One set of experts finds the answer to why certain youths engage in gang-related, especially violent, behavior mainly in the defects of the social, cultural, or economic environment rather than in the youth himself. To some extent this begs the question also of the variable extent and quality of criminal activity by gang members or by the individual gang member over time. The environmental perspective is reflected in learning theory, which states that joining a gang and adopting delinquent gang behavior are an outgrowth of a natural social learning process in certain low-income and/or transitional areas. Positive reinforcements exist for deviant gang behavior and joining a gang, and punishments for not participating in its activities. Such socialization takes place in the context of particular delinquent and probably gang groups and largely accounts for the patterns of delinquent behavior that result (Elliott, Huizinga, and Ageton 1985, pp. 33–35).

In this perspective, membership in the gang is simply normal and adaptive in a particular time and place.

> Here [in the gang] the gang member receives affection, understanding, recognition, loyalty, and emotional and physical protection. In this respect, the gang is psychologically adaptive rather than maladaptive. . . . Based upon 26 years of work with Hispanic gang members as a *barrio* gang group worker, probation officer and mental health therapist, the author has found that the vast majority of gang members are [relatively normal and] *not* mentally disturbed. (Morales 1982, pp. 140–141, 145)

Vigil suggested that the gang as an institution serves the same function as male initiation rites in other cultures (Vigil 1988b, pp. 5–8; see also A. Cohen 1955; Bloch and Niederhoffer 1958; W. Miller 1958). He explained that the youth gang, especially in the Mexican-American community in Southern California, is viewed as a collective resolution to multiple problems associated with "territory, age-grading, and gender socialization" (ibid.). Vigil stated also that the youth strives for self-identity in a social environment beset with difficulties. The gang youth is not regarded as the average or normal youth in a normal or socially healthy community (Vigil 1988b, p. 150).

Some analysts believe that gangs are composed of youths who have some social liabilities, but also certain social strengths. Gang members do have some cognitive relationships and cognitive disabilities. They are "less assertive. They are more reactive to false signals. . . . They tend to be neurotic and anxious, less gregarious and more narcissistic." However, the gang member is not characterized by "desperation in search of stable human relationships, nurturance and security. He seems rather to have worked out a reasonably realistic solution to his problems. The gang boy, in many respects, is a pragmatist" (Short and Strodtbeck 1965, pp. 231–233). Gordon considered gang behavior "not merely an expression of individual psychological disturbances or of group norms, but also as a complex of techniques through which boys in a group strive to elicit nurturant, accepting, and highly dependable responses from each other—perhaps to compensate for deprivation in their family backgrounds or other institutional contexts" (Gordon 1967, p. 48).

In the variants of a social environment explanation, the gang member's behavior is seen as functional to his survival in a particular social context that requires him to join and do the "crazy things" he does as induced by the gang's social status system. Few of these youths have experienced anything but severe economic or status deprivation. They find themselves on the brink of adulthood without education or training to compete successfully in the labor market. "Survival through 'hustling' or 'fighting' is a functional adaptation to an uncompromising social environment" (Krisberg 1974, p. 116).

Some of the gang theorists of the 1950s and 1960s rejected the idea that gang members were aberrant. They were neither psychopathic, sociopathic, or maladjusted, nor did they possess significant personally disabling conditions. Gang boys were not alienated from conventional norms and values—they were structurally or environmentally not permitted or enabled to achieve success goals or "make it" in a variety of conventional institutional contexts. Therefore, they found alternate means through the gang to achieve desirable societal objectives (Cloward and Ohlin 1960; see also Short and Strodtbeck 1965).

The most sanguine view of the social and emotional health of gang members is that of Walter Miller—at least in his earlier writings, which stressed the functional adaptation of gang youths to lower-class culture and the gang as preparation for a career in a marginal adult working class (Miller 1958; see also Moore 1978). Miller stated that gang youths "are not psychopaths, nor physically or mentally 'defective.'" They are competent and potential leaders; "in fact, since the cornerboy supports and enforces a rigorous set of standards which demand a high degree of fitness and personal competence, the gang tends to recruit from the most able members of the community" (1958, p. 17).

The exposure to certain social and cultural environmental pressures, rather than personal disturbance of the individual youth or his family, is the key factor in the youth's decision to join or naturally drift into the gang. Several analysts trying to explain Chinese youth gang-member phenomena emphasize this point:

> I'm certain that there are parents who are real bummers for their kids. But I think, in the main, the fellows are just trying to do the John Wayne thing. (Sung 1977, p. 42)

> My contention is that although social disorganization plays an important role in delinquency among Chinese adolescents, becoming a gang member invariably involves learning and internalizing Triad norms and values transmitted by the Tongs. (Chin 1990b, p. 101)

The Social Control/Maladjustment Perspective

In the social control or personal maladjustment perspective, the explanation for why the youth becomes a gang member and participates in gang-motivated delinquent behavior shifts from the social environment to certain characteristics of the youth. Control theory assumes that it is not external environmental pressures but the strength of internal controls that regulates behavior, and more important, that restrain the "natural impulse to delinquency" (Elliott, Huizinga, and Ageton 1985). The focus of control theory has been on the acquisition of norms by the individual that constrain and channel behavior in a legitimate direction. Weak internal controls may result from defects of socialization during childhood, particularly through weak family structure or a defective pattern of supervised parental relations. Delinquency results from a breakdown of previously established personal controls, particularly during adolescence, as well as from social disorganization or weakening of the legitimate sources of external control, more generally through school, peers, and community agencies (Elliott, Huizinga, and Ageton 1985, p. 16; see also Hirschi 1969). Vigil posed a series of interrelated personality-centered explanations:

> It is those Chicanos with the most fragmented egos who during adolescence are especially attracted to the gang as a source of self-identity. [The gang] . . . also helps reconcile inner psychological conflicts over different types of "identities," including *ideal* (what I would like to be), *feared* (what I would not like to be), *claimed* (what I would like others to think I am), and *real* (what I am). (Vigil 1988b, p. 15)

While Vigil and Long emphasize key components of Mexican culture as a context for gang youths to express and induce their aggression, they imply that personal conflicts and failures must be recognized:

Machismo in combination with *locura* (literally, craziness or wildness) as core values of the gang motivate violent conflicts with outsiders, especially rival barrio gangs. These conflicts often focus on protecting the streets of the home barrio from encroachment by other gangs and on violating other gangs' claims to similar control of their own barrios. Such fighting, in turn, provides gang youths with opportunities to release aggression and hostilities engendered by their marginal upbringing. Fighting and frequent partying together are the most noticeable activities of the barrio gang. (Vigil and Long 1990, p. 61).

In a greater emphasis on maladjustment, the gang is viewed as an aggregate of individuals with "shared incapacities"; aggression is "a coping mechanism that receives constant reinforcement within the gang" (Klein 1971, pp. 81–81). Gang members have "worse relationships than boys who do not have a criminal record . . . those boys appeared to be anxious to be accepted by their mates" (Sarnecki 1986, p. 20). Gang members tend to be more than normally "hostile, disruptive, defiant, aloof, distant, arrogant, and defensive" compared with other prison inmates (G. Camp and Camp 1985, p. 121; see also Jacobs 1977). Some analysts believe gang members are psychopaths or sociopaths. The gang is not only a useful channel for the expression of hostility but for the exercise of fanciful and megalomanic power (Yablonsky 1962). Certain gang members show a preference for aggression based on their feelings of inferiority and their fear of being rejected or ignored by others (Gerrard 1964). Core members are more troubled and troublesome than fringe members (Yablonsky 1962; Klein 1971). Older youths who provide leadership to younger gang members are particularly personally disturbed (New York City Youth Board 1960, p. 16).

The Need for Order, Structure, and Organization

Finally, what may best distinguish the personality or character of the gang member from that of the non-gang delinquent is a deficiency in the organization of his or her motivational system, including defects in personal control structure as well as in connections with external adult systems, whether legitimate or illegitimate. The gang youth is not so much a deviant or a rebel, attached to a set of different, deviant, or criminal norms and values and relationships, as he or she is unattached to criminal or conventional systems. He seeks a closer, more adequate connection, but does not know how, where, or when to establish such a connection. The gang represents for him an available structure of social attachment and connection during a period of adolescent identity crisis.

The gang permits him to identify with a status-providing system that emphasizes violence or threat of violence as a key means to resolve uncertainty, ambiguity, and the lack of connectedness. Gang violence is a way to define and establish boundaries of personality for himself within the group, between his gang and other gangs, and with the outside world. The greater or more frequent the violence, the sharper the boundaries and the more meaningful the structure, which signifies his social status and that of his gang, and especially the stronger the sense of himself. Violence or the threat of violence advertises to others that he and his group have an identity that is recognizable and strong. Violence becomes a basis for negotiating access to something of great symbolic value. Aggression against or retaliation for an attack from another gang, arrest, jail, fear of him and his gang by neighbors, criminal income—all signify identification with a structure that gives him meaningful identity and status. The gang youth is thereby no longer isolated, rejected, or doubtful about who he is or where he belongs.

The observations that the gang youth has low impulse control (Klein 1971, p. 85) or that he is a defiant individualist (Jankowski 1991, p. 24) are only partially correct. These perceptions do not provide an understanding of sources both within the individual and in the social environment producing tendencies to gang membership and gang violence; nor a sufficient basis for treatment, suppression, or social planning to control, prevent, or intervene in the problem.

After many years of research, Ianni, a psychoanalyst, concluded that it is lack of personal identity and isolation based especially on lack of structure that are the distinctive characteristics of the gang youth:

> . . . We found that gangs and other disruptive groups emerged where adult caretaking environments such as the family or the school did not provide a clear and accessible structure of social order and expectations. What seemed to bond the members of these various deviant groups was some shared sense of an unmet need for affiliation, a search for what Erik Erikson called "fidelity"; something or somebody to be true to.
>
> . . . What we concluded from years of observation of disruptive peer groups in general and street or fighting gangs in particular, is that they grow up in the cracks which appear in the social structure of communication under stress when their institutional systems are incongruent, unavailable, or even alien for the youngsters who live there. What the juvenile gang, and to some extent the adult criminal gang as well, provides for its membership is the certainty of a structure of social control which for some reason is missing in their contacts with the more conventional social structure of their communities. (Ianni, pp. 206–207, 211)

Conclusion

This chapter has presented a theoretical framework to explain mainly violent gang crime and to develop a basis for social planning, social control, and intervention. The failure of structure or connectedness is addressed at societal, community, interorganizational, and personality levels of analysis. Poverty-related theories, including classic opportunity and lower-class, as well as underclass theories, only partially explain the formation of delinquent subcultures and the development of gang crime. Social disorganization theory identifies another set of concepts, which more directly explain the origin of the gang problem. Social disorganization refers to the ineffective articulation of social and personality systems at and within various levels of value, action and relationship. It is the inability of a community, its agencies, and its families to mesh norms, relationships, and resources with the motivations of youths in such a way as to produce effective socialization for male youths.

Population change, especially the "incursion" of a minority ethnic group, and the exodus of the old or established population, may result in the disruption of existing institutional functions and agency service patterns. Family disorganization is a key factor in the development of pressures that contribute to the development of alternate structures, such as youth gangs, to meet socialization needs of youths. A strong sense of youthful isolation and personal distress begins with insufficient social support and control relationships developed in the context of the family.

Racism acts possibly more indirectly than directly in the creation of the gang problem, through segregated neighborhoods and deficient opportunity systems. However, the racism hypothesis is insufficient to explain why many youths in the same environment subjected to similar patterns of personal or systemic racism do not join gangs or participate in antisocial behaviors; nor why with the diminution of racism in many communities in recent years, gang violence has not decreased.

Certain factors of individual social-psychological development, especially deficiencies of personality organization. contribute to the gang member adaptation. The gang permits the youth to identify with a status-providing system that emphasizes violence or threat of violence as a key means of resolving uncertainty, ambiguity, and lack of social connectedness. Characteristics of the gang youth in particular are deficiency of personal identity, strong sense of isolation, and especially lack of structure in which to develop personal and social identity. How to organize an effective community set or structure of interrelated institutional arrangements that provide social support, control, and especially opportunity for vulnerable gang youths to achieve meaningful social status is the purpose of the analysis in the policy and program chapters that follow.

11

Planning for Youth Gang Control
and Violence Reduction

This chapter begins the discussion of issues and strategies for dealing with the youth gang problem, with special emphasis on community mobilization. It stresses the importance of defining the problem and creating policies and programs directed at particular types and levels of the problem. First, however, it summarizes strategies used during recent decades for dealing with delinquent groups and gangs, particularly at the community level. To a large extent, what is past is prologue. There are both continuity and change in the policies and practices that show promise in dealing with gang issues. The challenge is to create a new paradigm of action that modifies past approaches to make them relevant to current and evolving situations. I describe five strategies for dealing with gang problems in different community contexts. The discussion of planning focuses on definitions of the gang incident, assessment of community problems and resources, development of appropriate strategies and interorganizational structures, targeting of different gangs and gang youths, and setting of priorities.

Historical Considerations

Recent decades have produced four basic (and one subsidiary or modifying) strategies for dealing with youth gangs. Each strategy has assumed some dominance in a particular historical period, and each is related to different assumptions about cause and effect and what to do to reduce and control the gang problem. The strategies, in order of historical sequence and emphasis, are (1) local community organizing and mobilization; (2) social intervention; (3) social and economic opportunities provision; (4) suppression, including formal and informal methods of social control and incarceration; and (5) organizational or institutional change and development. The last strategy seeks to modify and elaborate each of the primary strategies through new mechanisms and tactics. It is a general and continuing bureaucratic or modernizing process, and I address it in the following chapters.

The four basic approaches are usually mixed and implemented through an array of evolving and changing policies, organizational and program arrangements, services, and procedures. Youth agencies, criminal justice agencies, local community organizations and schools, and increasingly city, state, and federal government agencies have been the institutional structures or means for development of these approaches. However, there has been little systematic evaluation of results. Program research was carried out mainly in the 1950s and 1960s in relation to the strategy of social intervention by youth agencies. Almost no research has taken place to determine the effectiveness of the law enforcement or gang suppression approach. Opportunities provision and community mobilization approaches have not been clearly formulated or until very recently targeted to the youth gang problem in the modern era, let alone evaluated.

Community Organization/Mobilization

The strategy of organizing local community is based on the idea of countering social disorganization. It was originally a response to the rapid population and institutional changes that were contributing to delinquent group and gang formation in the early part of the century. Urban ecologists of the 1920s and 1930s observed that great waves of immigration, mainly from Europe, were associated with problems of cultural and social adaptation (Thomas and Znaniecki 1918; Park and Burgess 1921; Shaw and McKay 1943). Family ties were weakened and community institutions were not strong in facilitating the transition of youths to social patterns acceptable to the new culture and larger established society. Adjustment was particularly difficult for first generation, mainly white ethnic, males. Delinquent groups and gangs grew and developed as residual or interstitial socialization structures in the inner-city areas where these populations usually settled (Thrasher 1936; Shaw and McKay 1943). The gangs were said to be products of insufficient supervision, insufficient social control, or inadequate processes of acculturation by the family, church, school, and youth agency.

The organized response to youth gangs before World War II involved mainly local groups taking on more responsibility for those immediate neighborhood conditions presumed to be influencing the creation of youth gangs and delinquent groups. The Chicago Area Project and its local community committees, and later the decentralized local welfare councils in certain cities, attempted to bind elements of local citizenry, local youth agencies, community organizations, and the criminal justice system into a collaborative response to the delinquent group problem (probably relatively mild compared with the current youth gang problem) strictly at the neighborhood level (Kobrin 1959; Schlossman, Zellman, Shavelson 1984). Emphasis was on community mobilization and coordination of available local resources, with special emphasis on utilizing indigenous leadership, even ex-delinquent group members or ex-convicts. A key goal was to restore a sense of local community through citizen involvement, support, and controls that would directly lead youths to more conventional youth behaviors. These efforts were not adequately analyzed or evaluated to determine whether the approach as a whole or specific components were effective for which types of communities (however, see Schlossman, Zellman, Shavelson 1984).

The development of the youth gang problem as a problem mainly of newcomer blacks and Hispanics in urban centers in the 1940s and 1950s brought with it more complex and formal efforts at national as well as at local levels to better coordinate agency efforts. Citywide or even statewide special projects evolved. Outreach social services were sponsored by welfare councils or coalitions of agencies as well as youth authorities (Crawford, Malamud, and Dumpson 1970; New York City Youth Board 1960) and county probation departments (Klein 1968). Citywide social welfare or youth service programs were introduced into local communities to deal with gang problems. The earlier stable base of local community or grass-roots organization characteristic of efforts to deal with the delinquency problem in white ethnic communities did not necessarily exist or at least was not mobilized in the poorer, weaker, more recently arrived, or rapidly expanding black and Hispanic communities in the northern urban centers. Specialized outreach organizations were established, often based on outside interest, direction, and authority. The strategies and interests of particular agencies (e.g., police and youth agencies) were distinct and at times clashed with each other, and did not contribute to a unified approach to the problem (Spergel 1969).

The pattern of separate, often specialized approaches intensified in the late 1950s and throughout the 1960s with the introduction of foundation and federal resources to deal with race, poverty, inner-city youths, and delinquency, despite reference to comprehensive community strategies. Local militant or community action strategies were stimulated by the civil rights movement and the Office of Economic Opportunity. Together with the policies of established youth agencies, police departments, and special interest groups, the result was an increasingly diverse and clashing set of values for addressing social issues, including a worsening youth gang problem. Labor markets were also changing. They no longer provided easy access to unskilled jobs and opportunities, traditional inducements for youths to leave the gangs.

Youth gangs grew larger and more complex probably due in significant measure to conflicting philosophies, policies, and uncoordinated agency programs in response to the changing gang problem (Moore 1978; Poston 1971). Gang members were viewed by some establishment groups and social advocates as legitimate citizen elements of local communities and even as community leaders to be involved in programs of urban development and citizen control of riots. They were not necessarily considered hoodlums or budding racketeers who had to be suppressed and incarcerated. This came later, at the end of the 1960s and in the 1970s, perhaps after too much political conflict and program failure were encountered. Local community organization and social planning efforts no longer clearly targeted delinquent or gang youths. Focus shifted to problems of housing, education, jobs, and empowerment of citizens in low-income areas.

The strategy of community mobilization in response to delinquency did not disappear in the 1970s and the 1980s. However, its character shifted to the interests of the "good" local citizenry versus the interests of the "bad" citizenry, mainly youth delinquents. Local crime prevention and crime control were more and more closely aligned with suppression approaches in the attack on crime (Roehl and Cook 1984; J. Wilson and Kelling 1982). Focus was no longer on the youth gang member or criminal but on the criminal event (Bursik and Grasmick 1993). Local community attention turned to the control of violence on school grounds. School staffs, parents, and students were mobilized to preserve safety and maintain security (Gottfredson, Gottfredson, and Cook 1983; Gottfredson and Gottfredson 1985). There was great concern about the safety of children as they traveled across gang territories to and from school and home.

In its most recent evolution in the late 1980s and early 1990s, the community organization or mobilization approach incorporates the development of coalitions of justice agencies with schools, community groups, and even former gang members (as workers or mentors) with local, state, and federal agencies and resources to deal collectively with the problem of gangs, especially gang violence and drug trafficking. The newer community mobilization idea elaborates notions developed in prior historical periods. Emphasis now is on community or problem-oriented policing, with law enforcement in key coordinating positions. Programs of the U.S. Justice Department and Housing and Urban Development [HUD], such as "weed and seed," dealt with the problem of drugs and gang violence focused on the collaboration of various youth agencies and grass-roots organizations with law enforcement. A 1989 initiative of the Office of Human Development Services, U.S. Department of Health and Human Services (Federal Register 1989), also emphasized the development of a consortia of human service agencies in dealing with the problem of juvenile gangs and drug use using a prevention strategy.

Social Intervention/Youth Outreach/Street Work

In the 1950s, social science theory and research served as a partial basis for social agency and research development of outreach services for deviant youths. The assumption was that lower-class communities, lower-class culture, and deviant youth groups were coherent and functional systems that could be somewhat modified or partially redirected. Certain lower-class communities and youth gangs were not disorganized, but stable, even positive phenomena (Whyte 1943; Kobrin 1951; W. Miller 1958; Suttles 1968). Gangs were viewed as serving a variety of adaptive needs of male youths in coping with status frustration, alienation, or social isolation in a middle-class-dominated world (A. Cohen 1955). Norms and behavior pertaining to group rivalries, insults, retaliations, colors, signs, symbols, and identification with turf did not, in the 1940s and 1950s, result in the high number of deadly street gang wars typical of today in certain cities. Drastic restructuring of social institutions seemed not to be required.

A key assumption of youth agency programs in this period was that youth gangs could be redirected to fit the expectations and needs of the larger society. Youth gang norms and values could be changed sufficiently with the aid of outreach supportive services, including street gang programs, special peer counseling and group development activities, and crisis intervention or mediation. The gang itself was to be the vehicle for its own transformation. The small gang or subgroup was to be the unit of attention of the street worker. The manipulation of gang structure through group meetings, recreation, group counseling, referral of individual members for services, and sometimes support from parent and community groups were at the heart of the efforts to co-opt or redirect gang values and behaviors. The juvenile gang had positive potential; only selected negative structural and process elements required modification. Workers who understood group dynamics were expected to be sensitive to the distinctive norms and patterns of gangs, and able to establish positive relationships with its aggressive and troubled members. The workers served as mediators in conflicts between gangs and with the conventional world. An important objective was to de-isolate youth, but first youth gangs had to be "reached" and worked with in their own setting and to some extent on their own terms (Spergel 1966).

Youth-outreach targeted specific gangs and gang youths. It was often not part of other youth service programs. Close relationships were established with gang youths, which led to a problem of some workers being viewed as overly identified with gang members. The police, committed to a suppression ideology, argued that youth or street workers actually cohered gangs and contributed inadvertently to an increase in gang crime. Klein's research supported the police view. He found that gang crime was reduced when street workers were withdrawn from service to youths on street corners, and when gang members were dispersed (1968). This view was not necessarily shared by other researchers (Gold and Mattick 1974).

Youth-outreach approaches were sharply curtailed, if not abandoned, in the late 1960s and 1970s as gang conflict problems seemed to grow more complex and intractable in a number of cities. Youth agencies, with the aid of federal justice system reform policy and resources, also turned their attention to other forms of youth deviancy, such as status offenses, particularly running away. It became evident that older youths and young adults were now part of gangs that had become criminalized and were not amenable to traditional street-work counseling or recreational strategies. A few programs remained, but social intervention and value transformation gave way to limited social control or mixed social intervention and suppression approaches in the form of citywide or areawide crisis network intervention programs in close collaboration with criminal justice agencies and sometimes grass-roots citizen groups.

Youth agencies became interested again in the youth gang problem in the late 1980s in response to community concerns and especially federal and state initiatives and resources. Youth agencies, however, began to target younger youths in efforts to prevent serious gang violence and criminal behavior, especially drug trafficking. Street workers emphasized mediation of intergang disputes to a more limited degree and now attempted to a greater extent to coordinate efforts with law enforcement and probation. Involvement of local citizens and former gang members in these control efforts characterized the newer youth-outreach approaches. The schools have also become a context for early intervention and preventive efforts. An implicit or explicit division of responsibility has developed, with law enforcement taking primary responsibility for dealing with older, hardened core gang members, now increasingly involved in drug trafficking, and youth agencies being responsible for work with at-risk younger youths.

The social intervention strategy has become increasingly varied in its contexts and methods of implementation. The strategy has been incorporated by a range of treatment organizations, criminal justice agencies, schools, and grass-roots groups, including churches, as well as youth agencies. Programs now include crisis intervention, outreach, diversion, counseling, role modeling, mentoring, group work, casework, drug prevention and treatment, presentence and postsentence services, tatoo removal, conflict resolution, intergang mediation, leadership development, referral for services, job training and development, temporary shelter, case management, and attempts at religious conversion. It is not at all clear, however, who an at-risk gang youth is and what services are appropriate to prevent or control the problem in particular social settings. An exceedingly broad range of youth from ages 3 to 18 years in low-income minority or immigrant communities have been targeted somewhat indiscriminately for prevention services.

Opportunities Provision

Concern with the rising rates of delinquency, unemployment, and school failure of inner-city youths in the 1950s and 1960s were the basis for a series of large-scale efforts initiated by foundations or federal agencies to change social institutions and establish new types of school and training programs directed to these youths. Some efforts emphasized the provision of new social opportunities for disadvantaged youths and the development of increased participation by local citizens, and a new relationship between the federal government and local neighborhoods toward the solution not only of delinquency, but of poverty itself. Traditional youth work strategies based on notions of changing the individual or youth gang were regarded as insufficient. Structural strain, lack of community resources, and relative deprivation were the key ideas that explained the causes of delinquency, including youth gang behavior, and provided a basis for social planning and action. Social and economic institutions, and the lack of sufficient legitimate means, rather than the criminal behavior of gangs and individual youths, were to be addressed (Merton 1957; Cloward and Ohlin 1960).

The opportunities provision strategy of foundations and federal government agencies in the 1960s came not to focus sharply on the youth gang problem. Recreational, social service, and treatment programs were also of secondary interest. The Ford Foundation, the President's Committee on Juvenile Delinquency and Youth Development, the Office of Economic Opportunity, the Labor Department, and local foundations stimulated the development of new programs through the schools, neighborhood organizations, special training, job projects, business, and industry toward the social and economic advancement of people, including youths, in disadvantaged inner-city and rural areas.

Broad-scale programs were to be initiated to deal with a variety of social problems. Grass-roots groups and social reformers occasionally tried to involve youths in a variety of militant social actions to deal with issues of lack of social opportunities and civil rights. Delinquents and gang members at times participated in marches and demonstrations by civil rights and cultural movement organizations to increase opportunities in the black and Hispanic communities. However, it was not clear that these multiservice programs, social movements, or reform social policies substantially benefited or directly served the social needs and interests of delinquents or gang members. While there is evidence that programs such as Head Start and Job Corps were generally successful in the socialization, academic development, and retraining of inner-city minority young people, and even in reducing delinquency, at least over the short term, it is less clear whether and how these programs targeted actual or potential gang members.

The idea of opportunities provision has grown more complex, more differentiated, and more difficult to implement in recent years. The involvement of gangs and gang youths in social movements, social reform, and community action is less frequently sought. Social services are no longer viewed as a simple or direct way of providing access to opportunities; counseling and various personal development activities per se are not accepted as equivalent to basic social and economic opportunities for gang or gang-prone youths in inner-city areas. Jobs, job preparation, job placement, job development, and various training, remedial tutoring, apprenticeship, and competence-building activities are regarded as opportunities. Moreover, social opportunities must be increased primarily through national policy or basic re-allocation of resources rather than simply through provision of social services, organizational changes, and local community mobilization. Gang youths, however, are generally not targeted in current opportunity provision plans or ideas, such as Job Corps or Urban Youth Corps.

Suppression

A philosophy of major institutional change and resource reallocation was replaced by growing conservatism in the 1970s and 1980s. With the decline of community and youth-outreach efforts, the inability or insufficiency of opportunity provision and social service approaches, and rising community alarm over crime, a dominant police suppression approach developed. The gang was increasingly seen as dangerous, evil, and beyond the reach of most community-based institutions or even national social policy. Vigorous law enforcement became a key strategy to protect local communities. Gang members were to be arrested, effectively prosecuted, and removed from society for long prison sentences.

Police and prosecutors came to play the primary response roles. Information systems, surveillance procedures, and tactical patrols by specialized police units directed to the gang problem were developed. Hard-core gang member prosecution divisions, intensive supervision, and vertical case management by probation departments were new organizational mechanisms created in the 1980s to meet the gang threat. State legislation provided increased resources for improved coordination of local justice system efforts. City, state, and national legislation was proposed or passed to enhance sentences for suspects convicted of serious gang-related violent or drug-related offenses. Interagency law enforcement task forces evolved and increasingly targeted older, hard-core youth. Local citizen groups and social agencies were requested to assist law enforcement with intelligence gathering and support for sweeps and arrests, particularly in public housing projects.

However, the results of suppression strategy have been associated not only with more arrests, more convictions, and longer stays in prison for gang members, but with continued growth and "spread" or development of gangs within prisons and neighborhoods and across cities. A sharp rise in gang-member-related drug trafficking has also occurred. The strategy of increased and targeted suppression has not, by itself, been adequate to reduce the gang problem and return "control of the streets"—the goal of law enforcement agencies—to local citizens. At the close of the 1980s and in the 1990s, many localities, states, and federal agencies were seeking better ways to deal with a worsening and an increasingly intractable youth and young adult gang problem.

Elements of a Community Planning and Mobilization Process

Recommended planning and community mobilization should vary according to the nature of the gang problem, and the distinctive social, economic, cultural, racial/ethnic, and other specific community factors precipitating and conditioning it. The history of community response to the gang problem and the nature of leadership and of interorganizational and community group patterns and resources have to be carefully assessed. Key elements of this process include: (1) specification of the problem, (2) selection of appropriate policy and program structure, (3) determination of strategies to be employed, and (4) targeting of the problem and prioritizing policies and services or procedures (see Appendix A).

Specification of the Problem

It is important to accurately identify, define, and understand the problem, in terms of its key components: (1) the criminal youth gang, (2) the youth gang member, (3) the gang incident, (4) the gang problem context, especially whether it is chronic or emerging, and (5) the nature of the specific relationship between gangs, violence and drug trafficking.

The Criminal Youth Gang. This group ordinarily comprises both juveniles and young adults who engage in a range of social and antisocial behaviors. Cliques or members engage repetitively, and at times unpredictably and spontaneously, in violent, predatory, and criminal gain, usually street-based, behaviors. The criminal youth gang may be located within a neighborhood or across neighborhoods and even cities. It may be loosely knit or well organized with established but not always consistently implemented rules of conduct. The youth gang may or may not have a name, turf, colors, signs, symbols, and distinctive dress. The values of the youth gang include mutual support among members, conflict with competing gangs, and lack of trust of established authority, especially the police.

Many street gangs continue to be traditional turf-based gangs established to build and protect the structure, integrity, reputation, and status of the gang within a framework of shared or communal values. Gang functions are increasingly complex and difficult to change. Some youth gangs are now more economic-gain oriented and more rationally organized than gangs of an earlier era.

The Youth Gang Member. The criminal youth gang includes some youths who are associates or at the periphery of the structure and conform primarily to conventional norms, but it also includes committed, especially hard-core members who engage in a range of criminal behaviors. Most gang members are in the age range of 12 to 24 years. This is not to deny that some pre-adolescents as well as a few persons in their 40s and 50s engage in street-gang activities. However, the most violent gang behavior tends to be committed by older adolescents and young adults. Some gang members may join for a period as short as a day, a week, or a month; others remain members for years. Some move from low to high gang status, from less serious to more serious gang behaviors, and vice versa.

Traditional gangs may have various roles or positions for their members: identifiable leader, core, regular, associate, soldier, peripheral, wannabe, floater, veteran or old-head. Of special interest, for purposes of intervention, control, and prevention planning, are two categories of gang youth: the more serious, hard-core, often older gang youth, and the younger, high-risk, often less committed gang youth. The characteristics of gang members are quite variable even in the same community. Multiple sources of up-to-date information should be used to identify the characteristics of gang members, such as gang member self-identification, statements by reliable witnesses, verification by a second independent agency source, and prior police records.

The Gang Incident. A gang incident is the unit for classifying and reporting an event as a gang crime, especially for law enforcement purposes. Reported gang incidents become the basis for determining whether a gang problem exists and for assessing its scope. The gang homicide is usually the key and most reliable measure of the seriousness of gang crime. Labeling or categorizing an incident (e.g., homicide, assault, or robbery), as gang related is neither a simple nor a standard procedure across jurisdictions. Two different procedures are generally employed to determine whether a gang incident has occurred, which give special law enforcement and public policy meaning to the event.

1. *Gang motivated.* In this procedure, focus is on the criminal act. An act is defined as a gang incident if it grows out of gang motivation, interest, or specific circumstances that enhance the status or function of the gang. Examples include: intergang violence, gang retaliation, turf protection, intimidation, robbery of gang paraphernalia, and recruitment. One or more members of the gang may be involved as a suspect, witness, offender, or victim. In classifying the incident, focus is on the details of the specific situation in which the act occurs, such as a drive-by shooting, throwing bricks at a car containing suspected members of an opposing gang, or yelling a gang slogan in the course of the crime, usually an assault.

Crimes such as burglary, car theft, prostitution, and drug trafficking by a gang member are thus less often recorded as gang crime, because they may be committed for personal gain under this definition. Many criminal acts serve individual member needs unrelated to gang interests. On the other hand, seemingly individual or self-serving crimes by gang or aspiring gang youth may be gang motivated. For example, a youth may be required or feel compelled to commit a particular property or person crime because of initiation or status pressures by the gang.

2. *Gang related.* This procedure focuses on the youth as gang member. A criminal or delinquent act is defined as a gang incident if the suspect, offender or victim, is identified as a gang member, regardless of gang motivation or circumstances. Usually any serious criminal act, especially of a violent, predatory, or drug trafficking nature, in which a gang member is involved is classified as a gang incident. For example, the crime of a gang member who steals from a store for personal reasons would

be classified as a gang-related incident. (See Glossary for a discussion of mixed situations and erroneous classification of group delinquency as gang crime.)

3. *Which definition to use.* The argument in favor of using primarily the gang-motivated definition is that it focuses sharply on the circumstances of the incident rather than identification of the individual as a gang member. It is more precise as to the scope of the gang problem and has greater validity than the broader gang-related definition. It withstands court challenges better. It also avoids excessive labeling or exaggeration of the gang problem.

A counterargument is that the gang-motivated definition minimizes the actual scope of the gang member's contribution to the crime problem. It encourages organizational or community denial of the problem. A key assumption by the proponents of the broader gang-related definition is that a gang member is likely to engage in a wide range of serious crimes because gang membership, per se, predisposes him or her to do so. Evidence for this argument is not clear, however.

Some police and prosecutors generally believe that it is desirable to identify gang members and their activities as comprehensively as possible for intelligence-gathering purposes. Some police units are particularly concerned that the full range of criminal activities of the gang member be available for efficient tracking and law enforcement purposes, to best protect the community; they are less concerned with issues of minimizing labeling or facilitating prevention, which might overlook or minimize certain types of gang member, non-gang, or gang delinquent behavior.

A gang-incident procedure should probably be devised that distinguishes between gang-motivated and non-gang-motivated crime committed by the gang member. All serious criminal incidents by repeat gang offenders should be clearly "flagged" on criminal justice computer systems. The presence of an effective computerized information system permits use of either or both procedures to track gang-motivated incidents and gang member crime and to plan a more complex and comprehensive approach to dealing with gang member behavior as well as non-gang criminal behavior.

Gang Problem Contexts, Chronic and Emerging. With the growth and spread of the youth gang problem, a twofold categorization of the problem context has come into use: chronic and emerging. The differences in these contexts can be a basis for the development of distinctive strategies, policies, and procedures for gang suppression, intervention, and prevention. Simply put, a more preventive or early intervention and less formal approach may be appropriate in the emerging gang problem context, whereas a more elaborate and formalized suppression, intervention, and prevention approach may be necessary in the chronic context.

CHRONIC GANG PROBLEM CONTEXT. Such a community context is characterized by persistent or periodic crises of major gang member violence and sometimes related drug trafficking extending over a multiyear period, even decades long. Youth gangs, or generations of youth gangs, are usually better organized in communities located in larger or older cities. These are likely to be impoverished, ghetto, or transitional areas or ports of entry. However, gangs are increasingly found in smaller cities and older suburban communities.

EMERGING GANG PROBLEM CONTEXT. This community context is characterized by less well-organized and persistent but at times serious forms of gang violence and gang member drug trafficking. The gang problem has usually been present and/or recognized for fewer than ten years, often fewer than five. To some extent, the development and spread of the problem may be traced to the influence of new settlers or gang entrepreneurs, including drug traffickers, who have moved from chronic problem cities or contexts. Youth gangs in emerging problem areas tend to be fewer in number and most often evolve out of, or are connected to, local delinquent, sometimes social, groups under conditions of population change and/or deteriorating economic or social situations, particularly for minority newcomers who become socially isolated.

The distinction between chronic and emerging gang problem communities, however, is not sharp. Indicators related to the time of onset of the problem, its duration, degree of gang organization, severity of gang violence, and related gang member drug use and trafficking patterns, as well as the nature of response to the problem(s), are not neatly categorized by the terms *chronic* and *emerging*.

Emerging gang problem communities may interact and develop into chronic; and chronic gang problem communities may go through periods of significantly diminished gang activity before the problem re-emerges. Different organizations or parts of a community or jurisdiction may be characterized by different stages or degrees of severity of the problem at a given time.

Variability of Gang, Drug Trafficking, and Crime Problems. It is important to understand for policy and program purposes that youth gangs involved in gang violence are not necessarily involved in drug trafficking. Some communities with high levels of youth gang violence may have relatively low levels of drug use and trafficking, and vice versa. Drug trafficking may or may not diminish patterns of youth gang violence. Drug dealing by gang members, especially older members, may provide the wherewithal to purchase weapons for younger members of the gang to engage in intergang conflict. Older gang members who are drug dealers, on the other hand, may indiscriminately sell weapons to members of an opposing gang as part of a drug deal.

Finally, high levels of general criminality in a community do not necessarily indicate high levels of gang activity. Some cities with the highest levels of youth homicide and drug trafficking may have relatively limited youth gang activity. For an assessment model of the different types of gang youths and problems to be addressed, see Appendix B.

Selection and Development of Appropriate Policy and Program Structure

Bursik and Grasmick (1993, p. 161), in part, suggest the need to elaborate community organization efforts to counter social disorganization. Strategies and activities should be designed not only to bring community adults into meaningful contact with local youths, but open up channels of communication between local residents and institutional representatives who might provide useful resources to the neighborhood and especially to vulnerable youth. A systemic community approach also requires involvement and interaction at interpersonal, youth and adult, indigenous and local institutional, as well as larger governmental levels. Furthermore, since the gang problem is systemic, both older and younger gang youth must be appropriately targeted. The interrelation of emerging and chronic gang problem contexts in a community must be recognized and dealt with as necessary.

A structure and set of strategies must be created for the development of policy and program across local organizational or agency and community group interests, as well as involve different government levels. Of special importance is the integration of policy among state and federal agencies that deal or should deal with various aspects of youth problems, including the gang problem. Interagency structures already exist at the national level, as suggested previously, for example in the Office of Juvenile and Delinquency Prevention of the U.S. Justice Department, but are often not used. Sometimes different units of the same large bureaucratic agency, locally or nationally, determine policies and programs without adequate communication or integration of efforts with other subunits of the agency.

At the local level, a policy structure must be developed to facilitate communication and to coordinate and integrate ongoing citizen and agency efforts based on the interests, needs, and present and potential resources of the particular community. Processes and mechanisms have to be created for the integration of the efforts of local criminal justice, community agencies, and grass-roots groups, including those community groups that are most affected by and involved with the problem. Local grass-roots groups are often less well organized, influential, or articulate than established agencies. Special local community or neighborhood councils, youth boards, or task forces should be generated (or authorized), if necessary, either by state law or by decision of the city council, mayor, or city manager's office. (In emerging gang problem jurisdictions, a less formal and more limited structure and set of strategies may be required.) Of special importance, especially in chronic problem communities, is the development of explicit procedures for the collection and sharing of appropriate information among diverse agencies and community groups about youths to be targeted and the development of appropriate standards for broad and reciprocal role functioning. Different race/ethnic, class, and organizational and interorganizational spects as well as different types and levels of the gang problem must be taken into account in fashioning appropriate local structures of community mobilization.

The structure in the emerging problem jurisdiction should:

- involve schools, youth agencies, and police as well as youths themselves as key actors in the development of an appropriate coalitional structure, supported by grass-roots organizations, business and industry, and other criminal justice agencies;
- stress that key programs should be centered in the schools with emphasis on prevention and early intervention, since gangs, gang leaders, and gang patterns are not yet well established; special attention should be directed to development of clear and meaningful risk indicators;
- emphasize the importance of local parent and neighborhood involvement in school-based efforts to deal with the gang problem;

- encourage neighborhood youth agencies to reach out to the schools in support of remedial academic programs directed to youth at high risk of gang membership or already involved in gang activities;
- assist police, school, and youth agencies to develop cooperative action or program arrangements for gang prevention, also involving parents and youths themselves with locus in the school to the extent possible;
- encourage civic associations, agencies, and churches to reach out to newcomer and minority groups in socially isolated neighborhoods where the problem is often most critical;
- approach coalition building among the key organizations through formal and informal means, including contacts at church and ethnic association gatherings;
- facilitate the development of a common approach to the gang problem among agencies and local groups, with emphasis on better utilization of existing resources on behalf of targeted youths and their families.

In the chronic gang problem jurisdiction, the structure should:

- be linked directly to the mayor's office, a public youth commission, a human relations department or a criminal justice coalition, led by a police or a probation department;
- involve a broad range of agency staff and community representatives at both policy and program levels in efforts to deal with the youth gang problem, including:
  1. Police (also from transit and public housing)
  2. Schools
  3. Churches
  4. Community-based youth agencies
  5. Employment (i.e., business, industry, and labor)
  6. Probation
  7. Judge
  8. Grass-roots organizations
  9. Corrections
  10. Parole
  11. Mayor/City Manager's Office
  12. United Way and private foundations
  13. Park Department
  14. Housing Authority
  15. State Criminal Justice Planning Authority
  16. Health agencies
- facilitate the development of special interagency mechanisms and activities by those organizations most directly addressing the hard-core gang problem, particularly police, outreach youth agencies, probation, and key local community group coalitions;
- encourage the development of advocacy committees comprising a variety of

different agency and community group representatives in respect to social opportunity and criminal justice policy issues bearing on the problem;
- focus not only on prevention and intervention with younger youths, but on outreach to older gang youths, for purposes of remedial education, training, and especially job development, referral, and placement;
- develop special advisory or operational committees that have special information sharing concerns about the problem (e.g., a criminal justice group concerned with older hard-core gang youth, a police-school-youth agency-grass-roots committee concerned with fringe, younger, or at-risk youth);
- advocate, along with grass-roots organizations, for increased resources and the development of crisis as well as long-term programs including remedial education, training, and jobs for gang members and high-risk gang-prone youths.
- focus on a variety of formal mechanisms to integrate or coordinate efforts across agencies and community groups at both policy and operational levels, on regional, citywide, and neighborhood bases.

Strategies

The four major lines of action and modifying strategy, already identified, must be combined in appropriate ways, depending on the specific problem context, the mission of the particular organization, and the kind of youths targeted for special attention. The nature and purpose of these five strategies for planning purposes may be elaborated as follows.

Community Mobilization. Involvement of local citizens, including former gang youth and even current gang influentials, community groups, and agencies and coordination of programs and functions of staff within and across agencies are essential in communities that produce criminal street-gang activity. Social disorganization, as described earlier, refers to the inability of key institutions to interact effectively with each other and socialize youths adequately, as well as to the fragmentation or lack of coordination of criminal justice or community service delivery systems within and across communities.

Opportunities Provision. The provision of additional social opportunities, that is, the development of a variety of specific educational, training, and employment programs targeted to gang youth, is the second most important component for the reduction and prevention of the youth gang problem, particularly when it is chronic. The schools need to provide remedial and enriched educational and other competence-building programs for gang-prone and hard-core young people, at elementary school, secondary school, and community college levels. Remedial education, training, and jobs are especially critical for older youths still in gangs who are not in school but who are at "positive risk" to leave the gangs or decrease participation in criminal gang activity. A key objective of these programs should be development of socially competent youths.

Social Intervention. Youth-serving agencies, schools, grass-roots groups, churches, and even police and other criminal justice organizations must "reach out" and act as links between gang youths, their families, and the conventional world. Staff or adult volunteers of these organizations must develop meaningful social relationships with the youths, relationships that emphasize in some integrated way positive communication, social development, and social control. Local community-based organizations need to create or facilitate a range of programs that contribute to socialization and also protection of the community, such as mediation, truces, crisis intervention, mentoring, referral for services, and especially training and social support to youths on jobs. Special efforts must be directed to mainstreaming gang youths. Advocacy, case management, and coordination of various agency efforts must be interrelated. They are key elements of the social intervention approach.

Suppression. Formal and informal social control procedures, including suppression and close supervision or monitoring of gang youths by agencies of the criminal justice system but also by community-based agencies, schools, and grass-roots groups are essential for community protection, social development of gang youths, and reduction of the gang problem. The control of youth gang member behavior involves not only law enforcement but a variety of other agencies and community groups separately and collectively in the targeting of, communicating with, sharing of information with, monitoring of, and supervision of gang crime offenders.

Arrest, prosecution, imprisonment, monitoring, and close supervision of gang youths, however, are insufficient unless joined with other community-oriented strategies, including community mobilization, social intervention, and opportunities provision, to make long-term as well as short-term impact on the problem. This means that community-based agencies and local groups must collaborate with criminal justice agencies in surveillance and sharing of information, under conditions that protect the community as well as the civil liberties of youths targeted. The police, prosecution, and other criminal justice agencies must also communicate and collaborate with each other as well as participate, and at times develop leadership, in social intervention, opportunities provision, and community involvement programs to supplement their primary mission of suppressing gang crime.

Organizational Change and Development. Finally, the foregoing strategies need to be appropriately organized and integrated on the basis of the nature and scope of the problem in the particular community and the mission of the particular organization. Organizational development and change require the most effective use and reallocation of available and potential resources, both within and across agencies. Common definitions of the problem, resident and client involvement, and coordination of objectives, procedures, tactics and services within as well as across agencies are required. Both community mobilization and organizational development strategies, whether in emerging or chronic gang problem contexts, should be closely interrelated to create efficient and cohesive systemic arrangements for dealing with the gang problem.

For a descriptive model of the way these strategies can be applied and interrelated across different types of organizations and in different community contexts, see Appendix C.

Targeting

To most effectively deal with the youth gang problem and conserve resources, it is important to target for attention certain communities, organizational contexts, gangs, core gang members, and clearly defined gang-prone youths, based on shared knowledge. Sampson, furthermore, has directed attention to the idea of life stages transition and turning points. He has linked temporality and context. Age-graded transitions for youth, e.g., leaving home for school, successful achievement in class, getting a job, marriage, and parenthood, are imbedded in certain institutional and community contexts, often through a process of programed as well as natural change. Social behavior is interactional (see Sampson, p. 432).

This suggests that the youth himself or the social context alone should not be separate objects of change. Policy and program must be based on appropriate targeting of both institutions and youth and also their relation to each other at a specific time and place, e.g., when the youth is entering the gang or ready to leave it and/or at the stage the gang problem is developing in the particular institution or community.

The problem of gangs must neither be denied nor exaggerated at local and national levels. The attention should include appropriate types and levels of control, support, and provision of resources and services for particular youths in particular group, organizational, and community contexts. Indiscriminate provision of additional resources, per se, may be inappropriate. The careful and sustained development of local programs must be based on a collaborative and balanced set of strategies and tactics in which program operators are held accountable for results.

Labeling. The development of relevant and accurate information systems is of special importance. Care must be taken, however, not to label youths as gang members unless reliable and valid confirming information is available. County, statewide, and national information systems, which are in process of development, should be careful to include only the names and records of convicted gang members and not simply everyone identified as a gang member, gang associate, or suspect. Juveniles should be afforded special protection, and should preferably be excluded from these systems except for extremely serious offenses. At the local community level, a narrow or gang-motivated rather than a broad definition of gang incident should be the principal means for assessing the scope and severity of the problem. Special precautions should be taken not to collect, share, and maintain names and information about gang members who may no longer be active or to assume that the gang problem is simply indicated by stereotypes of particular age, gender, race, ethnicity, or clothing style.

Targeting should be based primarily on shared organizational and community group information about the most delinquent or criminal gangs and serious gang crimes, with the intention of identifying specific syndromes and developing special approaches for these. Tracy, Wolfgang, and Figlio have observed that, "A juvenile justice and criminal justice policy that focuses on the few [most dangerous individuals] at the most propitious time has the greatest likelihood of effecting change. Social intervention applied to those few need not be merely restrictive and depriving of liberty; it can also be healthful for and helpful to those who are under control" (1990, p. 298). Therefore, most needed are "targeted programs focused on specific objectives and based on explications of how achieving specific program objectives will affect gangs" (W. Miller 1990, p. 281).

Priorities. The more violent or criminal youth gangs should be targeted. Particular gang youths should be provided with special controls, social services, and social opportunities and targeted in the following priority:

1. Leadership and core-gang youths, in order to weaken gang organization, protect the community, separate key influentials from gangs, and facilitate the social integration of these youths through proactive, community-oriented law enforcement, educational and job referral, job placement and development, and social intervention programming
2. High-risk, gang-prone youths, often younger or aspiring gang members, who give clear evidence of beginning participation in criminal gang activities, through intensive supervision and support services, particularly in the school context
3. Regular and peripheral gang members with special needs for social control and intervention, through a variety of special educational and socializing services

Nonexistence of Tested Models. Finally, a common assumption of policymakers and planners is that tested or proven ways of dealing with youth gang problems exist and one simply needs to apply these "tested" approaches and programs. But successful models do not exist. W. Miller observes that there have been hundreds of gang control programs during the past several decades. Few have been based on explicitly developed formulations and even fewer have received an adequate evaluation, using "hard" data rather than simply case examples. Program evaluation was more frequent for gang social intervention programs in the 1950s and 1960s. Miller states that the "virtual abandonment of sound evaluation of gang control efforts is a major reason for our [ongoing] failure to reduce gang problems" (1990, p. 273). The tendency in gang control and intervention policy and programming unfortunately is to continue with popular, simplistic approaches even after they have been shown to be ineffective. Klein recently speculated that community networking, coordination, and data sharing may result in "reinforcing elements of the problem"—a "problem of social and bureaucratic construction of the targeted problem" may occur (Klein 1992, p. 13). In other words, a great deal of commitment is required by policymakers, academics, researchers, and practitioners to determine systematically whether particular strategies and policies work, even community mobilization and targeted opportunities provision or suppression, and if they do not, to provide alternative or modified approaches to deal with youth gang problems.

Conclusion

Recent decades have produced four basic (and one modifying) strategies for dealing with youth gangs. In order of historical sequence and emphasis they are (1) local community organizing and mobilization of citizens, community groups, and agencies; (2) social intervention, often outreach counseling and detached work; (3) provision of social and economic opportunities, especially jobs, training, and remedial education targeted to gang youths; (4) suppression, including both formal and informal mechanisms of control; and a fifth modifying strategy: organizational or institutional change, especially emphasizing outreach, "vertical" case management, and collaboration within various organizations and programs.

It is important also to accurately interpret key reality components of the gang problem, so as not to exaggerate, deny, or mythologize them. These are: the gang, street or youth; the gang member; the gang incident; whether the problem exists in an emerging or chronic gang context; and the relation between gang violence and drug trafficking, if any. A more limited definition of the gang problem, focused on the gang-motivated incident rather than on gang membership per se, is preferred for purposes of accurately describing the scope of the problem and better targeting its critical aspects. Different policies and structures of community collaboration are recommended, depending on whether the problem is emerging or chronic in a particular community or organizational context.

The ideal plan of intervention and suppression, as well as prevention, depends on appropriate analysis of the community's gang problem and resources available and needed to deal with it. Community mobilization and opportunities provision generally should be emphasized, especially in chronic problem contexts. This is not to deny the importance of suppression and social intervention strategies and programs, but rather to stress the extreme importance of interrelating these strategies along with priority strategies of community mobilization and provision of targeted opportunities.

The more threatening and criminal youth gangs should be selected for special attention, based on shared organizational and community group information. Gang youths should be targeted for special controls, social services, and provision of social opportunities in the following order of priority: first, leadership and core-gang youths; second, high-risk gang-prone youths who give clear evidence of beginning participation in delinquent or criminal gang activities; and third, regular or peripheral members with special needs for social control and intervention through a variety of educational and socializing services. Finally, there is a great need to evaluate current approaches, including the process and outcome of community mobilization efforts, using "hard" data.

12

Criminal Justice System: The Police

The concepts involved in traditional strategies, policies, and programs dealing with the gang problem are useful as frames of reference for what organizations may do in the future to be more effective. Newer models for dealing with this problem are distinctive rather than categorically different from older models. This chapter and the following ones describe policies and programs that appear to be promising based on past experience, limited program evaluation and the theoretical framework used here. The chapter analyzes and compares mainly specialized police suppression approaches of the past two decades with evolving, more complex, community-oriented approaches.

Chapter 11 focused on relatively abstract strategies. Now, specific organizational patterns, procedures, and objectives need to be carefully described and analyzed within a particular time and community to understand past, current, and evolving policy and program models.

Suppression: "Recent" Traditional Law Enforcement Approaches

Specialized and clearly articulated law enforcement strategies directed to youth gang problems have developed in certain police departments in recent years, but analysis or reliable evaluation of such strategies is limited (however, see Collins 1979; Needle and Stapleton 1983; Jackson and McBride 1985). A vigorous "lock-em-up" approach appears to remain the key action of police departments, particularly in the larger cities with acknowledged gang problems. In this strategy the "primary focus is on apprehension and punishment of offenders to deter individuals and groups from engaging in crime" (Short 1990a, p. 211), ostensibly to protect and serve the community.

While the U.S. Department of Justice's "weed and seed" strategy and "The Violent Crime and Law Enforcement Act of 1994" to deal with street crime problems, especially violence, narcotics, and gangs, indicate some commitment to prevention and use of community agencies, suppression still appears to be the dominant strategy of the federal government and the basis for the disbursement of funds to states and localities.

> This strategy will consist primarily of enforcement, adjudication, prosecution, and supervision activities designed to target, apprehend and incapacitate violent street

189

criminals who terrorize neighborhoods, and who account for a disproportionate percentage of criminal activity. Criminals who qualify will be prosecuted under Operation Triggerlock . . . [the] Community-Oriented Policing Strategy . . . operates in support of the intensive law enforcement containment activities and provides a 'bridge' to the prevention, intervention, treatment component, as well as neighborhood reclamation and revitalization components" (California Office of Justice Programs 1990, p. 6).

Many federal, state, and local law enforcement officials and politicians believe that certain communities are in the midst of a "gang holocaust" (Burrell 1990). The periodic public message of the Drug Enforcement Administration (DEA), the Bureau of Alcohol, Tobacco, and Firearms (BATF), the Secret Service, the FBI, and local enforcement organizations from California to Washington, D.C. is that they are "gearing up for a battle of major proportions against the gangs that have turned parts of Los Angeles . . . into a Beirut" (O'Connell 1988, p. 1). The problems of gangs and narcotics trafficking have to a considerable extent become one global concept that ignores the complex and varying degree of gang involvement in violence, drug trafficking, and other criminal activities in different neighborhoods and cities.

Former Los Angeles Police Chief Daryl Gates urged President Reagan to declare a national emergency to fight drug use and gang violence. Gates claimed that the Los Angeles Police Department "is engaged in an effort to obliterate gang violence in the city. Gang violence has reached epidemic proportions [and] . . . is fed and nourished by the drug trafficking" (*Los Angeles City News Services* 1988). The established philosophy of law enforcement in the 1980s was to focus on hard-core sociopathic leaders of gangs who presumably led fringe members astray as part of a national gang criminal conspiracy. The suppression approach was and still is based on a "war model," especially in cities in California but also in many other states. Special equipment and procedures are required, such as battering rams, helicopters, task forces, sweeps, sophisticated intelligence, tracking systems, and specialist training. However, where the technology of "the war against gangs" has become most advanced, the scope and severity of the problem have often increased. As early as the 1970s some critics of a strict, specialized, and community-unrelated law enforcement suppression approach suggested simplistically that there might be a causal relationship between the changing gang problem and a technically advanced or at least more efficient suppression approach:

> In 1963, when Gang Control [of Philadelphia] was able to monitor 27 violent gangs, there were 4 gang homicides. Repeated violence mainly took the form of rumbles [planned gang confrontations, often without use of weapons], of which there were 46. There were only 13 shootings. . . . By the 1970s, all 105 [gangs] were being watched. . . . The number of shootings rose drastically and the number of rumbles plummeted. In 1973, there were 43 gang deaths, 159 shootings, and only 7 rumbles.
>
> A gang shooting is fast, low-visibility violence. It requires one gunman and a moment under cover of night. . . . (Lieber 1975, p. 47)

Police Policy and Gang Violence

The causal relationship between a police suppression strategy, specialized police organization, and use of sophisticated technology on the one hand and the rise in rates of gang violence on the other is probably spurious. Yet, it is not uncommon to blame—directly or indirectly—a worsening gang problem on law enforcement activities of various sorts. The rise of gang crime in Chicago in the late 1960s was attributed to the activities of the newly formed Gang Intelligence Unit of the Chicago Police Department (Sherman 1970). Gold and Mattick claimed that, because of media publicity generated by the Gang Intelligence Unit, the Blackstone Rangers gang (now the El Rukns) became widely known to many youth and street groups of Chicago's black neighborhoods. Furthermore, the Chicago Police Department (and more recently federal law enforcement authorities) have made periodic claims to the destruction of this gang since the late 1960s (Gold and Mattick 1974, pp. 335–336). In the final analysis, the police cannot be held responsible for basic failures of youth socialization; lack of social and economic achievement by families, deficiencies of schools, decreased employment opportunities for African-American youth, the extensive street presence and accessibility of sophisticated weaponry, and the extensive racism and social isolation that appear to be highly correlated with the gang problem in some low-income minority communities.

This does not deny that the police, as well as the media, can on occasion be responsible for a deviancy-amplifying process and contribute to increased social disorder. Stanley Cohen observed that the gang problem in England seemed to worsen when the police and media viewed certain street groups as "warring gangs." The police "tightened social control efforts" and expanded the definition of delinquency; the increased publicity and tension "prepared [the youths] more for potential conflict, for example, by carrying weapons. Such actions increased potential for serious violence" (quoted in Morash 1983, p. 328). It is likely that the media, including newspapers, records, TV, and most significantly the movies in their glorified portrayal of gang incidents, may be partially responsible—often unintentionally—for the spread of gang phenomena, for example, emerging and middle-class "copy-cat gangs." However, I do not consider the police or the media generally responsible for the more persistent and serious aspects of the gang problem.

Police, along with delinquents or criminals, occupy the same no-man's land that respectable society refuses to see or want to do much about. The police have been known to refer to themselves as a gang, sometimes facetiously. Furthermore, there is an old urban tradition of police teasing, taunting and attacking gangs, and vice versa (Asbury 1971). My own recent field observations indicate that police may cross out rather than expunge gang graffiti, or may add opposing gang graffiti. This sometimes triggers a turf battle. Police have been known to deliberately release gang youths in opposing gang territories to see what happens. Occasionally, a supervisory police officer will admit that his officers commit these provocative actions, but also imply efforts to control them: "We have problems like police officers acting like another gang. . . . Cops were snatching hats, urinating in them, stealing jackets . . . a clubhouse was burned down . . . shortly after two police officers left the building" (Hargrove 1981, p. 89).

The frequency of these police provocations and the seriousness of their consequences are unknown. On the other hand, there is ample evidence of effective intervention by well-trained police officers in the prevention, control, and breakup of specific gang situations and the solving of gang crimes. In fact, there has been a high rate of clearances of serious gang cases—as high as 90 percent—especially in those cases involving homicide in Chicago and Los Angeles during certain years. Traditional violent gang crimes tend to be public or street displays, with offenders often flaunting colors or gang paraphernalia and at times shouting their own names or gang slogans. Witnesses are usually present. Gang members may be only too willing to identify their own gang names or those of opposing gangs involved in the incident.

The key issue, however, is that the ideology of "hard-nosed" police suppression is often developed with little reference to other strategies. "Soft," "preventive," or community problem-solving strategies, until recently, have been downgraded or ignored. The recent "traditional" police approach to gangs is often expressed in terms of moral justification or organizational interest through an attack on sociological rationales or liberal juvenile court rehabilitative practices.

> There is no reason any citizen . . . be literally held hostage in his home by fear, afraid to walk his neighborhood. The solution is simply to take the streets back from the young thugs. As they make war on the citizens, we must virtually make war on them. We have waited on the great enlightened solutions from the sociological world and they have failed to materialize. It is now time to take control of our streets and place the blame squarely where it has always belonged—on the gang member and on his parents for allowing him to be what he has become—a street hoodlum. (Los Angeles Sheriff's Department 1985, p. 6)
>
> "Another major problem with the juvenile system response to the gang member who engages in narcotic offenses is due to the *parens patriae* reason in the juvenile court. . . .These offenders . . . have learned how to manipulate the system and avoid proper consequences for their actions. . . . Law enforcement continually expresses frustration when an arrested juvenile drug offender is almost immediately released back into the community pending adjudication. (Davidson 1987, p. 6)

Law enforcement may represent itself as doing personal battle against the "bad guys" who should get their just desserts (Pillsbury 1988). If the gang cannot be wiped out or destroyed, it must be at least neutralized, made illegal, and its members swept up and placed behind bars, out of sight. Sometimes, a policy of extreme suppression stems from legislative and state agency mandate. The police may be required to increase "the number of individuals identified as gang members and the number arrested for violent gang-related crimes [and] improve the clearance rate of reported crimes targeted as gang-related" (California Office of Criminal Justice Planning 1987, pp. 10–11). The police in California were operating under a broad inclusive definition of gang member and gang incident, accompanied by specialized, centralized, and suppressive tactics.

Police Organizational Arrangements

The police suppression approach becomes organized not only as a moral crusade but a military campaign. Simple objectives of control, reduction, or prevention of gang crime are regarded as insufficient. What is required is a full frontal or counterattack against a "vicious and evil enemy." The police consequently may become organized into units with names or acronyms that express a "cowboy," or "paratrooper" dimension of suppression, for example: Los Angeles Police Department, CRASH (Community Resources Against Street Hoodlums); Los Angeles County Sheriff's Department, GET (Gang Enforcement Team); San Bernardino County interagency task force, SMASH (San Bernardino County Movement Against Street Hoodlums).

Several years ago, Needle and Stapleton identified three police organizational forms that dealt with the gang problem: the youth service program, the gang detail, and the gang unit. These authors viewed different organizational arrangements as functions of the perceived differences in the scope and seriousness of the gang problem, police department size, and available resources. In the youth service, juvenile division, or community relations program model, personnel usually were not assigned gang control responsibilities on a full-time basis, but retained other duties. In the gang detail model, one or more officers were assigned responsibility to deal exclusively with gang control. In the gang unit form, a centralized, separate, and elite structure was developed to deal solely with gang problems. Sometimes both gang and narcotics-control functions were responsibilities of the same specialized unit. In a few of the large cities, complex gang units encompassed comprehensive intelligence, investigation, enforcement, prevention, community relations, follow-up, and liaison responsibilities (Needle and Stapleton 1983, p. 19ff). In the interest of further specialization, the Los Angeles Police Department created a narcotics subunit that was assigned responsibility for dealing with gang-related drug crimes. Simultaneously, a specialized gang unit to deal mainly with gang-related violence also existed.

The various types of police anti-gang organization have comprised anywhere from 1 to 500 or more personnel. The gang unit may be centralized in one location or decentralized in several, assigned as part of local-precinct or district operations. The units do not necessarily develop from less to more specialized structures. Nor do the very large cities necessarily have the most specialized, centralized, or largest gang units. Currently, the New York City and Philadelphia police departments do not consider the youth gang problem to be a large or serious one. Until recently only two officers were assigned full-time responsibility in the juvenile division in the New York City Police Department, and youth officers in the various city precincts dealt part-time with the problem. Approximately eight officers in 1988 were assigned to the Preventive Patrol Unit in the Philadelphia Police Department and had responsibility for gang youths as well as runaways, sexually abused children, and other special youth problems. On the other hand, the Los Angeles Police and Sheriff's department had specialized gang units each with about 200 gang unit officers in the late 1980s and early 1990s.

Chicago's gang unit in early 1992 contained over 500 specialized police gang officers, carrying out a variety of functions. In early 1993, however, the department underwent drastic organizational changes in response to a 1992 Booz, Allen, and Hamilton study that highlighted the need to eliminate specialized units. The gang crime unit was downsized, mainly to an intelligence group of approximately sixty officers. Many of the gang crime special patrol or field officers were sent to the twenty-five police districts to continue their focus on gang crime, but now somewhat within a community policing framework. Higher ranking gang officers, mainly detectives, were reconstituted as part of an Organized Crime Division to better fight narcotics racketeering, which at times involved gangs. The Booz, Allen, and Hamilton study noted that despite highly trained officers, "considered to be the best in the department," only "24 percent of arrests made by gang crime in 1991 were serious offenses and most of the arrested resulted in the suspect being back on the streets within hours" (Stein 1992).

Police gang suppression operations are increasingly part of cooperative community, county, state, and federal task force or interagency arrangements. Federal agency representatives, including the FBI, DEA (Drug Enforcement Administration), BATF, and INS (Immigration and Naturalization Service) may join the local law enforcement effort. The media reported, after the Cold War with Russia came to an end, that the U.S. Justice Department was deploying "300 former spy hunters . . . [to] 39 . . . cities, amounting to an 18.5 percent increase in manpower devoted to gang crimes. It was described as the largest reallocation of manpower in the FBI's history" (Briggs 1992). "Joint federal, state and local FBI sponsored task forces are now operating in 42 cities to counter gang- and drug-related violence" (Ostrow 1992). According to another media report, a growing number of suburban Cook County police departments were teamed up with federal immigration authorities "to use deportation as a weapon against criminal street gangs." In a ten- or eleven-month period, 870 immigrants were arrested for gang-related crimes in the suburbs (Houston 1992b). The U.S. Secret Service, best known for guarding presidents, recently indicated that it had "a plan to protect residents of the Cabrini Green public housing complex" from gangs, drugs, and crime (Long 1993).

Some skepticism has arisen about the value of federal involvement in controlling street gang crime. Local enforcement officers doubt that the FBI and DEA can effectively apply sophisticated anti-racketeering measures to "the primitive and loose-knit world of gangs. . . . In Los Angeles . . . drug wars play a very small part in gang violence and do not offer a useful avenue for combatting gang activities. . . . Of the 207 deaths investigated by the sheriff's department, only five were directly linked to drugs" (Mydans 1992). The chief hard-core gang prosecutor in Los Angeles County doubts the effectiveness of the INS program that deports gang offenders, particularly from the Los Angeles area, back to Mexico. He claims that most of the youth sneak back into the country and the local area in a matter of days.

Development of Specialized Information Systems

At the heart of a suppression strategy often is the assumption that most street gangs are criminal organizations and they must be attacked through an efficient gang tracking and identification system as well as multiagency law enforcement task forces. The information developed and exchanged within and among law enforcement units becomes the basis for a range of "strike" tactics. Special interest, if not urgency, has recently developed to expand gang information systems from local to state and national levels.

> The expansion of gangs and their importation of drugs throughout the state make it even more critical to design and develop a statewide gang information network and clearing house. The statewide system should provide local law enforcement officials with gang analysis files. The system would greatly improve communication, cooperation, and coordination among all criminal justice entities throughout the state. (Philibosian 1989, p. 55)

Gang information systems have become an important organizational status symbol and income resource at the national level. The DEA, the BATF, and the FBI were in competition with each other to establish a national gang network information center. The DeConcini bill in Congress in 1991 would have given the BATF a national gang analysis center. "It would be a national repository for gang intelligence that will provide information to law enforcement" (Drug Enforcement Agency 1991). The bill would also have given the bureau "seizure and forfeiture authority over drugs, money, and other property involved in crimes related to firearms and explosives" (Ibid.).

The traditional police suppression strategy is to quickly investigate, track, arrest, and assist in the prosecution and conviction of gang members—especially hard-core members or leaders—through tactics such as surveillance, stakeout, aggressive patrol and enforcement, follow-up investigation, the development of extensive intelligence, and infiltration of gangs or contexts in which gangs are found, such as schools (Davidson 1987, p. 1). Exchange of information; development of information systems; and education of prosecutors, judges, probation, parole, and corrections officers are key elements of this strategy.

Specifics of Local Data Systems. Increasing quantities and an improved quality of information are required to discover who is a gang member and what criminal activities are carried out or being planned by the gang. In consequence, extensive departmental and interagency computer information and gang tracking systems have been developed or are planned. Systematic exchange and checking of information about gang members are now carried out by increasing numbers of law enforcement units with each other and with county and state probation and corrections departments in many parts of the country. Increases in arrests and long-term reduction of gang-related crime are expected to be the payoffs of these more extensive and improved information systems (Guccione 1987). Gang information systems are expected to improve crime analysis, surveillance, communication, investigation, and other techniques to monitor gang activity, especially gang-related drug trafficking. Law enforcement officials argue that improved data systems and coordination of information across different justice system agencies will lead to more efficiency, more gang members being removed from the streets, more rapid prosecution, and more imprisonment with "less hassle" for longer periods. For example:

> Law enforcement officers with [computerized] information that the drunk suspect is on probation will generally be able to arrest the suspect. . . . All of a sudden, a simple drunkenness arrest can land a suspect in state prison rather than an early morning release on bail. . . . Probation violations are also easier to prosecute . . . there is no trial and the prosecutors don't have to prove the suspect is guilty within a reasonable doubt unless he is charged with a separate crime . . . the procedure is cost-effective . . . and by breaking up a group of drunken gang members with probation violation arrests, the law enforcement officer often stops potential crimes . . . [since] . . . most gang-related crime sprees begin with an innocent gathering of members. (McBride 1988; see also, Reiner 1992, p. 142)

Limitations of Gang Files. However, many problems and issues are inherent in computerized gang files. They are often quickly outdated, they are nonsystematic, or they contain erroneous information (Burrell 1990). Consequently, one recommendation has been that information on alleged crimes by alleged gang members be made available to the youth or guardian (under appropriate circumstances) so that it can be challenged and, if necessary, deleted. Occasionally, hearsay about gang affiliation that had been kept in the police officer's head or in personal files was incorporated indiscriminately into a computer data base (Guccione 1987). Serious impediments in certain communities were language barriers that reduced the amount of data or value of information systems, investigative tools and technology (i.e., wire taps, informants, and undercover operatives) (General Accounting Office 1989). There were several reasons also for the reluctance of gang victims, especially of Asian origins, to go to the police. In some Asian countries there is a traditional aversion to dealing with the police, who have been oppressive or corrupt. In addition, the victims were usually the owners of restaurants or stores who brought home large amounts of cash they wanted to shield from the Internal Revenue Service (Butterfield 1992a).

While some law enforcement data systems have become increasingly specialized, nearby police jurisdictions, sometimes dealing with the same highly mobile street gangs, have not necessarily developed compatible or easily accessible information systems. The data on particular gangs sometimes are not comprehensive, and different law enforcement departments do not necessarily develop collaborative or efficient information exchanges. Some of the difficulty resides in competition among departments, for example between the Los Angeles County Sheriff's Department and the Los Angeles City Police Department.

> The L.A.P.D. has never acceded to any arrangement which would leave it dependent on the L.A.S.D. for internal computer services. So it was quite predictable that the computerization of the L.A.P.D. gang files. . . would proceed on a separate track. . . .
> There are serious questions of jurisdiction, accountability, daily operations, and access—not to mention substantial investments in hardware. (Reiner 1992, p. 138)

Bureaucratic specialization and police unit self-interest extend to the development of specialized data approaches to gang-related narcotics activity. Narcotics officers often do not see street gangs as major players in their field and have not been interested in working closely with gang units, at least in the Los Angeles Police Department. A specialized Gang Related Active Trafficking System (GRATS) was created in 1988. It was established in the narcotics unit as a computerized system for tracking and locating gang-related narcotic activity, with the avowed purpose of reducing the flow of drugs among gang members. "To the surprise of no one in either gangs or narcotics, GRATS did not prove to be a break-through operation" (Reiner 1992, p. 152).

Specialized gang unit officers may not share information with tactical unit officers, or vice versa, about gangs or gang members. Both units may be in competition for such information, which is the basis for making arrests and obtaining credits or points for promotions.

Further, there are problems in the usual policy of expunging files of persons listed as gang members, if no repeat arrest takes place three to five years after the last listing (the time period varies with police jurisdiction). In most jurisdictions, informal files of those originally listed members are still kept by individual officers. Moreover, there is no clear policy by prosecution and probation for expunging the names of gang members from files after a particular time. This makes it extremely difficult to delabel gang members or former gang members, because information from these data systems is not regularly purged. An artificial aging of active or inactive gang members on files also occurs, which can lead to erroneous conclusions about the number of active gang members and the nature of the gang problem.

The issue of racism is raised when an extraordinary proportion of youthful blacks, 12 to 24 years of age, in certain cities (as many as two out of three in Denver) are placed on lists of suspected gang members by the local police. Many youths on these lists have not even been arrested (Dirk Johnson 1993). One recent survey indicates that 40 percent of police departments in cities receiving Department of Health and Human Service funds for gang and drug prevention can make no clear distinction between youth gangs and delinquent groups (Development Services Group 1993; chap. 4, p. 16).

Police Anti-gang Tactics

Police (also prosecution and probation) suppression tactics sometimes have been creative and extensive. They have included street sweeps; saturation policing; selective enforcement (often a euphemism for arresting youths identified as gang members in groups of two's or more); implementation of civil or nuisance abatement programs; special "notice of service" papers informing gang members that they will receive extra jail time if convicted for gang-related crime; intensified gang narcotics investigation; special gang-oriented victim–witness protection programs; use of ID cards, physical barriers, and extra or permanent anti-gang crime guards in public housing projects; seizure of assets of suspects accused of certain kinds of gang-related crimes; implementation of gang-drug-free zones, especially around schools, youth centers, and churches; driver's license suspension; foot and bicycle patrols in high gang-crime areas; special anti-gang decentralized units in parks and schools; neighborhood watch programs; and antigraffiti units. The FBI, DEA, BATF, and INS have established their own special gang units and procedures to deal with the gang problem. As suggested previously, the INS has developed gang units in some jurisdictions, arresting "hundreds of immigrant gang members and launched deportation proceedings for many" (Burgos 1991).

The cost efficiency of some of these tactics has been questioned. The Los Angeles Police Department sweeps of 1988 and 1989 produced so many arrests that the police were forced to set up mobile booking units at the Los Angeles Memorial Coliseum. One report indicates that close to half of those arrested were *not* gang members (Burrell 1990). Another report states that "about half of the weekend gang task force's cases . . . have been rejected for insufficient evidence. . . . Many of those arrested [were] back on the streets in 24 hours" (Gibbons 1988). Uninformed, insensitive, proactive police gang-fighting activity can also produce outrage by community residents, parents, and civil right organizations. One such community protest occurred when the Los Angeles authorities questioned and photographed students who wore blue bandannas—blue being the color of the CRIPS gang—which turned out to be a prank. In another campaign, Los Angeles police made random street stops of young people believed to be gang members, and photographed them for police files. In many instances, these youngsters had committed no crimes and were not even gang members (Burrell 1990). To what extent such practices contributed to the riots in the communities of Los Angeles city and county in the spring of 1992 is unknown.

The concept of targeting gangs and gang members only for suppression purposes is flawed. A series of questions has been raised in California and Illinois about the constitutionality of laws and practices that target people simply because they are gang members.

> Their membership in a gang is not unlawful. . . . It is . . . clear that under the law, you can't arrest somebody unless you believe they have committed a crime. . . . Making mass arrests on the basis of affiliation is clearly unconstitutional. Arresting someone because of their appearance would violate not only Fourth Amendment protection against unreasonable seizure but First Amendment provisions protecting the right to peaceful assembly. (McGarry and Padilla 1988)

The suppression strategy becomes a political tactic when a local government leader chooses to defy the court in respect to arrests of gang youth for loitering:

> Mayor Daley on Thursday lashed out at two judges who dealt a double blow to the city's efforts to combat gangs and graffiti, saying the judges "don't live in the real world."
> Meanwhile, Chicago Police have been instructed to ignore a Circuit Court associate judge's ruling and continue citywide enforcement of a ban on loitering by "known gang members" while the Daley administration appeals the ruling. (Spielman 1993)

The Chicago Housing Authority (CHA) admitted that gangs, drugs, and weapons were "virtually out of control" in some of its buildings. It was seeking court approval to allow its housing personnel, including security guards, "to search apartments, residents and their personal property for drugs and weapons." However, the local American Civil Liberties Union vowed to fight the requested charges in court, calling them "unconstitutional and measures that would turn CHA developments into internment camps" (O'Connor and Haines 1992).

A defense attorney in California, addressing the issue of probation detention, stated that there may be constitutional impediments if the primary basis for arresting and detaining an individual or group of individuals is their identification as gang members or associating with gang members:

> Detentions are sometimes premised on the officer's belief that the detained is subject to a probation condition prohibiting association with gang members, wearing "colors," or being present in certain parts of the city. The validity of such court-imposed conditions has not yet been determined in published decisions. Conditions addressing association, or free travel, may well be unreasonable restrictions on protected liberties. (Burrell 1990, p. 756)

Effectiveness. We have no systematic or reliable assessments of the effectiveness of a gang suppression strategy by criminal justice agencies, particularly law enforcement. One news reporter writes, "A decade of law enforcement crackdowns and get-tough policies has failed to curb the growth of gangs and their violence in Los Angeles and throughout Southern California, and defeated engineers of these efforts are now looking for more sweeping and fundamental social solutions" (Sahagun 1990b). On the other hand, anecdotal information suggests that an early suppression approach may have been effective in eliminating or stopping for a period of time the threat of gang formation, violence, and possibly drug trafficking, particularly in smaller or middle-sized cities, such as Flint, Michigan; Louisville, Kentucky; Fort Wayne, Indiana; and Tallahassee, Florida, where gangs have not yet established a foothold. Police ideology supports the notion that a proactive approach of arresting and harassing small gang formations—especially gang leaders—can successfully "nip the problem in the bud."

Philibosian stated that, "In Santa Barbara, gang membership has been reduced through targeted enforcement, vertical prosecution and public education. Officials estimate that these efforts have reduced gang membership by over 40 percent, which has resulted in a 30 percent reduction in crimes" (Philibosian 1989, pp. 10–11). In Joliet, Illinois, the police claimed that suppression had a positive effect on gang crime problems. "Increased foot patrols by police and tighter security in public housing are having an impact on gang-related crime . . . [residents say] now you don't have the gangs and dope dealers on each and every corner. They are staying on the outside of the projects" (Cerven 1991). However, the reliability of claims in favor of gang crime reduction through a simple suppression strategy remain questionable without adequate data.

Further, the effectiveness of specialized police organization in implementing a primary suppression strategy in dealing with the gang problem has not been demonstrated in large or small cities. The cities with the largest and most specialized gang units, Chicago and Los Angeles, appear to have much larger gang-crime problems than New York and Philadelphia, which have very small and less specialized units with more circumscribed suppression procedures for dealing with youth gangs. This is not to deny that gang forms, behaviors, and the reporting of gang incidents may not be readily comparable across these particular cities. Also, while it is possible to identify gangs in smaller cities in terms somewhat comparable to those in larger cities, a recent study suggests there is little reason to think specialized gang training and gang units will make a practical difference. To deal with the gang problem in highly specialized terms in a smaller community where the problem is not crystallized has not in fact been demonstrated to be an efficient police strategy (Klein, Maxson, and Gordon 1987, especially pp. 37–38).

Emerging Police Approach

A community, problem-solving police approach to youth or street gangs seems to be slowly emerging. This more complex, multidimensional, citizen-involved, and not always police-directed approach is not as widely accepted or practiced as the traditional police suppression approach. The newer strategy or set of strategies assumes that an arrest and lock-em-up strategy is not sufficient. The causes of the problem and answers to it must be defined in broader and more complex rather than simple law and order terms. What is required is an approach that emphasizes community mobilization and employs social intervention, opportunities provision, and suppression and related organizational arrangements in some appropriate and coordinated fashion.

The newer police strategy is a rational social control and community solidarity, social-institution-building approach that strives for the prevention and control of the gang problem on the basis of careful analysis of community and situational factors. This evolving approach assumes that local community groups and agencies—as well as gang or former gang members themselves—must bear responsibility for and participation in control of gang violence and criminal behavior. Successful policing results, in large measure, from "consent and holding the trust of the public" (Clarke 1987, p. 399). A process of joint involvement with key community organizations and established agency representatives is required, based on intimate knowledge of local neighborhood and gang patterns. When a gang-related crime occurs, it has to be put into context. The police officer should know who might be involved and what the basis of the crime might have been. This approach presumes a day-to-day working relationship with key community elements (Pillsbury 1988). It may involve collaboration with youth-serving agencies, probation officers, and schools, and with former and current gang members.

Community Gang Problem Policing

Henry Goldstein's recent work (1990) on problem-oriented policing is consistent with and supportive of the evolving community problem-solving approach to youth gangs. Goldstein notes that the "majority of changes that have been advocated in policing over the past several decades reflect a continuing preoccupation with means over ends; with operating methods, process, and efficiency over effectiveness in dealing with substantive problems" (p. 15). He advises that "the police must do more than they have done in the past to engage the citizenry in the overall task of policing" (H. Goldstein 1990, p. 21). He also notes that "conveying sound, accurate information is currently one of the least used, but potentially most effective means that the police have for responding to a wide range of problems" (H. Goldstein 1990, p. 14).

Trojanowicz adds that community policing "requires a department-wide philosophical commitment to involve average citizens as partners in the process of reducing and controlling the contemporary problems of crime, drugs, fear of crime, and neighborhood decay, and efforts to improve the overall quality of life in the community" (Trojanowicz 1990, p. 8). Community policing is not regarded as a synonym for police-community relations which is a limited means for reducing hostility toward those police, especially by minority group members. Community policing must also be systematic in dealing with a targeted problem. Cummings suggests that problem-oriented policing comprises four stages:

> scanning, which involves the identification of the problem; analysis, during which the relevant data about the problem are collected; response, which occurs when the problem is addressed; and assessment, in which responses are evaluated . . . problems must be defined in very specific terms . . . information about the problems must be collected from sources outside the police agency, not just from internal sources

... police agencies must engage in a *broad* search for solutions including various alternatives to the criminal justice process. (Cummings 1990, p. 63)

The concept of community must also include the notions, not only of police collaboration with local citizens, but of close collaboration with other justice system elements both within and outside the department. For example, it is critically important that court workers, police, and probation officers work closely at the front end of the justice system to share information and develop appropriate supervisory and social service approaches to particular gang youth. Otherwise the justice system remains fragmented and does not fulfil its potential as the public component of a preventive community control and support system.

The community policing cum problem-oriented approach must be appropriately structured depending on the needs, interests, and culture of the particular community, as well as police organizational law enforcement mission. Police officers have to be located geographically in and connected meaningfully to the area of operations. They have to be clearly identified as accessible in terms compatible with the expectations of the particular neighborhood. One example is an Asian Advisory Committee on Crime (AACC) that deals with gang and other crime problems. It is directly available to newly arrived city residents through police officers who are able to communicate in a language residents understand:

> Four outreach Public Information officers were established at strategic well-marked locations in the Laotian, Chinese, Vietnamese and Cambodian communities. They are staffed by bilingual police officers, AACC members and other community volunteers. The staff provides police services—taking reports, assisting citizens with the criminal justice process and making appropriate referrals to other agencies.
>
> ... The Asian Crime Committee ... is the sworn officer arm of the Advisory Committee ... the committee deals with organized Asian gang activity, disturbances with racial overtones and juvenile group violence. As a police officer in the community, Sgt. Chinn investigates crime and makes arrests, but he acts also as coordinator for the community-based organizations and feeds them the law enforcement information ... resulting in a vast increase in witness cooperation from the Asian communities. (Chinn 1990, pp. 128)

In many respects, the vision of community policing is to build the community. The police become a "resource for the community, aiding local residents and working with indigenous leaders to solve community problems, with special focus on the problems of young people. The goal ... is to promote the achievement of 'functional communities,' that is, communities in which family life, work, religion, education, law enforcement, and other institutional areas reflect and reinforce common values" (Short 1990a, p. 226). This goal, however, must be carefully operationalized.

A variety of devices can be employed to structure a closer relationship between police and community. For example, getting police, as in earlier times, to walk the beat, get to know local residents, develop informal and positive relationships with gang youths, even live in the area of patrol.

> The three officers live in the neighborhood to which they are assigned as part of the experiment inaugurated last June by Elgin Police Chief Charles Gruber. ... Gorcowski [a juvenile officer, tries] to get to know everybody in the hood. But you try to know the bad guys first. You want to know who's against you, who your enemies are, as

well as who your friends are. . . . Gorcowski's job involves walking the neighbor-hood, visiting its schools, talking to neighbors, and working with public and private agencies that serve the area. . . . He recalled one man, well known to police, who didn't trust him at first. The man told Gorcowski he wanted to work, but his police record kept him from getting a job. . . . "I called some people at factories around here and asked them to help," the officer recalled. "They gave him a job." (Houston 1992a)

It is possible to interpret certain initiatives of federal and local government as partial, indirect, or unintended yet beginning efforts at community policing directed to the gang problem. In recent years the federal government has been particularly concerned with improved coordination and communication across juvenile justice units in dealing with serious habitual offenders. The Office of Juvenile Justice and Delinquency Prevention, and more recently the Bureau of Justice Assistance of the U.S. Justice Department, has embarked on a series of programs to prevent serious gang offenders from falling through the cracks and avoiding appropriate justice sys-tem processing. Cooperation, the sharing of information including rosters and pro-files of targeted youths, and case management across police, prosecutors, schools, probation, corrections, and social and community aftercare services have been key goals of the Integrated Criminal Apprehension Program and Serious Habitual Offen-der Comprehensive Action Program (American Institute for Research 1988; *National Crime Prevention Institute 1988*).

Increasingly, the notion of community involvement, as well as interagency coor-dination and information sharing, has guided the efforts of law enforcement agen-cies, especially the police, in addressing the gang problem. The assumption that youth gangs can be eliminated and the gang problem resolved by simply jailing all gang members is no longer valid, let alone constitutional. Jackson and McBride, long-time gang police experts, observed that "experience and studies have yet to show an in-stance in which a street gang was dissolved or put out of action because of suppres-sive police action. When police pressure is intensified on a street gang, its members typically go underground and become secretive" (1985, p. 108).

New Police Structures and Programs

Police structures for dealing with youth gangs have included youth division, com-munity relations, homicide, violence, patrol, and detective units or task forces, as well as specialized gang units. Such units tend to state their objectives in somewhat broader terms than do specialized gang units. For example, Philadelphia's Preven-tive Patrol Unit aims to "render assistance and guidance to the youths of the commu-nity as well as the investigation and containment of acts of juvenile crimes in the area of organized crime" (Philadelphia Police Department, Preventive Patrol Unit 1987, p. 1); the basic responsibility is law enforcement (apprehension and arrest of violators), but emphasis is on "selective enforcement concomitant with community need" (ibid.). Effective enforcement not only serves the criminal justice system and the community, but also aids in the prevention and containment of the gang problem (Collins 1979, pp. 155–156).

A great variety of community-based, preventive, and developmental procedures are incorporated into the evolving community policing model targeted to the gang problem, including: school-based lecture programs; school and probation liaisons; broad-scale information dissemination about gang problems; recreation; job programs; counseling; referral of youths to social and community agencies; working with parents and community organizations in preventive and control efforts; and training teachers and agency and community representatives how to recognize and deal with gang members and gang problems (see Needle and Stapleton 1983).

Special broad-purpose coordination mechanisms may be created both within and outside of police units to assist troubled youngsters, including gang members. For example, a Gang Event Response Team was established in San Francisco to ensure a coordinated intradepartmental response to gang-related incidents. Representatives of the Narcotics, Gang Intelligence, Community Services, and Patrol units or divisions jointly investigate gang-related shootings. These resources are in addition to normal liaison with homicide and other police units as well as with district attorneys, probation officers, judges, parole and correctional officials, and still other law enforcement officers in overlapping jurisdictions to facilitate gang suppression and justice and correctional system processing activities.

There is no easy, precise set of responsibilities for law enforcement agencies dealing with the gang problem. The task can be an overwhelming and frustrating burden for a police department if approached in a way that focuses only on suppression. Police departments can be creative and their officers can experience great satisfaction if the task is approached in more flexible, multidimensional terms. For example, the Phoenix police sponsor many community programs that target at-risk youths, including gang members. Through a Police Activities League, members of the police force take young people on shopping trips; organize recreational, social, and educational programs; and arrange job opportunities. The police also sponsor a Boy Scout Explorer Post, with police officers volunteering as Scout masters or leaders (McKinney 1988). In Pasadena, California, a Youth Services Coordination and Intensive Care Unit was established with specially trained police officers to work on a one-to-one basis with juveniles who had gotten into trouble with the law. The police acted simultaneously as informal probation officers, counselors, and "Big Brothers." Some police officers actually obtained teaching certificates and were assigned to counsel and teach students in class (Oleisky 1981).

In Oakland, California, the Transit Authority joined with local civic leaders to attack graffiti and unemployment problems simultaneously. Gang leaders were offered jobs and encouraged to locate other potential youths to clean buses. As a result, the buses were cleaned, young people got jobs, and the word got out that marking up buses was not "cool" because cleaning them was tough work. Furthermore, an organization encompassing many youth gangs in the area, Bay Area United Youth, was established as part of the Community Values Program, Inc. In New York City, a somewhat similar effort, Inner City Round Table on Youth (ICRY), was encouraged by the police to bring representatives of gangs together "in terms of talking about training for the future . . . for a vocation" (Galea 1982, p. 228). In El Monte, California, the collaboration of the police and the Boys' Club resulted in special job development and job referral projects for gang members. The police were influential in prevailing upon local employers to hire gang leaders (Amandes 1979; Clayton 1983).

In Chicago's Little Village, a community oriented project, the Gang Violence

Reduction Program, has been recently initiated to target hard-core gang offenders, 17 to 25 years of age, in dealing with serious gang violence. The Chicago Police Department has contracted with the Cook County Probation Department and the University of Chicago's School of Social Service Administration in the development of an integrated team approach within a framework of outreach, church and community agency involvement, and social resource provision. Former gang leaders are collaborating with police and probation officers to mediate, prevent, and control gang conflicts as well as assist current hard-core gang youths to return to school, obtain jobs (which are being opened up for them), and obtain other appropriate services. Police, probation, and community youth workers coordinate their efforts, including joint field operations and sharing of information. Gang youths are fully aware of the purpose and nature of the project.

In Rochester, New York, a youth-outreach program was established by the police to:

> (1) hire and train youth-outreach workers; (2) afford the Rochester Police Department the opportunity to establish better community relations with the younger members of the community; (3) respond to the needs of area youths in proactive rather than reactive manner; (4) reach youths involved in organized groups/gangs who may or have become involved in illegal or disruptive behavior; (5) refer youths involved with gangs to agencies that can assist them with specific problems.
>
> The Rochester Police Department Teens on Patrol Program has hired over 60 teens that have been identified as youth-group members over the last three years. The workers have also been instrumental in forewarning the Department about planned confrontations between rival groups, and major problems have been averted. (Dunston 1990, p. 28)

Role of the Officer. The police officer in these newer approaches emphasizes the importance of both suppression and social intervention, obtaining information that will ensure proper prosecution and conviction, preventing youth gang crime, helping members leave the gang, and in a variety of ways contributing to their improved social functioning. Communication with gang youths to obtain intelligence and the development of positive relations with them are key elements of gang-oriented community policing that does not deny the value of suppression as part of social control.

> He has the responsibility of becoming knowledgeable as quickly as possible with the gang and its members; particularly the leadership of the gang. . . . In meeting or "rapping" with the gang, it will be his function to establish a trustful or quasi-friendly relationship that will elicit information and intelligence that can be utilized and still allow him to return and speak with the gang from time to time. The success or failure of a Gang Intelligence Unit [GIU] is dependent on the ability of a GIU officer to make inroads with the gang or its members by his ability to relate, identify with, and listen to the real or imaginary problems they present. (Collins 1979, p. 140)

Under the newer, evolving, community-oriented approach, the police officer can perform a variety of roles—assisting a youth to obtain a job, counseling youth in school, referring youths with personal and family problems for social services, mediating gang fights, and training other human service personnel and neighborhood residents on how to deal with gangs, as well as arresting and contributing to the prosecution of law-violating gang youths. Most important, he must be able to communicate with the gang youth in such a way as to demonstrate respect, acceptance, and concern for, as well as effective control of, the youth. For example:

> Galea, a police officer in the Gang Intelligence Unit in Brooklyn [developed a] curiously friendly relationship [with street clubs, i.e., gangs]. . . . He listened to their problems, tried to effect reconciliation with other clubs, [and] played softball with them. They pumped him for gossip on other clubs' activities, expected him to get criminal charges against them dropped, even demanded that he visit them in prison or write them job references. (Campbell 1984b, pp. 1–2)

Sergeant Galea's view of his own work was a little more complex:

> I have two roles. I am their [gang members'] friend, but also their foe. . . . I personally am responsible for many of them being locked up [but] they always come to me to help them . . . getting them jobs . . . back in school, we have got a couple into the armed forces. . . . They know that if they commit a crime they are going to be arrested. But they also know that they can come and talk about it to us. (Galea 1982, pp. 223–225)

Effectiveness. We do not yet know how effective this new (perhaps very old or more traditional) multidimensional, community involvement, problem-oriented, and gang-targeted approach is or will be. One long-time police gang investigator and analyst claims that:

> The investigators found that, as they applied firm but fair law enforcement and used their personal knowledge of the gang members backed by a demonstrated humanitarian concern for the status of the individual, violence within targeted gangs began to decline. . . . Many of the gangs targeted early in the program [also involving prosecution and probation] showed a 50% decrease in overall activity. (McBride 1993, p. 413)

Hard long-term evaluative data, however, are not available on police community problem-solving strategies that include prevention or social intervention and social opportunities provision, as well as suppression. In one limited evaluation of police assisting gang youths with job referrals, the results were mixed. Gang members found jobs as easily on their own as processed through a special police-sponsored job-referral program (Willman and Snortum 1982). More important, it was not clear that the program contributed to a reduction of gang and/or non-gang crime. However, other preliminary reports on the positive effects of community policing strategies are suggestive:

> Through a program launched February I, under the nickname "Operation Cul-de-Sac," police [L.A. city] have moved away from the hammer-like tactics that have characterized recent anti-gang sweeps, and instead have painted over graffiti, hauled away trash, attended high school dances and even hosted picnics, complete with piñatas and pony rides. . . . Officials say that since the program began, crime in the neighborhood has been cut 12 percent compared to the same period last year, from 483 major felonies to 425. Drive-by shootings have dropped 64 percent from 14 to 5 . . . [citizen fear of being hurt by gangs . . . had fallen]. (Jesse Katz 1990)
> Elgin's [Illinois] Gifford Park was a danger zone. . . . Drug dealers and gang

members were a fixture on nearby street corners. . . . A decision by the community and police department to join forces [was made]. . . . Elgin police, churches, community organizations, concerned mothers and even a gang banger-turned-preacher call it a success. . . . Gang-related crime in the city fell 19 percent in 1991, to 291 incidents compared with 358 in 1990 . . . gang-related fights dipped 24 percent. (Fountain 1992)

Reno [Nevada] adapted a community-based policing program in 1988, when drive-by shootings were running at roughly 40–50 per year. The following year the total dropped to seven. In the first half of 1991, there were none . . . [the program, however, apparently focuses on children or wannabes] . . . Kids are picked up before they become hardcore gang members . . . and returned to their parents. Churches and social service agencies are involved and available along with police to help . . . The police department backs up the basic effort with recreational programs and other gang projects [however, not adequately explained is the relation between the sudden cessation of drive-by shootings probably by older gang youth and the development of a prevention program addressed to much younger youth]. (Reiner 1992, pp.133–134)

The success of newer community-oriented police models probably will vary under different community conditions—including the scope and severity of gang problems; state law; the availability of strong police leadership; and especially, appropriate community interest and resources to support and develop alternate strategies, such as good school remedial programs and job opportunities. Obviously, a great deal more descriptive and evaluative research is required to determine the specific nature and effectiveness of these various police community gang problem strategies and programs.

Conclusion

This chapter analyzed traditional, often specialized police suppression and more complex community involvement and social development approaches to the street-gang problem. A vigorous "lock-em-up" approach appears to remain the key line of action of police departments, particularly in larger cities with acknowledged gang problems. Police departments in some cities in California, for example, have operated on the basis of a moral crusade against gangs, with law enforcement suppression programs with acronyms like CRASH, GET, SMASH. Large, specialized, centralized gang units were organized in certain large cities. Before its reorganization, the Chicago Police Department's highly suppression-oriented gang unit contained about 500 officers. It was the largest unit in the department.

At the heart of the suppression approach is the assumption that most street gangs are criminal associations that must be attacked through an efficient gang tracking, identification, and targeted enforcement strategy. Law enforcement officials have argued and demonstrated that improved data collection systems and coordination of information across different justice system agencies lead to more efficiency and to more gang members being removed from the streets, rapidly prosecuted, and sent to prison for longer sentences. However, gang problems remain, grow, and "spread." Further, a series of constitutional questions has been raised about targeting gangs without sufficient attention to the actual commission of crimes by individual members. Also, there is little evidence that the various specialized suppression programs and tactics have been effective in reducing the gang problem in either large or small cities.

A more complex multidimensional, citizen-involved, and sometimes police-directed community problem-solving approach seems to be evolving. This newer approach assumes that local community groups and agencies, as well as gang or former gang members themselves, must bear responsibility for and participate collaboratively in control of gang violence and criminal behavior. A variety of community-oriented police structures and programs is developing to deal with the gang problem, including school-based police lecture programs, counseling, referral of youths to social and community agencies, and work with parents, gangs, probation, and community organizations in gang violence prevention and control efforts.

Reality-based more limited goals, such as gang violence reduction, rather than the simple and naive goal of youth gang destruction, are now established. The police officer in these newer approaches emphasizes the importance of both suppression and social intervention, obtaining information that will ensure proper prosecution and conviction as well as prevent serious youth gang crime and help members to leave the gang and adapt socially. The police officer learns to communicate with gang youths in such a way as to demonstrate respect, acceptance, and concern for, as well as effective control of, the youth. Nevertheless, while a community problem-solving approach to the gang problem appears to be promising, systematic evaluation of its effectiveness is not yet available.

13

Prosecution, Defense, and the Judiciary

Prosecutors and judges are the criminal justice officials most likely to view the gang problem in straightforward and uncomplicated suppression terms. The key question that guides the prosecutor is, "How do we take the gang member who is committing crimes and successfully keep him behind bars" (Genelin 1993, pp. 1, 2). The prosecutor often tends to see his or her job as processing, convicting, and winning long sentences for gang youths on maximum charges as quickly as possible. Often judges in juvenile court believe that the youth-gang problem belongs in adult criminal court. State law may require automatic transfer of certain juveniles committing violent offenses and permit use of RICO (Racketeer Influenced Corrupt Organizations) statutes to combat gang crime. Judges have tended to consider gangs as a serious and organized threat to society. State law, political pressures, public opinion, and lack of firsthand knowledge of the problem largely determine these hard-line views and actions.

The problems inherent in gang cases have led to the development of new suppression tactics and new organizational forms for increased efficiency in maximizing convictions and sentences. The deliberate and increased use of the label "gang-related" by prosecutors in California and other states has had far-reaching ramifications. Gang offenders have been singled out for investigation and processing by special gang prosecution units. In response, the court sometimes and defense attorneys more often have had to develop special counter tactics and procedures. At trial, gang affiliation has raised a host of evidentiary problems for the judge and jurors. At sentencing, evidence of gang membership is almost sure to affect the judge's exercise of discretion (Burrell 1990).

The roles of prosecutors, defense attorneys, and judges in respect to the problem are very slowly evolving. Much practice by prosecutors is still suppressive (the approach of judges to gang cases is cautious and less clearly articulated). The procedures of defense attorneys are evolving more rapidly in response to the tactics of prosecutors. This chapter emphasizes descriptive and prescriptive roles of these court actors. The analysis and critique emphasize the need for greater attention by these court-based actors to a community-mobilized and opportunities approach, or at least for a closer court relationship to community-based organizations and institutions and focus both on rehabilitation of gang youths and protection of the community from them.

The Specialized Prosecution Strategy

The prosecutor represents the state as protector of the community's interests and guardian of the integrity of the justice system through vigorous enforcement of its laws. The prosecutor's ethical responsibility is to promote justice in its broadest sense, not simply to convict individuals or win legal battles. The lawyer's code of professional responsibility states that the responsibility of a public prosecutor differs from that of the usual advocate. The prosecutor's duty is to seek justice, not merely to convict. The prosecutor in the juvenile court, in addition, has the duty of maintaining the "community's and the legal system's commitment to the integrity of the family" (Fink 1987, p. 282) and the reciprocal rights and responsibilities of parents and children to each other. Finally, the prosecutor "represents the sovereign" and makes decisions affecting the public interests; therefore, he or she should "use restraint in the discretionary exercise of governmental powers," such as the selection of cases to prosecute (ibid.).

Gang cases pose special problems for prosecutors in regard to court jurisdiction, witness protection, and the value of suppression or threat of jail sentences. Such cases often involve juveniles and adults acting together, who are then prosecuted in different courts. Not only the offenders but also the victims are often members of gangs. The offenses are group or subculturally motivated. The acts committed are sometimes extremely violent. The prosecution of gang cases also must be specially concerned with consequences for the safety of witnesses and the potential for intimidation of jurors. Furthermore, gang defendants often are not deterred by prison sentences. All of this means that gang cases require that prosecutors have specialized knowledge about gang structure, gang processes, the current pattern of intergang relationships in particular community contexts and time periods, and complex understanding of both causes and remedies for the problem.

Much of the special prosecutorial approach to gang crime in urban jurisdictions throughout the United States is very recent and owes its origins to the pioneering experience and evolving suppression tactics of the Los Angeles County District Attorney's Office in the late 1970s. According to Genelin and Naimen:

> Gang cases are not easy to prosecute. Ten years ago, the Los Angeles District Attorney's Office was losing a large percentage of them because gang members did not want to testify against rival gang members. Instead, they preferred street payback. Furthermore, if non-gang witnesses were at the scene, they were either too frightened to cooperate or soon became so because of threats, actual physical intimidation, or murder. There was another factor: gang members talked a language unique to their culture. Attorneys did not maximize results because they did not know what questions to ask or how to ask them. (Genelin and Naimen 1988, p. 1)

Since the early 1980s, a few large and medium-sized cities, with the stimulus of federal funds, have created hard-core gang or vertical prosecution units, which pay special attention to gang crime suspects. The prosecutor had, until then, generally ignored the gang-related circumstances of a case for several reasons. The prosecutor earlier believed that the identification of a crime as gang-related tended to divert the jury's focus from the actual crime to the question of gang affiliation. This distraction was viewed as being counterproductive and therefore to be avoided. Furthermore, a prosecutor usually had incomplete information from the police or sheriff about gang-situational characteristics. He or she was not able to determine whether gang affiliation signified a greater or lesser threat to community safety.

The original system of vertical prosecution represented a rational, specialized, mainly deterrent outreach strategy by district or states attorneys. It assumed that gangs could be controlled best through an efficient and a somewhat community-based approach that is fully informed about gang events. It emphasized vigorous, proactive prosecution, particularly for the most serious, violent, or drug-related gang cases involving gang leaders and core members. The original premise was that "a few gang members commit a significant proportion of the crimes and negatively influence the behavior of other gang members. Effective deterrence was to incapacitate offenders through incarceration, particularly those leading other gang members in illegal, violent activities" (California Office of Criminal Justice Planning 1987, p. 4).

With the significant increase of gang members involved in drug-related and criminal gang activities across state lines, federal prosecutors have also become more and more involved. The "carrying capacity of the federal system," however, remains very small compared with local needs and efforts (Reiner 1992, p. 158). Because the Los Angeles County District Attorney's Office hard-core or vertical prosecution gang unit was established mainly to deal with felony violent cases (it has dealt almost exclusively with homicide cases in recent years), the Los Angeles City Attorney created its own vertical prosecution unit in 1987 to focus on hard-core gang-member misdemeanor cases (ibid., pp. 172–173).

With the great rise in gang cases of both the Los Angeles County and the Los Angeles City offices, the missions of both agencies have been overwhelmed and their functions increasingly focused on a suppression approach. The Hard Core Gang Division of the Los Angeles County District Attorney's Office handles only about half of all gang homicide cases. The huge homicide case load has also forced the hard-core prosecutors to eliminate time spent with police and sheriff's gang officers in the field (Reiner 1992, p. 169).

Vertical Prosecution

Under vertical prosecution, usually one prosecutor (rather than a shifting array of prosecutors) handles a case from its "inception until its disposition in the criminal justice system" (Daley 1985, p. 18). One assistant state's attorney or district attorney participates in the "full range of prosecutorial functions for any given case investigation, use of the grand jury, arrest, filing of charges, preliminary hearing, pretrial motions, plea conferences, trial, and sentencing" (ibid.). When both juveniles and adults are involved, the same prosecutor is used, often with the same police officers, to deal with the various cases. If selection of the more serious case is required, the adult participant is more likely to receive special attention. Elaborations of the vertical prosecution approach include special units directed to gang-related narcotics cases in Los Angeles (Los Angeles County Probation Department 1988, p. 10) and to juvenile drug-gang cases in San Diego (Davidson 1987).

Vertical prosecution organizations perform a variety of law-related and community leadership functions with respect to the gang problem.

The Institute for Law and Justice reported that in 1991, 32 percent of prosecutors in large jurisdictions (more than 250,000 population), but only 5 percent in small jurisdictions (50,000 to 250,000 population), had formed vertical prosecution units to focus on gang members. These units were usually staffed by two to four full-time attorneys. The Los Angeles County prosecutor's office, the largest in the nation, was staffed by 48 full-time attorneys (1994, pp. 1, 2–13).

Highly qualified prosecutors and special investigators are selected. Reduced case loads and special coordinating relations with law enforcement agencies are established to develop the most effective evidence for prosecution and also to provide protection to cooperating witnesses by preventing intimidation or retaliation by the defendant's gang associates (California Office of Criminal Justice Planning 1987, p. 4). The district attorney has increasingly been accorded a leadership role in the community's war against gangs, particularly in California. By California state law, the vertical prosecution attorney or senior attorney also acts as chairperson of an interagency gang task force in each county. The task force serves as a coordinating body not only for other law enforcement and supervisory authorities, such as police and probation, but also for school and community-based agencies concerned with gang problems. The task force is a communications mechanism, a policymaking organization, and a project-generating group. In Los Angeles County, this body has stimulated the development of an interagency gang information system, GREAT (Gang Reporting Evaluation and Tracking) as well as social programs funded by "Youth At Work" throughout the city.

In recent years, California law has been concerned primarily with law enforcement, prosecution, and deterrent probation efforts in dealing with problems of gang crime. Gang suppression has aimed at providing broad, clear, and strong procedures for bringing suspects and offenders to justice. The Los Angeles County District Attorney's Office has improved prosecution of gang cases by forbidding plea bargains . . . "in all felony cases involving weapons and/or violence whether or not they involve gang members" (Reiner 1992, p. 171). The inclusion of community-based organizations such as schools and youth service agencies has served mainly to extend and strengthen the investigative and information-gathering capacities of law enforcement. The provisions for special school curricula and services for youth at risk of gang membership have thus far received secondary attention and limited funding.

The California Street Terrorism Enforcement and Prevention (STEP) Act of 1988 has been a major instrument for the Los Angeles County and City District Attorney's offices to deter serious gang crime. The Act and its implementation procedures, particularly in Los Angeles County, have since become a basis for dealing with the problem in several states throughout the country. The Act not only "makes it a crime to engage in criminal gang activity, [but] subjects persons to sentence provision aimed at buildings in which criminal gang activity takes place and permits the prosecution of parents under a parental responsibility theory" (Burrell 1990, p. 745). Under the Act, law enforcement officers serve personal notices on gang members, who then become eligible for enhanced sentences. The notice ensures that the gang member has read and understands the Act and that he or she is aware of the gang's illegal activities and its legal status as a criminal street gang (Reiner 1992, p. 161).

Some analysts believe that the abatement provision of the Act has, in fact, had some deterrent effect:

> After L.A.P.D. served STEP notices in the Harbor Area, there was a 44 percent drop in gang-related crime from 1989 to 1990. The Jordan Down's Housing Project experienced a 50 percent drop in gang-related crime after notices were served in December 1989. In both cases, the notices were accompanied by other anti-gang measures (including targeted policing, the Community Reclamation Act and the L.A. City Attorney's Gang Civil Abatement Program . . .).
>   In San Fernando, a STEP-like process has been used to keep warring gangs out of a park. . . . Two warring gangs . . . claimed Los Palmos as their turf and had turned it into a free-fire zone. . . . An ordinance [was created] which imposes a fine of $250 on any criminal street gang member who enters the park. . . . [While the Act] is currently under legal challenge by the ACLU on grounds that it violates the rights of gang members . . . so powerful has been the deterrent effect that . . . three citations have been issued in six months. (Reiner 1992, pp. 162–163)

Sophisticated data gathering, planning, and coordination are at the heart of the prosecutorial suppression strategy to deal with the burgeoning gang problem. These include:

- the development of a central file of gang activity across city, town, and suburban community jurisdictions within the county and sometimes across counties to which all police departments would have access.
- the creation of a comprehensive tracking system of all gang-related crime from the time of arrest through prosecution;
- establishment of conferences and seminars that would supply intensive gang awareness training to police and prosecutors; planning and coordination objectives, mechanisms, and reports, often involving expert views that define the nature and scope of the gang problem and which make recommendations for official action (Kuczka 1991; Reiner 1992, pp. 211ff).

Characteristics of the vertical prosecution strategy, based on the Institute for Law and Justice national survey, includes emphasis on transfer of certain juvenile gang members to adult court. Seventy-one percent of prosecutors in large jurisdictions (including all 175 counties with more than 250,000 people) compared to 38 percent of prosecutors in smaller jurisdictions (including 193 prosecutors randomly selected from counties of 50,000 to 250,000 population) sought such transfers from juvenile to adult criminal court. Close to 35 percent of prosecutors in large jurisdictions and 11 percent in small jurisdictions undertook forfeiture of vehicles used in drive-by shootings. "Although 31 states have RICO statutes, only about 12 percent of large county prosecutors and fewer than 10 percent of small county prosecutors have ever used RICO against gang members. About 36 percent of prosecutors in both large and small counties are using state drug kingpin statutes against gang members. State conspiracy law has been used by 37 percent of large jurisdictions and 26 percent of small jurisdictions" (1994, p. 2–14).

The prosecutorial suppression strategy also gives some emphasis to early identification of children who are at risk of being recruited as gang members, and encourages social programs on their behalf. An assumption is that juvenile offenders, or even status offenders, progress in due course to gang membership. Such progression, however, has not been demonstrated in the findings of criminal justice research (see Kobrin and Klein 1983; Spergel and Hartnett, 1990). Furthermore, efforts to hold parents responsible for the gang activity of their children have generally not proven successful or constitutional, since "responsible parenting" is usually not defined. Civil liberties lawyers believe that "the problem of gang violence is great, but we do not need to abridge the Constitution in order to achieve peaceful streets" (Associated Press 1991).

Innovative Prosecutorial Tactics

The vertical prosecution strategy has been accompanied by a growing panoply of "gang law" and tactics to address difficult evidentiary and logistical problems that characterize the collective nature of gang offenses (Daley 1985, p. 2). Of special interest is the development of the law of accountability or accessoryship in which a gang member can be held responsible for the crimes of another committed outside his presence where it can be proved that he "advised, encouraged, aided, or abetted the perpetration of the crime" (ibid.). The law of conspiracy has been associated with the law of accountability so that "it is not necessary to show a formal agreement between the parties . . . it is sufficient to show a mutual understanding of the parties which may be established by direct or circumstantial evidence or combination thereof" (ibid., pp. 5–6). Innovative strategies and tactics have been developed by prosecutors and defense attorneys, respectively, to implement and challenge these laws or prosecutorial procedures. Some judges restrict the application of these statutes in homicide cases to those who actually kill or possess the intent required for murder, and intent must be more than imputed.

According to the findings of the national survey conducted by the Institute for Law and Justice (1994), prosecutors in large jurisdictions use more approaches than prosecutors in small jurisdictions against gang members. These tactics include participation in special gang enforcement initiatives with other criminal justice agencies, discouraging reduced charges brought against gang members, access to police computerized gang member-tracking systems and participation in broad-based anti-gang coalitions (p. 2–16).

The Hard Core Division of the Los Angeles County District Attorney's Office has developed a set of tools for prosecution of gang cases based on (1) the use of trained investigators, (2) widening the scope of the search warrant, (3) the selection and education of the jury, (4) the use of the police officer as expert witness, (5) setting bail, (6) dealing with recalcitrant witnesses and informants, (7) witness protection, (8) countering courtroom intimidation by gang members, and (9) establishing that gang members can be held accountable for a group criminal action (Reiner 1992, p. 162; see also Genelin and Naimen 1988).

Trained Investigators. Genelin and Naimen emphasize the importance of a well-trained gang-investigating officer who can read placa, or gang graffiti, and testify to its meaning in court. The investigator must be aware of gang processes and the current state of gang and intergang activities and relationships in the community. It is important not only that the investigating officer meaningfully interview witnesses, but also that the prosecutor personally interview gang witnesses and record testimony on videotape (whenever possible), which can be played later before the jury. One or more witnesses often will recant testimony because of a preference for personal payback—if the witness is a member of the opposing gang—because he or she (usually a non-gang member) was intimidated or because there is a general feeling that the police are the real enemies. The video or tape recording then becomes important as a backup.

Search Warrant. A special warrant is needed to obtain evidence. Gang members often retain items that can be of special value to gang prosecution, for example, weapons, photos, gang paraphernalia. "Gang members are proud of the fact they are in a gang. . . . They will paint their rooms with gang placa, have banners . . . books of photographs of themselves and other gang members flashing signs and displaying weapons." These items are viewed as good material for trial and the "critical task is to obtain it" (Genelin and Naimen 1988, p. 3) through an expanded search warrant justified (for example, searching for evidence of motivation for a crime) by an experienced investigator.

Selecting the Jury. The prosecutor should educate the jury about the distinctive characteristics of a gang case. Customs—such as payback, gang signs, graffiti, and intimidation—have to be stressed. The prosecutor needs to be alert to certain prejudices in jurors, which will hurt his or her case. For example, a juror who lives in the area of the gang member on trial may be too frightened to render a "people's verdict." Other factors that influence jurors' perceptions include whether the juror is related to gang members, the juror's prior membership in a gang, and his or her attitudes toward police (Genelin and Naimen 1988, p. 6).

Expert Witness. An expert witness is often used to establish not only that the defendant is a gang member, but also that a gang conspiracy exists to commit a crime. Case law holds that gang membership can be considered as circumstantial evidence of a conspiracy. A qualified expert can testify about membership in gangs, rivalry between gangs, common practices of gangs and gang members, gang terminology, street codes of conduct, and even specific and identifiable types of gangs. ". . . Interlinking gang evidence with the crime is a force for conviction, and explaining a witness's demeanor by way of gang affiliation can go a long way toward winning a case" (Genelin and Naimen 1988, pp. 5–7).

District attorneys are prone to use police gang-crime officers as gang experts. Genelin and Naimen have noted that "the law permits you to detail a gang's activities in general, the specific activities of the gang and even . . . emphasize singular facts . . . using the expert to hammer home all your evidence" (undated, pp. 5–6). Burrell, a defense attorney, however, writes that it is important to disassociate the defendant from a gang relationship, if possible. She attacks the notion of necessarily using any or all police as "experts," by definition:

> The fact that officers have been assigned to the "gang detail" or have made many arrests in gang-related cases is not sufficient to qualify them as experts. [The California] Evidence Code, Section 720(a) requires that the expert himself possess special

knowledge, skill, experience, training or education in the subject to which his testimony relates. Repeated observations of an event without inquiry, analysis or experiment does not turn the mere observer into an expert. (Burrell 1990, p. 770)

Bail. According to Genelin and Naimen, bail often should be set as high as possible to avoid inappropriate releases, to develop additional information, and to persuade reluctant witnesses to testify. Gang offenses may be very serious, and the defendant often has a long prior record. The defendant may attempt to flee; the victim may die; the defendant himself may be at risk of a payback. The solution, according to Genelin and Naimen, is to recategorize the offense as a more serious crime that allows a prereview, no-bail hold. An additional process may also be used if the funds for the bail were obtained through illegal means: "no bail bond shall be accepted unless the judge or magistrate is convinced that no portion of the security pledged was feloniously obtained by the defendant" (Genelin and Naimen undated, pp. 12–13). Furthermore, if a defendant is in jail, it may allow for the development of other evidence "by way of jailhouse informants, seizure of incriminating communications with co-defendants, or by simple observation of the defendant in a social milieu with other members of his gang" (p. 5).

Recalcitrant Witnesses. The prosecution of gang cases is particularly difficult because it requires not only the cooperation of victims and witnesses in the case against the suspected offender. However, inter-gang violence involves the suspect or defendant, victim, and other witnesses in a series of interchangeable and revolving roles (Institute for Law and Justice 1994, p. 7). Genelin and Naimen have elaborated the uses of bail or custody in California to persuade recalcitrant witnesses for the prosecution to testify against the defendant. "A magistrate may exact from each witness who testifies at the preliminary hearing a written promise that he will appear and testify or else forfeit the sum of $500 (Genelin and Naimen undated, pp. 11–12). The judge may also issue a "body attachment for the defaulting witness. . . . One night in custody is usually enough to ensure cooperation from a witness, or at least . . . appearance in court . . ." (ibid.).

Witness Protection. Special attention is often required in cases involving gang leaders or core members in order to protect witnesses for the prosecution. Witnesses, as already suggested, may be exposed to intimidation or undue influence from members of the opposing gang. If the witness is released, the investigators should keep track of him or her and what is occurring in the community, since the subject may be under great community pressure not to testify. "Careful consideration should be given to removing witnesses from the area and relocating them in safer neighborhoods" (Genelin and Naimen undated, p. 9). The Los Angeles County District Attorney's Office's Victim Witness Program provides special assistance to minority victims of gang violence (Reiner 1992, p. 167).

Genelin and Naimen believe and stress that most of the witnesses in gang cases are themselves gang members. They share common backgrounds: "They tend to have long prior records, they tend to be chronic drug users, they are currently in trouble with the law, and they are chronic liars" (undated, p. 13). Therefore, Genelin and

Naimen indicate the importance of the development of detailed collaborative evidence to make the testimony of the gang member as prosecution witness believable. Furthermore, if it is necessary to obtain testimony through a plea bargain with the witness for his own crime, the bargain should be a "measured and rational one. Total immunity should be given only as a last resort" (p. 14).

Courtroom Intimidation. A variety of techniques have been devised to prevent intimidation of witnesses and specifically to limit courtroom intimidation by gang members who are usually present for the proceedings. If witnesses are in jail, Genelin and Naimen advise: get them housed in different court modules than the defendant or the defendant's fellow gang members; don't transport members of opposing gangs in the same vehicle or house them together in the same court-holding cell. During the course of the trial, use additional investigators, police, or bailiffs; identify gang members to the judge and jury; frisk and remove gang members from court; police officers should request gang members present "to pose for a Polaroid picture" to be placed in the gang book; and arrest gang members in court, if they are discovered to be on probation or parole, for violation of provisions of nonassociation with gang members (Genelin and Naimen undated, p. 4).

Gang Accountability. Most important, the prosecutor is concerned with the issue of how to establish group intent and "how to attach criminal liability to the members of the group," (Genelin and Naimen undated, pp. 15–16) even if they were not present at the scene of the crime. California law, the same as Illinois law, makes it possible to prove an abettor guilty of a crime if the defendant "(1) acted with knowledge of the criminal purposes of the perpetrator, (2) acted with the intent or purpose of . . . committing, encouraging, or facilitating the commission of the offense, or (3) by act or advice promoted, encouraged, or instigated the commission of the offense. . . . The conspirator . . . is guilty not only of the offense he intended to facilitate or encourage, but also of any reasonably foreseeable offense committed by the person he aides or abets" (Genelin and Naimen undated, pp. 15–16).

Defense Attorneys

Defense attorneys, in turn, have begun to develop innovative techniques and procedures to counter vertical prosecution efforts. Major objectives of the defense are to disassociate the defendant from identification as a gang member and to prevent the crime the youth is accused of committing from being classified as gang related. The labels "gang," "gang member," and "gang-related crime" have far-reaching ramifications in a criminal case. At sentencing, evidence of gang membership ordinarily results in enhanced sentences or special probation conditions. Questions that therefore can be raised by the defense attorney include: the adequacy of the identification of the accused as a gang member; the indiscriminate practice of stopping or arresting youths on suspicion of being gang members and of having committed a crime; the nature of gang evidence admitted in court and its relevance to the crime committed; the qualifications of the gang expert witness; and the constitutionality of the law (for example, California's Street Terrorism Act).

Susan Burrell emphasizes the importance of the "discovery" of police records of gang affiliation. Mistakes are made in official information that attribute gang membership or affiliation to the accused. The counsel needs to find out what the police think, what they know about the defendant, the sources of information used, and especially the standards used for the entry of information into gang files, including procedures for updating and purging files (Burrell 1990). To avoid the dangers of identifying a gang member because of the clothes the youth wears, his demeanor, or other characteristics—and then arresting or detaining him—there must be "specific and articulable facts leading the officer to believe that (1) some activity relating to *crime* has taken place or is occurring or is about to occur, and (2) the person the officer intends to stop or detain is involved in that activity" (Burrell 1990, p. 755).

Burrell is particularly concerned with the use of evidence that is irrelevant to the case at trial. The defense needs not only to shield the defendant from any gang reference to the extent possible, but indicate that membership in an organization does not lead reasonably to any inference as to the conduct of a member on a given occasion. It is important to analyze carefully the prosecutor's theory of relevance, and object if it is spurious or goes beyond the purported theory. Even if gang evidence is relevant, it may be inadmissable if outweighed by prejudice to the defendant. The term "gang" could take on a sinister meaning when associated with group activities. Burrell concludes that gang evidence, "like other evidence, *is* admissible if it is (1) material to the fact sought to be proved or disproved; (2) relevant, in the sense that it . . . (3) is not inadmissible because of some other rule or policy. Evidence offered simply to show that the defendant is bad (and therefore committed the crime) is inadmissible" (p. 757).

Also, recent law used by vertical prosecutors has come under challenge, at least at the trial court level. The claim is that legislation such as the California Street Terrorism Act poses serious constitutional problems. Terms in the law that are essential to its application and enforcement are vague, particularly in regard to the imposition of civil or criminal penalties for mere association with others. Restrictions on associational freedom, unless drawn to meet some compelling government need, may be an intrusion in violation of constitutional rights guaranteed by the First and Fourteenth Amendments (Burrell 1990, pp. 774–778).

Vertical Prosecution Efficiency

There is little doubt of the efficiency in the processing and the short-term effectiveness of vertical prosecution of gang cases in recent years. An early evaluation of the Los Angeles County vertical prosecution unit found that, in cases involving gang-related murders, an increase occurred in the conviction rate to 95 percent compared with a preprogram period when it was 71 percent and with contemporaneous nonvertical prosecution that was 78 percent (Dahmann 1983, chap. 6, p. 26). A substantial increase in trial conviction and incarceration rates also occurred (ibid., chap. 6, p. 33). Comparable achievements have been described in Cook County, Chicago (Daley 1985). On the other hand, it should be noted that a relatively small number of gang offenders are subjected to vertical prosecution. While over 71,000 gang members were arrested in California counties in fiscal year 1986–1987, only 546 defendants were vertically prosecuted (California Office of Juvenile Justice Planning 1987, pp. 17–18). Furthermore, the large majority of gang arrestees were accused of minor offenses (ibid.).

The Los Angeles city attorney involved in vertical gang prosecution claimed that conviction rates had soared for gang misdemeanors involving civilian witnesses. Normal conviction rates for such cases were in the range of 77 to 81 percent but for gang section cases were in the range of 87 to 100 percent. However, conviction rates did not increase for cases that involved only law enforcement witnesses. The length of sentences for gang misdemeanor cases did increase from 153 days, with normal prosecution, to 252 days with vertical prosecution (Reiner 1992, pp. 172–173). Bruce Coplen, supervisor of the gang unit in the Los Angeles city attorney's office, also claimed a 33 percent reduction in gang crime in the Cadillac Corning neighborhood, compared with other areas of Los Angeles, after aggressive use of nuisance abatement laws (Coplen 1988). The strategy apparently was not extended to other neighborhoods, however, and the number of gang incidents and homicides continued to climb throughout the city—raising questions about the original claim of success.

Critics of vertical prosecution suggest that prosecutors do not have sufficient understanding of barrio or ghetto life and the peer pressures that lead a youngster to accompany a group of youths in a drive-by shooting. Extreme sentences by prosecutors are requested for, and sometimes accorded to, naive, impressionable juveniles who happen to be present on such occasions and may not be gang members (Hicks 1988). Despite the increased efficiency of vertical prosecution, it has not been accompanied by a general decline in gang activity or a reduction in gang crime or gang-crime arrests in the community.

The relative proportion of prosecutions for gang-related drug offenses compared to gang-related violence has been rising. The deterrent effects of vertical prosecution, if they exist, probably have been overwhelmed by community changes and urban conditions facilitating gang activity, including immigration, population movement, poverty, and drug trafficking, over which prosecutors have no, or almost no, control. Vertical prosecution does not necessarily address the consequences of long-term sentences and prison overcrowding for the gang offender or for the community when the offender returns. Also, while there is growing recognition by prosecution that the gang problem must be addressed through broadened governmental and community efforts and through federal, state, and local justice systems, prosecutors still generally favor prosecution and punishment over a more comprehensive approach.

Recommendations for a Broader Prosecutorial Approach

Some analysts have recommended that the district or states attorney's approach be broadened to include preventive services, social intervention, social advocacy, and community-mobilization strategies that affect younger gang members as well as older, more serious offenders. In some communities, support groups, educational campaigns, and twenty-four-hour hotline reporting and advice services relative to the gang problem have been established by vertical prosecution units. In Los Angeles County, a community or social agency referral service was at one time planned for persons concerned with or implicated in a variety of gang-related problems, but it is unclear that it was implemented.

Attorney General Reno has recently suggested broadening the prosecutorial function, although her frame of reference is still restricted to the child or juvenile:

> I feel very strongly that it is imperative that we look beyond the role of prosecutor and understand what causes delinquency problems in the first place. I don't think that there's any one point at which you can intervene in a child's life to make a significant difference. Instead, it is essential that we view a child's life as a continuum and provide a consistent support system for those times when the family is unable to provide that support on its own. (John Wilson 1993, p. 2)

Attorney General Reno also seems to imply the possible extension of this broad rehabilitative reasoning to older youth, perhaps gang members, in the future development of the role of the prosecutor:

> We can't simply punish young offenders and return them to the community where the problem arose and think that they are going to succeed—particularly if they don't have a strong family system and are living in circumstances rife with risk factors. For these reasons I support programs with job training and placement, treatment, counseling services, aftercare and follow-up to help juvenile offenders reenter the community. (ibid. p. 6)

Court Attention to the Problem

A tradition of individualism and a strong desire to remain neutral or objective have probably contributed to the paucity of statements by judges about the gang problem. The lack of adequate court attention is especially noticeable and serious in large jurisdictions with inner-city ghettoes and newcomer and low-income populations. Judges in the juvenile court in addition are not only deprived of the knowledge, but also of the resources, they need to handle gang-related cases, in part because of their inexperience. Juvenile courts tend to have high judge turnover. They may be required by law to refer juvenile gang cases automatically to adult court, particularly in violent and drug-related juvenile cases. Thus, specialized legal expertise, knowledge of the gang problem, and skill in use of local resources appropriate for addressing the gang problem may not be generally developed in juvenile court.

Judges may deny or avoid recognition of the problem in order not to bias consideration of cases. Judges prefer that information about gang relatedness of the offense or offender not be admitted. Judges may attempt to rule such information out of order, unless specifically germane to the facts of the case at hand. However, information about gang-related characteristics and pressures, often from other sectors of the criminal justice system, does intrude and probably influences judges' general attitudes toward gangs and gang crime. Further, probation reports of the social circumstances of youth, including gang affiliation and prior gang offense history, are viewed as quite appropriate in presentencing investigations.

The National Council of Juvenile and Family Court Judges and its Metropolitan Judges Committee seem to take a highly suppressive view about how judges should deal with youth gangs. These bodies recommend a set of punitive options based on unsupported, if not fanciful, evidence that youth gangs are widely involved in sophisticated and organized drug trafficking. "These gangs have become interstate, regional, and national organizations commanding economic resources and able to bypass collaboration with or challenge more traditional organized criminal networks" (Metropolitan Court Judges Committee 1988, p. 29). Judges are urged to simply and strictly "mandate severance of the gang affiliation as part of its sanctions and remedies" (p. 30).

In some juvenile court jurisdictions, however, judges have tried more realistically to use the court as a center for a coordinated rehabilitative approach in which representatives of a variety of community, school, family, and justice system organizations are called on systematically to address the special needs of the juvenile gang member (see Reiner 1992). These comprehensive community-oriented approaches attempt to integrate social-control, intervention, and opportunity-provision approaches with respect to the juvenile gang member. Some judges believe that the criminal gang behavior of youth fundamentally originates through problems of home, school, and defective community structures, and therefore they need to be directly addressed by the court in the specific cases that appear before them. The mechanism to be employed by the juvenile court has not yet been clearly worked out or tested, however.

It should be noted that the juvenile court's traditional approach to non-gang cases has been benign with respect to dependent, neglected, abused, and other kinds of delinquent children and youths, including those who are physically or sexually abused, exploited, runaway, and incorrigible, as well as truants and school dropouts. In such cases the juvenile court has recommended

> the establishment of a working and effective partnership of courts and public agencies with the full involvement of businesses, labor, private foundations and agencies, and citizen volunteers. Also regarded as essential is an emphasis on prevention and sensitivity to the rights of the individual child, the family, and the rights and responsibilities of the parent as well as those of the courts, agencies, and legislators. (Metropolitan Court Judges Committee 1986)

The juvenile court, however, has not yet recognized that gang and non-gang juveniles may not be fundamentally different. Much depends on the individual situation. Gang youths may differ only in degree from non-gang youths. Their behavior, as aggressive or violent as it can be, should not necessarily be treated differently from that of other types of deprived, problematic, or troublesome youths. The long-term consequences of such differential juvenile court treatment for gang and non-gang juveniles, in terms of both protecting the juvenile and the security and welfare of the community, need to be carefully addressed by the juvenile court.

Court Functions and Issues

There appear to be few guidelines available to judges in juvenile or adult court about how specifically to deal with gang cases other than legislatively mandated enhanced sentencing requirements in a growing number of states. Much effort, however, is needed to adapt existing and develop additional court principles and procedures for dealing with gang cases. Identified here are certain court conditions, processes, and situations to which special judicial attention is required.

Lack of Resources. A key problem within the court is the lack of resources to carry out its varied justice system functions. The court is overburdened with cases, particularly in chronic gang problem contexts that are usually characterized by heavy population density and high rates of many kinds of social problems. Judges in these areas have little time to focus adequately on individual cases or follow-up. After adjudication or at sentencing, the court is not always aware of the nature of the particular role the youth plays in the gang nor of distinctions in terms of crime patterns of the different gangs in the various communities. Additionally, most judges receive no information (e.g., recidivism data) on how individuals fare after their cases are disposed of by the particular court. The flow of data between the police and court is often slow and incomplete. The police are not always aware that a gang leader or core gang member has been returned to the community on court supervision. Court data systems need to be efficiently computerized so that correct and appropriate gang-related information is available for judicial decision-making and quickly relayed to police authorities. Court orders to the police (e.g., probation conditions) about specific gang cases are often not issued or delivered in a timely manner.

Court resources to provide both for the social adjustment and development of gang youths and protection of the community are often not available. As a result, certain justice system distortions tend to occur. The judges may decide to sentence the youth to a correctional facility because sufficient probation arrangements or adequately trained staff are not available to supervise gang youths properly, primarily because of heavy case loads. In other instances the judge may decide to certify the youth to adult court or sentence him to a residential facility because specialized resources such as strong or intensive supervision, outreach probation, vocational training, and family counseling are not available to juvenile gang delinquents. The resources required to deal effectively with gang youths may not be developed because the court system, the legislature, and the community at large do not fully understand the nature and scope of what needs to be done.

Attorney General Reno advises a better organization and integration of court and community services, and the exercise of greater leadership by the court:

> It is time to recognize that juvenile court judges need more say in structuring programs that fit the needs of the child [and youth]. Judges would be more effective if they had a comprehensive evaluation and assessment of the child and of the child's needs. And if the social service components in youth service programs were better linked with the court and the court had more of a say in the program, the entire juvenile justice system would work together better and be more accountable to the community. (Wilson 1993, p. 2)

Certification of Youth to Adult Court. An early and primary consideration for the judge in juvenile court is whether a case should be transferred to the adult criminal court. In a number of jurisdictions, as indicated, juvenile court judges are required to or will readily transfer or waive gang cases to the adult court. However, gang membership or the nature of the gang incident per se should not ordinarily be a sufficient basis for certification. The U.S. Supreme Court in *Kent* set rigid standards for transfer of any juvenile case (which should include both gang and non-gang cases) to adult criminal court, and the Supreme Court required that:

1. a hearing be held on the transfer motion;
2. a full investigation be made;
3. a child be afforded counsel;
4. counsel have access to all records to be considered in reaching decisions;
5. the court issue a statement of reasons for the transfer.

A sixth requirement has been added since *Kent*—that the court must find probable cause to believe that the child has committed the offense charged against him. Furthermore, in the development of grounds for transfer or certification, which usually grow out of the investigation report, the following factors should be considered:

- amenability of the child to treatment in terms of age, prior record, presenting offense;
- the degree of sophistication of the child;
- the likelihood of successful rehabilitation through the juvenile justice system;
- the fact that the juvenile loses the right to juvenile detention and confidentiality of proceedings by such transfer;
- the general consequences that a transfer outcome usually has for the prospects of rehabilitating the youth and protecting the safety of the community within the judge's particular jurisdiction.

Detention and Release. The concerns of judges in both adult and juvenile courts may be quite similar in the determination of whether to detain or release gang offenders. The juvenile court judge, however, has the option only to detain or to release the juvenile (to the custody of the parents). In adult court, the judge can detain, set bail, and release a suspect or defendant. Judges in both courts, because of lack of current or sufficient data, are often unable to base their decisions on: the seriousness of the particular offense; the general propensity for violence of the gang member; the need to ensure protection for the suspect as well as the witness; and the present state of criminal activity and conflict between warring gangs of which the suspect or defendant may be a member. Judges can order detention for adult recalcitrant (gang member) witnesses in certain states if they are likely to recant testimony.

One means to address this dilemma, particularly in adult court, is the development of a system of pretrial services providing both social services and controls for selected chronically violent gang youth awaiting trial. Trials in overburdened courts conducted by skilled defense attorneys may take a year or more, during which period the status-conscious and personally disorganized gang youth is likely to engage in further violent offenses. The Cook County Circuit Court has developed such a system, but pretrial supervision is still not appropriately and consistently used by judges in cases where youth have not been adjudicated.

Court Hearings. Conduct of the trial in a gang case is, furthermore, no easy matter. The judge has to maintain the integrity of trial proceedings both inside and outside the courtroom. This is particularly important in adult criminal court where proceedings are public, in contrast to the juvenile court where proceedings are generally private. The judge needs to be alert to the presence of other gang members during the adult court hearing. Their presence and actions may be distracting, particularly when gang members use hand signals or wear gang colors and symbols. As suggested previously, often outright gang intimidation may occur, whether in the courtroom, in the hallway outside, or in the community. Special police arrangements should be made to protect witnesses and suspects. The judge can order that appropriate charges be brought against such disruptive or intimidating gang members, including violation of probation or parole by youths causing the disturbance, if they are under supervision.

Evidence

The judge needs to be especially concerned about the quality of evidence brought to the court that identifies the youth as a gang member and the incident as gang related. The judge has to be knowledgeable about the different levels of proof required to establish the validity of these terms and particularly careful not to accept hearsay evidence as sufficient. The quality of police reporting and the reliability of police files has to be determined. Ideally, the background characteristics of the youth would be irrelevant unless directly related to the motivational circumstances of the incident (e.g., gang retaliation). The judge should make sure the jury understands that if the defendant is charged with a gang offense, the offense must directly and clearly grow out of gang motivation and specific related circumstances. The judge understands that the identification of the suspect as a gang member may be prejudicial.

The accuracy of testimony by witnesses who are members of an opposing gang also needs to be meticulously examined. Gang members may manipulate testimony to either falsely incriminate a suspect or withhold evidence that could lead to a dismissal of charges. As previously suggested, in the discussion of vertical prosecution, the aggrieved gang member or witness may prefer to have his gang "settle the score" later on the street. Further, the burden of directly establishing the facts may fall more heavily on the juvenile court judge than on the adult criminal court judge since, in most states, a jury trial does not occur in juvenile court. The juvenile court judge, therefore, must be particularly well informed about gang conditions in the community to apply the appropriate burden of proof to the facts at hand for proper adjudication.

Sentencing

Sentencing is probably the most critical function performed by judges in our current era of rapid increase in prison populations. "Between 1980 and 1988, for example, the population of federal and state prisons nearly doubled," although remarkably, "homicide, robbery and burglary rates declined by nearly a quarter in the same period" (Morris and Tonry 1990, p. 47). Sampson and Laub indicate that current court policies that sentence youths to prison produce unintended criminogenic effects, particularly when sentences to prison are excessive. "Length of incarceration in both adolescence and adulthood has negative affects on job stability, which in turn leads to later crime and deviance . . . it is critical that individuals have the opportunity to reconnect to institutions like family, school, and work *after* a period of incarceration" (1993, p. 275).

A central question confronting judges under these circumstances is, "To what extent can community-based punishments be combined with conditions of treatment to create punishment that both control and treat and are interchangeable with incarcerative sentences and with ordinary probation to create a comprehensive sentencing system?" (Morris and Tonry 1990, p. 180). Morris and Tonry have suggested a pattern of interchangeable "intermediate punishments" that provide the judge and the probation administrator with "a menu of choices . . . house arrest . . . intensive supervision [which] may or may not be monitored electronically . . . fine and community service and obligations of attendance at treatment programs." (ibid., pp. 212–213). A continuum of punishment and treatment interchangeable at various points, should be formulated and implemented in such a way as to contribute to rehabilitation as rapidly and effectively as possible.

In coming to a decision, the judge considers the current offense and the gang youth's previous criminal history. Recommendations by the probation officer, the defense attorney, and other interested and responsible representatives have to be assessed by the judge in the development of a rehabilitation program for the juvenile or young adult, even the serious and chronic gang offender. The judge must understand that gang membership and gang offenses tend to be time limited. Most gang youths are committed members only for a short period, usually between the ages of 14 and 18 years, particularly if conventional alternative opportunities are available. Key questions a judge should ask are: What can be done to transition the youth out of the gang? How quickly and by what means? The judge must be especially sensitive to precisely when and why a youth is ready to give up the gang lifestyle, and what community circumstances exist to pressure and support such a decision.

Of primary importance in the judge's sentencing decision should be the weight given to specific factors that can assist the youth to develop social competence and at the same time protect the community from further acts of gang violence. While these two criteria can be closely related, much depends on the availability of adequate resources to the court, the community, and the correctional institution to serve these purposes. In regard to rehabilitation, a key objective in the sentencing decision should be to provide the youth with a social environment in which value change and behavioral modification can occur. Integral to this change process is the provision of opportunities for remedial education, training, and the availability of jobs, as well as appropriate, sometimes intensive, forms of community-based supervision.

Placement on Probation

If the judge places the gang youth on probation, special arrangements must exist that guarantee an appropriate level of supervision, including protection of life and property of the youth and members of the community, restitution on behalf of the victim, and the delivery of suitable services to the youth and his parents. Supervision can be enhanced by the use of special orders that allow the probation officer to enforce a discontinuation of violent or criminal gang activity. Such orders often require that the probationer not associate with other gang members involved in criminal activities; not participate in gang-related behavior including wearing of gang attire, of colors, or use of gang symbols; and observe curfews, especially during periods of high criminal gang activity. Additionally, fines and community service can be mandated. Search and seizure powers can also be provided to be used by the probation officer.

The court should require participation by the youth and his or her parents or spouse in activities designed to improve chances for a successful social adjustment preferably in a community setting. Such conditions must emphasize, as appropriate, school attendance and special tutoring, provision of health care (e.g., physical/psychiatric examination, tatoo removal, substance abuse treatment), job readiness and vocational training, age-appropriate employment, recreational activities linked to youth group activity sponsored by youth service agencies, and parental or spousal participation in special gang awareness and social skill training classes. With regard to parents of juvenile gang members, contempt of court powers can sometimes be utilized to enforce many of these conditions. When the juvenile's family situation is highly disorganized, alternative arrangements may need to be made to place the youth in a more socially constructive and structured or restrictive environment.

Placement within a Correctional Institution

If the judge decides to sentence a youth gang member to a correctional institution, care must be taken to ensure that the youth is placed in a protected and secure environment that reduces gang-related opportunities and provides viable competence-building activities as an alternative to the gang lifestyle. Certain youths, because of their physical demeanor or gang specific affiliation, may be placed in danger if sentenced to a particular institution. Judges in jurisdictions where the gang problem is just emerging must take special care not to place gang youth in "chronic" gang-problem institutional settings where the youth may develop a more entrenched and sophisticated gang identity and lifestyle. Parole and probation officers may be a good source of information on these matters. Youth who do not receive appropriate remedial education, vocational training, and social skill development services in the institution are probably more likely to go back to gang affiliation and gang-related criminal behavior when they return to the community.

According to Judge Schiller, formerly of the Cook County Adult Criminal Court, if the offense is not probationable and he must sentence the youth to an institution, certain questions arise. Can the youth survive in an institution? If so, in which kind of institution? It is important not to sentence the youth to a particular correctional institution that, for one reason or another, will provide an inimical environment. There are special gang, racial/ethnic, and behavioral characteristics of institutions that can be harmful to particular youths. A correctional environment should reduce gang-related opportunities for the youth. In Illinois, as in California and elsewhere, it is not uncommon for certain institutions to be identified with a particular, dominant gang. Also, certain juvenile institutions may serve as recruiting grounds for gangs, sometimes under the influence of older gang members who are in adult prisons. The juvenile correctional institution may serve as a vehicle to recruit or solidify juvenile ties to both prison and street gangs.

Under ideal conditions—particularly if a youth can be placed on probation—specific community arrangements should be made that provide alternate legitimate opportunities for peer affiliation, social status, and support in place of what the gang provides. Not only training and job opportunities should be offered, but also links to local neighborhood organizations, social agencies, fraternal groups, and even local political clubs that are neighborhood based should be assured. Such ties could induce gang youths to stay away from former gang peers and/or constrain these youths from becoming again involved in crime-generating situations. Local community agencies or precinct police, in conjunction with probation, could conceivably be assigned by the judge to fulfil social support as well as surveillance functions for gang offenders and better restructure and reintegrate them into conventional patterns within the community (Schiller 1988).

Use of Probation and Special Court Review

The judge should carefully consider *all* of the information provided by the probation officer in the dispositional process and be prepared to enforce his or her own court orders. Probation officers must also be allowed access to the bench so they can inform the judge about their capacity to implement court orders and how they plan to carry them out. To adequately supervise the youth gang member in the community, the court should expect the probation officer to communicate clear expectations and provide adequate oversight; follow-up; and swift, consistent enforcement of consequences if the youth violates a court order. The following options should prove particularly useful in juvenile court:

- Intensive probation that places the juvenile gang member under close surveillance. This option, when combined with mandated parental participation, may be especially promising. Electronic monitoring or day custody in lieu of placement in the institution may also prove cost effective as well as promising.
- Regular court review, usually monthly or bimonthly, whereby juvenile gang members appear in court and their compliance with their court orders is reviewed (e.g., through special court checks of school attendance, grades, and conduct).
- Allowance of a petition by the parents or guardians requesting the court to assume custody of the youth gang member who is deemed incorrigible. If the child violates court conditions, the court can enforce consequences such as detention.

The judge may delay final court disposition of the case in order to review the youth's attempt to make a satisfactory social adjustment. Postponing sentence may be a useful device to avoid long-term institutionalization of the gang youth and his development of the "rep" as an official offender in the eyes of his gang peers. A "stiff" sentence may enhance rather than reduce the youth's standing as a "proven" gang member. An elaborated juvenile court review process also requires the youth, the parents, probation officer, teachers, and significant others to appear in juvenile court periodically to attest to and present documentation that the youth is making social progress, for example, is no longer affiliated with a gang or engaging in delinquent activity. Court review also allows the judge to determine whether services and social support are being provided to the youth and his family. It can be used also as a way to sustain pressure on outside agencies, including the school, to meet the social needs of the youth and his family.

Trial and Appellate Decisions

Trial and appellate court decisions bearing on laws that address the gang problem have begun to appear. They are generally concerned with lack of clarity of statutes, inadmissibility of certain kinds of evidence, their overreach and failure to protect the gang youth's rights of freedom of association:

> Judge Miller, Chief Justice of the Illinois Supreme Court, recently states that the General Assembly should clarify the "gang transfer" provision of the Juvenile Court Act . . . which allows the prosecutor to file a petition or motion for transfer to adult court if a minor aged 15 or older who had been previously adjudicated delinquent for a felony is accused of a forcible felony in furtherance of criminal activities by an organized gang. The court noted that legislation is unclear on the standard of proof required and suggested the standard be probable cause. (B. Miller 1992, p. 6)
>
> The Los Angeles City Attorney, James Hahn . . . filed a civil suit against 300 unnamed members of the Playboy Gangster CRIPS. Hahn would have prohibited, among other things, the suspected gang members from wearing gang clothing. . . . He would have imposed on them a 7 p.m. to 7 a.m. curfew and made the 300 subject to arrest for being in public more than five minutes at a time—or for two or more of them to be seen together. . . . In dismissing Hahn's suit, Superior Court Judge Warren Deering characterized it as "far, far overreaching" and said that "many, many of these provisions violate basic constitutional liberties." . . . Judge Deering suggested the way to handle an alleged criminal is "just go ahead and file a criminal charge." (Goldberg 1988)
>
> Even if gang evidence is relevant, it may still be inadmissible. Probative value is sometimes outweighed by the prejudice to the defendant, particularly where the evidence would come on a tangential point. . . . Thus, *Williams v. Superior Court* [in California] suggested that evidence of common gang membership to link separate offenses "might very well mitigate *against* admissibility of one offense in the trial of the other," since it would be of limited probative value, yet would create a "significant danger of unnecessary prejudice." (Burrell 1990, pp. 764–765)
>
> The right of association protects the right of individuals to pursue a variety of political, social, economic, and recreational interests without governmental intrusion. The first and fourteenth amendments prohibit the imposition of civil or criminal penalties for mere affiliation with others . . . Any restriction on associational freedoms must be narrowly drawn . . . The lack of precision and inherent subjectivity of the anti-gang legislation demand careful attention to the underlying validity of the statutes. . . . (Burrell 1990, p. 777)

Conclusion

Suppression characterizes evolving strategies and practices of prosecutors and to some extent judges dealing with the youth gang problem. Prosecution is concerned traditionally and currently with establishing the guilt of gang suspects or defendants, particularly adults. The system of vertical prosecution developed in the 1980s rcpresents a rational, specialized, mainly deterrent strategy. Prosecutors have emphasized proactive prosecution, particularly of the most serious, violent, or drug-related cases involving gang leaders and core members. Under vertical prosecution, usually one prosecutor handles a case from inception to disposition.

The vertical prosecution strategy has been accompanied by a growing panoply of "gang law" and procedure to address difficult evidentiary and logistical problems that characterize the collective nature of gang offenses. Of special interest is the development of the law of accountability or accessoryship, in which a gang member can be held responsible for the crimes of another if it can be proved that he advised or aided in the perpetration of the crime. The Hard Core Division of the Los Angeles County District Attorney's Office, the pioneering vertical gang prosecution unit in the country, has developed a set of tools for "effective" prosecution of gang cases including use of trained investigators, widening the scope of the search warrant, selection and education of the jury, use of the police officer as expert witness, setting bail, dealing with recalcitrant witnesses, witness protection, countering courtroom intimidation by gang members, and establishing that gang members be held accountable for a group criminal action.

Defense attorneys have also developed a set of innovative techniques to counter those of prosecution. A key objective of defense is to disassociate the defendant from the gang or at least his action as gang related. In this regard, strong "discovery" efforts are made to test the reliability of police records. Recent legislation, which targets gangs and provides for enhanced sentencing of certain offenses, is challenged as unconstitutional, based on first and fourteenth amendment rights. In general, few data support the effectiveness of specialized or vertical prosecution in deterring or reducing gang violence in the community, although there is evidence of increased efficiency in prosecution of the relatively small number of cases targeted.

Both juvenile and adult courts continue to emphasize a suppression approach, that is, incarceration, enhanced sentences, and close monitoring or supervision of gang youths. There seem to be few appropriate or balanced guidelines available to judges in juvenile or adult court for dealing with gang cases. A key problem has been the lack of justice system resources to carry out its varied functions, particularly when it is so overburdened with cases. Court data systems are often undeveloped and inefficient, making it difficult for the judges to make good decisions and then carry them out. State law and the juvenile court have not yet developed an appropriate basis for certification of suspected juvenile offenders, often gang violent offenders, to adult court.

Of special concern is the development of greater options for the judge in the sentencing decision. Ideally, sufficient resources should be available to develop a comprehensive system of interchangeable punishments and rehabilitation options to meet the needs of particular youths. The options include curfew, intensive supervision, house arrest, use of electronic monitoring devices, fines, community service requirements, and compulsory attendance at treatment programs. Judges play or can play a special leadership role in educating the public to the complexities of the gang problem and the need to develop appropriate services and a range of punishments to deal with the problem.

14

Probation, Corrections, and Parole—After Care

Probation, corrections, and parole are concerned mainly with management of gang youths either in the institution or the community, generally once the youths have been adjudicated or penetrated the justice system. Limited national experience exists on how best to control and rehabilitate gang youths. The complexity of efforts required and the lack of resources present daunting problems to those system workers who would change the behavior of gang youth. The nature and extent of postadjudicatory and some preadjudicatory programs seem to be highly varied. Only California appears to have addressed the gang problem systematically across a range of strategies for both youth and young adult offenders over a sustained period, particularly in Los Angeles County. Remarkably, some probation and correctional agencies are beginning to address the gang problem through a range of strategies, including prevention as well as intervention and suppression.

Recent concern with rapidly increasing numbers of gang youths and the extraordinary expense of incarceration have encouraged innovative and expanded efforts by probation and correctional institutions in local communities. One analyst observes, however, that entrepreneurship and politics per se may be more important than the interest by justice system agencies in front-end prevention or social intervention strategies. It is difficult, furthermore, to envision how a goal of reducing the number of youths known to the justice system can be reconciled with a prevention strategy that could result in labeling as gang members youths who are not yet arrested (Reiner 1992, pp. 209–210).

This chapter attempts to describe traditional and evolving strategies and procedures of probation, corrections, and parole or after-care agencies for dealing with gang youths. The discussion is confined largely to the development and implementation of such programs in a few states. Newer strategies of community-based programming for adjudicated or incarcerated offenders are likely to be addressed mainly to non-gang delinquent youth, however. Probation, correction, and parole authorities continue to emphasize suppression rather than rehabilitation of gang offenders. The question of how to structure and implement integrated suppression and social intervention strategies, whether in the institution or the community, has not yet been satisfactorily resolved.

Probation

The earliest specialized probation program directed to the youth gang problem, the Los Angeles County Probation Group Guidance Project, evolved from community concerns about the Zoot Suit Riots during World War II. It utilized outreach work with youths and their parents as a major social intervention method that emphasized group discussion, counseling, and recreational activities. The approach lacked comprehensive community involvement as well as effective collaboration with grass-roots agencies, community agencies, and other units of the justice system, particularly with law enforcement. This detached probation worker program was evaluated negatively (Klein 1968). The program, however, was terminated as a result of interorganizational conflict between the Los Angeles County Probation and the Los Angeles City Police Department rather than because of lack of positive outcome for gang members or probationers served (see also Chapter 15).

Specialized Gang Programing—Mainly Suppression Oriented

Los Angeles County Probation Department, nevertheless, has retained its interest in gang programs. It is the largest probation department in the world. In 1992 it operated three juvenile halls, nineteen probation camps, one secure treatment facility, and sixteen adult/juvenile investigation and supervision field offices throughout Los Angeles County. It supervised 91,000 adult and 20,000 juvenile probationers. In recent years, in response to escalating drug and gang problems, it has increasingly integrated its efforts with law enforcement as well as, to a lesser extent, community-based agencies. In October 1980, the Los Angeles County Board of Supervisors approved a Specialized Gang Supervision Program. Improved probation control and surveillance and the return of offenders or probation violators to court for appropriate disposition became key strategies.

The Specialized Gang Supervision Program in the early 1990s served 2,000 to 2,400 probationers 14 to 25 years of age. Separate juvenile and adult jurisdictional distinctions were avoided so that the gang problem could be treated in integrated, gang structure- and process-relevant terms. The program had forty probation officers in six units, each unit dealing with 400 gang offenders. No more than 50 to 60 cases were prescribed per officer, in contrast to a normal case load of 150 to 300 for the regular probation officers in the department. However, the case load of 50 to 60 was regarded as much too large for the varied tasks required of probation officers with difficult gang offenders. The specialist gang probation officers were expected to be on duty in the evening and on weekends, and to make their presence known in the community and in schools. The probation officers participated in "ride-alongs" with police agencies, were on patrol during special community events, and interacted with members of the County District Attorney's hard-core units as well as with the City Attorney's gang prosecutors (Nidorf 1988, undated; Reiner 1992, p. 164).

Specialized gang probation officers were also expected to participate in a range of court duties, community-based activities, drug prevention classes, presentations at schools, and interagency coordination and networking. Primary emphasis, however, was on strict supervision of, visitation to, and search of the homes of youths, as necessary. Traditional counseling, job referral, and the conduct of truce meetings between gangs were minimized (see Duran 1987). Funding had been requested but apparently was not available for leadership training and social development programs, at least for the older probationers.

The actual operational nature of this project and its effects, however, remain somewhat unclear. Despite the fact that serious gang violence was relatively more characteristic of older teenagers and young adults, the Specialized Gang Probation Unit's case load was 70 percent juvenile. A large proportion of the youths it served were peripheral gang members who did not get involved in violent activity but were "typically . . . unmotivated youths . . . [who were] into drug use, graffiti writing, truancy, and [had] low social achievement. Most of the efforts of the unit were in the prosecution of technical violations and petty offenses" (Duran 1987, p. 25). One "specialized Gang Suppression Program" progress report concluded with a recommendation for a change in policy to target more "hard-core violent youths" similar to the youths served by the Los Angeles Police and Sheriff's gang units (Duran 1987).

The Los Angeles County Probation Department has developed other gang-suppression projects targeting hard-core gang-related probationers. The Gang/Drug-Pushers Project sought to reduce the criminal activity of probationers who were gang members known to be involved in drugs. It has utilized intensive monitoring activities, such as electronic surveillance and accelerated handling of violations, to ensure prompt removal of gang/drug-pushers from the community when appropriate. The department has provided "increased sanctions, restrictions, and electronic surveillance of the activities of adult gang members known to be involved in the use and sale of drugs and narcotics" (Duran 1987, p. 8). "Probation also operated a small intensively supervised Probation (ISP) program which focused on the hardest of hard-core offenders" (Reiner 1992, p. 164).

The department is also pursuing a variety of initiatives emphasizing early intervention and prevention. An Early Gang Intervention Program was established "to focus preventive resources on first-time youthful offenders with limited peripheral gang involvement" (Los Angeles County Probation Department 1988, p. 7). The School Crime Suppression Program (SCSP) was mandated by the Los Angeles County Board of Supervisors in 1981. The Gang Alternative and Prevention Program (GAPP) includes group counseling, tutoring services, and job/development/training on selected school campuses. Six GAPP units have thus far been organized. The latest probation service program for gang youths, the Drug Treatment Boot Camp (DTBC) organized in 1990, emphasizes vigorous physical exercise and work to provide a basic foundation of structure and discipline for probationers. Drug-using 16- to 18-year olds are targeted, but many gang offenders are also included in the program.

The Los Angeles County Probation Department also received funding from the U.S. Justice Department's Office of Juvenile Justice and Delinquency Prevention to develop a multi-justice system and community organization project for the coordination and development of programs dealing with gangs in an "emerging gang-problem city" (Los Angeles County Probation Department 1988, pp. 5–11). This effort seemed to have potential for addressing the gang problem through a comprehensive approach but was funded only for an eighteen-month period, with a second year of funding to assist in the transition of the program to local community agencies. A third year of funding was subsequently provided by the Los Angeles County Board of Supervisors.

The Los Angeles County Probation Department, like many other probation departments, is caught between two general missions: suppression and community protection on the one hand and rehabilitation and prevention on the other. The dilemma has been severely aggravated by a "law and order" public clamor, inadequate funding, and the need to provide a "low-cost alternative to incarceration for a larger and much higher-risk group of criminals that society would really prefer to lock up if only it has the space" (Reiner 1992, p. 164). Consequently, the Los Angeles County Probation Department, like other probation departments, has had to make hard choices, which usually means the abandonment of close supervision for most youths and adults on probation, with the exception of a hard-core violent few. Some justice system observers charge that the Los Angeles County Probation Department has given up on the provision of quality probation that emphasizes social services and rehabilitation.

Evolving Comprehensive and Community-Based Probation Programs

An early California probation-coordinated approach, still in existence and emphasizing a suppression approach, was the Intensive Juvenile Gang Supervision Program of the Santa Clara Probation Department, which proposed "to reduce the impact of youth-gang violence in Santa Clara, Santa Cruz, and Monterey counties by enhancing Probation/Parole services, coordinating with other justice agencies, and promoting public protection and providing assistance to victims and witnesses" (Santa Clara County Probation Department 1984, p. 1). A key assumption was that inadequate justice system processing of gang offenders was due to a lack of coordination between criminal justice agencies, especially law enforcement, district attorney, probation, and parole. The coordination of these agencies was regarded as essential to cope with the mobility of gangs across justice agencies' jurisdictions. Before this approach, according to the Santa Clara Probation Department, these conditions resulted in a lack of continuity in case handling through the different phases of justice system processing of the youth.

The Santa Clara Probation Department's activities to achieve the goal of reducing recidivism included: vertical case management, that is, the assignment of one officer to pursue a case through all stages of the probation or parole process; intensive investigation and supervision of gang cases; imposition of special court orders; commitment to rehabilitation facilities; and services to victims and witnesses, including referral to community resources and maintenance of secure court waiting areas (DeWitt 1983). Sufficient time has elapsed since the start of this project to permit some evaluation. After five years of operation, local officials claimed that the number of gangs decreased from fifty to twenty, with only ten to twelve active on a regular basis. There was also a shift of concern from Hispanic gang violence to black gang involvement in drug trafficking and Vietnamese youth gang participation in residential burglaries and robberies, commercial robberies, and vehicle thefts. Moreover, the shift from extreme violence to serious property crime was viewed as an improvement in the crime situation (Creamer 1988).

The California Orange County Probation Department planned a project that would have been one of the most comprehensive in the nation. Strategies of social intervention, opportunities provision, and community mobilization were to be integrated with a deterrent approach for younger gang members. The prevention and intervention objectives of the proposed intensive probation supervision program were to include: the diversion of 11- to 14-year-old juvenile gang offenders from detention and incarceration experiences to community-based alternatives; the use of a comprehensive case management approach to deal with families and youth at risk of gang involvement; the provision of special opportunities to encourage at-risk youths to remain in school and dropouts to return to school; the linkage of current and potential youth gang members with conventional types of organizations or activities within the county; and the involvement of parents, families, and organizations in community activities designed to change environmental factors that promote youth gang involvement (Orange County 1989, pp. 18–19).

A continuum of supervision levels had already been established by the Orange County Probation Department, dependent on the assessed risk of the youth engaging in further delinquent or gang-related behavior. It included field supervision, intensive field supervision, house arrest, electronic monitoring, mandatory substance-abuse treatment, detention, and incarceration in a juvenile institution. Specific indicators of gang membership were also explicitly identified, including: self-admission; the wearing of gang colors and tatoos; the writing of gang graffiti or placa; having a family member in a gang; and knowledge that a minor associates with a gang member.

The Orange County plan proposed that a separate gang school be established for its young gang probationers to provide remedial education, job readiness, and job placement experiences. It also recommended an intensive academic program, with a focus on bringing minors up to grade level and an emphasis on language skills. The special school program would focus on classroom social skills development, teaching the minor on probation how to gain positive attention in the classroom, how to ask questions comfortably, and how to obtain extra help when needed so that he does not need to avoid class or fail to complete assignments. Each of the young gang probationers would remain in the special school setting for approximately one semester. The minor's transition back to his neighborhood school would be carefully planned by establishing ongoing relationships with the minor's teacher, guidance counselor, and the principal so that progress begun in the special school could be continued.

A consortium of support agencies and organizations was also to be formed to target problems within the gang youth's family and to mobilize key business, community agency, and governmental units to deal with issues of education, jobs, and other matters specifically affecting conditions closely associated with gang development. The provision of child care for the minor's younger siblings would be included in this proposed Orange County project; child care would be provided adjacent to the special school site to enable parents to participate in counseling and skill development for the family. In addition, the consortium of agencies would provide adult education and vocational training for parents to improve parents' overall ability to cope with problems through links with local community college programs (Orange County 1989).

Effects. Recent innovative efforts by probation to deal with the gang problem have not yet been properly evaluated. Claims for success exist, however. The Philadelphia Crisis Intervention Network was probably the earliest and best of the coordinated community-based programs developed to address the youth gang violence problem in a major urban area during the 1970s. It included a community-based probation/ parole unit as well as the development of various community groups. Relationships with schools, police, and other agencies were developed. The probation/parole component focused on the control of older youths or young adults likely to influence younger gang members. Probation officers worked with street workers on a daily basis. The results of the program apparently were associated with a sharp reduction in gang homicides. Its positive results were sustained for over a decade (see Chapter 15).

It is not always easy to distinguish the separate effects of probation, correction, and after-care efforts in a comprehensive community-based program. There is some preliminary evidence, however, of the success of a probation or parole strategy that emphasizes community-based social intervention efforts with gang youths. Reiner observes that "an El Monte 'Project Return' has been judged successful . . . in cutting the rate of recidivism among juveniles returned to the San Gabriel Valley after detention by the California Youth Authority and the Probation Department . . . [also] Boot Camp is three times as effective as other camps in preventing recidivism, a record [the Los Angeles County Probation Department] . . . believes is partially due to aftercare" (1992, p. 208).

We are less sure, however, about the results of one of the more recent probation prevention programs that, although specialized and community based, did not target serious gang youths for social intervention services. An evaluation of the Gang Alternative Prevention Program (GAPP) of the Los Angeles County Probation Department seems to have produced mixed results, despite the agency's claim of "valuable impact." While student grade point averages increased and truancy was reduced, the experimental probation group produced higher rates of recidivism on number of arrests, citations, short-term law contacts, and convictions than the comparison group. To what extent the research is adequate in terms of appropriate comparison group and control of age factors may be questioned (Agopian 1991). The rationale and value of a probation strategy of prevention in a school or other community setting for youths *with no prior arrest or court contacts* has not been adequately determined or tested. A danger exists, not only of excessive justice system contact and labeling of officially nondelinquent youths, but also of replacing the school in its basic mission of socializing youths, including problem youths. A full range of intermediate punishments has not yet been developed and implemented in respect to many probation programs directed to gang youths. Probation programs should continue to direct attention to the social needs of gang offenders who become probationers, but avoid unintentionally widening the net of justice system contacts for potential or peripheral gang youths.

Corrections

Prisons, juvenile correctional institutions, jails, and detention centers have been viewed often as training schools for crime. State prisons repeatedly have made a significant contribution to the development of sophisticated criminal gang organization both in the institution and on the streets (Jacobs 1977). Prisons may also have produced a deviancy amplifying effect since gang members are now spread widely across local communities, many states, and federal institutions. Imprisonment or incapacitation—while it is a simple short-term solution—may have produced increased gang cohesion and membership recruitment (Reiss 1987), and perhaps more rather than less gang crime when the incarcerated gang youth returns to the community. We cannot be sure.

Distinction between Prison Gangs and Street Gangs

The precise nature and extent to which current prison and street gangs communicate, interact with, and influence each other is not reliably known. There is undoubtedly much individual gang-member-related communication and interaction across prison walls, but we are not clear about the specific nature and significance of these contacts and how serious a threat they constitute to prison and community safety and security. Knox claims that the influence is considerable and that both law enforcement and correctional authorities should closely interface with each other to avoid major problems of social disorder. Gangs on the inside can influence to some extent the actions of street gangs on the outside, and gangs on the outside can presumably order "hits on inmates and guards inside a prison" (Knox 1991a, p. 514).

On the other hand, Reiner (1992) suggests that, although connections between prison gangs and street gangs exist, there are important distinctions. The character and purposes of the two types of organization need to be understood, and concerns about a general criminal conspiracy should not be exaggerated:

> Prison gangs, be they Black, Latino, or Anglo, are more akin to organized crime networks than to street gangs. . . . In general, fears of a prison/street gang nexus seem to be overblown. No law enforcement authority interviewed . . . saw any trend toward prison gang control over street gangs. Individuals often belong to both types of gangs, and may move back and forth between them. . . .
>
> Turf-oriented gangs are extremely parochial. Their members may affiliate with a prison gang for protection and companionship on the inside—and they may stay in touch when they get out—but once back in the old neighborhood, few try to push an agenda that transcends the loyalties of the barrio or the "hood." (Reiner 1992, pp. 50–51)

To complicate the discussion, the authors of a recent small-scale prison gang interview study in California indicate that the linkages between street and prison gang activities are complex and volatile. In their report of that study, Hunt et al. state that "whereas previously there were four or five major gangs, today there are nine or ten new groups, each with its own network of alliances and loyalties. These cross-cutting and often conflicting allegiances have a significant impact on prison life" (1993, p. 404). Life in prison for gang members may be increasingly fragmented, disorganized, and unpredictable, at least in California.

The influence by prison gang members across institutions in various city, state, and national jurisdictions, and on the streets, is probably stronger in reference to illegitimate business activities of the criminal organization than to traditional status and turf-based activities. Gangs do, however, constitute an increasing violence and crime problem in terms of basic prison institutional responsibilities, which are:

1. insuring stable control of the facility;
2. incapacitation, i.e., separation of youthful offenders from the community as a sanction for their offenses, thus protecting the community from crime during their incarceration;
3. insuring the physical, social, and mental well-being of youths while in the custody of the institution; and
4. providing services to youths which promote noncriminal adjustments within the institution and when they return to the community. (Regulus 1992, p. 19)

Regulus writes further:

Gang youths pose special challenges to these correctional mission responsibilities because of their organization, solidarity, and commitment to violent and criminal lifestyles. In extreme cases, youth gangs can usurp control of the facility; threaten the well-being of non-gang youths and staff; conduct and coordinate serious crime within the institution and the community; and destroy the rehabilitative climate of the facility. Appropriate design and implementation of gang suppression and intervention activities are therefore essential. (ibid.)

The Prison Gang Problem and What to Do About It

A variety of reasons for why prison gang problems exist have been proposed, including overcrowding, poor inmate living conditions, defective administration, violence-inclined gang leadership, gang competition and conflict, lack of resources, turmoil in the community and political environment outside the institution, and racism.

Hunt et al. believe that overcrowding and disorganization are key factors accounting for the current development of street gangs in California prisons. "Since 1980, the California prison population has increased dramatically from 24,569 to 97,309 [through 1991]. . . . Currently the inmate population stands at 91,892, while bed capacity is only 51,013 . . ." (1993 p. 402).

The National Institute of Corrections states that, while "disturbances involving groups of inmates who threaten the security, safety and order of a correctional facility . . . have become more frequent and more serious" (1991, p. 13), they are probably more often due to institutional disorganization than inmate disorganization. The culture of an institution may be the crucial ingredient in determining whether specific conditions will lead to a disturbance. According to the National Institute of Corrections, some of these conditions are as follows:

1. Ineffective management
   a. Vague lines of responsibility
   b. Lack of visibility and accessibility of administrators
   c. Practices or policies seen as unfair or based on favoritism

    d. Staff perceived as not in control
    e. Inconsistency in application of rules and guidelines
  2. Inmate inactivity
    a. Lack of programs
    b. Lack of work opportunities
    c. Idleness
  3. Inadequate inmate services
    a. Poor or insufficient medical care
    b. Poor food service
    c. Overly restrictive visiting opportunities
  4. Facility problems
    a. Unsafe, sanitary conditions
    b. Crowded conditions
    c. Outdated or poorly maintained facilities

The precipating event may be a sudden change, rumor, or occurrence that substantiates a set of grievances or ongoing concerns that are perceived by inmates as a "turning point, a signal that there is no longer an alternative to violence. . . . Administration must limit the impact of a precipitating event by correcting perceptions quickly" (ibid., p. 14).

Two general suppression views seem to prevail among prison or correctional agency administrators about how to address the gang problem. The first is a somewhat impulsive reaction to gang members who cause trouble, which is to transfer them out of the local or state institution to another institution as soon as possible. Knox observes that no standards currently exist from the American Correctional Association on the appropriate techniques for handling gang problems (Knox 1991a, p. 16). Until recently, juvenile correctional institutions "did not consider gang problems a high priority for specific policies and programs" (Duxbury 1993, p. 427). Clarence A. Terhune, a director of the California Youth Authority, on the other hand, believes that a state correctional system has responsibility for being "better organized than the gang, i.e., having a 'delivery system' [for example] that can respond to feuding between rival gang members confined to the same institution" (McKinney 1988, p. 4).

Regulus suggests that gang problems in institutions have four sets of causes: (1) youth gang population relationships, including institutional turf rivalry, member recruitment, competition over control of contraband or illegal activities, interracial or ethnic conflicts, and intragang, often leadership conflicts; (2) individual gang member deficits in their personal and social development, such as inadequate education, employment, training and job placement experiences prior to the institutional stay, as well as ongoing family problems; (3) institutional deficits including overcrowding, lack of adequate educational, vocational, and social programs, staff shortages, inadequately trained staff, staff racism, rapid and unexplained policy and rule changes, and an overly repressive and depriving environment; and (4) community-related problems, including gang and racial/ethnic conflicts that spill over to the institution, and illegal activities such as drug operations and contract violence that are managed either from prison or community that interactively affect both settings.

Prison issues of what to do about gangs and which approaches to use are similar to those faced by other justice system and community-based representatives; however, the issues are more sharply drawn. The gang problem is clearly more concentrated and serious in adult than in youth corrections, and different responses are necessary, but the distinctions can be exaggerated—particularly since the majority of inmate gang members are probably still in their 20s in most correctional institutions. Gangs in prisons cannot easily be ignored, and the consequences of wrong decisions by administrators can be severe. Unlike their position in other criminal justice agency settings, gang members must be considered full-time participant members of the structure and organization of the prison or training school.

Screening. Management of the gang or potential gang problem requires appropriate intake and classification of inmates. All incoming youths need to be assessed and objectively classified as a gang member or in some other category. Risks for escape, suicide, and violence must be determined. Classification of needs includes such factors as educational skills, academic achievement, vocational experience, history of drug and alcohol abuse, health and mental health problems, and general level of social maturity (Duxbury 1993, pp. 428–429).

An early operational problem is defining the significance of gang membership for the entering inmate. What should be administrative policy? "One school of thought proposes that gang membership, in and of itself, is not sufficient to warrant official sanction. As long as individual gang members do not violate the rules of institutional conduct they may participate in activities available to other inmates and move about the institution as do other inmates" (C. Camp and Camp 1988, p. 9). Another perspective, increasingly dominant, is that the presence of members of gangs or of any unauthorized criminal-oriented organization in prison or youth correctional institutions constitutes a threat and a challenge to the administration. In this more suppressive stance,

> any inmate identified as a gang member will be segregated from the general population. This policy requires provision for enough segregation cells . . . a plan for how segregation units are to be operated, including contingency plans for gang warfare. . . . This strategy puts great emphasis on screening for gang membership upon admission and the development of detailed official criteria for establishing gang identification. (C. Camp and Camp 1988, p. 13)

The issues of gang identification and recognition and the development of appropriate information systems are viewed as critically important for the control of the gang problem, both internal and external to the institution. Is it desirable, for example, to distinguish between "acknowledgement and recognition of prison gangs" (C. Camp and Camp 1988, p. 12)? Acknowledging the presence of gangs as illegitimate organizations but not formally acknowledging their existence as legitimate organizations minimizes the risk of providing credibility to the gang and their manipulation of the institution's control system. Camp and Camp's recommendation is that detailed information on gang membership and gang-activity characteristics, inside and outside of the institution, be placed on computer systems. Such information should be shared with a variety of other justice system representatives to enhance control and prevent violence and other gang crime (ibid.).

Issues of prisoner rights and due process also arise, however. Labeling an inmate as a gang member for the purpose of singling him out for special attention, deprivation, or punishment in the absence of observed criminal behavior may be unlawful. Inmates cannot be excluded from prison activities or deprived of regular privileges because they are gang members without due process. Another dilemma is that the prison administration must protect a prisoner who is not a gang member, or a gang member who seeks to leave a gang, from harm by "predatory gang prisoners" (C. Camp and Camp 1988, p. 19).

Mainstreaming. Regulus believes that systematic schemes to manage gang youths should be developed with special emphasis on mainstreaming within the institution:

> Gang youths should be involved in the same programs and services as non-gang youths (mainstreamed) to the extent possible. Program services and residential assignments should be based on individual youth service and security needs as delinquent or criminal youths, not gang membership per se. Gang membership should be used as an additional and important but not exclusive focus for correctional suppression and intervention. Gang youths benefit from general involvement in quality institutional programs and services. Mainstreaming also reduces special status which can inadvertently be provided because of gang membership. (Regulus 1992, p. 37)

There are limits to mainstreaming of gang youths, however, depending on particular circumstances:

> In some correctional facilities, mainstreaming may not be appropriate for some gang youths where their gang-related behavior, i.e., intimidation and recruitment of non-gang youths or other program disruption, cannot be managed within the normal treatment, service, and housing program of the facility. Separate residential housing and programming may be necessary in such circumstances. This gang option should be used with extreme caution. The concentrating of difficult to manage gang youths in the same programs and housing facilities can facilitate consolidation of . . . gang problems. (ibid.)

Suppressing Criminal Gang Behavior

A variety of deterrents and incentives have been considered in order to limit criminal gang behavior in the institution. The average length of stay in a California Youth Authority facility has nearly doubled, from 10 months in 1968 to 21.1 months today (McKinney 1988, p. 5). Consequently, the California Department of Corrections has considered awarding "good time" to inmates—including gang members—leading to early release. Police in Chicago, however, claim that the early release of gang members (without alerting the police) led to a renewal and escalation of the black gang problem in Chicago public housing projects in the early 1980s. Prison administrators have been increasingly likely to utilize deterrents, such as: vigorous criminal prosecution for crimes by gang prisoners, use of technologies to reduce introduction of drugs through visiting areas, inmate drug testing, strengthening of controls over inmate funds, stricter restrictions for inmates confined in segregation units, and making gang membership an aggravating factor when sanctions are applied for rule violations (C. Camp and Camp 1988, p. 56; see also Baugh 1993). State prison officials in Connecticut have begun to monitor "all phone calls made by inmates except their conversations with their lawyers" (*The New York Times* 1994).

Maintaining Social Order. Success in maintaining order in adult correctional institutions, according to Camp and Camp, depends on the efficient implementation of a formal and an informal organizational approach that minimizes the impact of gang structure. Adequate numbers of staff are necessary, and experienced, professional line staff must be available to enforce prison rules in a professional manner. Guards must avoid implicit or explicit pressures not to enforce rules for gang members in exchange for helping to keep the peace as a quid pro quo. Gang inmates, especially gang leaders, should not be given any notoriety within the system or in public, and they should ordinarily not be combatted with any strategy that acknowledges gang structure or values. Inmate clubs or organizations should not be permitted to meet privately, since thereby the institution may abdicate control of any room or area to a gang. Prison staff and administration should not ordinarily speak through gang leaders to their memberships (C. Camp and Camp 1988, p. 45).

A key control weapon, as suggested earlier, is the transfer of negative gang leadership out of one institution to another, where the gang member's ties and patterns of influence may be reduced. "Separating and isolating gang leaders interrupts communication and can serve to fragment and cripple a gang operation" (C. Camp and Camp 1988, p. 49). On the other hand, the interinstitutional transfers of hard-core gang members may in fact spread the gang problem without necessarily alleviating a current gang problem, particularly where a line of secondary leadership in the gang has already developed (C. Camp and Camp 1988, p. 47). To what extent these various elements of a supposedly efficient suppression strategy have been, in fact, implemented and how successful they have been in dealing with the prison gang problem are not clearly known.

Increasingly, corrections officials believe that once gangs have become entrenched within a facility or a system, "strategies are better geared toward their control than their elimination" (National Institute of Corrections 1991, p. 9). The practice of segregated housing for gang members furthermore has been ruled improper by the courts. The California Department of Corrections provided separate housing only for those gang members considered "hardcore." Illinois rotates gang leaders through the system (ibid., pp. 10–11).

A strong suppression approach seems to be based primarily on the assumption of actual or threatened violence created by gangs in a prison. Another approach argues caution, since prison violence may not always be a direct result of intergang friction. The presence of gangs may be a convenient rationale for frequent, erratic lockdowns and shakedowns (Caponpon and Tagatac 1985). Several wardens with successful experience in dealing with prison gangs conclude that "good security cannot be established without good treatment and good treatment cannot be maintained without good security." The key tactics for establishing or regaining control of a prison are "awareness, automated recordkeeping, and networking with other criminal justice agencies" (Baugh 1993, p. 3).

Alternative Approaches

One alternative and more socially oriented strategy encouraged by administration, staff, and inmates is well-designed housing that "may not only deter gang violence but also reinforce constructive behavior" (C. Camp and Camp 1988, p. 27). A key to the improved ability of the staff to supervise inmate activity and improved inmate satisfaction in part may be smaller housing units. They provide "more options for housing assignments [and] reduce gang member contacts . . ." (ibid.). The use of smaller units and dispersing of both the general and the gang inmate population "reduces the likelihood of housing units being labeled as one particular gang's 'turf' and . . . makes communication within the gang more difficult" (ibid.).

A more complex and balanced prison/community approach may be evolving. This approach is based not only on notions of effective coordination with law enforcement officials outside the institution to deter the interaction of institutional and street-based gang activity, but also on effective communication between correctional officials and inmates. Social intervention programs are emphasized—especially values change as well as the provision of internal institutional opportunities such as education, training, and jobs—and external community-based involvement and support programs. Good communication and rapport with inmates are nurtured within a framework of effective supervision of inmate activities and sound organizational and community relationships.

A variety of innovative social control mechanisms and social development activities are being tried. Formal collaboration between staff and inmates, coupled with individual and group treatment, has been advised as a mechanism for controlling inmate violence, at least in juvenile institutions. Increased communication may enable staff to control violence, reduce deprivation, increase freedom, and foster less exploitive inmate relationships (Feld 1981, p. 363). The development of a self-help movement focused on ethnic or racial cultural themes and issues has also been viewed as of value in facilitating constructive changes in inmate attitude and behavior (Moore 1978, p. 135). Other techniques have emphasized communication with external system and community representatives. For example, victims of gang violence or parents of victims may be brought into the institution for discussion with inmate gang violence offenders (Terhune 1988). Youth agencies and community organizations have been invited to provide a variety of services, including education, training, and preparation for social reintegration into the community. The process of adjustment back to the community should commence before the youth leaves the correctional facility.

The Draper Hall Experiment. An experimental social services approach, specially directed to gang youths, was developed by the Wisconsin Department of Health and Social Services, Division of Corrections. The program for hard-core gang offenders in their late teens, many of them drug traffickers, was established at its Ethan Allan Boys School in Wales, Wisconsin. A particular cottage, Draper Hall, was the locus of the experiment. The rationale for the program was that "youth can eliminate delinquent behavior and disassociate themselves from gangism as a means of socialization. . . . The program within Draper Hall is individually designed while utilizing the power of group dynamics" (Shade 1988, p. 4).

The program addressed four general categories of intervention: psychosocial, educational/vocational; family/community functioning; and program evaluation. The treatment plan was designed for a maximum of twenty-six youths in a seven-month program involving intensive counseling, monitoring, and group participation. The staff anticipated some problems, as well as a few benefits, in the concentration of youths from different gangs in the same residential location. On the one hand, it created risks and generated some management challenges, but on the other hand, "the very design keeps the gang behavior from going underground and undetected, which then enables the staff to directly confront the resident in his activities, its purpose, and its negative results—creating the opportunity to challenge gang values and participation" (Shade 1988, p. 18). The program at the Ethan Allan School is not unlike a variety of programs developed at other juvenile institutions and many public schools in communities throughout the country that emphasize conflict management and mediation through improved communication and cognitive problem-solving skills— at least where the structure of intergang relationships and violence has not solidified.

A key design aspect of the Draper Hall program was individual and group counseling based on "the application of the Behavioral Errors in Thinking" procedure that requires the youths to keep logs, identify behavior resulting from an error in thinking, and develop an alternative strategy that would be successful. The program also used group training sessions to encourage successful communication and values clarification. After-care services were provided through a private counseling service and intended to help youths finish their education, find employment, and receive health care services (Conley 1991, pp. 74–75). The Draper Hall experiment was in sharp contrast to other youth institutional system arrangements where officials either are not aware of gang problems, deny their existence, or simply emphasize the maintenance of orderly institutional routines rather than gang-related rehabilitation. The Wisconsin program appeared to have been a genuine attempt to change attitude and behavioral patterns and to prepare the gang youth for outside living and social achievement in the community.

Program processes, effects, and youth participant outcomes in this experiment, however, were not apparently systematically researched, although anecdotal accounts and occasional verbal reports indicated a "successful" program. Conley notes that "Of the 41 participants released during 1989, only 17 percent had subsequent police contacts during the year and only 17 percent were observed in the company of gang. . . . Data for 1988 through 1990 show that only 6 of 130 program participants released during the same period were subsequently incarcerated in an adult correctional facility" (Conley 1991, p. 75). A further, more recent, verbal report from the director of the Draper Hall experiment indicated that of all 107 youths who participated in the special cottage program over a period of three years, only 6.7 percent came into contact with the Wisconsin adult correctional system and only 17.7 percent were known to probation (K. Miller 1992). Such reports are intriguing but inadequate for purposes of reliable program evaluation and policy development. Complete and systematic data or analyses were not provided. No comparison groups were identified.

An apparently important idea and articulated program for gang youths has not yet been properly researched.

A somewhat similar program that emphasizes social orientation or rehabilitation was developed at the MacLaren School program in Woodburn, Oregon. "It mixes straight talk with tough action. It is open to the whole campus but is targeted on gang members and focuses on gang issues. The program is a mix of group and individual counseling aimed at developing positive self-images, cultural pride, job skills, communication skills, and the ability to accept responsibility for one's actions . . ." (Conley 1991, pp. 73–74). We are aware of no systematic evaluation of this particular program.

Parole—After Care

There appear to be few parole after-care programs or projects directed specifically to the gang problem, either by correctional or social service authorities. Community-based supervised programs directed to released offenders generally have undergone considerable attrition due to lack of funds in recent years. Resources are in short supply to deal specifically with gang parolees. Many of the issues relevant to probation strategies and procedures of intensive supervision apply to gang or former gang youths on parole. By and large, paroled youths have been more serious offenders and possibly more integral to the gang structure and committed to the gang lifestyle than probationers. Parolees have generally been incarcerated for longer periods of time and therefore require additional and sometimes special social assistance and use of techniques of social control to facilitate adjustment. Attention to problems of community reentry, including temptations to rejoin the gang, and special living and work support arrangements are required.

A traditional suppression-oriented project of the California Youth Authority is the Gang Service Project, a specialized parole unit located in Compton. The parole agents specialize in the direct supervision of

> known, sophisticated, hard-core gang members on parole. Each ward assigned to an officer has a history of gang violence and a special parole condition regarding non-gang association. The condition is aggressively enforced. Parole agents work flexible schedules—conducting surveillance as well as monitoring parole behavior, often with the assistance of local law enforcement. The goal of the unit is to be highly visible in the community and hold gang members accountable. (Lockwood 1988, p. 4)

Duxbury notes that electronic monitoring for gang youths released back to highly active gang communities may have unanticipated positive consequences for youths attempting to avoid peer pressure to return to the gang, or at least avoid gang violence. "Some young people on field supervision have expressed a wish to begin or continue electronic monitoring so that they have an excuse when their friends urge them to join in gang banging" (1993, pp. 435–436).

The California Youth Authority has also created a transitional group home as a "safe house" in San Diego County, the *CASA* program for wards who have made the decision to leave the gang lifestyle. The program serves older parolees, 17 to 24 years old, who "desire to get away from the negative gang environment" (Lockwood 1988,

p. 4). Parolees in this residential program receive weekly therapy and drug counseling. They are also provided with the resources of a local employment specialist to assess their training needs and assist in job development. The minimum stay in the house is three to four months. Parolees are not allowed to move out of the facility until they have gained steady employment. Approximately 37 percent of the house residents complete the program (Lockwood 1988, p. 5).

Some youth correctional and parole or after-care programs are now also attempting to develop activities that are coordinated, if not highly interrelated, with a variety of community-based youth service and developmental programs. Consortia of detention staff, law enforcement officers, youth service agencies, and neighborhood groups are evolving to deal with problems of youth violence, often directed to or inclusive of youths recently released from correctional institutions. A variety of social support and treatment referral services and special educational programs are provided. One such program provides "after-care support to those released from MacLaren [School, Oregon] as well as community outreach to the families and youths vulnerable to gang involvement and serves as a place [community center] where gang members, regardless of their affiliation can come and talk. Local law enforcement officers drive by and assure that peace is maintained" (Conley 1991, pp. 73–74).

The development of day treatment programs also may be promising when directed to younger gang youth on probation or in transition as parolees back to the community. Special attention to participation of parents may be provided.

> The different program types can include evening and weekend reporting centers, school programs, or specialized treatment facilities. . . . Day Treatment can focus more on the family unit and the youth's community behavior. . . . Participation of parents in support groups and the treatment of their child is an essential program component because significant changes in the youth's behavior will only last if a change has occurred in the family unit. (American Correctional Association 1994, pp. 2–3)

One of the earliest gang-focused and still one of the most unique community-based involvement programs has been the Gang Violence Reduction Project of the California Youth Authority using parolees as staff who earlier were active and violent gang members. The primary methodologies of the project consist of mediation and community development. Conflict resolution procedures tailored to the culture of the barrio are employed by former gang influentials—assigned to the gangs with which they were originally identified—to find alternatives to gang violence. A variety of community-oriented program activities, such as trips, athletics, neighborhood meetings, gang and drug prevention discussions and lectures in elementary schools, referral of drug abusers for treatment, and involvement of local businesses and parent groups, are employed. The project is supervised by professional parole agents and has received a positive review by some researchers and justice system agency personnel, but not by others. While the project is closely identified with community groups and some social agencies, it remains a source of controversy because of the workers' possible overidentification with gangs still engaged in, or stimulating, serious violent activity.

Further, though there is evidence that probation, correctional, and parole agencies are increasingly involved in local community efforts at control and rehabilitation of gang youths, or even prevention programs, coordination across these programs in the same communities by these justice agencies apparently has not occurred. For example, while the California Youth Authority, like the Los Angeles Probation Department, appears to have a variety of programs directed to youth-gang members, the nature of their interrelationship and the degree of coordination of these two major gang offender supervisory agencies at administrative or field levels are not clear. The California Youth Authority, through its Information Parole Coordinators, "collects gang information whenever Youth Authority parolees are involved within their respective jurisdictions. . . . The designated agents attend local law enforcement gang meetings, compile records on the activities of gang members, and exchange information with local authorities" (Lockwood 1988, p. 4). But it is not clear that such information is shared with probation authorities. California state legislation does not appear to accord a key or integral role to parole—as it does to probation and law enforcement—in the development of a comprehensive local system to deal with the gang problem.

Finally, despite the development of a variety of innovative programs to provide community-based treatment and intensive supervision for offenders, there have been serious questions about their implementation and effectiveness. These questions are relevant to dealing with gang as well as non-gang offenders. The head of the Crime and Justice Foundation in Boston states that "for purely political reasons, those who are most in need of halfway house services are routinely denied them. . . . Inmates who have committed violent crimes generally are not even considered for the programs" (Pérez-Peña 1993, p. A20).

The Rand Corporation evaluation of intensive supervision programs (ISP) in fourteen jurisdictions in nine states revealed that the programs were well implemented but were not successful at decreasing the "frequency of seriousness of new arrests but did increase the incidence of technical violations and jail terms . . . and drove up program and court costs. . . . [Nevertheless] development of an array of sentencing options to create a graduated sentencing system should justify continued development and testing of ISP programs" (Petersilia and Turner 1993, p. 281).

Conclusion

The earliest gang control program by the Los Angeles County Probation Department was developed in the late 1940s as a consequence of the Zoot Suit Riots in World War II. Since then, specialized gang control, rehabilitation, and even prevention programs have been developed by the agency, focused on hard-core as well as younger gang youths or initiates, in collaboration with youth agencies and schools. Probation and parole programs directed at gang youth and others in California and elsewhere have become increasingly complex and comprehensive, involving a range of intermediate punishments and rehabilitation measures, but still generally emphasize punishment or supervision more than treatment.

Gangs constitute an increasing problem in prisons. Unlike other settings, gang youths are integral members of institutional organizations and programs. Four sets of causes for problems of gangs in prisons have been identified: youth gang conflicts, often over control of contraband activities; inadequate personal and social development of individual members as they affect gang behavior; institutional problems of overcrowding and lack of resources; and problems that spill over from the community, whether gang tensions or racial/ethnic conflicts.

Evolving prison approaches include use of small, well-designed inmate housing that not only deters gang member contacts with each other but reinforces constructive behavior, improved communication with gang inmates, and effective coordination with law enforcement to deter the interaction of institution and street-based gang activity. Quality social, educational, and training programs; use of parent groups; and youth agency and local community organization contacts with gang youths and officials in the correctional institution have also been regarded as useful in maintaining social control and contributing to successful community reintegration of inmates when they are discharged.

Few parole or after-care programs exist directed specifically to the gang problem, mainly due to lack of funding. Where these programs are present, however, many of the same issues relevant to probation and corrections apply. Gang parolees tend to be more serious offenders than probationers and are incarcerated for longer periods of time. They therefore may require additional or special assistance and control techniques in facilitating their community reentry and rehabilitation. Most parole or after-care programs, like recent probation or correctional programs, directed to gang youths have not been adequately evaluated. A recent evaluation of intensive supervision programs for a general population of serious offenders indicated lack of significant success. It is not clear which approach or combination of strategies is most promising in the reduction of recidivism of gang youths who have penetrated the justice system.

15

Social Intervention

Social intervention, as discussed in this chapter, signifies social programming, mainly social services, to deal with the gang problem. Youth serving agencies, such as Boys' and Girls' Clubs, YMCAs, social settlements, special youth projects, and youth development authorities, have a long tradition of dealing with youth gangs through in-house and outreach activities and services. These programs predate the more recent specialized law enforcement and other justice system efforts directed to the problem. The older programs were in a state of decline through much of the 1970s and 1980s, but have recently experienced some resurgence, more complex design, innovative program or case management, and the availability of additional, mainly federal and state, resources. Many of the newer or reinvigorated programs emphasize prevention and intervention for younger or at-risk adolescents, unlike the older programs that more often focused on hard-core gang youths, particularly on efforts to mediate or prevent disputes between warring gangs.

The youth gang problem has become far more serious and intractable than it was in an earlier era. Not only has it spread from large inner-city areas to suburban communities, to middle-size and small communities across the country, but it is now characterized by a different range of sociodemographic and organizational factors. The age of gang members is somewhat younger, but also older. Youth gangs have become deadlier, more criminal in character, better organized, and very difficult to deal with. The problem, in its various manifestations, has become hard to ignore by social and community agencies even when they decide not to address it directly. The impact of the gang problem is pervasive and no longer deniable.

A great many human service agencies, schools, community groups, and law enforcement organizations are now engaged in efforts to deal with the problem in some fashion. However, traditional strategies largely prevail, and old policy and practice issues remain unresolved, for example, acceptance or denial of the problem in particular program, organizational, or community contexts; recognition of the gang as a potentially legitimate social group or community structure versus suppression of the gang as a criminal organization; redirection of the activities of the criminal gang versus separation of youths from gangs; and program efforts either in relative isolation from or in close collaboration with other agencies. Despite several excellent evaluations of outreach programs in the 1960s and 1970s, current understanding of gang processes and what programs are effective is extremely limited. The following summarizes findings of earlier outreach or street-gang programs and discusses current program efforts with attention to those evolving strategies that show some promise of reduction of the problem.

Traditional Approaches: Street-Gang Work

Street-gang or outreach programs—the most salient of the social intervention or social service programs addressed to the gang problem—have been subjected to more evaluation than any other strategy. Klein (1971) described and analyzed traditional street work programs, and attributed their early failure to a variety of program defects. Goal priorities were confused. Program designs were not clear as to whether the central goal was control of gang fighting, treatment of individual personality problems, provision of access to social opportunities, alteration of basic values, or prevention of delinquency (see also Spergel 1966). Gang programs still tend to be process rather than goal oriented and theoretical or "blandly eclectic," producing "inconsistency, random or uncoordinated programming and uncertainty" (Klein 1971, p. 53). It is still difficult to determine what approach or activities were actually employed and what effective program process or outcome measures should be used (see also A. Goldstein 1993, p. 27).

Youth agencies and their workers have often subscribed to activities for gang youths because of certain untested program values, because of moral imperatives, and at times because they served the economic survival or expansionary interests of agencies, with little or no relation to delinquency, gang control, or prevention (Klein 1971, p. 53). Consequently, a model of inadequate and disorganized program intervention has been produced that is characterized by "flexibility with respect to client targets, intervention techniques, and theoretical postures" (Klein 1971, p. 150) and extreme reliance on generalized counseling techniques and group programming, with emphasis on group activities, sports, dances, and camping trips. Klein observed that the purpose of these approaches and activities was mainly value transformation or attitude change, and worker–client identification or role modeling. He wondered—his earlier wonderment is still relevant today—why traditional youth service approaches and programs addressed to gang youths have continued, despite repeated evaluations that prove them worthless. He concluded that a major function of youth agency control and prevention programs might be "to sustain rather than to solve [gang] problems" (ibid., p. 150). This is probably an exaggeration of the negative or positive influence of youth agency programs.

The Value of Street Gang Work Programs

Klein's position was based on considerable research. Others asserted, on the basis of speculation but little research, that the street work approach had positive value. For example, Cloward and Ohlin (1960) referred to two "successful" street work projects —the New York City Youth Board Project and the Roxbury Project in Massachusetts. They stated that "the advent of the street-gang worker symbolized the end of social rejection and the beginning of social accommodation" (1960, p. 176). They also observed that "a successful street-gang program . . . is one in which detached workers can create channels to legitimate opportunity; where such channels cannot be opened up, the gang will temporize with violence only as long as a street worker maintains liaison with them" (p. 177). This approach was supposed to ensure a connection between the presence of a street-gang worker and access to opportunity for the youth. In fact, the New York City Youth Board Project—the largest in the country, which endured for at least a dozen years in the 1950s and 1960s—was never systematically evaluated. We still don't know whether the Youth Board Project was successful.

Walter Miller modified his initial claims for the success of the Roxbury Project. He later concluded, after a completed evaluation, that the project had not reduced delinquency. The Roxbury street work project, begun in the late 1950s and early 1960s, included a comprehensive set of intervention components: community organization, family case work, detached work with gangs, organized group work, recreation, and job referral. Miller's evaluation, using comparison groups and a variety of data sources, indicated no reduction in immoral, law-violating behavior or in court appearances; the project's impact was determined to be negligible (W. Miller 1962).

Short and Strodtbeck, in their observations of YMCA-detached workers, at one time speculated that the presence of workers "makes less frequent the need for status-maintaining aggression by [gang] leaders . . . the gang also recognizes its obligation to the worker as a quid pro quo for services performed by the worker and the additional status within the gang world that accrues to a gang by virtue of their having a worker" (1965, p. 197). However, Short and Strodtbeck did not provide any data to support such claims. Later in their study report they noted ambiguously that, "Whatever the effectiveness of the detached worker . . . it seems to arise from his monitoring of the flow of events, rather than his effectiveness in changing personality or values of gang boys" (p. 270).

The Chicago Youth Development Project (CYDP) sponsored by the Chicago Boys' Club, conducted between 1960 and 1966, was based on the same general assumptions as the New York City Youth Board (1960), Roxbury street work (W. Miller 1962), and Chicago YMCA-detached worker (Short and Strodtbeck 1965) projects. The Chicago Youth Development Project emphasized both "aggressive street work and community organization" (Gold and Mattick 1974, p. 257) and worked with groups rather than with individuals. Results indicated that the target areas continued to account for "more than" or "at least their share" of delinquency (ibid.). This project, like the others, failed to support a key expectation that an intensive (or "tight") worker–youth relationship was positively related to effective outcome. Rather, those youths who said they were closest to their workers continued to be most often in trouble with the police (Gold and Mattick 1974, p. 189).

One bright spot of street work in the Chicago Youth Development Project was that street work seemed to raise youths' educational aspirations significantly; a measurable reduction in delinquency existed in a subgroup of youth that was helped with their school adjustment (Gold and Mattick 1974, pp. 205, 265). Overall, however, the evaluators were pessimistic about the value of a detached or street worker approach for the gang member's social adjustment:

Despite the successful efforts of the staff in finding jobs, returning school dropouts, and intervening in formal legal processes, the youth unemployment rate remained at about the same level. The school drop-out rate increased slightly and the arrests of youngsters in the CYDP areas increased over time, with a lesser proportion of them being disposed of as station adjustments. . . . On balance, and in the final analysis, the "experimental" population resident in the action areas of the CYDP seemed to be slightly worse off than the "control" population resident in a similar area selected for comparative purposes. (Gold and Mattick 1974, pp. 296–297)

Yablonsky's project to control delinquency and gang activities in the Morningside Heights area of New York City was developed at about the same time as the other projects, although it was never formally evaluated. Yablonsky's observations about the largely recreation-oriented street work he sponsored were consistent with the findings of other projects: "to direct the gang's energies into constructive channels such as baseball did not seem necessarily to change the Balkans and their patterns . . . working with them . . . to play baseball resulted mainly in bringing some additional 'baseball players' into the gang" (1962, p. 53).

The Wincroft Youth Project in the United Kingdom also used a street outreach approach; a variety of group and casework services were supplied by a large volunteer staff (Smith, Farrant, and Marchant 1972). While there was no overall reduction in delinquency rates, the younger youths (14 years old and under) with low maladjustment scores who had never been convicted before appeared to fare the best. This may or may not be contrary to the findings of the other outreach projects, since most of them generally focused on more serious delinquents or committed gang members.

The Los Angeles Group Guidance Project (mentioned in the previous chapter), a four-year detached-worker effort under the auspices of the Los Angeles County Probation Department between 1961 and 1965, was similar to the Roxbury Project in its emphasis on group programming, including use of parent clubs. A "transformational approach"—change of gang member values, attitudes, and perceptions through counseling and group activities—was the key strategy. Klein concluded that the "project was clearly associated with a significant increase in delinquency among gang members" (1968, pp. 291–292). The gangs that were served most intensively did the worst; also, the delinquency increase was greatest at the lower age levels. He attributed much of the rise in delinquency to an increase in programming, especially group activities that increased gang cohesion and commitment (especially by younger youths) to delinquent patterns (Klein 1968). This study contradicted the findings of the Wincroft Project.

Klein (1971) developed and conducted a follow-up project to test the idea that reduced group programming and the provision of alternative individualized services or opportunities would reduce cohesion of the group and thereby lower delinquency rates. The quasi-experimental project lasted eighteen months with a six-month follow-up period. Klein found that the overall amount of gang delinquency was lowered, but the delinquency rate of individual gang members remained unchanged. The size of the gang was reduced by completely stopping the entry of new members. Group cohesion was thereby partially reduced. Klein viewed his project as promising, but concluded that cohesion reduction was not sufficiently achieved, and therefore the hypothesis was not adequately tested (1971, pp. 301–307).

Other analysts have endorsed the strategy of reducing gang cohesion as a means to control and prevent gang delinquency. Yablonsky, for example, noted that sometimes the street worker can unintentionally provide services that give a "formerly amorphous collectivity structure and purpose," thereby increasing cohesion and delinquency (1962, p. 290). Lo, a Hong Kong social worker and researcher, recommended that gang subgroups should be kept apart and worked with as independent subsystems, especially avoiding communication and cooperation between younger and older members (1986). "Some older gangsters . . . likely to grow out of delinquency" should be "accelerated" out of the gang and "fringe gangsters, isolated members, scapegoats, outcasts, and new members [should be] weaned away" (Lo 1986, pp. 94–97).

Group-work and value-transformation approaches, nevertheless, have persisted, with perhaps greater focus on the reduction of gang violence than general patterns of delinquency. The California Youth Authority sponsored a parole agency-gang violence reduction project that was evaluated between 1979 and 1981, and for a three-year follow-up period from 1982 to 1984 (Torres 1985). The project resolved antagonisms between gangs, provided positive group activities, particularly sports and recreation, and employed gang consultants who were older but still influential members of the gangs (Torres 1980). While the results of the California Youth Authority project reportedly were positive, a close analysis suggests that these findings are ambiguous. Claimed reductions in gang homicides, for example, may have resulted from a decision to exclude from the analysis offenders and victims whose gang affiliations were unclear (Torres 1985, p. 8). There is also some dispute about whether incidents of gang violence began to decline even before the project started. In the mid-1980s the project shifted emphasis to preventing youngsters from joining gangs and promoting their involvement in community improvement activities (Torres 1985, p. 1).

Use of Gang Structure. An extreme case of failure of a social intervention or rehabilitation approach based primarily on use of the gang structure or gang leadership to prevent and control gang crime, especially violence, was the Youth Manpower Project of The Woodlawn Organization in Chicago. This highly controversial million-dollar project, conceived by a staff member of the Community Action Program of the U.S. Office of Economic Opportunity and implemented by the Woodlawn Organization, a militant grass-roots organization in conflict with Mayor Richard J. Daley's office at the time, was conducted for only one year, from 1967 to 1968. The chief goals of the project were manpower development, including job training and job referral, "reduction of gang violence," and lowering the risk of riots then breaking out in many urban areas of the country. The project was staffed, in hierarchical fashion, by leaders and subleaders of the two major gangs: the East Side (Devil's) Disciples, which evolved into the present-day Gangster Disciples, and the Blackstone Rangers, which evolved into the notorious El Rukns. Each gang was originally assigned control and responsibility for staffing of two training centers. The Woodlawn Organization supervisory staff consisted of only four professionals, too few to deal with both a gang staff of approximately 30 young adult gang leaders or influentials and 600 gang member program participants, 16 to 19 years old.

The Youth Manpower Project stirred great community and political controversy and hostility. The police, Chicago City Council, community agencies, national legislators, and the news media took sides in praising or condemning the project. Finally, the Office of Economic Opportunity, under extreme congressional pressures, refused to provide funding for a second year. Key leaders of one of the gangs were later charged and successfully prosecuted for fraud by the Regional U.S. Attorney's Office. The available data indicate that while there was an overall decline in crime in the target gang communities during the project period, there was also a rise in aggravated batteries and gang homicides and no evidence of abatement of gang conflict. Program success in job training or placement was also not achieved (Spergel et al. 1969; Spergel 1972). The two gangs served by the project continue to thrive twenty-five years later, despite claims to the contrary by law enforcement.

Gang-staffed economic or social development projects were also part of a national grass-roots and community development movement in the late 1960s and early 1970s. Especially noteworthy were programs established in New York, Philadelphia, Los Angeles, and Chicago. Gang leaders or ex-convicts with gang backgrounds were involved in important staff and decision-making positions in social agency programs, manpower development, housing rehabilitation, and community planning and economic development. Several gangs, with the help of a few social reformers, attempted to develop a national association of youth-gang organizations called Youth Organizations United (Poston 1971). No systematic evaluation or comparative analysis of these programs exists, however. Recent gang summits in Chicago, Kansas City, Los Angeles, St. Paul, and Pittsburgh are reminiscent of these early efforts to organize representatives of diverse gangs from black inner-city communities to control gang violence, in collaboration with various churches, civil rights groups, private foundations, and some public officials.

A variety of anecdotal reports indicate that all of the street work–community development type programs of the 1960s and 1970s eventually foundered. Most were not well conceived or designed; they were poorly implemented, and malfeasance often occurred (Poston 1971). Kahn and Zinn reported that in a few cases ex-convict gang members took over some of the programs. "Gangs, especially Mexican Mafia, have infiltrated drug treatment and other social programs, [and] committed bank robberies in Los Angeles, starting in the early 1970s" (1978, pp. 59–63). G. Camp and Camp described a 1976 government funded project in Los Angeles that relied heavily on gang leaders and gang structure to carry out a service and community development program. A key objective was to help ex-convicts, mainly gang members, "to readjust to living in society" (1985, p. 98). Funds apparently were misappropriated for vehicles used in gang homicides and in the purchase of heroin before the project was finally investigated and shut down.

Interest and faith in a nonfocused, non-closely supervised or coordinated, helping, outreach, social services, and social advocacy approach for gang youths did not die easily. Just before the development of a prototype Crisis Intervention Network program in Philadelphia (description follows), a series of outreach social service efforts was attempted in that city. Youths, many of them from gangs, were recruited from the streets and directly enrolled in or referred to counseling, educational, and employment programs. The premise of one of these programs in Philadelphia was that simple delivery of social services to gang youths would be sufficient to curtail violent gang disruption by providing alternative incentives and activities (Royster 1974). Evaluators concluded, however, that such highly individualized service referral programs were not effective. Rates of gang homicides rose. Services to youths did not improve. The failure of the program was attributed to "poor management techniques, lack of visibility in the community, [and] lack of ability on the part of workers to deliver services" (ibid., pp. 4–17).

It is difficult to agree with recent scholars or revisionists who claim that classic detached worker programming was not a failure, and that in fact, its efficacy remains unknown (Goldstein et al. 1994; see also Bursik and Grasmick 1993, pp. 153, 157). Claims that such programs suffered from failures of program integrity, intensity, and comprehensiveness; absence of relevant techniques; and "program prescriptiveness" are not correct in terms of the best knowledge and available resources either then or presently (Goldstein et. al. 1994, pp. 36–37). Furthermore, a missed key issue is that a detached worker strategy, or an elaborated outreach counseling or social service approach, by itself, is unable to deal with a complex structural problem requiring other strategies and relevant resources, for example, remedial education, jobs, controls at various levels, racism, and community and interinstitutional mobilization.

Philadelphia's Pioneering Programs

A major innovative structurally oriented program that evolved in the 1970s was the Crisis Intervention Network of Philadelphia. It integrated local community groups and a probation unit with a street work program for integrated purposes of providing services and opportunities as well as control and supervision of both younger and older influential gang members. A variety of related mothers' groups and grass-roots organizations were closely involved in various crisis intervention, mediation, and community education activities. A suppression or surveillance strategy was added to a social intervention or youth-outreach approach within a community mobilization framework in which all key elements of the community, legitimate and illegitimate, joined to reduce the level of gang crime. While a formal evaluation was not conducted, police data indicate a substantial reduction in gang incidents and especially gang homicides from 1974 well into the 1980s (Needle and Stapleton 1983, p. 81). Again, some questions remain: Did the decline in gang homicides begin before the initiation of the program? The adequacy of gang incident reporting by the Philadelphia police in this period was also questioned. Furthermore, other community organization activities conducted at the same time may have contributed to the substantial decline of the traditional turf-based gang violence problem in Philadelphia.

A unique program in Philadelphia coexisting with the Crisis Intervention Network was the House of UMOJA (a Swahili word for "unity"), a resident and nonresident program for gang and other delinquent youths that created "a sanctuary, a sheltered environment" for black gang youths (D. Fattah 1987, p. 4). The program required adherence to strict house rules and a signed contract. Individual counseling and assistance with educational development, job development, and personal problems were provided to each youth. The program was comprehensive and addressed health and recreational needs. It was based on the importance of the notion of the extended family and was at the same time a "modern adaptation of African culture" (ibid., p. 38).

Earlier, the House of UMOJA had been successful in its gang-summit and gang-mediation strategy, particularly as it mobilized and involved all sectors of the community. "UMOJA . . . called for a summit meeting on gang matters . . . 75 percent of the gangs responded. Over 500 members . . . were in attendance, along with social workers, ministers, police, teachers, and other interested persons. The meeting produced a 60-day truce in which no one died from gang warfare" (D. Fattah 1987, p. 39). Organizers solicited the support of gang members in prisons throughout the entire state before the summit was called. A "no gang war" poster became the symbol of a citywide campaign in which state and city authorities, as well as businesses, participated. Continued peace meetings were held in schools, police stations, and campsites throughout 1974. Young people apparently responded positively and massively (S. Fattah 1988, p. 9). Again, while these anecdotal news media reports indicate a high degree of success in the House of UMOJA program, no systematic evaluation was available as of 1988. A replication, however, was planned in Wilmington, Delaware, through the Juvenile Education Awareness Program. The House of UMOJA was also operating a similar program in Portland, Oregon, as of 1991. The UMOJA programs were by then focused more narrowly on residential programming and social services rather than on broad-scale community mobilization to deal with gang violence.

Gang summits, mediation meetings, and truces continue to be tried on a more limited basis in a variety of contexts, with mixed results. Sometimes they appear to succeed for a brief period. It has been argued that mediation meetings and peace treaties buy time for a cooling-off period, separating gangs and confining them to their respective turfs, particularly with organized community involvement to reinforce truce conditions. On the other hand, one knowledgeable law enforcement gang expert has stated, "From time to time, these 'accords' have averted intergang turmoil, but there hasn't been a peace treaty to date that can prohibit the disorder that breaks out when a gang leader summons his 'boys' to retaliate against any foe who offends him, or dishonors the gang" (Collins 1979, p. 64). Many, but not all, gang analysts and practitioners subscribe to Haskell and Yablonsky's statement that "violent gangs should not be treated by any official community program as a 'legitimate' societal structure" (1982, p. 457). The belief is that giving credence to an illegitimate structure feeds gang leader megalomania and legitimizes the possibility of further violence.

The significant reduction in gang violence in Philadelphia over a sustained period in the 1970s and 1980s is an important milestone in the development and elaboration of street work approaches. However, some caution in interpreting the cause(s) of the reduction is required. Whether the activities of the Crisis Intervention Network, the efforts of other community organizations or agencies, special police task forces, the development of peace treaties or meetings, or primarily the development and availability of an alternative criminal opportunity system—drug trafficking— was responsible for the reduction in gang violence in Philadelphia remains unclear. A major decline in gang activity occurred in New York City at about the same time apparently without benefit of special crisis intervention programs or community efforts. In New York City, good access to drug markets, an improving economy, and more concerned and developed social policy and programming may have been instrumental in the conversion of gangs or posses to more lucrative gain activity.

Other Coordinated Community-Based Approaches. Support for a mixed social intervention or crisis intervention approach, with strong deterrent and community involvement characteristics, however, was also obtained from a brief nine-month field experiment in Humboldt Park, an extremely violent gang-ridden community of Chicago. Ecological and individual-level analyses indicated that the program exercised significant control over violent gang activity in comparison with three other similar parts of the city, but had little effect on non-gang crime. The effectiveness of the program appeared more evident for juveniles than for young adults (Spergel 1986). Contemporary street work programs in Los Angeles and Chicago apparently have not fared as well as the earlier Philadelphia Program, possibly because they deemphasized the combined deterrence, community-involvement, and crisis-intervention strategy and replaced it with a more traditional, nontargeted social services gang prevention, value transformation, or group work model (see Klein and Maxson 1987). Some emphasis on local community citizen involvement seems to have occurred in the Los Angeles Street Work project, California Youth Group Services (CYGS), with some apparently positive results. No formal evaluation of this program has been conducted, however. Gang violence across the city and county of Los Angeles has remained at an extraordinarily high level for years.

Limits of Preventive and Counseling Approaches

A recent street work program in San Diego that emphasized traditional counseling, job referral, and work with existing gang structures was also not clearly successful. Gang-related felonies decreased by 39 percent in the target area over two 1-year periods. However, such crimes were also reduced by 38 percent in the control area during the same periods. Furthermore, it should be noted that while the street work program was in operation, the probation department and the district attorney's office were independently also concentrating on gang crime. It is not known what the separate effects of the detached-worker program in comparison to the effects of law enforcement were. The gang problem appeared to abate in San Diego in the early 1980s (Pennell 1983). The gang and drug problem, however, grew more serious in the middle and late 1980s, and stronger deterrent approaches were being implemented in this city.

With greatly increased societal concern about youth gang problems in many parts of the country in recent years, there remains a strong focus on group and individual counseling with younger youths, alongside a generally unrelated even stronger deterrent emphasis by law enforcement, probation, and parole agencies with older youths. These differential and independent approaches may reflect a traditional division of labor in which community-based youth service agencies serve younger, peripheral gang youths, based on a prevention or early intervention model, while established control agencies focus on older, core gang members, based on a suppression model. This duality was still largely apparent in the strategies of prevention and crisis intervention programs and law enforcement anti-gang programs in Los Angeles and Chicago. The effectiveness of a strategy that does not take into consideration the fact that the gang problem is systemic and involves older and younger youths and requires the efforts of criminal justice, youth agencies, schools, employment, and citizen groups, interactively and interdependently, remains to be demonstrated.

Gottfredson (1987) reviewed the results of a series of experiments on peer counseling approaches in schools and community agencies. He concluded that they lend "no support to any claim of benefit of treatment, with the possible exception that the treatment may enhance internal control for elementary school students. For the high school students, the effects appear predominantly harmful" (p. 710). Furthermore, he suggested that "it may be useful to avoid delinquent peer interaction entirely rather than to attempt to modify its nature" (ibid.). Community-based peer group experiences seem to be somewhat successful when small group activities integrate a limited number of young delinquent or predelinquent youths into small groups that are dominated by conventional youths and guided by conventional youth leaders (Feldman, Caplinger, and Wodarski 1983).

Individual counseling approaches with gang youths, at least of a general nondirective form, where evaluated, have also produced poor results. The individual gang member is more strongly influenced in what he does by gang norms and gang pressures than by what he promises to do during individual counseling sessions (Short and Strodtbeck 1965). Caplan reported that "over time, individual subjects repeatedly demonstrate a tendency to nearly succeed in adopting final change behaviors advocated by the treatment plan . . . remotivation remains a major hurdle to overcome in reorienting the activities of urban [gang] youths" (1968, pp. 84–85).

In sum, traditional social intervention programs, whether agency-based, outreach or street work, or crisis intervention, have shown little effect or may even have worsened the youth gang problem. Such programs seem somewhat more effective and produce some positive results when they are designed as part of a comprehensive or mixed set of strategies. Multiple-agency service approaches—including value-transformation, deterrence, and opportunity provision strategies, closely integrated with local citizen involvement but fashioned in different ways in different communities for targeted younger and older gang youths—may be promising. Newer approaches of techniques and contexts for dealing with the gang problem must take past experience and insight into consideration.

Recent Innovative Approaches

The Los Angeles riot of 1992, together with the growth of violence and gangs in urban areas throughout the country, has brought a heightened awareness of the complexity of the gang problem and the need for effective youth service programs. Slowly coming to consciousness in the public mind is the realization that explosive pressures now exist in society because of the arrival and concentration of poorly educated and trained older youths from various minority groups in inner-city areas at a time when few meaningful jobs are available for such youths. The threat of violence and urban disruption by youths without access to educational, social, and economic opportunities and adequate legitimate social control systems has led to a recent increase in resources and a diversity of approaches to deal with these youths, including gang members.

Whether the newer social intervention programs are indeed innovative, are significantly different from past efforts, and constitute an effective strategy is unclear. Many of the new-wave programs have been stimulated and supported by the Departments of Justice, Health and Human Services, Labor, and Housing and Urban Development; Commission on National and Community Service; and a number of major foundations. New urban conservation and youth service, educational, and work opportunity programs plan to reach high-risk and criminal youths. The Commission on National and Community Service was expected to parcel out $65 million for such programs in 1992, the most federal money allocated to youth programs since the "Roosevelt Administration's 1930s creation of the Civilian Conservation Corps (CCC) to fight the Great Depression" (*Youth Today* 1992, p. 22). A significant proportion of federal funds was to focus on social intervention, including youth and community service.

Crisis Intervention and Youth Empowerment

The newer social intervention approaches attempt to seek out and work with youths at high risk of gang involvement or serious gang offenders in their own social milieus, largely on terms relatively acceptable to deviant youths. The current—like the old—program assumption appears to be that such youths require mainly nonjudgmental social support and assistance with a variety of personal, school, or work problems as youths define them. Little attention is paid simultaneously or interactively to the imposition of social controls, directly or indirectly. The workers in these programs continue to be, as in traditional street work practice, in only nominal contact with law enforcement and traditional youth-serving agencies. Workers are highly identified with and often protective of gang youths regardless of their antisocial behavior.

Much effort continues to be directed to maintaining the peace among increasingly sophisticated and well-armed street groups that are pervasive in some city neighborhoods. The straight social services or social intervention model with greater emphasis on mediation or truce arrangements remains. Morales and Sheafer observed that Community Youth Guidance Counselors had fourteen street teams in Los Angeles and

> were able to convince forty-four of 200 gangs they worked with to come to the table to develop a "peace treaty." During the period the peace agreement was in effect, from Thanksgiving of 1986 through the New Year's holidays of 1987, there was only one act of violence among the forty-four gangs. The "peace treaties" model can "buy time" for all concerned, but if society does not respond with the needed resources (jobs, training, physical health-mental health services, education) peace treaties are very difficult to maintain. (Morales and Sheafer 1989, pp. 608–509)

Such approaches are valuable in maintaining communication with often extremely alienated youths, sustaining the few channels available for normalized relations and the limited possibilities of mainstreaming gang youths into conventional roles in the community. Some analysts also continue to emphasize the positive functions of gangs on their own terms for the development of "self-esteem, peer acceptance, increased pride, feelings of empowerment, hopefulness, social skills, and sense of family" when other institutions have failed to provide these necessities for youth development (Dunston 1990, p. 45). Some of the street work efforts have incorporated a limited entrepreneurial model that aspires to economic and career development based on youth enterprises or businesses that youth themselves control. This latter approach has not been widely developed or evaluated. Generally insufficient resources appear to be infused into, or are ultimately produced by, these nonprofit operations (p. 36).

Nevertheless, street work programs, because they are so free-wheeling, marginal to other community agencies, and often lacking in adequate field supervision of workers, continue to cause crises of confidence in relationships with other agencies, especially law enforcement. Limited relationships with police and probation are further weakened over time. Many of the gang workers continue to be former gang members or influentials, are poorly trained, and succumb not only to patterns of over-identification with gang youths but frustration at difficult work, low pay, and lack of opportunities to upgrade their own job career possibilities. Under pressures from law enforcement and funding agencies, street work programs have again pulled back from sustained crisis intervention and close contacts with older gang youths. More and more effort is going into work with younger youths and preventive efforts, to the detriment of systemic or simultaneous working relationships with older, more active, and dangerous gang-bangers in recent initiatives of the Department of Health and Human Services.

Family/Parent Focused Programs

A variety of youth-serving and family agencies have currently sought to deal with serious problems of family breakdown associated with younger youth gang members, youth alienation, and growing juvenile violence. An outreach family support concept is usually employed, focused on gang membership and drug-related activities, particularly for families in high-risk areas. Emphasis is on the development of the family's capacity to structure controls and sanctions, as well as on support for youths vulnerable to gang influence. Frequent home contacts and the creation of parent support groups are part of this approach. Sometimes twenty-four-hour hot lines are available to assist parents deal with their "problem" children. Ongoing assessments of family problems and intensive and comprehensive services focused on both the family and the youth are usually recommended, but it is not clear if they are carried out.

Hawkins claimed that the most effective of the family-oriented programs for reducing delinquency and drug abuse must be based on: early childhood education that teaches individual parents the basic skills of socializing children and managing families and at the same time teaches children skills of how to get along with peers from an early age (e.g., first and second grades. Parents need to learn how to set clear expectations for child behavior, bonding children to the family through various family-focused activities (Hawkins 1989, p. 19). However, at least one experienced youth-gang worker claims that working with parents of older gang youths is not successful and may not be a practical approach. "By the time their sons are involved with a gang, the parents have lost control. While some parents might have good intentions and want to be involved, they usually are not going to be part of the solution" (Conley

1991, p. 54). More likely is that variable patterns of parent–gang youth relationships exist and require different social intervention techniques and approaches, taking into consideration race/ethnicity, economic community, gang youth age, and other interpersonal factors.

Peer Group Interventions

A variety of group interventions in different contexts, including correctional institution and school continue to be popular in delinquency prevention programs. A recent review of the outcome research literature continues to suggest that the least promising approaches include, "increasing self-esteem without touching anti-social propensity . . . increasing the cohesiveness of anti-social peer groups . . . and attempts to focus on vague personal/emotional problems that have not been linked with recidivism" (Andrews et al. 1990, p. 374). Andrews and his colleagues observe that

> higher levels of services are best reserved for higher-risk cases and that low-risk cases are best assigned to minimal service. . . . Appropriate types of service typically, but not exclusively, involve the use of behavioral and social learning principles of interpersonal . . . [and] include modelling, graduated practice rehearsal, role playing, reinforcement, resource provision, and detailed verbal guidance (making suggestions, giving reasons). (ibid.)

Hollin concurs that "the type of intervention program is important. The more structural and focused approaches, including behavioral, skill-oriented and multimodal treatment, appear to be more effective than less structured and focused approaches, such as counseling." He adds that "intervention programs conducted in the community have a greater effect on offending behavior than do residential programs" (Hollin 1993, pp. 73–74). However, the reality is that many inner-city areas tend to be chaotic, with institutional arrangements highly fragmented. Offenders in such contexts are hardly connected to structured community situations other than the gang, which is not ordinarily a model of stable structure and activity.

New Social Contexts and Team Arrangements Required

Gang youths need to be integrated into community development programs and "secure meaningful, productive, long-term employment" (Dunston 1990, p. 29). This can be achieved through involving gang youths in a range of social situations and related experiences, appropriately timed—from medical services providing tatoo removal, to conflict mediation experiences in school, and even to "spiritual" opportunities for beginning another, better life. Morales also observed that when "there is a major *structural* change in their lives, such as entering into a marital relationship, having a child, obtaining a steady job, re-enrolling and attending school, or becoming a 'Born Again Christian,' they seem to abandon the gang" (Morales 1989, p. 439).

A variety of new contexts, within which social intervention is practiced, are necessary. New agency structural and program combinations and professional specializations are required. Youth workers need to operate out of grass-roots or tenant organizations providing a range of services to youths, parents, and public housing managers in regard to gang problems. Liaison with schools is important to assist school administrators and teachers to improve conditions of safety for children and youths in and around school and improve educational tutoring opportunities for at-risk and already committed gang youths. Increased parent involvement is required in the formal education of younger youths, as well as social and educational support to parents, and coordination with teachers.

Teams of diverse professionals—youth center, mental health agency, and law enforcement personnel—need to work together to establish common goals and objectives on behalf of at-risk youths and to form anti-gang coalitions to carry out a developmental model (Advisory Centers 1990, pp. 6–7). Social service, school, law enforcement, correctional, and other justice agency personnel need to develop new collaborative arrangements for assisting parents and supplementing their social control and developmental roles with at-risk and core gang members. In the process, a network of intervenors in new contexts should be established. For example, Morales and Sheafer suggest the development of special hospital outreach crisis teams, modeled after or interrelated with SCAN (Suspected Child Abuse and Neglect) teams. One member of such a team would be a specialist, responsible for coordinating treatment of the gang member and/or his family in situations of gang victimization:

> In working with gang members who have been seriously injured as the result of gang assault, the author has found that often this is when their psychological defenses are down as they are suffering adjustment disorder or post-traumatic stress disorder symptoms (PTSD). . . . During this acute stage which may last about six months, they are quite motivated to abandon "gang banging" (gang fighting). . . . It is at this point that the social worker can also obtain needed employment, educational, recreational, or training resources for the vulnerable gang member.
>
> The parents may also be emotionally vulnerable having just gone through an experience in which they almost lost their son. They may be more willing to accept services for themselves if needed, and/or younger siblings who might be showing some early behavioral signs of problems (deteriorating school performance, truanting, aggressiveness). . . .
>
> If there are adolescent gang members in the family, they may be quite angry and want to retaliate and get "even" for their brother's or sister's death . . . the social worker would call upon community gang-group agencies to assist in reducing further conflict. (Morales and Sheafer 1989, pp. 611–613)

Such structural reorganizing of services requires not only the development of innovative techniques but a willingness to coordinate efforts across disciplines and agencies and examine outcomes through evaluation procedures. Reiner notes that such coordination or collaboration is extremely difficult. *"The turf wars among prevention [or intervention] agencies can be almost as fierce as those among gangs . . . not infrequently, there are profound differences in style and fierce competition* between agencies doing quite similar work. . . . In part, this is because the field attracts true believers" (Reiner 1992, pp. 230–231). Youth agency personnel and other social intervenors tend to be powerful, self-convinced, missionary personalities committed to social action and saving individuals, neighborhoods, and societies, yet who do not usually examine their premises, actions, or program outcomes. Under what conditions social intervenors and also law enforcement officials can modify their beliefs and actions remains to be determined. Ongoing research and evaluation of gang member rehabilitation, prevention, and control programs might be one requirement for funding large-scale social intervention efforts.

Conclusion

Social intervention signifies social programming, mainly the application of a range of social services, to deal with the gang problem. Street-gang work or outreach programs, the most focused of the social intervention approaches, were subjected to a considerable amount of "high quality" research in the 1960s and 1970s. The demonstration programs were essentially evaluated as not effective. They often relied primarily on the gang structure to redirect gang member orientations and behaviors from criminal to conventional norms, values, and activities. Many of the programs may not have been well conceived, designed, or implemented.

Several promising social intervention programs did evolve, however. They attempted to integrate deterrent as well as community mobilization strategies. A comprehensive and coordinated set of programs in Philadelphia in the 1970s was associated with a significant decline in the gang violence. However, other factors may have been associated with this outcome, since it occurred in other cities as well. Most succeeding efforts at gang control and individual gang member rehabilitation were neither comprehensive, well coordinated, nor adequately researched.

While there has been a significant expansion of resources to local human service agencies to address the spreading and worsening gang violence problem in the 1980s and 1990s, there is question as to how different or innovative the newer programs really are compared with traditional programs. New agency structures and professional specializations are probably required in the development of comprehensive approaches. Youth workers need to operate out of grass-roots, tenant, and local community organizations as well as in collaboration with schools, criminal justice agencies, public housing, and employment settings in the provision of a range of services to both older and younger gang youths. The development of new arrangements for the delivery of a greater range of more complex outreach gang services requires a higher level of coordination across professional disciplines and types of agencies, better trained and educated workers, and a strong commitment to long-term research and evaluation, to determine which social intervention arrangements and techniques are, in fact, effective.

16

Social Opportunities:
Education and Jobs

The provision of social opportunities is one of two critical components of a promising approach for both reducing and preventing the youth or street-gang problem. The other component is community mobilization, that is, the concerting of organizational and citizen energies, including perceptions, definitions, communications, and actions, in reference to particular gang problems. Community mobilization, including interagency coordination, must be integrated into the provision of social opportunities at national as well as local levels. But it is at the local level that political and governmental organizations, along with citizen groups, must take major responsibility for development of overall gang violence reduction efforts. This chapter describes and analyzes national and local policies and programs in the provision of social opportunities, particularly education, training, and job development and placement.

I believe that it is important to define the policy or program strategy of social opportunities in somewhat restrictive terms, in part to avoid confusion of the strategy of opportunities provision with that of social intervention or community mobilization, or even, at times, deterrence. In practice, these strategies are often mixed and interactive, but the distinctions among them are critical for conceptual and policy clarity and effective program development. A tradition in human services equates social opportunities with social intervention, and tends to overemphasize the values of counseling, mentoring, recreation, and other social support services without sufficient reference to their important linkage, but still not equivalence, to basic institutional opportunities. Youth services, juvenile detention, child welfare placement, physical and health services, have sometimes been regarded as directly providing social opportunities, since they afford contexts for learning social or recreational skills, placing youths in a stable environment and enabling them to deal with or overcome physical or emotional problems and handicaps.

My concern with social opportunities is at two different levels: macro and micro. I discuss first large-scale federal and state plans for resource infusion to change or expand education, training, and job means or opportunities (the macro level), and then examine policy and program for local community school improvement and job development (micro level). In the short and long term, school and job opportunities must be closely interrelated and appropriately directed at a range of types of gang youths, younger and older, at risk and hard core. A social opportunities approach, in the sense in which I use it, requires that programs of social intervention and deterrence also be provided and interconnected. Further, a social opportunities approach to dealing with the gang problem must be conceptualized and structured in such a way as to avoid socially isolating gang youths from mainstream educational, social, and career developmental opportunities. It is critical to interrelate, to the optimal extent possible, various mainstream and special gang-focused educational, training, job development, and social competence-building programs.

Macro Level Educational Perspective

A report of the Quality Education for Minorities Project (1990) is relevant to a discussion of the academic needs of gang as well as non-gang youths in socially deprived contexts. The report concludes that what is necessary is a comprehensive "set of strategies, sustained national leadership, and commitment to high-performing schools and educational equity" (p. 3). Schools need to be restructured in such a way that they enable "people [to] learn in different ways and pursue countless paths to reach their educational goals" (ibid.). Gang youths often have experienced school failure. Often they have been labeled and separated out from the earliest years of schooling by teachers on the basis of perceived low academic interest or ability or antisocial behavior. These children and youths are sometimes victims of low teacher expectations, based on inappropriate understanding and insensitivity to minority cultural backgrounds, the foreign languages students speak, or teacher misperceptions of students' home life. They may be placed in low-ability or remedial tracks or special schools, which later may be extremely difficult to escape (Quality Education for Minorities Project 1990, p. 17).

Restructuring Schools

A central approach to providing educational opportunities for gang youths is not only to change teacher and student attitudes, values, and behaviors but to restructure schools. Berlin and Sum emphasized the integration of relevant educational and training opportunities into actual work opportunities. While

> we are generally acknowledged to have one of the finest systems of higher education in the world, practically no attention is paid to the severe inadequacies of our vocational training and apprenticeship systems. We have the least well articulated system of school-to-work transition in the industrialized world. . . . In Austria, Sweden, West Germany, and Switzerland, it is virtually impossible to leave school without moving into some form of apprenticeship or other vocational training. (Berlin and Sum 1988, pp. 22–23).

We have as yet no

> national system capable of setting high academic standards for the non-college bound. . . . America may have the worst school-to-work transition system of any advanced industrial country. . . . [Other country systems] operate comprehensive labor market systems which combine training, labor market information, job research, and income maintenance for the unemployed. We do not. (National Center on Education and the Economy 1990, p. 4)

Hahn and Danziger observed that no institution or set of personnel in the United States has taken the lead in specifically coordinating and defining a response to the needs and difficulties of "estranged youth." This is not true in other countries. "In Japan, for instance, the few dropouts (less than 7 percent) are given assistance by school-based job counselors and are placed in jobs providing extensive lifelong training. In Germany, the apprenticeship system furnishes skills training and certification for students and dropouts alike" (Hahn and Danziger 1987, p. 52). Further, these authors stated that youths who are severely damaged socially may require

> a long, costly multidimensional response. Recovery from a tragic childhood cannot happen instantly. Successful treatment may require psychological and social services, family support, individualized learning of basic skills at the student's pace, a measured and patient exposure at work and ongoing social and vocational counseling while the youngster is on the job. That's a large order. But this is a very big problem. (Hahn and Danziger 1987, pp. 60–61)

A variety of foundation reports suggest slightly different or more detailed recommendations based, however, on the same strategy of a targeted opportunity provision:

> The [Grant] Commission recommends expansion of flexible, long-term and comprehensive education, training, and employment programs specifically designed to give truly disadvantaged young people added chances to succeed. These programs should be tailored to individual needs and provide the assistance that will make success possible, including help with day care, transportation, housing, health care, and training allowances. (Grant 1988a, p. 122)
>
> Long term objectives should include establishing appropriate standards with bonuses and other incentives to reward high-performing schools teachers, and students. . . . [This means that we must] . . . focus our efforts on all children, but give special attention to economically disadvantaged and minority children who are deficient in both basic skills and higher-order thinking skills.

> • Offer a continuum of services for both parents and children in recognition of the intergenerational causes of low basic skills.
> • Address the phenomenon of summer learning loss, especially during the neglected middle years when students learn the basic academic skills they need for a lifetime of learning and working.
> • Develop standards that hold institutions accountable while leaving room for local officials to exercise autonomy.
> • Smooth the transition from school to work for high school graduates who are not college bound.
> • Improve the quality and availability of the nation's second chance job training and community college programs. (Berlin and Sum 1988, p. 58)

Several school systems, abroad and in this country, have been restructured and provide examples of the characteristics of school reform that could be applied to controlling or preventing the youth gang problem. In Germany's comprehensive schools, teams of teachers for each grade are responsible not "merely for teaching their subjects but for the total education of their children, for making sure that their students succeed, personally and academically. . . . The teacher teams and their students stay together for 6 years, from the time the students enter the school in grade 5 until they earn their learning certificate at the end of grade 10" (Quality Education for Minorities Project 1990, p. 48).

Models for Gang-Prone Younger Children

American models emphasize community-based as well as system change. Conley suggests two program models that show promise in communities with serious gang problems. Both are aimed at improving "youths' attachment to school, increasing the responsiveness of the schools to the full range of student needs and improving the relationship of schools to their communities" (Conley 1991, p. 51). The School Development Program of Professor James Comer and his colleagues at the Yale Child Study Center stresses community and agency participation. It includes three groups: a school planning and management team (e.g., comprising a principal, parents, teachers' aides, counselors, and support staff); a mental health team (e.g., comprising a psychologist, teachers, the principal, a nurse, counselors); and a parent's group (e.g., the PTA) (ibid.).

In the model developed by Professor Comer, schools "paid attention to child development and established a basic participatory school management system in which the principal shared power with parents, teachers, and professional support staff" (Quality Education for Minorities Project 1990, p. 50). School staff in this experiment observed that "behavior problems result mainly from unmet needs rather than from 'willful badness' and that actions have to be taken to meet these needs" (ibid.).

The Program Development Evaluation method, created by Gary and Denise Gottfredson at the Center for Social Organization of Schools at Johns Hopkins University, emphasizes a more structured school management strategy "aimed at identifying school problems and managing them. A School Improvement Team comprising teachers, parents, school administrators, and district-level staff follow a set of predetermined steps to identify school problems, establish goals and objectives, develop programs and monitor the implementation process" (Conley 1991, p. 52). Hahn and Danziger have also suggested the development of a "comprehensive assessment of each child's social and economic conditions outside of school. This will involve extensive consultation with parents, periodic home visits, and joint planning with parent groups, community organizations, and youth-serving agencies" (1987, pp. 28–29). The integration of education and comprehensive services, case management, and long-term follow-up to ensure progress for each child is stressed in each model.

A more recent model emphasizes the development of "school-linked comprehensive service systems," "shared governance among the schools and various service-delivery systems . . . a flexible menu of services . . . collaborative funding . . . and reducing referrals to service agencies . . . to concentrate on developing sustained relationships with students and their families" (Quality Education for Minorities Project 1990, pp. 50–51). This latest model provides flexibility for staff to move across agency barriers to meet the needs of clients.

In these evolving models, bonds between home and school, especially at the elementary school level, are strengthened. The students' problems, whether physical, social, or emotional, are dealt with interactively through home and at school. The school becomes a base or center to coordinate the social, health, and vocational services that children and families need, including health care, literacy training, day care, and employment and training (Quality Education for Minorities Project 1990, p. 54). The Head Start programs have already demonstrated the importance of early child care and educational assistance for inner-city 3- to 5-year-olds before school entry, if later social problems are to be prevented or reduced. But a longer term, more sustained effort is required for certain youths during the middle grades, when gang problems begin to surface. Berlin and Sum have underlined the importance of the "intergenerational effect of the parent's education on the child's" (1988, p. 36). They urge that equal priority be placed on education and academic remediation for the parent. Children may be helped as much, or even more, by helping mothers and fathers. Therefore, turning schools into community education facilities that remain open evenings and weekends to serve the needs of adults, especially parents of children at risk, may be extremely important.

Models for Adolescent Gang Youths

Gang or gang-prone youths require a well-structured intense learning experience and deep, sustaining concern by teachers for their social and emotional needs. The special school or work-training program, especially in the adolescent period, therefore requires small school and class size; strong principals; and teachers who participate in counseling youths; as well as in-school management; clear standards, rules, and regulations; and extensive opportunities for learning by doing. Drop-out prevention for older youths, according to Hahn and Danziger, requires a "cohesive, integrated effort" that includes mentorship, an array of social services, health care, "family planning education and infant care for the adolescent mother . . . concentrated remediation using individualized instruction and competency-based curricula . . . effective school-business collaboration . . . improved incentives . . . [and] the involvement of parents and community organizations in drop-out prevention" (1987, p. 31). In this regard, there is question as to whether short-term limited efforts, such as the Summer Training and Education Program (STEP), can make a significant impact on the long-term educational, job, or sociobehavioral adjustment of youths. An extensive field study of the program demonstrated that disadvantaged urban students "who spent two consecutive summers working and learning for pay fare no better in the long run than those who did not participate in summer education programs" (*Youth Today* 1992, p. 7). Furthermore, youths in the program continued to participate in "risky behaviors" at a high rate.

School–Work Linkage. The building of vocational career bridges between school and work as suggested here is of special relevance to gang youths who generally are in their middle or older teen years. The development of school–business–industry agreements that establish connections and mutual responsibilities that contribute to the social integration of these youths into mainstream society is critically needed. The schools should make sure that vocationally oriented students meet attendance and achievement standards and that business and industry employers agree to hire preferentially the students so accredited. Few American schools have developed such links for those youths who are neither prepared nor desirous of pursuing further academic education after (or even before) graduation from high school.

In this system of school–work linkage, business and industry would make clear and precise the nature of qualifications for jobs needed by inner-city youths, with special attention to gang youths. Both schools and industry would structure attitudinal, classroom, and work-site training around cooperative learning and preapprentice and apprentice opportunities for hands-on learning (Quality Education for Minorities Project 1990, p. 74). Cooperative learning and work experiences may be especially important for gang youths who depend on and quickly develop associations and identification with a group. A successful work experience can signify a transfer of the identification of the youth from the gang to the work group at the office or plant. All such positive bonding must also be based on and guided by sensitive, warm, supportive relationships with adults in the immediate learning and work environment.

For gang youths or older youths at risk, it is especially important to consider and plan opportunities for long-term learning through the establishment of a National Youth Service that would strengthen skills and knowledge and develop a sense of the unity of youths across different economic, social, and ethnic backgrounds. The capacity of the Job Corps should also be expanded, so that gang youths are included in training programs focused on providing a "mix of remedial education and skills training delivered in a residential setting" (Quality Education for Minorities Project 1990, p. 75). Finally, expanded basic educational and training services through the Job Training Partnership Act need to be improved with the interests of gang youths in mind. Such programs offer "second chance" learning based on the combination of work and education through individual "competency-based, open-entry, open-exit," and alternative-learning modalities (ibid.).

The growing federal allocation of funds for conservation and service corps, as well as school-based volunteer services, augurs well for a concerted strategy to integrate training, jobs, and services for older youths, including gang youths. Approximately $58 million was recently provided by the Commission on National Community Service for such projects as "recruiting African-American, Latino, and Asian youths in South Central L.A. to assist the rebuilding of riot-burned buildings and constructing parks and gardens in vacant lots," and efforts to "integrate instruction in community-based service work" with school curricula and graduation requirements. Students were to be required and taught how to complete meaningful volunteer projects in community service programs in order to graduate (*Youth Today* 1992, p. 22).

Local School Programs

Local school district policy planning for socially disadvantaged and newcomer youths often does not pay sufficient attention to the specific interests and needs of gang youths. Yet local schools, along with parents and neighborhood institutions, bear principal responsibility for socializing and resocializing youths. Elementary and middle schools are an integral part of the local community life of families with children. Schools can become a context for gang formation, gang recruitment, planning of fights, drug use, and sometimes drug selling. While gang fights and gang-related criminal acts are more likely to occur outside than inside the school, they are often planned at school. The density of gang graffiti and frequency of trespass on school property may be indicators of the level of a gang problem in a school and its neighborhood.

Many school systems initially prefer to ignore the problem, which if recognized could create loss of status and embarrassment for administrators and teachers and involve a difficult and expensive process of organizational change and development. School administrators often claim they have other more serious social problems to contend with, such as teenage pregnancy, drug abuse, and dropouts, and that insufficient resources exist, including teacher and staff understanding and skills, to deal with a gang problem that may be less overt, at least in the school setting. When the school system does recognize the gang problem, it tends to react almost exclusively in security terms. Security arrangements may involve stationing police youth division officers in selected "dangerous" schools or employing outside firms to safeguard school employees and students and to protect property. Furthermore, state legislation and criminal justice planning agencies increasingly recommend close cooperation between schools and law enforcement agencies in dealing with gang problems inside, or outside but near, schools. Emphasis is on apprehending youths or adults who violate state laws pertaining to the possession and/or use of weapons or drugs on or near school property. Enhanced sentences are often provided under such legislation.

Traditional Approaches

Operation SPECDA (School Program to Educate Drug Abusers), a cooperative program of the New York City Board of Education and the New York City Police Department, operated in over 150 schools, serving students and their parents from kindergarten through grade 12. Police helped provide classes and presentations on drug abuse in the schools, but also concentrated on enforcement within a two-block radius of schools to create a drug-free corridor. Many arrests were made of youths in groups or gangs selling drugs or possessing firearms (McConnell and Bricker 1987, p. 70). The relationship between police and schools over the issue of gangs, crime, and law violation is, nevertheless, not easy to establish to the mutual satisfaction of representatives of both types of agencies. "Educators and law enforcement groups often have had difficulty in finding common ground for distinguishing between what is a crime and what is a disciplinary problem. When does the child cease to be the responsibility of the school and begin to come under the jurisdiction of the police?" (Summerhays and Lindbloom 1989).

A call for school security may result in an elaborate suppression strategy that also brings in outside criminal justice agencies, including probation. The School Crime

Suppression Program, recently approved by the Los Angeles County Board of Supervisors, called for "a 40 percent reduction in gang crime, with a primary emphasis on gang activities on school campuses. Probation officers assigned to the program were present on campus everyday" (Los Angeles County Probation Department 1988, p. 17). Probation officers were expected not only to supervise minors who were gang members known to the court, but also to "engage in prevention of gang activities on the campus as a whole" (ibid.).

The Portland school system developed a systemwide approach that focused on deterrence. It included provisions for "closely monitoring school campuses for signs of gang behavior . . . searching lockers or students whenever there was any indication of weapons or drugs . . . [recognizing] the display of certain clothing or adornments that indicated gang membership . . . [and] strictly monitoring visitors to school campuses" (McKinney 1988, p. 7). Portland also developed in-school support groups and counseling programs for students who displayed characteristics that might lead to gang battles, as well as for their parents (ibid.). At the high school level, programs stressed helping high-risk students find better than minimum-wage employment. But the Portland school system also focused significantly on the youth gang problem beyond school boundaries. It "is providing leadership and full cooperation with community, city, county, state, and federal agencies to thwart gang activities and criminal behavior" (Prophet 1988, p. 3). School police officers developed sufficient gang deterrent expertise to become Portland's major resource for information and intelligence on youth gang activities—not just activities affecting the schools, but activities affecting the entire community" (ibid.).

Preventive Programs. Many of the preventive programs that focus on elementary grade students point out the dangers of gang activity and urge students not to join them. "The Alternatives to Gang Membership" curriculum of the city of Paramount in Los Angeles County not only provides comic books, posters, and discussion opportunities for students that address the gang problem, but also sponsors neighborhood meetings led by bilingual leaders. The program sponsors informal counseling for individual youth who appear to be at special risk of gang involvement. The fifth-grade anti-gang curriculum, introduced in the Paramount Unified School District in 1982, identifies and encourages students to participate in constructive youth activities in the neighborhood. A significant number of cities in California have developed school gang diversion programs modeled after the Paramount plan.

The Santa Ana City Council approved a school anti-gang program "aimed at students in the fourth, fifth, or sixth grades. Students were to receive weekly 1-hour lessons on gangs intended to counteract the "glamorizing" they may be offered by older students already in gangs" (Schwartz 1988). The Los Angeles Unified School District inaugurated an ambitious Gang Resistance Education and Training curriculum in grades 3 through 9, with the capability of expanding the range from kindergarten through grade 12 by changing the instructional vocabulary and recommending age-appropriate conventional activities. The program was designed so that the "classroom teacher can further enhance students' self-esteem and their ability to solve problems without violence or negative behavior. Topics for lessons include resisting pressure to join a gang, alternatives to gang activity . . . how to recognize and manage stress in school . . . and communication skills in situations where the student must be assertive with peers and adults" (Los Angeles County Probation 1988, p. 11).

Evolving Approaches

Increasingly schools are part of multilevel or multifaceted consortia of agencies and community organizations that develop prevention and early intervention activities. A case management or coordinated approach is often proposed. Children 11 to 14 years old are usually targeted for educational tutoring, social service, health counseling, and recreational activities. Life skills, drug and alcohol education, and sometimes training for youth leaders in resolving conflict among students also may be provided. In many school systems, particularly at the high school level, standards of student behavior have been set by school administration to prohibit a variety of deviant behaviors, including gang activities and use, sale, or possession of drugs or alcohol, on school premises. In some communities and schools, every student and parent is required to sign a contract to uphold school standards. Violations of these standards may lead to parent conferences, possible suspension, and referral for special services.

George McKenna, the former principal of George Washington Preparatory High School in Los Angeles and later superintendent of the Unified School District in Inglewood, California, innovated many student and parent involvement activities to deal with the gang problem. Gangs initially controlled parts of the school, but under McKenna's leadership, parents became more active in school affairs—they even helped monitor hallways and restrooms. McKenna not only urged parent participation in daily classroom activities but pushed for the location of probation, medical, and human services directly on school premises (President's Child Safety Partnership 1987, pp. 69, 107; McKenna 1990).

More and more schools aim at helping build self-esteem among high-risk minority youths in socially disadvantaged and high-gang-crime urban areas. Key objectives are to strengthen decision-making skills and teach techniques for resisting peer pressures to join gangs, sell drugs, and engage in violent activities (Reiner 1992, p. 185). The Los Angeles Unified School District has recently inaugurated a program that also focuses on the development of self-esteem in parents and teachers, rather than only on gang youths. The program differs from the usual DARE (Drug Awareness Resistance Education) or SANE (Substance Abuse Narcotics Education) school prevention programs that center attention on youths at risk of gang membership. This program aims rather at building self-awareness and competencies among parents and school staff "for the purpose of passing these attributes on to students, who may be potential gang members and drug abusers" (Los Angeles Unified School District 1989, p. 7). In addition, the School District has a special interest in enhancing the self-esteem of girls and women.

Chicago developed an innovative early-intervention program, albeit for a short period of time. A project provided not only a curriculum to counter gang influence and special security arrangements to deal with school disorder and maintain school discipline, but also a crisis outreach program in two middle schools in a very high-gang-crime, inner-city community. The school employed paraprofessional outreach workers, specialist teachers, and counselors and targeted forty gang youths in sixth, seventh, and eighth grade who were having serious academic and behavioral difficulties. Many of the youths were known to the police, and some had official delinquency records (up to 30% in one school). Youths were provided with remedial academic assistance and special counseling and social service referral, which was also extended to their parents. Crisis intervention at the school and in the immediate neighborhood was provided during actual or potential gang fighting situations. Gang youths generally were not suspended from school but were required to complete class work and subjected to special tasks, surveillance, and discipline within the school. The development of a community advisory group and parent meetings, as well as special recreational activities and visits by the targeted youths to jails and drug clinics, were part of the program (Spergel and Curry 1988).

One of the most significant school programs to address the youth gang problem has been in the East Los Angeles Skills Center, operated by the Los Angeles Unified School District. The program is highly decentralized and community based. The Skills Center serves around 1,200 students, the bulk of them aged 16 to 21 years; however, only 10 to 15 percent of the student body are gang members. The Center is a combination adult education day/evening center and nonresidential Job Corps program. It combines education and vocational training and pays special attention to gang youths, but at the same time mainstreams them. The Center has established close relationships with a host of local and countywide organizations, from local parent groups to criminal justice agencies that focus on the gang problem. The philosophy of the Skills Center is not to eliminate gang members from the program but to communicate with them, through extensive counseling, the serious negative consequences of gang membership. Of those who complete the combined high school education–work preparatory program, over 90 percent are said to be placed in jobs (Reiner 1992, pp. 189–190).

One of the most innovative, all-encompassing proposals for dealing with a range of problems of the inner city, including gangs, drugs, teen pregnancy, and parental indifference, is a plan proposed by academic leaders in Chicago. The strategy recommended is "housing elementary and high school students from gang-infected neighborhoods in urban boarding schools. . . . The idea is to take them out of their violent environments and give them round-the-clock exposure to academics, athletics, cultural programs, positive role models and discipline. . . . The project will provide counseling, medical care, internship, job training . . . and . . . other support services to students and their families . . ." (Haynes 1994, p. 1). How economically and politically realistic such a plan is, particularly how focused on the gang problem, and the extent to which it would involve local community leadership and participation, is unclear, however.

Evaluations of School Anti-gang Programs. Few evaluations of school anti-gang programs have been conducted, and the results thus far have been ambiguous, as much due probably to the limitations of the research—often in-house—as to the programs themselves. Most school programs are directed to "wannabes"—marginal or peripheral younger youths. We know little about the effects of interventions with youths who are older or committed to the gang lifestyle. The evaluations of Paramount's

"Alternative to Gangs Program," based on student questionnaire responses, indicate that the attitudes of elementary and middle school children about gangs can be changed positively after exposure to the special anti-gang curriculum. Hard data are not available on behavioral outcomes. According to one set of news accounts, the number of active gang members in Paramount dropped from 1,000 to 200 since 1981 (Schwartz 1988). Another set of media reports, however, refer to an increase in gang cases known to the police in Paramount City, from 286 in 1986 to 396 in 1987 (Donovan 1988).

A recent three-year Gang Risk Intervention Pilot Program (GRIPP) in Los Angeles County, based in the school system, was at best a mixed success. The program was funded for more than a million dollars per year in each of three years, ending June 30, 1993. Its purpose was to "reduce or reverse" the "rising tide of gang violence," with the focus on young at-risk students in selected public schools. The targeted youth were exposed to positive sports and cultural activities, and were encouraged to affiliate with local agencies. They and their families received counseling and other services. A variety of claims of success were made. The evaluator adds, however, that "very few GRIPP-identified/targeted students were among the hundreds and/or thousands of youths in their city's juvenile age group who had been arrested for 'gang-related' crimes" (Hughes 1994, p. 5).

Most of the school antidrug or anti-gang programs appear to be useful in changing attitudes or increasing knowledge about gang issues. It is unclear, however, that behavioral change occurs. Hard-core youths may not even participate in these special school anti-gang activities. Attitudinal effects also decline sharply over a period of years. Reiner observes that while the DARE programs have had a "positive influence on student's [gang] knowledge . . . gang violence in the city of Los Angeles has risen almost every year since DARE began in 1983" (Reiner 1992, pp. 185–186).

Macro Level Employment Perspective

The placement of gang youths and young adults in jobs is critical to a reduction of the gang problem. Older adolescents and young adults tend to remain in gangs long after they are ready to leave them because adequate job opportunities and linkages to employment are not available. A national gang conference several years ago warned that youths are becoming more active in gangs largely "due to competition for the lucrative drug trade" (McKinney 1988, p. 1). Intensive and long-term prevention and intervention programs, including increased training and job opportunities, were necessary to keep at-risk youths from joining gangs or even older hard-core gang youths from converting gangs to criminal organization in the drug trade (ibid., p. 5).

Research findings strongly suggest that, unless a major national employment strategy evolves, we will have a continuing, if not cataclysmic, erosion of adequate job opportunities for disadvantaged minority young adult males, particularly gang youths, violent offenders, and organized street criminals in the near future. Berlin and Sum stated that "Young male adults [ages 20–24 years] in 1984 had real median incomes that were one-third less than young adults of the same age group eleven years earlier. . . . Among black dropouts [20–24 years] in 1973, only 14.2 percent reported no earnings, but by 1984, a whopping 43 percent reported no earnings" (1988, pp. 7–

8). Berlin and Sum analyzed the transformation of employment structure and its consequences for young adult minority males:

> It was this "silent firing" of young workers—those who were never hired to replace returning workers—that is the big untold story underlying the decline of the manufacturing sector. Those were frequently the jobs in which one could earn enough to support a family, even if one did not have a strong education. . . .
>
> The post-1973 period was especially damaging for minority youths. In 1973, more than half (55%) of all 20 to 24 year old black males had earnings adequate to support a family of three above the poverty level. By 1984, less than one-quarter, 23 percent, had such earnings. The experience of Hispanic men was similar. Sixty-one percent were able to support a family of three above the poverty level in 1973 versus only 35 percent a decade later. (1988, pp. 12–14)

At the same time, demographic changes at work would favor employment of this age group on condition that potential employees possess required educational background and advanced work skills. Projections are that the young adult population, 18 to 24 years old, will have decreased by more than one-fourth between 1979 and 1995. A higher proportion of this small total will be composed of minority and economically disadvantaged groups. "Thus, those at the bottom of the distribution curve of skills and schooling will increasingly hold the key to the future of America's performance" (Berlin and Sum 1988, p. 24). It is possible to argue that the decline in prospects for employment in the legitimate sector of the economy for disadvantaged youths has been associated with the growth of gang and drug problems, especially the increased involvement of older gang youths in more elaborate gang structures. The failure of the legitimate economy to employ especially African-American youths has been associated with their increased participation in the illegal street economy, particularly, drug trafficking.

> For many young men the drug economy is an employment agency superimposed on the existing gang network. Young men who grew up in the gang, but now are without clear opportunities, easily become involved; they fit themselves into its structure, manning its drug houses and selling drugs on street corners. . . . With the money from these "jobs," they support themselves and help their families, at times buying fancy items to impress others. (Anderson 1990, p. 244)

Youth gangs or street gangs for youth or young adults at a certain age are substitutes for the employment market. Currently, Latino young adults in major violent gangs in Little Village on the southwest side of Chicago hang on street corners and claim they need jobs. One particular group of young adult gang members regularly appears on a street corner beginning at 1:00 or 2:00 A.M. each morning to take what they call the third shift; they are well armed and their main occupation is protecting turf from opposing gang members who are marauding on foot or by car through the area. The world of gang violence is no longer simply an experience accompanying teenagers growing up, but a substitute for the job world, in varying degree articulated with an underground drug-dealing economy.

Chin writes that ganging is "simply a way of *win saik*, meaning making a living" (Chin 1990b, p. 103). A wide range of criminal gain activities are available to Chinese gang youths in New York City, including protection, extortion, robbery, prostitution, and drug trafficking. The local "booming" and integrated legitimate and illegitimate economy provides Chinese gangs with distinct criminal opportunities: "There are many businesses to be extorted, as well as considerable numbers of gambling houses that need protection. Thus, protection and extortion are the most prevalent crimes in the Chinese communities" (ibid.).

Sullivan observed that white gang youths have the most favored legitimate (and also illegitimate) job opportunities available to them. When they reach older adolescence and are prepared to move out of street gangs, such passage therefore is more accessible to them than is the case for African-American and Puerto Rican youth gangs in Brooklyn. "Hamilton Park youths . . . had more employment both in the middle teens and during the work establishment period than the other two groups. . . . They also had much greater opportunity for theft from the workplace. . . . They also had far less involvement in street crime and consequently far less protracted involvement in the criminal justice system" (Sullivan 1989, p. 96).

By definition, if gang youth, particularly young adults, are engaged in full-time employment, they ordinarily have less time available to hang on the street and get into trouble. Furthermore, if the jobs are meaningful and youths are treated positively and with respect, new personal and social identities are encouraged. While minority and low-income youths cannot readily rely on a network of employed friends and relatives to gain access to a job that offers potential for a future (Hahn and Danziger 1987, p. 48), even minority youths with partial access to job opportunities—perhaps through public programs—may find such opportunity "life-turning" events that draw them gradually away from "street life and all of the more personally dysfunctional activities" that go along with it (Vigil 1988b, pp. 30–31). The employment picture for minority youths with limited education may not be entirely bleak. Many low-level service or status positions in restaurants, hotels, hospitals, and nursing homes, including janitorial, maintenance, and even building or office security, offer better than minimum wage levels. However, the jobs require appropriate attitudes and behaviors, especially of self-discipline and adequate job-finding skills, by gang youths and social support from others.

Employment and Training Strategies

In recent years, poorly educated and jobless youths, including many gang members and offenders, have not generally been targets of federal employment and training efforts. Furthermore, the diverse characteristics of a large socially disadvantaged youth group require different strategies to "improve their employability, productivity, and earnings" (Levitan and Gallo 1990, p. 229). Even youths who have mastered reading, writing, and arithmetic but have little labor market experience may "benefit from learning basic job-search skills" (ibid.). Disadvantaged youths can profit from programs providing a high school equivalency degree, job readiness, work orientation, and vocational training.

In recent years, the primary means for addressing unemployment of youths and adults has been the Job Training Partnership Act (JTPA). Implementation of this federal initiative, however, has resulted in inadequate targeting and insufficient inclusion of socially handicapped youths in many of the available skills and employment programs. The "introduction of cost and job-placement performance standards, severe restrictions on stipends and support services, reduced funding, and an expanded business role have made creaming [or selection of the most qualified and employable youths] common under JTPA" (Levitan and Gallo 1990, pp. 241–242). Hahn and Danziger reported that "Under the [earlier] Comprehensive Employment Training Act (CETA), young dropouts comprised well under 20 percent of most youth program participants and, today, under the Job Training Partnership Act (JTPA), the share of dropouts in youth programs has declined further. . . . The relatively small number of participants in 'second chance' programs is attributable to a 'creaming' process" (1987, p. 51). Only 5 percent of eligible youths are currently served.

JTPA programs direct their efforts to the young people who are "easiest to reach, teach, and place" (Grant 1988a, p. 4). The least educated and experienced youths are weeded out. Part of the failure of these programs was the need to generate "success" statistics to ensure survival of the contracting organization (Latimore 1985, p. x). More collaborative, mission-oriented, and good-faith efforts are needed on the part of the funding agencies in these training and employment programs.

Remedial education is extremely important to the career development of gang youths. However, only limited opportunity exists for remedial education connected with skill or job training, sometimes because of lack of funds. Many job-training programs reject candidates without basic educational achievement. The Job Corps program, on the other hand, has been remarkably successful in providing an "equal share of educational and occupational training" for socially disadvantaged youths (Levitan and Gallo 1989, p. 15). Levitan and Gallo remind us that "quality classroom training has a proven track record for cost effectively improving participants' long-term job prospects, as indicated by analyses of CETA (Comprehensive Employment Training Act) and the impact of the Job Corps" (1990, p. 243). However, the Job Corps at the present time does not accept youths on probation or known gang members with records of violence.

Job Corps is reported to do well with gang youths who manage to enter and graduate from the program. Most decide to "move away from the gang, and wannabes. Experience suggests that only about 10 percent of the gang affiliates remain actively involved with their gangs after joining the Job Corps program" (Conley 1991, p. 59). Reiner indicates that "maintaining one person in Job Corps for one year costs about $20,000. Roughly two-thirds of all graduates are placed in jobs, with an additional one in six going on to further education [but] . . . entering the program is not the same as graduating . . . there is a very substantial failure/drop-out rate" (1992, p. 189). Job Corps can be an ideal program for gang or potential gang youths. It is a "comprehensive program providing occupational skills training, basic (and remedial) education, counseling, health care, and job placement to youths. . . . Participation resulted in decreases in criminal activity, as indicated by rates of arrest during program participation and decreases in seriousness of crime in the post-program period" (Betsey, Hollister Jr., and Papageorgiu 1985, pp. 9–10).

Focus on Community-based, Comprehensive Programs. The social and economic complexity of job training and placement opportunities requires a comprehensive focus, not only on the youth but also on the family. Social intervention and social opportunity strategies must be better integrated. Levitan and Gallo have suggested, in community-based programs, that a case manager should be family focused and facilitate the use of available job program opportunities for both the youth and the family (1990, p. 253). Hahn and Danziger (1987) stated that genuine job programs for troubled young people require linkages between the various service delivery agencies and some form of case management. A one-to-one case-work approach for particularly troublesome youths may also be necessary. Also, classroom training, combined with work experience, helped dropouts more than pure work experience.

The U.S. Department of Labor recently initiated a Youth Opportunities Unlimited Challenge Program, which attempts to avoid the pitfalls of traditional, fragmented job-training programs through comprehensive community-based demonstration efforts. According to the federal RFPs (Requests for Proposals) statement, the local demonstration programs "must generate an integrated series of initiatives—including school-based and second chance services—which are designed to address the various needs of each and every young person in a target area" (United States Department of Labor 1990, p. 1). The challenge grants are to have the following features:

1. **Measurable and attainable community goals**, with positive community impacts, including "reduced school drop-out rate, decreased teenage pregnancy, increased young adult employment rates, reduced drug abuse, increased school attendance, increased enrollment in post-secondary education, decreased juvenile delinquency and gang activity, and reduced criminal activity in the neighborhood" (U.S. Department of Labor 1990, p. 1).
2. **Focus on a small neighborhood**. The idea is to select "a small enough area so that all youths in the community will be significantly and positively affected" (ibid.).
3. **Visible center of activity**. "The demonstration is to have a physical site . . . for example, a newly established alternative school, a community learning center, or a youth construction corps center. . . . Services must include assessment, individual and family counseling, mentorship, drug prevention, recreation activities, health services, education, housing . . . job training, and employment assistance" (ibid., p. 2).
4. **Emphases on integrated multiple services**, including concepts of core programs, such as alternative schools, community learning centers, youth construction corps, and regional work/study colleges; and complementary programs, such as school-to-apprenticeship programs, teen-parent centers, summer remediation and employment programs, middle colleges, and community youth centers.
5. **Strong state, local, and community roles**, including links with existing programs (such as JTPA); commitment to extra police protection; restructured junior and senior high schools; drug prevention, sports, and cultural programs; local advisory groups; and key organizational participation (ibid.).

Other Strategies. Levitan and Gallo observed that the discrimination faced by minority youths often may be overcome by "partially subsidizing employers for on-the-job training costs and by vigorous enforcement of equal opportunity laws" (1990, p. 229). A significant strategy for providing access to work opportunities for socially disadvantaged youths is subsidies for various types of businesses. A growing number of businesses have received local government subsidies—"tax abatements and credits, low interest loans, favorable zoning decisions, attractive bond issues, and other advantageous incentives—to build, reconstruct, or operate enterprises that are supposed to benefit local communities" (Grant 1988b, p. 98). Under terms of these contracts, builders and entrepreneurs agree to set aside a certain percentage of jobs for low-income youths. A significant number of gang youths may be included with appropriate support and supervisory arrangements.

Some policy analysts and legislators have suggested the development of a new-style Works Progress Administration (WPA). A large-scale federal pilot program should be developed to employ young people in community service jobs. Such a program would be inclusive of hard-core disadvantaged youths, including gang members, with appropriate social support and control arrangements:

> Supporters of a new style WPA say it would be a sure-fire way to address some of the nation's needs in the 1990s, while developing self-esteem and a work ethic in those who've been dealt a hard-luck hand in life. . . . Emphasis would be on the clean up and repair of public property and community projects. . . . In Philadelphia, residents can call [the Philadelphia Youth Service Corps, a public-private partnership, one of the country's growing number of community service programs] . . . hotline and suggest neighborhood projects. (Jouzaitis 1992)

The most recent large-scale youth development program is AmeriCorps, which has begun to include a small number of gang youth.

> Modeled after the Civilian Conservation Corps of the 1930s and the Peace Corps of the 1960s, the National Civilian Community Corps (NCCC) offers youth ages 18 to 24 opportunity to serve in return for educational or financial awards and provides human and logistical resources to sponsoring communities, counties, cities, states, and federal agencies, and non-profit community-based organizations.
> . . . NCCC concentrates its resources on four broad areas of public service . . . environment . . . education . . . human needs . . . public safety . . .
> Youth ages 18 to 24 are invited to join NCCC as a corps member for a minimum of 11 months. . . . If selected, NCCC members receive six weeks of basic training before being assigned to a specific work team.
> All members live on NCCC campuses, often downsized or closed military bases, and travel to specific locations where NCCC has been asked for assistance. NCCC provides housing, meals, medical coverage, child care, and uniforms, and members earn an additional $8,000 during eleven months of service for expenses. Members may also earn an educational award of $4,725 for college, graduate school, or training program, or $2,362 in cash. (OJJDP News Notes 1994)

Local Employment

In addition to large-scale, federal and state training and employment programs such as Neighborhood Youth Corps, Job Corps, JTPA, and AmeriCorps, which have thus far only peripherally addressed the employment needs and problems of gang youths, there have been locally generated job programs. A handful of these have even provided a mixture of social support and controls for the youths to allow them to adjust satisfactorily to the job. In the 1960s, the YMCA in Chicago established special job support for gang youths as part of its detached-worker youth program. Once the youth was on the job, the program continued to provide counseling and other support services. The outcome of this federally sponsored project, however, was not clear, and its success was quite modest (Caplan 1968). Another approach was a New York City Courts' employment program that formed a "self-sufficient but supervised company manned by ex-offenders and gang members. The company's construction contracts— most of them with the city of New York—exceeded $1 million" (Sampson III 1985, p. 23).

Ad hoc employment programs of youth agencies and local businesses have usually been short-term and modest, focusing on such projects as cleanup or painting out of graffiti (Pearl 1988). However, the owner of a gas pipeline construction business in Los Angeles claimed that he employed gang members successfully over long periods. His approach was based on a combination of outreach, personal support, and strong authoritative counseling. Base pay was good and gang youths graduated in due course to higher paying jobs (Baker 1988b). A labor contracting company in Chicago began matching low-skilled, unemployed, inner-city workers—including some gang or former gang members—with manufacturing jobs in the suburbs. The contractor provided on-site training, group transportation, and steady work for beginning pay of $5.00 an hour (Casuso 1989).

Most of these local programs have not been carefully evaluated. The Boys' Club of San Gabriel Valley, California, reported that more than 1,000 jobs were provided to gang members, delinquents, and others through the efforts of the El Monte, California, police community relations unit, in collaboration with over 100 local businesses and community organizations. Factory employers in El Monte were said to depend on the pool of gang youth referred by the Boys and Girls Club project (Spergel and Chance 1990). Nevertheless, a comparison of 100 participants in the program with a control group of similar youths found no difference in criminal outcomes. "It appeared that both groups simply matured out of criminal gang behavior. There is also a question about the kinds of young people referred for jobs . . . whether they are all (or even predominantly) gang members or simply youths at-risk" (Reiner 1992, pp. 191–192).

One locally generated effort specifically addressed to the gang problem was the planned Dane County Juvenile Court Prevention Program in Wisconsin. The project was funded with the aid of the recent U.S. Department of Health and Human Services Juvenile drug-gang initiative. Under the aegis of the juvenile court, and in cooperation with the Dane County Youth Conservation Corps, the project was expected to generate different levels of paid conservation jobs for gang youths aged 14 to 18 years. The program was supposed to target both core gang members and youths at risk and would involve not only skills training but also alcohol and drug abuse education. Youths were to be matched with job opportunities and mentors in the private sector—including small businesses and homeowners in the Madison County area— and organized into small groups. Career awareness and skills training also were to be part of the experience. Court programs related to the gang-oriented employment and training project planned to include a variety of housing and camping services, as well as justice system deterrents, including shelter care, home detention, adventure challenge, and youth restitution (County of Dane 1989).

Another promising local community youth employment project was the San Jose, California, Youth Conservation Corps. The program, connected to the juvenile court and funded by state and private sector grants, provided employment to justice-system-connected youths aged 18 to 22 who wanted a job. Many gang youths were involved in this program, which had a capacity of fifty job slots. The court's program participants were required to be periodically drug tested. Local boosters of the program complained that its quick success had some drawbacks, because good workers quickly advanced to project supervisory positions and left for jobs in the regular job market. Plans were under way to expand the number of job slots and to include not only youths who were on probation but also youths who graduated from local correctional-ranch programs. More involvement and cooperation by private businesses, however, were required. Systematic evaluation of this and other local work programs, nevertheless, was desirable.

Business and publicly sponsored programs of training and work for gang youths are essential for reduction of the gang problem. Such programs are at high risk of failure, however, Reiner advises caution in some cases: "When a program decides to depend on ex-gang members as part of its staff, experience dictates that this must be treated as a job training program in its own right with all the extra support, preparation and strict supervision that such programs entail" (Reiner 1992, p. 194). The widespread assumption is that most gang youths would like to be employed when they reach a certain age (Reddick 1987). In fact, even many of the gang youths who are currently involved in drug dealing would "prefer decent paying jobs to the gang life, but they lack the skills and the attitudes to get and hold them" (*Insight* 1988, p. 17). Again, there is evidence that gang youths who obtain jobs are less likely to remain in the gang (Klein 1971; Hagedorn 1988). Even part-time jobs are viewed as helpful for many gang youths; some of whom may still be in school (Williams and Kornblum 1985).

Conclusion

The provision of social opportunities is a critical component of policy and program to prevent and reduce the youth gang problem. Social opportunities are defined as specialized or remedial education and training and job readiness, development, and placement, directed to the interests and needs of gang youths. A central approach is to restructure schools, particularly in terms of a well-articulated system of school-to-work transition. Several program models show promise in communities with serious gang problems. They are aimed at improving youths' attachment to schools, increasing the responsiveness of schools to gang youths, and improving the relationship of schools to their communities. In these evolving models, bonds between home and school, at both the elementary and high school level, have to be dealt with interactively.

Increasingly schools need to become part of multilevel or multifaceted consortia of agencies and community organizations that develop prevention and intervention activities. Varied, sufficient, and adequately coordinated anti-gang school programs have to be developed that stress collaboration with criminal justice and social service agencies. Many of these efforts thus far have been directed to prevention of elementary school children from joining gangs. Few evaluations have been conducted. Results suggest that attitudes of children can be modified but not necessarily that gang behaviors of youths can be readily changed, particularly if youths are already committed to antisocial gang activities.

Job placement of gang and gang-prone youths, especially adolescents, is critical to the control and reduction of the gang problem. Research findings strongly suggest that, unless a major national employment strategy evolves, we will have a continuing, if not cataclysmic, erosion of job opportunities for gang youths. It is possible to argue that the decline in prospects for employment in the legitimate sector of the economy for disadvantaged youths has been coordinate with the growth of the gang problem. By definition, if gang members, particularly gang adults, are engaged in full-time employment, they have less time available to hang on the streets and get into trouble.

The social and economic challenges of job training and placement require a complex focus, not only on the youth but also on the family, and a series of service-delivery organizations. Social opportunities, social intervention, and community mobilization strategies must be better integrated. Some policy analysts and legislators have suggested the development of a new-style Works Progress Administration or National Youth Service, e.g., AmeriCorps, that would also include gang members, with appropriate social support and social control arrangements for them. There is ample evidence that gang youths would like to become employed, and in fact most find employment in due course. The lack of decent jobs and gang member access to them, and the lack of appropriate gang member academic and vocational skills and social attitudes, are problems that have to be resolved at both national and local levels for a reduction of the gang problem.

17

Local Community Mobilization and Evolving National Policy

If the major causes of the gang problem are social disorganization and poverty or their various patterns of interrelationship, then logically we should address these causes in relevant ways. In the last chapter the focus was on the development of social and economic opportunities. This chapter deals with issues to counter social disorganization. The focus is on policies that serve to cohere or organize community participation and coordinate agency programs. The chapter examines efforts that operate across local citizen or community groups and governmental and nongovernmental agencies at local, state, and federal levels. Organizations often address the gang problem in separate, particularistic, and sometimes contradictory ways. Mobilized and coordinated approaches occur when organizations and significant units within them develop similar perceptions of the problem and establish related or interdependent policies, programs, and practices.

The federal government is or will be critically important in this process, not only in the provision of resources but in requiring that various forms of integrated policy and program take place at both national and local levels. This concluding chapter addresses experiences at local community and state levels for mobilization of citizen and organizational efforts, but it recommends more substantial federal policy to support such local mobilization. Federal agencies, such as Justice, Health and Human Services, Labor, Education, and Housing and Urban Development, must do a better job coordinating their programs within and across departments. Agreement also needs to occur within local organizations among board, staff, and volunteers on the nature and definition of a gang problem and what needs to be done about it. Local interagency task forces, including criminal justice, local community agencies, citizen groups, schools, and businesses, as well as former gang members and selected influential gang members—all concerned with reducing violence—need to better interrelate their efforts in planning, implementing, and coordinating gang prevention, intervention, and suppression strategies and tactics.

Local Citizen and Organization Mobilization

In recent decades a variety of ad hoc neighborhood programs have arisen to deal with gang problems. These efforts are in the American tradition of grass-roots organiza-

281

tion and local advocacy to deal with a range of human problems (Tocqueville 1954). They include spontaneous citizen attempts to "take back the streets" from gangs and/ or to meet youths' social needs so they will not become gang members. The grass-roots programs are as yet largely independent of governmental initiative and funding support, at state or federal levels. These efforts may be sponsored by, or closely associated with, local community-based agencies, private foundations, churches, or the mayor's office. They are often led by concerned and charismatic individuals. They often serve the interests of particular local community groups or aspiring political leaders. After a while many of these grass-roots anti-gang activities veer off course and come to focus on other, usually more manageable, social or community concerns.

A good deal of recent theory and research exists about citizen involvement in general antideliquency programs, particularly where there has been outside stimulus and resource input. However, there has been little specific interest or focus on the relationship between the reduction or control of gang crime and citizen involvement. The key purpose of these programs is to "implant" more effective systems of local crime control. This "implant hypothesis" has been tested in Neighborhood Watch and other community crime programs, and the results are not entirely positive. Their achievement has been largely a reduction of fear of crime rather than of crime itself. The evidence also indicates that in most high-crime, usually low-income, and some-times mixed racial and ethnic neighborhoods, local citizens do not substantially participate in community crime control activities. Furthermore, when citizen mobilization is somewhat successful or when awareness and participation in dealing with the crime problem increases, fear of crime may rise rather than decrease. The effects on the rates of crime either are unclear or figures are not available (Rosenbaum 1987). The problems of mobilizing citizen participation specifically against gangs are considerably greater when serious violence and crime, such as drug trafficking, are the sources of concern. Intimidation and attacks against local citizens by gang members may occur.

Nevertheless, there are examples of local groups of mothers, fathers, neighbors, and even gang or former gang members mobilizing, with or without the aid of established agencies, to control or reduce gang problems. These groups tend to develop when family members, the gang members themselves, or their property are attacked or threatened. In large cities such as New York, Chicago, Philadelphia, and Los Angeles, and in many smaller cities and suburban communities, local groups have patrolled streets and supervised social events such as house parties, street festivals, and dances to prevent gang disorders (*Insight* 1988, p. 9).

Local groups have sometimes taken credit for driving gangsters out of the neighborhood. These activities may have a vigilante character, and at the extreme may even involve the destruction of gang member property and the "defensive" shooting of gang members (*Insight* 1988, p. 11). Local citizen anti-gang activities may include intrusion into school buildings, the surveillance and intimidation of teachers and students suspected of using or selling marijuana, and the destruction of businesses or houses suspected of selling weapons to gang members. Organizations, such as the Guardian Angels or the Black Muslims, may not "shrink from interrupting drug deals, throwing dealers and buyers up against the wall, and searching them or surrounding and detaining them while the police are called" (ibid., p. 12).

Fagan has documented other, less militant, forms of local citizen involvement against gangs:

> Residents in one neighborhood formed an emergency information network that served as an early warning system when gang conflicts were about to erupt in violence. Relaying news that one group was about to set on another, the residents intervened through mediation and involvement of law enforcement to diffuse conflict situations. . . . In another neighborhood, residents arranged truces and sponsored events where gang members turned in their weapons and pledged nonviolence for specific periods during which turf conflicts and other disputes could be resolved through negotiation and conciliation. The authority and neutrality of the neighborhood organization made possible the trust and cooperation of gangs who were bitter enemies. (Fagan 1987, pp. 59–60).

Mothers' or parent's groups have on occasion been active in the local battles against gangs. During 1973 and 1974, the mothers of gang members in Philadelphia were reported to have been effective in intervening—or, literally, interposing their bodies—between groups of youths about to attack and shoot each other. Mrs. Frances Sandoval organized a group in Chicago, Mothers Against Gangs (MAG), patterned after Mothers Against Drunk Driving, which now has chapters in several neighborhoods of Chicago and other Illinois cities. Mrs. Sandoval, a mother whose son was killed in a gang fight, mobilized citizens and other mothers in the largely Mexican-American Pilsen area of Chicago to volunteer and provide group support to those mothers whose children had been victimized by gangs. Visits to court to testify against gang members were encouraged. Lectures to students and discussions with teachers were conducted at local schools. Advocacy efforts included campaigning for gun restriction laws, improving safety at school, and pressuring police and special anti-gang youth programs to be more active. Parents Against Gangs, an offshoot of MAG, was also a chapter of Parents Against Murdered Children which was established in Chicago. Another such group is Mothers Against Gangs in Communities (MAGIC) in Los Angeles. It "hopes to overcome community fear of gangs and even reach the parents of gang members to turn in their own children [to the police] to save lives" (Crust 1988, p. A3).

A very recent effort in Chicago is Neighbors Against Gang Violence. This is a program involving churches, youth agencies, job agencies, the alderman's office, block clubs, and parents concerned with hard-core gang youth 17 to 25 years of age. The group also supports the efforts of a team of police, probation officers, and outreach youth workers to control violence through an interactive strategy of suppression, opportunities provision, social support, and community mobilization. The author of this book has been instrumental in the development of this model.

East Los Angeles Experiences

Some of the grass-roots organizations have served a watch-dog function to make sure that existing public and voluntary agencies are genuinely committed to and achieve objectives related to gang control and violence reduction.

> UNO [United Neighborhood Organization in Los Angeles] leaders graded each agency involved in the project, giving good evaluations to representatives of the Sheriff's

Department, Community Youth Gang Services, and Soledad Enrichment Action, a church-based counseling and education program. . . . The County Probation Department came in for criticism for not even knowing where several "gang hot-spots" are, not keeping a high visibility in "strategic areas" and not making sure that kids who are a danger to the community are taken off the streets. (*Los Angeles County Sheriff's Department* 1991)

The East Los Angeles Concerned Parents Group, formed in the early 1970s, was probably the longest running grass-roots organization and possibly the most successful in confronting the youth gang problem. The organization started as a support group for the parents of young men who had been killed in gang-related violence. Brother Modesto Leon, a monk of the Claretian Order, encouraged members to become proactive and communicate with each other across gang turfs to deal with impending gang fights and to better control their own children. The Concerned Parents Group learned to trust the authorities, to call the police when necessary, to work closely with probation officers, and, if necessary, to have their own children placed in jail to protect them. These parents were involved in mediation meetings to bring about peace between warring gangs and organized mutual support activities to prevent and control drug trafficking activities by their own children and those of their neighbors. The group inaugurated a program of visitation to and discussion groups with youths in correctional institutions, as well as with their parents.

For a period of more than ten years, between the middle 1970s and the late 1980s, these efforts, along with those of other local organizations and community groups, appeared to contribute to a significant reduction in gang homicides in the East Los Angeles community (Spergel and Chance 1990). In recent years, however, the area has reverted to extremely serious gang violence, setting all-time gang homicide records. The return to gang violence may have resulted from several factors, including the presence of a new generation of immigrants, a fragmentation of local relationships between and among the new population groups, the lack of coordinated agency programs, and an increase in local poverty problems.

Limits of Local Organizations

Fagan has observed that it is difficult to "motivate families to participate in the lengthy developmental process of forming and sustaining an effective organization against gangs and crime," especially when parents are faced with "more immediate, concrete issues: housing, clothing, and child care" (1987, p. 60). Many of these action groups, if they survive, tend to move on to other activities that are less threatening, more feasible, and more generally acceptable to various elements in the broader community, such as recreation and tutorials for younger children, especially those who are less delinquent.

Sometimes local grass-roots efforts have been closely integrated with those of criminal justice agencies, and have even developed under their aegis. The Los Angeles Reclamation Project (CRP), sponsored by the Los Angeles County Probation Department and funded by the U.S. Justice Department, attempted to coordinate service delivery and develop cooperative arrangements across law enforcement, community agencies, business groups, and neighborhood organizations in the prevention and control of the gang problem in the South Bureau police district of the city. After approximately eighteen months, the project's impact on crime rates was at best mixed. Gang-related crime rose in the area, while it dropped in other nearby areas. Reiner concludes: "Coordination is easy on paper but hard in practice. Coordinating programs is much simpler if they are all part of the same organization. Rivalries, personalities, style, priorities, funding requirements, and a host of other problems can make it extremely difficult for community based organizations to work together" (1992, p. 223).

It is extremely difficult for a local neighborhood group or citizen's organization, by itself or even with the help of outside agencies, to sustain its efforts and deal with an established or chronic gang problem, in part because the youth gang is usually better organized and able to meet and sustain youth member needs and interests through gang solidarity and drug trafficking. In the process it readily counters weak community pressures. Adequate, long-term citizen, agency, and even local government efforts to fight gang activities are extremely difficult to develop and maintain. Agreement by gangs with neighbors and public officials to control gang activity are difficult to keep. For example, several years ago, two neighborhood parks were built with federal grants in Pomona, California, to provide young people with a variety of recreational alternatives. They evolved into:

. . . graffiti-covered havens for gang violence and drug dealing that should be demolished. . . . The two parks dedicated in 1972 . . . are named for the city's two oldest Latino gangs. . . . For two decades, the two gangs have exchanged drive-by shootings. . . . Bryant served his first term on the city council between 1964 and 1973, said he was partly responsible for the park's creation. . . . Bryant and a council colleague [spoke] with members of the two gangs. . . . They said they wanted a park . . . the gangs promised in return they'd knock off the garbage and start acting like people . . . they never kept their end of the bargain. (J. Miller 1988, p. 1)

Community Youth Organizations

More inclusive local youth organizations, including youth gangs themselves, and other agencies have sometimes expressed an interest in and attempted to control or reduce the level of gang violence and certain types of gang crime in neighborhoods. They have tried to prevent fights and vandalism, and especially to prevent disorders at public events such as festivals, dances, and block parties. In times of urban crisis, riots, or rebellions, youth patrol efforts may be organized by local youth agencies, churches, businesspeople, or adult citizen groups to prevent or control the spread of these disturbances. Youth organizations, including gang members, have even had the support—and sponsorship—of law enforcement representatives. One such federation of youth organizations is the Inner City Roundtable of Youth (ICRY) in New York City, which has been in existence for over fifteen years. It sought to bring "all the gangs in the city of New York together under one umbrella—together in terms of talking about training for the future" (Galea 1982, p. 228). ICRY evolved into a nonprofit organization and became a means of obtaining funding from various sources for small business development opportunities as well. Prominent public officials and business leaders sat on its board, and apparently both supervised and facilitated the work of the organization (ibid.).

The Federacion de Barrios Unidos, a federation of gangs or barrios, was formed in East Los Angeles in 1971. Its purpose was to mediate gang disputes, control gang violence, and combat drug sales and use. It used former gang influentials as the basis for organizing community improvement associations, which then involved gang members in such activities as repairing and painting old buildings, sponsoring a boxing program, and opening up "opportunities to do something in the community which met the basic psychology and needs of the gang barrio member (care, acceptance, love, achievement, recognition, responsibility, self-esteem, and self-actualization)" (Pineda 1974, p. 42). Reportedly, the federation was successful in its mediation efforts between warring gangs, and the California Youth Authority's Gang Violence Reduction Project modeled itself after it.

As discussed earlier in Chapter 15, a variety of projects in the late 1960s and early 1970s attempted to use the gang structure as a basis both for gang violence reduction and gang member rehabilitation, in addition to community improvement and manpower development. Few if any of these projects were successful in achieving long-term objectives. Many provoked community controversy and particularly police opposition (Poston 1971; Spergel 1972; Perkins 1987). Youth patrols—sometimes involving gang members under police supervision—also received a mixed review during the urban riots of the 1960s. They were often not particularly well organized, sustaining, or effective, although they were not necessarily a base for criminal activity (Knopf 1969). They may have served as opportunistic, ad hoc, and short-term devices to divert and provide jobs to troublesome youths.

More recent "United in Peace" efforts or gang summits have evolved in Los Angeles, Chicago, St. Paul, Kansas City, Pittsburgh, and elsewhere to control and reduce the level of violence problem among certain gangs, particularly in the African-American community. Gang members, particularly older former members, in coalition with representatives of churches, gang crisis intervention agencies, local community organizations, selected civil rights leaders, celebrities, politicians, and public officials have arranged peace meetings, mediated intergang conflicts, and attempted in various ways to reduce gang violence.

These efforts may be successful for short periods, but gangs are diffuse and not well-organized entities. Not all gangs are covered by truce arrangements, and there are "renegades" even among the gangs covered. Truce or peace arrangements can be used also as a means by gang or ex-gang leaders or social activists for claiming influence, who now want to be power brokers and community decision-makers. A variety of social and economic schemes to benefit the local community are sometimes put forward, including job training, small business development, improved health care, and improved school curriculum. Large demonstrations are sometimes conducted. However, such peacemaking and community development efforts are usually based on the presumed legitimacy of gang structure and often arouse the ire of police and established political, agency and community leaders. They may thus encourage further community fragmentation.

Gang war truce efforts can be maximally useful if they involve a broad range of citizenry and representatives of legitimate organizations as well as gang leaders and gang members in *collective* efforts to deal with problems such as gang violence, jobs, education, and health. They are useful if individual gang members are also thereby assisted to obtain remedial education and jobs and in due course move away from criminal activity and the general influence of gang structure in their daily lives. These community movement and social action efforts should not, therefore, become a basis for sustaining gang structure or attachments to the gang over the long term. As a rule, the gang—committed to violent and criminal activity—cannot be redirected through its own structure to legitimate and effective organizational activity, despite claims to the contrary. A key problem also is lack of skills and attitudes appropriate to the conduct of a legitimate enterprise. The gang's rationale for survival and development over time would cease thereby to exist. The gang system itself, because it is largely dependent on threat, intimidation, and violence, would be destroyed.

Key operational problems remain in efforts to incorporate gangs, gang leaders, and gang members in community mobilization to control or reduce the gang problem. Despite periodic concern with the heightened level of gang violence by the community, law enforcement, and gang members, the survival and developmental needs of the gang and the police cannot be readily bridged over the long term. The gang as an interstitial institution is concerned primarily with protection and development of its illegitimate interests in one form or another in today's rapidly changing society. Law enforcement is concerned primarily with community protection and organizational maintenance through high rates of arrest and prosecution. Periodically the two find common ground in their mutual interest in reducing levels of violent crime and flagrant drug dealing, among other forms of crime.

State-Level Mobilization

State (and incresingly federal) legislation and policy constitute a major framework for dealing with youth gang problems. Legislatures or city councils in various states and cities, for example, California, Indiana, Illinois, Florida, Georgia, Louisiana, Washington, Minnesota, and Ohio; Los Angeles, Miami, Chicago, and Joliet, have completed reports and passed laws or ordinances to address public concerns over increases in gang membership, gang-related violence and graffiti, narcotics trafficking near or in schools, the use of beepers by students, and the need to share information on gang member activity across agencies and jurisdictions.

As of 1991, 14 of 50 states had enacted new statutes specifically directed at criminal street-gang activity. There have been two different approaches to gang legislation: One is to adopt a gang statute such as California's Street Terrorism Enforcement and Prevention Act, based on the RICO model; the other is to amend existing criminal codes to add gang offenses. Special legislation attempts to link three definitions, "criminal street gang," "pattern of criminal gang activity," and "participation in a criminal street gang (Institute for Law and Justice 1994). Sentence enhancement has been characteristic of both approaches.

Thus far, however, policy has been mainly reactive, fragmentary, and focused on suppression. Two states, California and Illinois, appear to have been most active in the development of comprehensive legislation. California, the state with the most severe and diverse gang problems, has probably produced more gang legislation than all the other states in the country combined. Its approach may be characterized as proactive and community oriented, with, however, primary interest in suppression and only secondary interest in educational and social service strategies. The Illinois approach has been more fragmented and at times unimplemented: its original intention to pursue social support and social development has been replaced by mainly suppression policies.

California

Public concern and governmental action with respect to the gang problem is far more advanced and also more alarmist in California, particularly in Los Angeles County, than elsewhere. Speaker Willie Brown of the California House of Representatives noted in the late 1980s that "gangs are increasingly violent despite more than 80 bills passed by the legislature in recent years directed at them" (Sample 1988, p. A3). The Los Angeles County Supervisor, Kenneth Hahn, considered requesting the assistance of the National Guard to patrol neighborhoods affected by gang violence, and California Governor George Deukmajian offered at one point to authorize a $10,000 reward to encourage victims and witnesses of gang violence to come forward to press charges and testify against gang offenders. He also successfully promoted the passage of legislative bills to increase the severity of sentences for such offenders.

The California approach was initiated and continues to be driven by the interests of prosecution and law enforcement agencies seeking tough remedies to the gang problem. The California legislature acted in 1981 to improve the ability of district attorneys to address gang activity (California Penal Code, chap. 35, sec. 13826, et. seq.). Between 1982 and 1986 the law was amended to classify law enforcement, probation departments, school jurisdictions, and community organizations as eligible for funding, with a clear mandate to implement a suppression approach. A statewide Gang Violence Suppression Program was established and administered by the California Office of Criminal Justice Planning:

> The purpose of this program is to reduce the level of gang violence in the community and to divert potentially dangerous gang activity into more positive and constructive behavior. The program also strives to keep open lines of communication between law enforcement agencies, prosecutors' offices, community-based organizations, probation departments, schools, the community, and family members of gang or potential gang members. This is accomplished by swiftly identifying, prosecuting, and removing perpetrators from the community and by preventing incidents of gang violence. This approach works to incapacitate gang members already involved in violence and deter other young people who may be under "criminal influence". (California Office of Criminal Justice Planning 1987, p. 2)

California legislation requires that criminal justice agencies, schools, and community organizations work together in planning and coordination, especially through local task forces, under the supervision or guidance of the prosecutor's office. The roles of the Department of Corrections and California Youth Authority, as well as the role of judges and defense attorneys, are absent from the legislation and are touched on only briefly in the guidelines of the California Office of Criminal Justice Planning. The amended California legislation of 1985 and 1986 and other recent bills suggest the possibility of a broader and even more comprehensive approach providing a significant role for social intervention and especially prevention through school programs, beginning at an early age. For example, the legislature finds, among other things, that:

> There is an increasing percentage of school-age pupils involved in gang activity. . . . There is no statewide funded educational program developed to implement programs designed to prevent youths from becoming involved in gang activities. . . . There is evidence that the parents of gang members lack appropriate parenting skills. . . . There is evidence that gang members have no contact with positive role models. . . . There is evidence that most gang members lack basic educational skills. (California Penal Code 1988, 13826.1, chap. 3.5)

Thus the California legislation, its implementing structure, and its funding arrangements indicate some recognition, but less than full understanding, of the need for and commitment to a policy that emphasizes social intervention and social opportunities, and long-term prevention. It is possible that the California model, unless balanced substantially with strategies in addition to suppression, may contribute unintentionally to a costly process of criminalizing young offenders and ultimately of increasing gang activity—exactly the opposite of what the legislation fundamentally intends.

Illinois

Illinois' legislative approach to dealing with the gang problem appeared, at least initially, to be somewhat more benign. The early approach was directed to the provision of social opportunities and social intervention as well as suppression. Unfortunately, the legislation did not provide funding or an implementing structure for the programs envisioned. Legislation passed in 1985 called for the Department of Commerce and Community Affairs to make "grants to community groups in order to improve the quality of life in low- and moderate-income neighborhoods" (Illinois Revised Statute, chap. 127, para. 3301 et. seq.). Qualified recipients of funds were required to provide alternatives to participation in juvenile gangs in one of the following ways: creating permanent jobs; stimulating neighborhood business activity; providing job training services; implementing youth recreation and athletic activities; and strengthening community-based organizations whose objectives were similar to those listed above.

Additional legislation directed the Department of Children and Family Services to "conduct meetings in each service region between local youth service, police, probation and parole workers to develop interagency plans to combat gang crime . . . [and] . . . develop a model policy for local interagency cooperation in dealing with gangs" (Illinois Revised Statute, chap. 23, para. 5034.2). These actions were not taken. In 1986 the legislature broadened its efforts to combat gangs by adding gang-related responsibilities to two other state agencies. The State Board of Education was called on to ". . . enter into contracts for the establishment of three social group work demonstration projects in school districts" (Illinois Revised Statute, chap. 122, para. 2–3.72). The board was required to consider the need for reductions in gang crime activity in selecting sites for the projects. Companion legislation called on the Department of State Police to create an Office of Coordination of Gang Prevention to "consult with units of local government and school districts to assist them in control activities and to administer a system of grants to units of local government and school districts which, upon application, have demonstrated a workable plan to reduce gang activity in their area. . . ." The department was also required to "establish mobile units of trained personnel to respond to gang activities" (Illinois Revised Statute, chap. 127, para. 55 a-3, 9–4, p. 1926).

Funds for these above programs were not provided. However, a small gang unit was established within the Department of State Police, and the State Board of Education did make a small grant to the Chicago school system for a study of the city's gang problem. This latter effort predated the actual legislation by more than a year (Spergel 1985). A state law was also created to deal at least in part with the gang problem in Chicago: the automatic transfer of a minor defendant charged with unlawful use of a handgun on school grounds from juvenile court to adult court. The law established "safe school zones in and around school property and deals severely with the bringing of firearms, the selling of . . . hard drugs in and around schools [and] with adults trying to recruit juveniles into . . . gangs" (*People* [Illinois] *v. M.A.* [A Minor Appellee] 1988, p. 143). Since the mid-1980s, the Illinois legislature, furthermore, has "whittled at the jurisdiction of juvenile courts." The Illinois Supreme Court recently upheld a law approved by the legislature which requires "judges to allow a 15- or 16-year old suspect to be brought to trial as an adult if prosecutors show a prior finding of delinquency in Juvenile Court and providing that the new charges are gang-related" (Grady 1991, pp. 1, 20).

Need for National Policy

Only the beginnings of a national and comprehensive approach to dealing with the gang problem may be discerned. On the basis of his observations of gang policies and programs over several decades, Walter Miller claimed that, compared with the concerns and efforts of the federal government in the early 1960s, especially the conduct of the President's Committee on Juvenile Delinquency and Youth Crime, current developments in policy and program (at least until the late 1980s) represented a major step backward. "The sophistication of national efforts to cope with gang programs has not kept pace with the increasing seriousness of the problem . . ." (W. Miller 1990, p. 269).

Miller viewed the failure of the United States to deal effectively with the youth gang problem as resulting from two sources: the "lack of a comprehensive national gang strategy" (1990, p. 270); and the lack of a central national agency to gather or distribute information "on the location, character, and effects of gang control efforts. No one knows, for example, how many gangs and gang members there are in the United States, the location and seriousness of gang problems, how much crime, and what kinds of crime gang members are responsible, or the social characteristics of gang members" (ibid.).

At present what we have is a variety of local perceptions of the problem. A few national, law enforcement-oriented studies have been completed. Local projections of the scope of the gang problem are sometimes made. The Los Angeles County Sheriff's Department, for example, not only regularly reports on its local or regional gang problems but on the sightings of its local gang members outside the region. "Last year a map kept by the Sheriff's Department . . . contained more than 70 dots— including ones marking York, Pennsylvania, Hobbs, New Mexico, and Ashton, Idaho, population 1,200, where a drive-by shooting was linked to a gang member who had moved from Long Beach" (Olen and Lieberman 1991). The Gang Crime Unit of the Chicago Police Department was regularly contacted by police in other cities who believed that gangs with the same name as gangs from Chicago were operating in their cities.

A federal gang-tracking bill was pending in Congress in 1991 that would address the problem of lack of knowledge nationally about the gang problem. The recommended tracking system would have referenced an estimated "450,000 gang members under such categories as names, aliases, modes of operation, favored weapons and businesses used as fronts" (ibid.). Such a bill, unless targeted mainly to adult convicted gang offenders, would probably exaggerate, if not aggravate, the problem.

Basis of Current Policy Planning

Single causal assumptions or theories and particularistic strategies, mainly suppression but also social intervention, are still the basis of national policies. Protection of community and punishment of offenders remain the key components of the continuing "war model" in dealing with the gang problem (Burrell 1990, p. 741). Miller noted two decades ago that ideology was the "hidden agenda of criminal justice" and that its influence on the policies and procedures of the agencies that conduct the system or nonsystem were largely unrecognized (W. Miller 1973, p. 142). The media have also been a key institutional force generating single dimensional assumptions and views that contribute to failed policies. Joan Moore has observed that "public concern about gangs and drugs is usually so intense and moralistic that police and media actually define the phenomena, quite apart from reality" (Moore 1990, p. 60). The media's responsibility for distorting the gang problem may be examined in such films as "New York City," "Colors," "The Warriors," and "Boyz in the Hood," which have provided generally simplistic and exaggerated views of the nature and emphasized or glorified the significance of violent gang life. The media have directly fed stereotypes that sustain "moral panics," justifying a suppression strategy. Hagedorn noted that instead of facts guiding policy, "policy reacts to the images and definitions of gangs by the media and law enforcement" (Hagedorn 1988, p. 157).

The basic question for planning should not be "how to most expeditiously remove" gang members from the community but ultimately "how to integrate them into the larger social structure so that their talents will be employed in socially constructive ways" (Shannon et al. 1988, p. 22). A comprehensive policy at national or local levels requires a preventive as well as a suppressive approach. Prevention, furthermore, must be directed to changes in institutional arrangements for the socialization of gang youths. Effective policy requires focus not only on particular youths but also on the specific social environmental conditions that foster gang development. The concept of social control in particular must be viewed in broader terms, including not only coercive controls, which use or imply force (legal or legitimate) but controls that consist also of the development of individual, group, and neighborhood self-regulation (Mayer 1983, p. 24). These changes must be developed interactively within the individual and across collective institutional levels.

While the youth or street-gang problem is related in complex ways to more basic social policy issues that must be effectively addressed, it is a mistake to assume that as "larger" issues such as gun control, prohibition of assault rifles, or even hand-guns, restrictive immigration policy, expanded minority economic development, restoration and development of urban infrastructure, improvement in the quality of education for minority youths, provision of jobs and training for adolescent youths and young adults, and improvement in coordination of units of the criminal justice system are addressed, the gang problem will automatically be reduced. The gang problem varies at different times and places and must be dealt with on its own terms as well as in relation to these other fundamental urban and national problems. It must be addressed directly as well as indirectly.

It is important, therefore, that the approach to the gang problem be neither too broad nor too narrow. Criminal justice policymakers and administrators should not marginalize their efforts and isolate their program interests from related national social problem concerns. In turn, legislators, chief executives, and social policy generalists must attend to significant subsets of problems such as youth gangs on the assumption that a variety of component problems in fact comprise the larger youth, national economic, or developmental problem or issue. General social policy, for example in the national adult and youth manpower retraining area, should be developed in terms relevant to the special employment needs of gang youths. This may require policies, programs, and procedures that do not exclude hard-core gang members from a range of training opportunities, including youth with prior records of gang-oriented violence. Obviously, special safeguards or controls and social support services are also required for this subset of socially disadvantaged or socially disabled youth.

Prevention

The notion of prevention must be specified across several domains: the individual, the family, the school, the peer group, a variety of organizations, and the community. These risk factors must be addressed in institutional as well as in personal terms developmentally, both when individual behavior is being formed, usually in the early teen years, and after it has become crystallized, usually in the late teen years or young adulthood. Furthermore, gang behavior must be addressed in some interrelated fashion across age groups as well as collaboratively across institutions. Ianni has stressed the positive value of a comprehensive approach to delinquent group and gang problems, including a variety of interactive strategies by agencies dealing with both at-risk and hard-core youths:

> When programs did work, they were oriented toward an interactive social development approach looking to multiple causes, rather than focusing on some single factor thought to be causal in and of itself and the program used a variety of interrelated means of resocializing the adolescent. Some of the techniques were developmental such as psychological and life-skills counseling and encouraging new peer networks

among program participants as well as between participants and more conventional institutional settings. Other techniques, such as providing job training and education, were empowering, so that participants could function more successfully in those environments and feel some sense of competence. But others were more controlling, reducing the teenager's interaction with deviant peers and adults, setting firm and consistent standards for performances in the program, and demanding accountability rather than simply dispensing treatment and support without an evaluation of their individual and collective effectiveness. And some techniques were clearly based on negative reinforcement, lowering the opportunities for young people to get involved in deviance and, at the same time increasing the costs to individual adolescents and their caretakers when they did. (Ianni 1989, pp. 220–221).

Federal Agency Policy Coordination

A variety of federal agency and local community approaches are evolving to deal with the gang problem, often directed or related to street drug trafficking. These approaches are founded as yet on notions mainly of suppression, some social intervention and coordination across mainly law enforcement agencies, and local resident participation. Limited federal-local partnerships are the framework for the implementation of these initiatives. However, little cross-federal or even state agency policy related to a broad-scale, integrated focus on the gang problem has yet developed.

U.S. Justice Department. The Bureau of Justice Assistance, Office of Justice Programs, U.S. Justice Department developed an approach, "weed and seed," intended to be a comprehensive and coordinated multiagency approach focused on law enforcement as well as community revitalization (Bureau of Justice Assistance 1991, p. 3). The emphasis was first on "intensive law enforcement efforts to remove and incapacitate violent criminal and drug traffickers from targeted neighborhoods and housing developments," and second on "seeding" or restoring the community by providing "economic and social opportunities developed in cooperation with other federal, state, and local agencies" (ibid.). The local U.S. Attorney in the particular region had a central role in the weed and seed program and would be responsible for all law enforcement efforts (see also National Institute of Justice 1992).

The Justice Department programs also appear to interface, to some extent, with programs of Housing and Urban Development (HUD) directed to improved public housing security and local citizen and community development programming. The National Institute of Justice recently indicated that it has established a series of partnerships: "with the U.S. Department of Education in preventing and controlling crime and drug abuse in and around schools; with HHS in implementing the Health and Justice Initiative; and with the Office of National Drug Control Policy in controlling and preventing the spread of drug abuse across the Nation" (National Institute of Justice 1994, p. 7).

It is indeed possible that a comprehensive, systematic, and sustained set of model gang interventions and evaluation efforts may result from research and development programs of the U.S. Justice Department—such as the Office of Juvenile Justice and Delinquency Prevention's (OJJDP's) National Youth Gang Suppression and Intervention Program, the short-term existence of OJJDP's National Juvenile Gang Clearinghouse, more general violence reduction efforts of the Bureau of Justice Assistance, and research of the National Institute of Justice. However, these programs seem as yet to be somewhat unrelated to each other, representing spasmodic federal agency interest, and little sustained effort. Increased earmarking of funds to particular favored local community agencies with long-term and effective political ties to the Department and congressional representatives appears to have also occurred.

The recent comprehensive gang response initiative by OJJDP appears to be especially promising. A set of large-scale coordinated efforts is planned and includes a *National Gang Assessment Resource Center*, a "multi-site demonstration" of the *Comprehensive Community-Wide Approach to Gang Prevention, Intervention, and Suppression Program*, and an independent *Evaluation of the Comprehensive Community-Wide Approach*, as well as *Training and Technical Assistance* and *Targeted Acquisition and Dissemination of Gang Materials* (Office of Juvenile Justice and Delinquency Prevention 1994). OJJDP is also establishing an interagency consortium for the coordination of federal efforts. The agency, uniquely, has had long-term concern with the gang problem and interest in the development of gang research and intervention programs (Howell, 1994).

Department of Health and Human Services. The Office of Human Development Services, Administration on Children, Youth, and Families (ACYF), U.S. Department of Health and Human Services, created a Youth Gang Drug Prevention Program based on the assumption that "concerted and comprehensive efforts are needed at the community and grass-roots levels to prevent and reduce further the recruitment and involvement of at-risk youths in gangs" (Federal Register 1989, p. 15108). Emphasis in this program was based on the "coordination of city, county, and state services and systems with those of community-based organizations" (Federal Register 1989, p. 15108). Recipients of the initial awards included state, county, and city government offices—including manpower, departments of human resources, school systems, housing authorities, and recreation departments—as well as a range of nonprofit agencies—such as settlement houses and family and youth service projects. The federal share of project costs for the larger groups of government and community consortia ranged between $700,000 and $800,000 for the first year, and the possibility of more than a single year's funding existed in 1991. More recently, some of the consortia type programs have been funded for a five-year period.

While coordinated public, voluntary, and nonprofit agency programs may be evolving in these Department of Health and Human Service programs, little direct grass-roots involvement appears to have occurred. Also, the police, probation, court, and correctional agencies seem to be involved only secondarily. Focus is on prevention and early intervention, parent education and counseling, and various forms of youth-outreach and referral, such as drug and gang awareness counseling, preapprenticeship programs, and limited job experiences. These programs do not generally reach youths at high risk levels or hard-core older gang youths. A variety of existing socialization programs, emphasizing recreation and athletics of established social agencies, will undoubtedly be strengthened. Whether such programs will, in fact, provide a targeted, comprehensive approach involving the full range of significant individuals, community groups, and organizations dealing with the problem is questionable.

The Department of Health and Human Services programs appear to represent a positive step in the development of more organic, cross-agency approaches to combat the youth-gang problem in distinctive local community settings. But there are serious limitations, and it is not clear that very much will be learned from the demonstration efforts. It was not evident that these programs would be adequately monitored or evaluated. A limited amount of in-house research evaluation was encouraged, and a national evaluation was commissioned years after the programs began. The development of specific, well-conceived prevention or intervention models prior to program operations, and their systematic testing, is yet to occur, although various criteria of successful process, impact, and effectiveness have been identified.

Lack of Interagency Coordination. Federal agencies, such as Labor, Education, Health and Human Service, Housing and Urban Development, as well as the Justice Department, do not appear as yet to be significantly and interactively involved in each other's various initiatives such that they can contribute to a comprehensive program of prevention and reduction of the youth gang problem. The approaches of these agencies seem not to be systemic in reaching older and younger youths, parents, community residents, and former gang members as well as a variety of other agencies at federal and local levels through a set of interactive social development and social control strategies. Although the interrelated ideas of community mobilization and interagency coordination appear to be simple and logical, and are critically important to dealing with the youth gang problem, the existence of a tradition of strong independent-agency self-interest and a larger political and governmental tradition of fragmented powers clearly works against the integration of various programs.

The most serious gap in federal policy continues to be not only the general failure to understand the complex relationship of the gang problem to larger problems of poverty, housing, desegration, immigration, population movement, and lack of adequate educational, training, and job opportunities for young people, especially older minority adolescents, but also the failure to focus on the organization of local community efforts in disorganized inner-city and suburban communities. These gang-producing conditions have hardly been articulated in their full complexity, let alone addressed.

Conclusion

This chapter examined local community programs, state legislation, and evolving national policy dealing with the youth gang problem. A variety of ad hoc neighborhood programs and even gang organizations have attempted to control gang violence. These efforts are part of the American tradition of addressing social problems and community crises through local organizational advocacy and grass-roots mobilization. It is doubtful that these programs by themselves have been or can be successful. It is extremely difficult for local neighborhood groups to deal with established or chronic gang problems, in part because the youth gang may be better organized, or at least more present and persistent, than the groups. Local groups also are not able adequately to meet gang-member social and economic needs, especially providing access to legitimate resources.

From time to time, local gangs or federations of gangs reach a point of gang violence saturation. With the aid of local agencies or community organizations, gangs may then create mechanisms for controlling and limiting the violence, for example, truces. Such truce or peace arrangements, however, are usually of short duration; they are most effective when they also involve a range of citizenry and representatives of legitimate organizations.

An increasing number of states and cities have passed legislation and ordinances to control criminal gang activities, especially violence. Such legislation usually emphasizes enhanced sentences for violent crimes committed by gang offenders. California has produced the must elaborate laws, procedures, and arrangements for suppressing gang problems, with some secondary interest in community mobilization and development of other important strategies.

Only the beginnings of national and comprehensive approaches to the gang problem may be discerned. The basic question for federal planners should be not simply how best to remove gang members from the community, but how to integrate them into the larger social structure so that their energies and talents are employed in socially constructive ways. Because the youth or street-gang problem is related in complex ways to other basic social policy issues, it may not be effectively addressed unless concerns about poverty, racism, gun control or elimination, quality education, training, and jobs for minority youths in disorganized inner-city communities are also dealt with.

Prevention and reduction of the gang problem, however, must be specified across several domains: the individual, the family, the school, peer group, a variety of organizations and the community. A variety of federal and local agencies must focus on dealing with gang problems through integrated strategies of social opportunities, social intervention, and community mobilization, as well as suppression. Yet federal agency policy generally remains largely uncoordinated and simplistic. New institutional cross-agency and cross-jurisdictional arrangements must evolve, and new policies and programs must be developed and then rigorously and widely tested, so that we will know what truly works and what does not.

Community Mobilization/Planning: Selected Structure and Process Summary

A. *Problem Recognition*

Social/moral leadership initiatives
Articulation of the problem
Organization of concern and use of the media
Networking
Holding of community hearings

B. *Assessment*

Evaluation of nature, scope, seriousness of problem
Development of ongoing data bases
Involvement of key community organizations and groups
Resources made available to deal with problem: laws, agencies, manpower, motivations/concerns
Provision of incentives for organizations to participate
Countering of agency manipulative tendencies

C. *Construction of Interagency or Community Anti-gang Structure*

Identification of power figures at political, governmental, grass-roots, agency, and bureaucratic levels
Decentralization of the structure to point of impact of problem
Establishment of a range of policy and program level staff and cross-agency and community group committees and relationships
Development of funding relationships
Creation of meaningful goals and objectives
Setting of program targets, priorities, and strategies
Development and maintenance of relationships among agencies and groups
   1. *Power Relationships to Achieve Objectives*
      –Use of inducements: persuasion, money, prestige, morality, anger or protest, governmental leadership
      –Use of constraints: authority, law, policies and procedures, political and agency interests

–Overcoming denial, opportunism, and interorganization conflict
–Maintenance of communication with all key elements related to the
  gang problem, including gang youths

2. *Organizational Internal Development*
   Setting up of an agency community board, working groups directed
     to the problem
   Development of wide citizen participation
   Selection of qualified staff, both indigenous and professional
   Citizen and agency leadership rotation
   Purposeful agenda
   Avoidance/management of competitive internal agency group
     processes
   Timing of the development of collaborative mechanisms among staff

3. *Stimulation/Management of Conflict, Control of Problem,
   and Development of Resources*
   Identification of conditions and policies that impede attack on the
     problem
   Use of appropriate social action tasks: strike, march, petitions, use of
     the media (publicity), grass-roots (including gang youth)
     as appropriate
   Use of conflict resolution: negotiation, legal decisions, political and
     funding pressures, and inducements

D. *Community Mobilization Programming*

   Increase in communication among community groups and with gang youths
   Use of distinctive but overlapping emerging and chronic community
     programming approaches
   Coordination of agency and community group efforts
   Use of field team approaches

E. *Training and Knowledge Development*

   Citizen leaders
   Program participants
   Use of experts/university participation
   Cross-agency staff and community leadership training

F. *Funding*

   Knowledge and use of multiple funding sources
   Use of consortia arrangements
   Funding leadership by public agencies at state and national levels

G. *Monitoring and Evaluation*

   Monitoring by state agencies
   Adequate record keeping
   After-event brainstorming
   Outcome evaluation and use of hard data

Nature and Level of Youth Gang Member Problems to Be Addressed

Youth-Gang Member Characteristics	Emerging: High-Risk Gang-Prone (Wannabe, Fringe)	Chronic: Gang Member (Leaders, Core Members)
Age	Mainly 10–16 yrs	Mainly 15–24 yrs
Gender	Male or female	Mainly male
Race/ethnicity: African-American (low-income/segregated community)	Very high likelihood	Very high likelihood
Other black (low-income)	High likelihood	Moderate likelihood
Hispanic, specifically Mexican-American, Puerto Rican (low-income/partially segregated community)	Very high likelihood	Very high likelihood
Other Hispanic	Moderate likelihood	Moderate likelihood
Asian (low-income newcomer)	High likelihood	Moderate likelihood
White/European origin (low/middle-income)	Low/moderate likelihood	Low/moderate likelihood
Other racial/ethnic groups (low-income newcomer)	Low/moderate likelihood	Low/moderate likelihood
Peer relationships	Partially important	Highly important
Gang organization	Limited, partially developed	Extensive, well-developed
Street presence	Limited	High
Drug/use/Drug selling	Limited	Sometimes high
Home (parent involvement)	Partially unstable, partially supervised	Unstable, unsupervised
School adjustment	Partially involved, partially satisfying	Uninvolved, unsatisfactory
Police contacts	Limited	Extensive
Other justice system contacts	Limited	Extensive
Youth agencies	Partially involved	Uninvolved/exploitive
Other human service treatment agencies	Limited contact	No contact
Grass-roots organization contact	Limited	Very limited
Employment training program	Limited involvement	Limited involvement

Selected Strategic Activities/ Structures for Particular Settings (Organizations)

Setting/Agency	Suppression	Social Intervention	Opportunities Provision	Organizational Change and Development	Community Mobilization
Street hotspots, parks	Targeted gang surveillance, monitoring, communication, warning, setting limits, dispersal, arrest, sweeps, incarceration	Outreach, contact with target youth (gangs), brief counseling, crisis intervention, mediation, referral for services, recreational programming	Referral for training, jobs, paid community service projects, e.g., graffiti removal, beautification, side walk/street repair, painting, clean-up	Staff availability—evenings and weekends; use of beepers and field supervision, mobile service vehicles for crises intervention	(Networking) multiagency team patrols, availability of citizens as role models and mentors, use of agency workers and citizens to facilitate and supervise street events
Home (parents)	Advice and supervision by schools, community-based youth agency staff, probation/parole officers; visits by grass-roots groups e.g., parent groups	Counseling, support, advocacy, parent education regarding gangs, referral for services, including drug treatment, medical services	Referral for jobs, training, and educational development	Case management by a particular agency to coordinate service to families of gang youths	Parent participation in school and community anti-gang meetings; citizen patrols; community action to deal with crime and community improvement
Police	Investigation, intelligence, analysis and appropriate information sharing, gang problem surveillance, enforcement, education of criminal justice, community-based agencies and grassroots groups, as to scope and seriousness of problem; close collaboration with prosecution	Mentoring of at-risk and gang youths, brief counseling, referral for social services, mediation, case conferences around specific youth, conduct of anti-gang programs at school and community (e.g., DARE, SANE)	Referral of gang youth for jobs, training education, job development, supervision of youth in special training and job projects	Development of specialist gang officers, gang units, law enforcement task forces, computerized information systems, internal agency coordination of policies and procedures; increasing emphasis on community involvement around gang problem solving	Participation in inter-agency community task forces, collaboration with grassroots patrols and community agency and business anti-gang programs
Schools	In-school monitoring, use of metal detectors, uniform discipline code (including gang offenses), communication and application of	For students: DARE, SANE, and other anti-gang educational programs, conflict resolution instruction, peer group	Remedial and enriched educational programs for gang youths with academic problems; vocational and apprentice training, joint	Gang security units; school-social service, community agency teams focused on gang problems; special system-wide curriculum,	School-community advisory groups, participation in anti-gang community task forces, development of policies and procedures

302

	fair rules re: gang symbols, dress, activities; use of in-school suspension, parent contacts, street patrols, collaboration with criminal justice agencies	counseling (re: gang problems), crisis intervention, provision of school based social and health services, after-school recreational programs ***** For parents: outreach, referral for services, parent education regarding gangs	school-work experiences, tutorial and mentoring, field visits to business/industrial settings	social development coordinating structures	for sharing certain kinds of student information with other agencies, development and use of parent patrols and volunteers to assist with gang intervention, control and prevention
Prosecution	Investigation, case selection, knowledge of gang-applicable law, and development of recommendations for new gang laws, collaboration with police, development of case strategies (re: bail, detention, waivers, use of witnesses, witness protection, disposition recommendations)	Development of community service resource manuals for gang offenders, parents; focus on sentences directed to rehabilitition and use of community-based treatments to the extent feasible	Collaboration with business groups and chambers of commerce in job development for gang youths	Special unit vertical prosecution; also development of policy and procedure for general prosecution re: gang processing, collaborative information sharing across law enforcement agencies and jurisdictions	Coordination with other criminal justice and community organizations, leading and assisting in the formation of task forces, communication with media re: nature of problem and potential social solutions that are community based
Judges	Ensure that gang member obtains a fair hearing, concern both with protection of community and youths from violent gang activities, pretrial supervision for chronic	Court orders to facilitate rehabilitation (e.g., diagnostic testing, psychiatric treatment, compulsory school attendance) recommendation of family services to gang youths and parents,	Recommendation of special programs, and pressures on schools, agencies, and advising businesses to provide appropriate education and training opportunities for gang youths	Regular supervisory meetings with probation officers; meetings with groups of proba- tioners, access to com- puter information on gang youth history and social adjustment	Provision of community leadership on gang problems and need for more resources, sitting on community boards in advisory capacity and avoiding conflict of interests situations

Setting/Agency	Suppression	Social Intervention	Opportunities Provision	Organizational Change and Development	Community Mobilization
	offenders, appropriate sentencing especially to community-based institutions, limited use of waivers of juveniles to adult court	pretrial services for chronic offenders			
Probation	Use of range of intermediate and flexible control procedures; close supervision of gang youths, enforcing court orders, appropriate use of detention, home confinement, collaboration with police (joint patrols), parole and prosecution; home and neighborhood visits	Counseling, referral for individual, family, mental health, medical and dental services, teaching of conflict resolution skills, mediation, and crisis intervention, organization of parent support groups of probationers; parent education as to gang problem; development of special programs for younger and older offenders, in collaboration with schools and youth agencies	Provision to youths of court-sponsored vocational assessment, training, and job opportunities; special remedial academic programs; referrals for jobs	Development of risk/ needs assessments, computer information systems (re: gangs and gang members, and available community resources), intensive supervision, vertical case management; outreach to employers, schools, youth agencies re: control of, and collaborative services to, gang youths	Organization or stimulation of community groups, including parents, former gang members, to form community anti-gang patrols; sponsorship and coordination of community agency and grass-roots collaborative programs, including job development; participation in interagency community task forces
Corrections	Identification, and close supervision, of gang youths; application of clear policy (re: participation in gang activity in institutions),	Values change programs, conflict resolution instruction; drug/alcohol programs, personal and group counseling, use of	Remedial and advanced educational programs, training and job opportunities within institution and outside facility	Special staffing/team arrangements in institutions with serious gang problems, development of information systems on gang members/	Involving community groups in institutional living programs, participation in interagency and community task forces

	dispersion of gang members throughout institution, if feasible; collaboration with police, prosecution, parole (re: information sharing and joint approaches), transfer of selected hard-core gang youths as appropriate to other institutions	volunteer mentors, referral for services, including psychological, medical, dental		incidents, and risk/needs assessments	
Parole/after-care	Close supervision of gang youths, enforcement of parole orders, appropriate use of detention and revocation of parole, collaboration with probation, police, other justice system officials, home, neighborhood visits	Individual, group counseling, referral for social, medical, psychological services, development of parent support groups, developing housing arrangements, family counseling, crisis intervention, teaching conflict resolution skills, close case collaboration with institution prior to youth release	Provision of training and remedial education opportunities, direct job referrals, job development; close collaboration with schools, employers, to sustain youth in programs	Developing risk/needs assessments; use of case managers, trainers, specialized gang parole officers	Collaboration with a variety of agencies and development of services and job opportunities in respect to parolees; participation in community task forces re gangs
Employment and training	Liaison with probation, parole, awareness of gang culture and potential problems; clear rules (re: proscribed behavior) in training and on job	Career counseling, peer worker support arrangements, collaboration with mentors, referral for services, social support for parents and family, crisis management	Intake screening and assessment, tutoring, work acclimation training, job placement, and follow-up, academic and job skills training and/or referral	Integrated school/job training, multifunctional staffing, use of neighborhood mentors, monetary incentives for youths to participate in education, training, and special job preparation programs	Collaboration with various agencies (re: recruitment of gang youth and development of support services), participation as member of interagency and community task forces

Setting/Agency	Suppression	Social Intervention	Opportunities Provision	Organizational Change and Development	Community Mobilization
Community youth-based agency	Setting clear, fair rules and implementing them; monitoring and supervising youths in agency and community hot-spots, appropriate collaboration with police, probation, parole, and other justice system officers; contracting with justice system to provide services under prescribed conditions	Limited use of supervised recreation and group work activities; individual, group, family counseling, parent education (re: gangs); referral for services; job support; crisis intervention, mediation; home visits; victim assistance	Tutoring, remedial education, job training, job development and placement, provision of small business opportunities, close collaboration with schools, re: involvement of gang youths and their families in the educational process	Case management, outreach, decentralized centers, as appropriate for gang youths; use of paraprofessional and professional teams of workers; joint patrols with police and probation	Neighborhood gang prevention and control activity sponsors, member of interagency task forces, advocate for additional services and resources on behalf of gang youths, organizer of parent patrols in collaboration with schools and police
Grass-roots organization (especially churches)	Collaboration with police, probation, and other justice agencies, organizing parent patrols, advocate of improved law enforcement supervision of youth activities in the neighborhood, supporting more victim involvement at court in prosecution of gang cases	Counseling, tutoring, referral of youths for services, parent education (re: gang problem), sponsor of youth activities, crisis intervention and mediation	Sponsoring special training, educational, and job development programs for gang youths; stimulating local business development for job opportunities for gang youths	Outreach programs to youths, including gang youths, use of specialist gang worker, use of court watchers at gang cases	Sponsor local interagency and community gang task forces, advocate improved agency services, support parent patrols especially in school areas; social action for greater official attention to, control of, and better use of resources directed to gang problems; organization of block clubs and parent support groups
Emerging gang problem context emphasis	Identification and close supervision of juvenile gang members, and those at specific risk for	Counseling, recreation programming, family services, SANE, DARE, anti-gang curricula,	Referrals for part-time jobs and volunteer services, coordination of training and better use	Outreach to newcomer and/or race/minority ethnic groups in community, use of local	Development of informal as well as formal links among agencies and community groups

	gang membership; arrest and prosecution of older gang members	parent education programs	of existing job opportunities	citizens and volunteers, focus on generalized or mainstream rather than specialized approach to problem	Development of formal interagency and community anti-gang councils, monitoring of agencies so that they target hard-core gang youths as well as high-risk gang-prone youths
Chronic gang problem context emphasis	Targeting older gang youths and leaders as well as younger high-risk gang-prone youths; collaboration between justice system and community-based agencies	Crisis intervention, mediation, special service support projects to core-gang youths at school and in neighborhood	Development of major job programs, alternative schools and special educational mainstream programs for gang members to extent possible	Facilitation of specialized outreach worker units and procedures; use of computer information systems; development of multi-agency field teams	

Glossary and Discussion of Terms

There is much variation in the definition of *youth gang* or its equivalent terms depending on particular agency, city, or region of the country; race/ethnicity; gang generation; and cultural factors. The terms *delinquent group*, *gang*, and *criminal organization* are overlapping but need to be distinguished for policy, program, and research purposes to the extent possible.

Gang. Generally refers to a group or collectivity of persons with a common identity whose members interact on a fairly regular basis in a clique or sometimes as a whole group. The activities of the gang may be regarded as legitimate, illegitimate, or criminal in varying combinations.

• **Street gang.** Term preferred by law enforcement; it emphasizes the organized character of a group of persons on the street, often engaged in significant illegitimate or criminal activity. The ages of members of these street gangs vary—some authorities report arrests of members in their 30s, 40s, and 50s. Some street gangs and their members are more street based than others.

• **Youth gang.** May refer to a youth segment of a street gang or even a criminal organization, the youths usually being between the ages of 12 and 24. *Youth gang* is often used as equivalent to *street gang*, but community-based agencies, including schools, prefer "youth gang," since they deal primarily with younger youths.

• **Traditional youth gang.** Refers to a gang with sections of adolescents, juveniles, and some young adults concerned primarily with issues of status, prestige, turf protection, and group solidarity. The youth gang may have a name, a hangout, codes of conduct, colors, special dress, signs, symbols, dues collection, and so on. Traditional youth gangs tend to have a leadership structure (implicit or explicit), but differ in degree of commitment to criminal and noncriminal gang activity. They may persist over several generations.

• **Posse/crew.** Terms sometimes equivalent to the term *street* or *youth gang*. The posse or crew, more often than the traditional youth gang, is characterized by a commitment to criminal gain activity, particularly drug trafficking, rather than to status- or territorial-based concerns. It may be loosely organized and/or connected to an adult criminal organization.

• **Other types of youth "gangs."** "Quasi" gangs that may include stoners, punk rockers, Neo-Nazi Skinheads, hate groups, satanic groups, motorcycle gangs, and prison gangs. They may be similar to traditional or street-youth gangs in various ways, but have distinctive organizational, cultural, political, religious, and institutional lifestyles, perspectives, and biases. They can be loosely organized, ephemeral, or long enduring. They can engage in group-oriented violent or criminal behavior to sustain or defend their beliefs.

309

• **Other youth group considerations.** It is important to distinguish delinquent or criminal gangs and ganglike groups from youth or street groups of an earlier era, which still endure today. These latter groups have been called street clubs, youth organizations, and social and athletic clubs. They are not usually regarded as delinquent by local residents. They serve to socialize lower-income, working-class youth, and sometimes first-generation adolescents to adult roles. Their activities may constitute mischievous yet acceptable behaviors that are considered normal rites of passage in a particular community.

"Copycat" gangs may be increasingly present in some lower-income and middle-class communities, often located in smaller cities and suburban and rural areas. Youths in these groups may identify and attempt to imitate the mannerisms and behaviors of youth gangs in urban centers. Identification with gang culture, in significant measure through media influence, may be a basis for novel experience and excitement for these youths. The activities of copycat gangs may sometimes have serious violent or criminal consequences.

Most street-based youth groups, sometimes identified as gangs, are in fact ephemeral, engage in relatively minor delinquent acts, and have little if any actual or ongoing contact with youth or street gangs. The threat that these groups pose to the community and to the social development of their members should be carefully assessed so that a gang problem is not created or exaggerated.

Delinquent group. Refers to a group or collectivity, mainly of juveniles and/or adolescents, sometimes engaged in less serious or in a wider range of law-violating behavior, particularly with respect to property crimes, than those of youth gangs, posses or crews, and other "pseudo" gangs. The delinquent group is usually younger, less organized, and more ephemeral than a youth gang. It is characterized by few of the special characteristics of gangs such as turf, gang structure, tradition, distinctive dress, colors, and signs or symbols. The delinquent group is the most prevalent of all deviant youth groups in most communities. The terms *youth gang* and *delinquent group* may not be mutually exclusive in many circumstances.

Criminal organization. Usually a relatively well-organized, stable, and sophisticated clique, group, or organization of youths and/or adults committed primarily to systematic income-producing activity of a criminal nature. Its members are essentially employees of a criminal business. The criminal organization may at times use intimidation and violence to achieve or protect its economic interests. Such organizations may provide illegal services or goods to and acquire rewards or payments from local residents in mutually acceptable and reinforcing ways. The posse, crew, triad, and Mafia are subtypes of criminal organization. This type of organization also develops a certain social solidarity.

Gang clique, set, klika. *Gang clique* and *set* are terms sometimes used as equivalent to *youth gang*. On the other hand, a *klika* on the West Coast may represent an entire cohort or age sector of youths (e.g., 13- and 14-year-old males) who join or are "jumped into" a street gang. The clique in its smaller size connotation may signify a tight grouping of two or three youths who have similar characteristics or criminal interests. At times it is identified as separate from the large gang grouping.

Youth gang member. Can indicate various types of members who engage in a range of legitimate, illegitimate, criminal, and/or violent behaviors. Leaders and core members of youth or street-gangs are often (but not always) more serious and frequent offenders than are other kinds of gang members. Arrested gang members are more likely to become career criminals than arrested non-gang delinquents.

The following represent membership categories of the so-called traditional turf based gang in various communities, with regional and generational exceptions. In the course of a gang member's career, he or she may take on different roles at different times:

• **Gang leader.** An individual who makes central or symbolic decisions that affect the gang's behavior. The leader may be formally recognized as President, King, Queen, Prince, Governor, Ambassador, Section Chief, Enforcer, Old Gangster, or have no title, simply regarded as a shot-caller or influential. Leadership may also be a function shared by different members of the group, depending on particular situations, such as initiating a social or athletic affair; starting or sanctioning a gang fight; conducting a drug transaction; or negotiating criminal deals.

• **Core or hard-core gang member.** An attribution assigned, often by law enforcement, to gang members who engage consistently in gang violence and other serious gang-motivated crime (e.g., a shooter). It refers to the few gang members who are most influential in the development or implementation of the gang's violent patterns of criminal behavior, or who contribute to the development of gang solidarity and maintenance of rules and gang discipline.

• **Regular member.** A gang member who participates in the gang's criminal and noncriminal activities on a consistent and frequent basis. He or she is recognized as a member in good standing or status.

• **Associate.** Refers to a youth who occasionally associates with gang members on the street or elsewhere but who neither recognizes himself nor is usually, or fully, recognized by others as a gang member, except sometimes by law enforcement officials when a gang crime is committed and the particular youth is located nearby and arrested. The terms *gang member* and *associate* are sometimes used as equivalent.

• **Soldier or peon.** A reliable but low-status gang member.

• **Peripheral or fringe member.** A gang member who participates periodically and selectively in gang events. He or she usually does not have high status and is not regarded as a reliable or committed gang member. The peripheral member may readily leave the gang and be excused from participation in many of the gang's activities.

• **Wannabe (Shorty).** Refers ordinarily to a younger youth who wants to join the gang. He or she may be a friend or relative of a gang member or former gang member, or may already be a member of a "tot" or juvenile gang-related group.

• **Recruit.** Usually a younger and sometimes an older youth who is recruited for certain skills or talents useful during crises (e.g., gang fighting) and who may sometimes be requested to join for a limited time.

• **Youth at risk of gang membership, or gang-prone youth.** Usually a younger youth who is not yet a gang member. He or she may or may not explicitly aspire to gang membership, or be a target for gang recruitment. However, certain social characteristics and conditions in combination within his or her immediate environment make the youth likely to become a gang member, such as:

Living in a gang neighborhood;
Having a family member in a gang;
Experimenting with drugs;
Defiance or unruliness;
Committing delinquent acts;
Failing at school;
Having certain physical or social attributes that are attractive to the gang;
Being knowledgeable about gang lore;
Occasionally flashing gang signs or wearing gang colors;
Occasionally hanging out with or being suspected by school or police of being a
  gang member.

Again, these characteristics or conditions, singly, may be insufficient to predispose the youth to gang membership or actually identify him or her as a gang member. *A gang prevention program should be primarily concerned with high-risk gang-prone youth or incipient gang members who give clear evidence of likely or actual delinquent or criminal gang involvement.*

- **Floater, go-between, broker (criminal or non-criminal).** A youth or adult who is ordinarily not a member of a specific gang, but is well known and has high status or respect among several gangs in the community. He or she has ongoing knowledge, certain talents, or resources useful to gangs (e.g., access to other gangs, capacity to mediate a gang fight, ability to counsel in respect to personal problems, provider of legal advice, or special access to legitimate or illegitimate jobs, weapons, or drugs).

- **Veterano, Old Head, O.G. (Old Gangster), Senior, Advisor, Counselor.** Often an honorific title assigned to or taken by a young adult who was (or was reported to be) a gang member when he or she was younger. They may now be junkies, drug dealers, informers, racketeers, legitimate business operators, human service workers, a parent, or other respected members of the community. At times, older gang members with gang reputation and prison records still influence the group or its membership to maintain gang tradition, increase gang violence, and pursue illegitimate adult careers. Some former "gangbangers" may encourage younger gang members to become socially or politically active.

Group delinquency and gang crime incidents. Not all group delinquency or crime should be classified automatically as a gang incident (e.g., purse snatching, disturbing the peace, mob action, group assault by non-gang members)). Group delinquent acts are often incorrectly classified as gang-motivated incidents, particularly in emerging gang problem contexts. Officials often do not clearly recognize or understand the distinctive character of the problem. Authorities may initially overreact and classify co-offending youths as members of a gang when their delinquent activity is neither gang motivated nor gang related.

References

Advisory Centers. 1990. "Proposal for a Youth Gang Drug Prevention Program." Grand Rapids, MI: Advisory Centers, Inc. (24 pp. mimeograph.)

Agopian, Michael W. 1991. "Gang Alternative and Prevention Program Evaluation Report." Los Angeles County Probation Department. May 11.

Allen, Robert. 1981. "Discussion: The Youth's Experience." In *Youth Crime and Urban Policy*, edited by Robert L. Woodson. Washington, DC: American Enterprise Institute for Public Policy Research, p. 74.

Amandes, Richard B. 1979. "Hire a Gang Leader: A Delinquency Prevention Program That Works." *Juvenile and Family Court Journal* 30:37–40.

American Correctional Association. 1994 (January). "Day Treatment Development: Getting Off the Ground." *Juvenile Justice Day Treatment Newsletter* 2:2–3.

American Institute for Research. 1988 (January). "Evaluation of the Habitual Serious and Violent Juvenile Offender Program. Executive Summary." Office of Juvenile Justice and Delinquency Prevention, U.S. Justice Department. Washington, DC: U.S. Government Printing Office.

Anderson, Elijah. 1990. *Street Wise*. Chicago: University of Chicago Press.

Andrews, D. A., Ivan Zinger, Robert D. Hoge, James Bonita, Paul Gendreau, and Francis Cullen. 1990. "Does Correctional Treatment Work? A Clinically Relevant and Psychologically Informed Meta-Analysis." *Criminology* 28(3):369–404.

Anti-Defamation League. 1986 (June). "Extremism Targets the Prisons: A Special Report." New York: Anti-Defamation League of B'nai B'rith, Civil Rights Division.

———. 1987 (November). "Shaved for Battle. Skinheads Target American Youth: A Special Report." New York: Anti-Defamation League of B'nai B'rith, Civil Rights Division.

———. 1990. "Neo-Nazi Skinheads: A 1990 Status Report." An ADL Special Report. New York: Anti-Defamation League of B'nai B'rith.

Applebome, Peter. 1993. "Skinhead Violence Grows, Experts Say." *The New York Times*, July 18, p. 18.

Asbury, Herbert. 1971. *Gangs of New York: An Informal History of the Underworld*. New York: Putnam. (Originally published 1927, New York: Alfred A. Knopf, Inc.)

Associated Press. 1990. "Youth Gangs Stir Soviet Ethnic Unrest." *Chicago Tribune*, June 7, Sec. 1, p. 16.

———. 1991. "Law on Parent Liability for Crime Is Voided." *The New York Times*, December 23, p. 1.

———. 1992. "Homicide Records Set in 3 Big Cities." *The New York Times*, January 3, A9.

Ayres, B. Drummond, Jr. 1994. "In a City of Graffiti, Gangs Turn to Violence to Protect Their Art." *The New York Times*, March 13, p. 8.

Baca, Chris. 1988 (June). "Juvenile Gangs in Albuquerque." Paper presented by the Albu-

313

querque Police Department at the Coordinating Council Meeting, Office of Juvenile
    Justice and Delinquency Prevention, Albuquerque.
Bach, Robert. 1993. *Changing Relations. Newcomers and Established Residents in U.S.
    Communities.* New York: Ford Foundation, p. 1.
Baker, Bob. 1988a. "Gang Murder Rates Get Worse." *Los Angeles Times,* April 10.
———. 1988b. "Tough Boss Shows Gang Members New Way of Life." *Los Angeles Times,* April
    15. See also, "Homeboys: Players in a Deadly Drama." *Los Angeles Times,* June 26.
Barringer, Felicity. 1992. "White-Black Disparity in Income: Narrowed in 80s, Census Shows."
    The New York Times, July 24, pp. A1, A10.
Bastian, Lisa D., and Bruce M. Taylor. 1991 (September). *School Crime.* A National Crime
    Victimization Survey Report. U.S. Department of Justice, Office of Justice Programs,
    Bureau of Justice Statistics.
Baugh, Dennis G. 1993. *Gangs in Correctional Facilities: A National Assessment.* Laurel,
    Maryland: American Correctional Association, April 12.
Beavers, Gerald. 1988 (September). "Survey Interview." National Youth Gang Suppression
    and Intervention Project. School of Social Service Administration, University of Chi-
    cago.
Beck, Allen, Daniel Gilliard, Laurence Greenfield, Caroline Harlow, Thomas Hester, Louis
    Jankowski, Tracy Snell, James Stephan, and Danielle Morton. 1993 (October). *Sur-
    vey of State Prison Inmates.* 1991. U.S. Department of Justice, Office of Justice Pro-
    grams, Bureau of Justice Statistics.
Bell, Daniel. 1953. "Crime as an American Way of Life." *The Antioch Review,* Summer:131–
    154.
Berkeley, Bill. 1992. "JHERI Kurls" Trademark of Uptown Gang." *The National Law Jour-
    nal,* February 28, p. 8.
Berlin, Gordon, and Andrew Sum. 1988 (February). *Toward a More Perfect Union: Basic
    Skills, Poor Families, and Our Economic Future.* Occasional Paper, Number Three.
    Ford Foundation Project on Social Welfare and the American Future. New York: Ford
    Foundation.
Bernstein, Saul. 1964. *Youth on the Streets: Work with Alienated Youth Groups.* New York:
    Association Press.
Berntsen, Karen. 1979. "A Copenhagen Youth Gang: A Descriptive Analysis." In *New Paths
    in Criminology,* edited by Sarnoff A. Mednick, S. Giora Sloham, and Barbara Phillips.
    Lexington, MA: Lexington Books.
Betsey, Charles L., Robinson G. Hollister, Jr., and Mary R. Papageorgiu (eds.). 1985. *Youth
    Employment and Training Programs.* The YEDPA Years. Washington, DC: National
    Academy Press.
Blau, Robert, and John O'Brien. 1991. "Rise and Fall of El Rukn-Jeff Fort's Evil Empire."
    Chicago Tribune, September 2, pp. 1, 2.
Bloch, H. A., and A. Niederhoffer. 1958. *The Gang.* New York: Philosophical Library.
Block, Alan A. 1991. *Perspectives On Organizing Crime.* Dordrecht, Holland: K. Luwer
    Academic Publishers.
Block, Carolyn B. 1985 (July). "Lethal Violence in Chicago Over Seventeen Years: Homi-
    cides Known to the Police 1965–1981." Statistical Analysis Center, Illinois Crimi-
    nal Justice Information Authority.
———. 1991. "Lethal Violence in the Chicago Latin Community." Statistical Analysis Cen-
    ter. Illinois Criminal Justice Information Authority, March 7 (draft).
———, Rebecca Block, and Richard Block. 1993 (December). "Street Gang Crime In Chi-
    cago." *Research in Brief.* National Institute of Justice, Office of Justice Programs,
    U.S. Department of Justice.

Blumenthal, Ralph. 1992. "Growing Number of Bystanders Caught in Cross-fire, Police Say." *The New York Times*, August 31, p. B12.

Blumin, Stuart M. 1973. "Residential Mobility Within the Nineteenth Century City." In *The Peoples of Philadelphia. A History of Ethnic Groups and Lower-Class Life, 1790–1940*, edited by Allen F. Davis and Mark H. Haller. Philadelphia: Temple University Press, pp. 37–51.

Bobrowski, Lawrence J. 1988 (November). *Collecting, Organizing, and Reporting Street Gang Crime*. Chicago Police Department, Special Functions Group.

Boston Housing Authority. 1989. "Youth Gang and Drug Prevention Project for Public Housing Developments." Application submitted to the Administration for Children, Youth and Families (ACYF), Department of Health and Human Services, June 13.

Bowker, Lee H., Helen Shimota Gross, and Malcolm W. Klein. 1980. "Female Participation in Delinquent Gang Activity." *Adolescence* 15:509–519.

Breen, Lawrence, and Martin M. Allen. 1983. "Gang Behavior: Psychological and Law Enforcement Implications." *FBI Law Enforcement Bulletin* 52(2):19–24.

Briggs, Michael. 1992. "FBI Adds 18 Agents Here to Fight Gangs." *Chicago Sun-Times*, January 10.

Brody, Jane E. 1992. "Report Says Rape Leads Rise in Violent Crimes." *The New York Times*, April 20, p. A13.

Brown, Waln K. 1977. "Black Female Gangs in Philadelphia." *International Journal of Offender Therapy and Comparative Criminology* 21(3):221–228.

Buentello, Salvador. 1992. "Combatting Gangs in Texas." *Corrections Today* 54(5):58–60.

Buhmann, Elizabeth T. 1991 (June). *Gangs in Texas Cities*. Austin, TX: Texas Attorney General's Office.

Bureau of Justice Assistance, Office of Justice Programs, U.S. Justice Department. 1991. "Weed and Seed. A Conceptual Framework." Washington, DC: Office of Justice Programs, October 30.

Burgos, Frank. 1991. "Feds Spur Suburb Gang Crackdown." *Chicago Sun-Times*, May 3.

Burns, John F. 1993. "Gangs in Sarajevo Spread Terror, Unchecked by the Cowed Leaders." *The New York Times*, October 22, pp. A1, A5.

Burrell, Susan. 1990. "Gang Evidence: Issues for Criminal Defence." *Santa Clara Law Review* 30 (Summer):739–790.

Bursik, Robert J., Jr. 1988. "Social Disorganization and Theories of Crime and Delinquency: Problems and Prospects." *Criminology* 26(4):519–551.

Bursik, Robert J., Jr., and Harold G. Grasmick. 1993. *Neighborhoods and Crime*. New York: Lexington Books.

Butterfield, Fox. 1992a. "Youth Gangs are Attacking Families Near Boston." *The New York Times*, February 7, p. A12.

———. 1992b. "Are American Jails Becoming Shelters from the Storm?" *The New York Times*, July 19, Section 4, p. 4.

California Penal Code. 1988. "Street Terrorism Enforcement and Enforcement and Prevention Act," Sec. 186.20, Chap. II, Title 7, Part 1, pp. 3182–3187.

California Office of Criminal Justice Planning. 1987 (July). "California Gang Violence Suppression Program. Program Guidelines." Sacramento, CA.

Caltabriano, Michael L. 1981 (August). "National Prison Gang Study." Unpublished Report to the Federal Bureau of Prisons. Quoted in *Prison Gangs: Their Extent, Nature and Impact on Prisons*, 1985 (July), edited by George M. Camp and Camille G. Camp. Washington, DC: U.S. Government Printing Office.

Camp, Camille Graham, and George M. Camp. 1988 (September). *Management Strategies for Combatting Prison Gang Violence*. South Salem, NY: Criminal Justice Institute.

Camp, George M., and Camille Graham Camp. 1985 (July). *Prison Gangs: Their Extent, Nature, and Impact on Prisons*. Washington, DC: U.S. Government Printing Office.

Campbell, Anne. 1984a. "Girls' Talk: The Social Representation of Aggression by Female Gang Members." *Criminal Justice and Behavior* 1(1):139–156.

———. 1984b. *The Girls in the Gang*. Oxford, United Kingdom: Basil Blackwell.

———. 1990. "Female Participation in Gangs." In *Gangs in America*, edited by C. Ronald Huff. Newbury Park: Sage Publications, pp. 163–182.

Candamil, Maria T. 1990. "Female Gangs." U.S. Department of Health and Human Services, Administration for Children, Youth and Families. Washington, DC. (Unpublished paper.)

Caplan, Nathan S. 1968. "Treatment Intervention and Reciprocal Interaction Effects." *Journal of Social Issues* 24(January):63–88.

Caponpon, Victor and Geronimo Tagatac. 1985 (July). *A Joint Legislative Hearing on Violence at Folsom Prison*. Sacramento, CA: The California Senate Office of Research.

Cartwright, Desmond S., and Kenneth I. Howard. 1966. "Multivariate Analysis of Gang Delinquency: I. Ecological Influence." *Multivariate Behavioral Research* 1(3):321–337.

———, Barbara Tomson, and Hershey Schwartz. 1975. *Gang Delinquency*. Monterey, CA: Brooks/Cole.

Casuso, Jorge. 1989. "Contractor Puts Jobless to Work by the Busload." *Chicago Tribune*, August 7. Sec. II. pp. 1, 8.

Cerven, Jennifer. 1991. "Gangs, Drug Dealers Targeted by Joliet." *Chicago Tribune*, July 11, Sec. 2, p. 6.

Chein, I., D. L. Gerard, R. S. Lee, and E. Rosenfeld. 1964. *The Road to H: Narcotics, Delinquency, and Social Policy*. New York: Basic Books.

Chesney-Lind, Meda, Nancy Marker, Ivette Rodriguez Stern, Allison Yap, Valerie Song, Howard Reyes, Yolanda Reyes, Jeffrey Stern, and Jo Ann Taira. 1992. *Gangs and Delinquency in Hawaii*. Center for Youth Research, Social Science Research Institute, University of Hawaii at Manoa, January 3.

Chicago Board of Education, Center for Urban Education. 1981 (August). *The Chicago Safe School Study. A Report to the General Superintendent of Schools*. Chicago: Chicago Board of Education.

Chicago Sun-Times. 1992. "Bond Denied for 2 Female Gang Members." *Chicago Sun-Times*, May 16, p. 15.

Chicago Sun-Times. 1994. "Editorials. Weekend Under Fire Fingers Gangs' Toll." *Chicago Sun-Times*. August 30, p. 21.

Chicago Tribune. 1991. "English Gangs Continue Nightly Violence." *Chicago Tribune*, September 13, p. 9.

Chin, Ko-Lin. 1990a. "Chinese Gangs and Extortion." In *Gangs in America*, edited by C. Ronald Huff. Newbury Park, CA: Sage Publications, pp. 129–145.

———. 1990b. *Chinese Subculture and Criminality. Non-traditional Crime Groups in America*. New York: Greenwood Press.

Chinn, Ignatius. 1990. "Comments." *Community Mobilization*. Conference Proceedings. Sacramento, CA: Office of Criminal Justice Planning, pp. 128–129.

Clarke, Michael J. 1987. "Citizenship, Community, and the Management of Crime." *British Journal of Criminology* 27(4):384–400.

Clayton, Wayne. 1983. "The El Monte Plan—Hire a Gang Leader." El Monte Police Department, Los Angeles County, CA, March 1.

Cloward, Richard A., and Lloyd E. Ohlin. 1960. *Delinquency and Opportunity: A Theory of Delinquent Gangs*. Glencoe, IL: Free Press.

Cohen, Albert K. 1955. *Delinquent Boys: The Culture of the Gang*. Glencoe, IL: Free Press.
———, and James F. Short, Jr. 1958. "Research in Delinquent Subcultures." *The Journal of Social Issues* 14(3):20–37.
Cohen, Bernard. 1969a. "The Delinquency of Gangs and Spontaneous Groups." In *Delinquency Selected Studies*, edited by T. Sellin and M. E. Wolfgang. New York: John Wiley & Sons, pp. 61–111.
———. 1969b. "Internecine Conflict: The Offender." In *Delinquency Selected Studies*, edited by T. Sellin and M. E. Wolfgang. New York: John Wiley & Sons, pp. 112–137.
Cohen, Stanley. 1972. *Folk Devils and Moral Panics*. London: MacGibbon & Kee.
Coleman, James S. 1990. "Rational Organization." *Rationality and Society* 2(1):94–105; Supplement 106–113.
Collins, H. Craig. 1979. *Street Gangs: Profiles for Police*. New York: New York City Police Department, pp. 14–55.
Commission de Police du Quebec. 1980. *Motorcycle Gangs in Quebec*. Quebec: Ministere des Communications.
Community Research Associates. 1994. "AmeriCorps National Civilian Community Corps Offers Opportunities for Youth and Resources for Community Approaches." *OJJDP News Notes*. August, p. 2.
Conley, Catherine. 1991. *Street Gangs: What They Are and What Is Done About Them*. Bethesda, MD: Abt Associates Inc. (draft).
Coplen, Bruce R. 1988. "Field Interview." *National Youth Gang Suppression and Intervention Project*. University of Chicago, School of Social Service Administration and the U.S. Office of Juvenile Justice and Delinquency Prevention.
Coplon, Jeff. 1988. "Skinhead Nation." *Rolling Stone*. December, pp. 52–94.
County of Dane, Juvenile Court Program. 1989. "Gang Prevention Project . . ." Madison, WI, June 13.
Covey, Herbert C., Scott Menard, and Robert J. Franzere. 1992. *Juvenile Gangs*. Springfield, IL: Charles C. Thomas.
Cowell, Alan. 1994. "Where Crosses Stand, A Swastika Intrudes." *The New York Times*. National. May 17, A6.
Crawford, Paul Z., Daniel I. Malamud and James R. Dumpson. 1970. *Working with Teenage Gangs*. New York: Welfare Council of New York City.
Creamer, Robert. 1988 (November). "Survey Interview." National Youth Gang Suppression and Intervention Project. School of Social Service Administration, University of Chicago
Cressey, Donald Ray. 1972. *Criminal Organization: Its Elementary Forms*. London: Heinemann Educational Books.
Crust, John. 1988. "Magic Comes to Mean Streets." *Los Angeles Herald Examiner*, April 8, pp. A3, A13.
Cummings, D. Brian. 1990. "Problem-oriented Policing and Crime-Specific Planning." *The Police Chief*, March, pp. 63–64.
Curry, G. David, and Irving A. Spergel. 1988. "Gang Homicide, Delinquency and Community." *Criminology* 26(August):381–405.
———, and Irving A. Spergel. 1992. "Gang Involvement and Delinquency Among Hispanic and African-American Adolescent Males." *Journal of Research in Crime and Delinquency* 29(3):273–292.
Curry, G. David, Robert J. Fox, Richard A. Ball, and Darryl Stone. 1992. *National Assessment of Law enforcement Anti-Gang Information Resources*. (Draft, 1992, Final Report). Morgantown, WV.

————, Richard A. Ball, and Robert J. Fox. 1994. "Gang Crime and Law Enforcement Recordkeeping." *Research in Brief.* National Institute of Justice. Office of Justice Programs, U.S. Department of Justice. August.

Dahmann, Judith S. 1983 (September). *An Evaluation on Operation Hardcore: A Prosecutorial Response to Violent Gang Criminality.* Alexandria, VA: Mitre Corp.

Daley, Richard M. 1985. *Gang Prevention Unit.* Report. Chicago: Cook County State's Attorney's Office.

Dannen, Frederic. 1992. "Revenge of the Green Dragons." *The New Yorker,* November 16, pp. 76–99.

Davidson, John L. 1987. "Juvenile Gang Drug Program." Grant Proposal to Office of Criminal Justice Planning, Sacramento, CA, September 28.

Davis, Allen F., and Mark H. Haller. 1973. *The People of Philadelphia.* A History of Ethnic Groups and Lower-Class Life, 1790–1940. Philadelphia: Temple University Press.

Davis, Robert. 1991. "Anti-Gang Plans Need Work, Aldermen Say." *Chicago Tribune,* October 26, Sec. 1, p. 5.

————. 1992. "City Moves to Control Pay Phones." *Chicago Tribune,* June 4, Sec. 2, p. 6.

Davis, Roger H. 1982a. "Outlaw Motorcyclists: A Problem for Police (Part 1)." *FBI Law Enforcement Bulletin* 51(10):12–17.

————. 1982b. "Outlaw Motorcyclists: A Problem for Police (Part 2)." *FBI Law Enforcement Bulletin* 51(11):16–22.

Dawley, David. 1992. *A Nation of Lords. The Autobiography of the Vice Lords,* 3rd ed. Prospect Heights, IL: Waveland Press.

De La Rosa, Mario, Elizabeth Y. Lambert, and Bernard Gropper. 1990. *Drugs and Violence: Causes, Correlates, and Consequences.* NIDA Research Monograph 103. Bethesda, MD: U.S. Department of Health and Human Services. Public Health Service. Alcohol, Drug Abuse, and Mental Health Administration. National Institute on Drug Abuse.

Delfs, Robert. 1991. "Feeding on the System." *Far East Economic Review,* November 21, pp. 28–30, 34–35.

————. 1992. "Why Pick on Us?" *Far East Economic Review,* March 5, p. 27.

Dellios, Hugh. 1993. "U.S. Street Gangs Serving as Mercenaries for Mexico's Drug Lords." *Chicago Tribune,* July 11, Sec. 1, p. 3.

————. 1994. "Black-Latino Rivalry Accentuates L.A. Change." *Chicago Tribune,* Sec. 1, pp. 19, 24.

Deukmajian, George. 1981 (June). *Report on Youth Gang Violence in California.* Sacramento, CA: Department of Justice, State of California.

Development Services Group Inc. 1993. *National Evaluation of the Youth Gang Drug Prevention Program.* Final Report. Vol. 1: Parts I, II, III (draft). Bethesda, MD, November 22.

DeWitt, Charles B. 1983. "Gang Crimes Investigation/Supervision Unit." A project proposal submitted to the Office of California Justice Planning by the Santa Clara County Justice Division and Department of the Youth Authority.

Dinitz, Simon, and C. Ronald Huff. 1988. *The Figgie Report. Part VI: The Resources of Crime. The Criminal Perspective.* Richmond, VA: Figgie International.

Dolan, Edward F., Jr., and S. Finney. 1984. *Youth Gangs.* New York: Julian Messner.

Dold, Bruce R. 1990. "Gangs Simmer in City's Melting Pot." *Chicago Tribune,* June 10, pp. 1, 18.

Donovan, John. 1988 (August). "An Introduction to Street Gangs." A paper prepared for Senator John Garamemdi's Office, Sacramento, CA.

Dorney, Sean 1990. *Papua New Guinea.* New South Wales, Australia: Random House Australia, pp. 286–319.

Downes, David M. 1966. *The Delinquent Solution.* New York: Free Press.

Drug Enforcement Agency. 1991. "Police Organization Lobbies for Gang Violence Legislation." *Drug Enforcement Report*, February 25.

Dunston, Leonard G. 1990. *Reaffirming Prevention*. Report of the Task Force on Juvenile Gangs. Albany, NY: New York State Division for Youth, March 1.

Duran, Miguel. 1987. "Specialized Gang Supervision Program (SGSP) Progress Report. Los Angeles County Probation Department.

Duxbury, Elaine B. 1993. "Correctional Interventions." In *The Gang Intervention Handbook*, edited by Arnold Goldstein and C. Ronald Huff. Champaign, IL: Research Press, pp. 427–437.

Elliott, Delbert S., David Huizinga, and Suzanne S. Ageton. 1985. *Explaining Delinquency and Drug Use*. Beverly Hills, CA: Sage Publications.

———, and Marvin L. Voss. 1974. *Delinquency and Dropout*. Lexington, MA: Lexington Books.

English, T. J. 1990. *The Westies. Inside the Hell's Kitchen Irish Mob*. New York: G. P. Putnam's.

Erickson, Maynard L., and Gary F. Jensen. 1977. "'Delinquency Is Still Group Behavior!': Toward Revitalizing the Group Premise in the Sociology of Deviance." *The Journal of Criminal Law and Criminology* 68(2):262–273.

Esbensen, Finn-Page, and David Huizinga. 1993. "Gangs, Drugs, and Delinquency in a Survey of Urban Youth." *Criminology* 31(4):565–587.

Fagan, Jeffrey. 1987. "Neighborhood Education, Mobilization, and Organization for Juvenile Crime Prevention." *Annals American Academy of Political and Social Science* 494(November):55–70.

———. 1988 (July). "The Social Organization of Drug Use and Drug Dealing Among Urban Gangs." Criminal Justice Center, John Jay College of Criminal Justice, New York.

———. 1989. "The Social Organization of Drug Use and Drug Dealing Among Urban Gangs." *Criminology* 27(4):633–669.

———. 1990. "Social Processes of Delinquency and Drug Use Among Urban Gangs." In *Gangs in America*, edited by C. Ronald Huff. Newbury Park, CA: Sage Publications, pp. 183–219.

———, Elizabeth Piper, and Melinda Moore. 1986. "Violent Delinquents and Urban Youths." *Criminology* 24(3):439–471.

———, and Sandra Wexler. 1987. "Family Origins of Violent Delinquents." *Criminology* 25(3):643–669.

Faison, Seth. 1994. "U.S. Says 17 in Bronx Gang Rented Rights to Sell Heroin." *The New York Times*. May 27. B16.

Farrington, David P., Leonard Berkowitz, and Donald J. West. 1982. "Differences Between Individual and Group Fights." *British Journal of Social Psychology* 21:323–333.

Fattah, David. 1987. "The House of Umoja as a Case Study for Social Change." *Annals of the American Academy of Political and Social Science* 494 (November):37–41.

Fattah, Sister Falaka. 1988. "Youth and Violence: The Current Crisis." Written Statement. The Select Committee on Children, Youth, and Families. U.S. House of Representatives, March 9.

Federal Register. 1987. "Juvenile Gang Suppression and Intervention Program." Office of Juvenile Justice and Delinquency Prevention (OJJDP), Justice. Vol. 52, No. 133, July 13, pp. 26254–26259.

———. 1989. "Availability of FY 1989 Funds and Request for Applications. Youth Gang Drug Prevention Program." Administration on Children, Youth and Families (ACYF), Office of Human Development Services (OHDS), U.S. Department of Health and Human Services, Vol. 54, No. 71, Friday, April 14, pp. 15108–15129.

———. 1992. "Youth Gang Drug Prevention Program; Availability of Funds and Request for Applications; Notice." Administration on Children, Youth and Families (ACYF), U.S. Department of Health and Human Services. Vol. 57, No. 55, Friday, March 20, pp. 9865–9897.

Feld, Barry C. 1981. "A Comparative Analysis of Organizational Structure and Inmate Subcultures in Institutions for Juvenile Offenders." *Crime and Delinquency* July, pp. 336–365.

Feldman, Ronald A., Timothy E. Caplinger, and John S. Wodarski. 1983. *The St. Louis Conundrum. The Effective Treatment of Anti-Social Youths*. Englewood Cliffs, NJ: Prentice-Hall.

Fink, Janet R. 1987. "Determining the Future Child: Actors on the Juvenile Court Stage." In *The Role of the Juvenile Court, Vol. I*, edited by Francis X. Hartman. New York: Springer-Verlag, pp. 270–307.

Fountain, John W. 1992. "Elgin Shows the Way in Evicting Street Gangs." *Chicago Tribune*, January 16, Sec. 1, pp. 1, 24.

———. 1994. "On Canvas of death, City gangs only part of picture." *Chicago Tribune.* June 13. Section 2, pp. 1, 4.

Friedman, C. Jack, Frederica Mann, and Howard Adelman. 1976. "Juvenile Street Gangs: The Victimization of Youth." *Adolescence* 11(44):527–533.

———, Frederica Mann, and Alfred S. Friedman. 1975. "A Profile of Juvenile Street Gang Members." *Adolescence* 10(40):563–607.

Galea, John. 1982. "Youth Gangs of New York." In *Aggression and Violence*, edited by Peter Marsh and Anne Campbell. New York: St. Martin's Press, pp. 215–228.

———. 1988. Personal communication.

Gallagher, James P. 1992. "As Law Enforcement Crumbles, Russian Crime, Gangs Proliferate." *Chicago Tribune*, September 2, Sec. 1, p. 6.

Genelin, Michael. 1993. "Gang Prosecutions: The Hardest Game in Town." In *The Gang Intervention Handbook*, edited by Arnold Goldstein and C. Ronald Huff. Urbana, IL: Research Press.

———, and Loren Naimen. 1988. "Prosecuting Gang Homicides." *Prosecutor's Notebook.* Vol. X. California District Attorneys' Association.

———. Undated. "Concerns in Trying the Gang Homicide Case." *National Law Enforcement Institute*. Santa Rosa, CA.

General Accounting Office. 1989 (September). *Non Traditional Organized Crime*. Report to the Chairman, Permanent Subcommittee on Investigations, Committee on Governmental Affairs, U.S. Senate.

Gerrard, N. L. 1964. "The Core Member of the Gang." *British Journal of Criminology* 4:361–371.

Gibbons, Sandi. 1988. "Half of Gang Cases Are Rejected." *Van Nuys (CA) Daily News*. April 12.

Giordano, Peggy C. 1978. "Girls, Guys, and Gangs: The Changing Social Context of Female Delinquency." *The Journal of Criminal Law and Criminology* 69(1):126–132.

Goering, Lawrie, and Flynn McRoberts. 1992. "Gang Colors, Fashions, Paint Good Kids as Bad." *Chicago Tribune*, April 13, Sec. 1, pp. 1, 17.

Gold, Martin. 1987. "Social Ecology." In *Handbook of Juvenile Delinquency*, edited by Herbert C. Quay. New York: John Wiley & Sons, pp. 62–105.

———, and Hans W. Mattick. 1974. *Experiment in the Streets: The Chicago Youth Development Project*. Ann Arbor, MI: Institute for Social Research, University of Michigan.

Goldberg, Danny. 1988. "Curbing Liberties No Way to Fight the Gang Problem." *Los Angeles Herald Examiner*, March 15.

Goldstein, Arnold P. 1993. "Gang Intervention: A Historical Review." In *The Gang Intervention Handbook*, edited by Arnold Goldstein and C. Ronald Huff. Champaign, IL: Research Press, pp. 21–51.

———, Barry Glick, Wilam Carthon, and Douglas Blancero. (1994). *The Prosocial Gang*. Thousand Oaks, CA: Sage Publications.

Goldstein, Henry. 1990. *Problem-Oriented Policing*. Philadelphia, PA: Temple University Press.

Goldstein, Paul J. 1985. "The Drugs/Violence Nexus: A Tripartite Conceptual Framework." *Journal of Drug Issues* Fall:493–506.

Gonzalez, David. 1992. "Teen-agers Send a Message of Hate." *The New York Times*, January 16, p. A16.

Gordon, Robert A. 1967. "Social Levels, Social Disability, and Gang Interaction." *American Journal of Sociology* 73(1):42–62.

Gott, Ray. 1988 (June). "Statement." Coordinating Council Meeting, Office of Juvenile Justice and Delinquency Prevention, U.S. Dept. of Justice, Washington, DC.

Gottfredson, Gary D. 1987. "Peer Group Interventions to Reduce the Risk of Delinquency Behavior: A Selective Review and A New Evaluation." *Criminology* 25(3):671–714.

———, and Denise C. Gottfredson. 1985. *Victimization in Schools*. New York: Plenum.

———, Denise C. Gottfredson, and Michael S. Cook (eds.). 1983 (June). *The School Action Effectiveness Study*. Second Interim Report, Part 1, Report No. 342. John Hopkins University, Baltimore, MD.

Grady, William. 1991. "State High Court Upholds a Tough Anti-gang Law." *Chicago Tribune*, November 1, pp. 1, 20.

Grant, William T. Foundation, Commission on Work, Family and Citizenship. Youth and America's Future. 1988a (January). *The Forgotten Half. Non-College Youth in America*. Washington, DC: Commission Office.

———. Foundation, Commission on Work, Family and Citizenship. Youth and America's Future. 1988b (November). *Final Report*. Washington, DC: Commission Office.

Griffin, Jean Lutz. 1992. "Trauma Centers Feel Gang Fallout." *Chicago Tribune*, March 3, p. 3.

Guccione, Jean. 1987. "Computer on Gang Members Being Readied." Office of Criminal Justice Planning News File, December 30.

Hagan, John. 1992. "Juvenile Justice and Delinquency in the Life Course." *Criminal Justice Research Bulletin*. Vol. 7, No. 1. Huntsville, TX: Sam Houston State University Criminal Justice Center, pp. 1–4.

Hagedorn, John. 1988. *People and Folks: Gangs, Crime and the Underclass in a Rust Belt City*. Chicago: Lake View Press.

———. 1990. "Back in the Field Again: Gang Research in the Nineties." In *Gangs in America*, edited by C. Ronald Huff. Newbury Park, CA: Sage Publications, pp. 240–262.

———. 1992. "Gangs, Neighborhoods, and Public Policy." *Social Problems*, 38(4):529–542.

———, Perry Macon, and Joan Moore. 1986 (December). "Final Report, Milwaukee Gang Research Project." Urban Research Center, University of Wisconsin-Milwaukee.

Hahn, Andrew, and Jacqueline Danziger with Bernard Lefkowitz. 1987 (March). *Dropouts in America*. Washington, DC: The Institute for Educational Leadership.

Hamm, Marks. 1993. *American Skinheads: The Criminology and Control of Hate Crime*. Westport, CT: Praeger.

Hargreaves, David H. 1967. *Social Relations in a Secondary School*. New York: Rutledge & Kagan Paul.

Hargrove, Sergeant James. 1981. "Discussion: The Youths' Experiences." In *Youth Crime and Urban Policy*, edited by Robert L. Woodson. Washington, DC: American Enterprise Institute for Public Policy Research, p. 89.

Harris, Mary G. 1988. *CHOLAS, Latino Girls and Gangs.* New York: AMS Press.

Haskell, Martin R., and Lewis Yablonsky. 1982. *Juvenile Delinquency,* 3rd ed. Boston: Houghton Mifflin Company.

Haskins, James. 1974. *Street Gangs. Yesterday and Today.* New York: Hastings House Publishers.

Hawkins, David. 1989. "Risk-Focussed Prevention: Prospects and Strategies." A Presentation at the June 23 meeting of the Coordinating Council on Juvenile Justice and Delinquency Prevention. Office of Juvenile Justice and Delinquency Prevention and the School of Social Work, University of Washington, Seattle.

Hayes, Ronald. 1983. "Testimony before U.S. Senate Subcommittee on Juvenile Justice." *Gang Violence and Control.* Committee on the Judiciary, 98th Congress, 1st Session. Hearings, February 7, 9. Sacramento, CA, p. 65.

Haynes, V. Dion. 1994. "Schools to try room, board and education." *Chicago Tribune.* August 20. Section 1, pp. 1, 10.

Herman. 1992. "Suburbs Map Gang War." *Chicago Sun-Times,* September 18, pp. 1, 17.

Hickey, Maureen, (ed.). 1993. "Survey of Inmates Shows Figures on Gun Use, Gang Involvement." *Compiler.* Illinois Criminal Justice Information Authority, Summer, pp. 3, 7.

Hicks, Jerry. 1988. "D.A.'s New Special Prosecution Team Plans to Fight Gangs on Its Own Turf." *Los Angeles Times,* April 25.

Hinshaw, Dwayne. 1988 (September). "Survey." National Youth Gang Suppression and Intervention Project, School of Social Service Administration, University of Chicago.

Hirschi, Travis. 1969. *Causes of Delinquency.* Berkeley, CA: University of California Press.

Hollin, Clive R. 1993. "Cognitive-Behavioral Interventions." In *The Gang Intervention Handbook,* edited by Arnold P. Goldstein and C. Ronald Huff. Champaign, IL: Research Press, pp. 55–85.

Hollopeter, Clayton. 1988 (November). "Survey." National Youth Gang Suppression and Intervention Project, School of Social Service Administration, University of Chicago.

Horowitz, Ruth. 1983. *Honor and the American Dream.* New Brunswick, NJ: Rutgers University Press.

———. 1987. "Community Tolerance of Gang Violence." *Social Problems* 34(5):437–450.

———. 1990. "Sociological Perspectives on Gangs: Conflicting Definitions and Concepts." In *Gangs in America,* edited by C. Ronald Huff. Newbury Park, CA: Sage Publications, pp. 37–54.

Horwitz, Sari. 1991. "Violent Gangs 'All Over City,' D.C. Chief Says." *The Washington Post,* September 29, pp. A1, A8.

Houston, Jack. 1992a. "New Breed of Cops Taking Their Work Home." *Chicago Tribune,* February 3, Sec. 1, pp. 1, 8.

———. 1992b. "Deportation Gaining as Gang-Fighting Tool." *Chicago Tribune,* July 16, Sec. 1, pp. 1, 7.

Howell, James C. 1994. "Recreating Gang Research: Program and Policy Implications." *Crime and Delinquency* 40(4):495–515.

Howenstein, G. Albert, Jr. 1988. "From the Executive Director." *Newsletter,* Office of Criminal Justice Planning, Summer 3(2):1, Sacramento, CA.

Huff, C. Ronald. 1988. Youth gangs and public policy in Ohio: Findings and recommendations. Paper presented at the Ohio Conference on Youth Gangs and the Urban Underclass. Ohio Stte University, Columbus.

———. 1993. "Gangs in the United States." In *The Gang Intervention Handbook,* edited by Arnold P. Goldstein and C. Ronald Huff. Champaign, IL: Research Press, pp. 3–20.

Hughes, Howard C. 1994. *Final Evaluation Report.* Gang Risk Intervention Pilot Program. Santa Rosa, CA: Hughes Associates Consulting, February 9.

Hunt, Geoffrey, Stephanie Riegel, Tomas Morales, Dan Waldorf. 1993. "Changes in Prison Culture. Prison Gangs and the Case of the 'Pepsi Generation.'" *Social Problems*, 40(3):398–409.

Hutcheson, Ray. 1993. "Blazon Nouveau: Gang Graffiti in the Barrios of Los Angeles and Chicago." In *Gangs: The Origins and Impact of Contemporary Youth Gangs in the United States*, edited by Scott Cummings and Daniel Monti. New York: State University New York Press.

Hyman, Irwin A. 1984. "Testimony before the Subcommittee on Elementary, Secondary, and Vocational Education of the Committee on Education and Labor." U.S. House of Representatives, January 24, p. 82.

Ianni, Francis A. J. 1974. *Black Mafia*. New York: Simon & Schuster.

———. 1989. *The Search for Structure. Report on American Youth Today*. New York: Free Press.

Illinois Criminal Justice Information Authority. 1994. "Juvenile Offenders and Violent Crime." *On Good Authority*. May, pp. 1–4.

Ima, Kenji, and Jeanne Nidorf. 1990 (April). "A Profile of Southeast Asian Refugee Delinquents: The San Diego Experience." San Diego State University. Paper prepared for the Annual Conference of the National Association of Asian Pacific American Education (NAAPAE). (draft.)

Inciardi, James A. 1990. "A Crack-Violence Connection Within a Population of Hard-Core Adolescent Offenders." In *Drugs and Violence: Causes, Correlates and Consequences*, edited by Mario de la Rosa, Elizabeth Y. Lambert, and Bernard Gropper. NIDA Research Monograph 103. U.S. Department of Health and Human Services, Public Health Service, Alcohol, Drug Abuse and Mental Health Administration, National Institute on Drug Abuse, pp. 92–111.

Insight. 1988. "Neighbors Join to Roust the Criminals in the Street." *Insight*, November 28, pp. 8–21.

Institute for Law and Justice. 1994. *Gang Prosecution in the United States*. National Institute of Justice, Office of Justice Programs, U.S. Department of Justice. August.

Jackson, Robert K., and Wesley D. McBride. 1985. *Understanding Street Gangs*. Costa Mesa, CA: Custom Publishing Company.

Jacobs, James B. 1974. "Street Gangs Behind Bars." *Social Problems* 24(3):395–409.

———. 1977. *Stateville: The Penitentiary in Mass Society*. Chicago: University of Chicago Press.

Jankowski, Martin Sánchez. 1991. *Islands in the Street. Gangs and American Urban Society*. Berkeley, CA: University of California Press.

Jansyn, Leon R., Jr. 1966. "Solidarity and Delinquency in a Street Corner Group." *American Sociological Review* 31(5):600–614.

Japanese Ministry of Justice. 1984 (December). "Annual Report on Crime (Summary")." Tokyo: Foreign Press Center.

Jencks, Christopher, and Paul E. Peterson (eds.). 1991. *The Urban Underclass*. Washington, DC: The Brookings Institute.

Joe, Delbert, and Norman Robinson. 1978. "Chinese Youth Gangs: An Investigation of Their Origins and Activities in Vancouver Schools." A paper presented at the Annual Conference of the American Educational Research Association. Toronto, Ontario, March.

———. 1980. "Chinatown's Immigrant Gangs." *Criminology* 18:337–345.

Johnson, Bruce D., Terry Williams, Kojo Dei, and Harry Sanabria. 1988. "Drug Abuse and the Inner City: Impact of Hard Drug Use and Sales on Low Income Communities." New York State Division of Substance Abuse Research, October 31.

Johnson, David R. 1973. "Crime Patterns in Philadelphia, 1840–70." In *The People of Phila-*

delphia. A History of Ethnic Groups and Lower-Class Life, 1790–1940, edited by Allen E. Davis and Mark H. Haller. Philadelphia: Temple University Press, pp. 89–110.

Johnson, Dirk. 1993. "2 Out of 3 Young Black Men in Denver Are on Gang Suspect List." *The New York Times*, December 11, p. A7.

Johnstone, John W. C. 1981. "Youth Gangs and Black Suburbs." *Pacific Sociological Review* 24(3):355–375.

Jouzaitis, Carol. 1992. "WPA-Type Programs May Help People Off Welfare." *Chicago Tribune*, August 16, pp. 1, 15.

Justice Research and Statistics Association. 1993. *Violent Crime and Drug Abuse in Rural Areas: Issues, Concerns, and Programs*. Washington, D.C.: Bureau of Justice Assistance, Office of Justice Programs, U.S. Department of Justice. September.

Kahn, Brian, Project Coordinator, and R. Neil Zinn. 1978. "Prison Gangs in the Community: A Briefing Document for the Board of Corrections." County of Sonoma, CA, June 14.

Kass, John, and George Papajohn. 1994. "Group's rapid success and real inside story." *Chicago Tribune*. July 24, Section 4, pp. 1, 5.

Katz, Jack. 1988. *The Seduction of Crime: Moral and Sensual Attractions in Drug Evil*. New York: Basic Books.

Katz, Jesse. 1990. "Officers' Folksy Tactics Pay Off in Gang Domain." *Los Angeles Times*, November 5, pp. B1, B6.

Kifner, John K. 1991. "New Immigrant Wave from Asia Gives the Underworld New Faces." *The New York Times*, January 6, pp. 1, 13.

Kinzer, Stephen. 1992. "Youths Adrift in a New Germany Turn to Neo-Nazis." *The New York Times*, September 28, p. A1.

Klein, Malcolm W. 1968. *From Association to Guilt: The Group Guidance Project in Juvenile Gang Intervention*. Los Angeles, CA: Youth Studies Center, University of Southern California and the Los Angeles County Probation Department.

————. 1969. "Violence in American Juvenile Gangs." In *Crime of Violence* series, Vol. 13, *National Commission on the Causes and Prevention of Violence*, edited by D. J. Mulvihill, M. M. Tumin, and L. A. Curtis. Washington, DC: U.S. Government Printing Office, pp. 1427–1460.

————. 1971. *Street Gangs and Street Workers*. Englewood Cliffs, NJ: Prentice-Hall.

————. 1989. Personal communication. February 21.

————. 1992. "Twenty-five Years of Youth Gangs and Violence." Social Science Research Institute, Los Angeles: University of Southern California, February 9.

————. (Forthcoming.) *The American Street Gang: Its Nature, Prevalence and Control*. New York: Oxford University Press.

————, and Lois Y. Crawford. 1967. "Groups, Gangs, and Cohesiveness." *Journal of Research in Crime and Delinquency* 4(1):63–75.

————, and Cheryl L. Maxson. 1987. "Street Gang Violence." In *Violent Crime, Violent Criminals*, edited by M. E. Wolfgang and N. Weiner. Beverly Hills, CA: Sage Publications.

————, Cheryl L. Maxson, and Lea C. Cunningham. 1988 (May). "Gang Involvement in Cocaine 'Rock' Trafficking." Project Summary/Final Report, Center for Research on Crime and Social Control, Social Science Research Institute, University of Southern California. Los Angeles.

————. 1991. "'Crack,' Street Gangs, and Violence." *Criminology* 29(4):623–650.

————, Cheryl L. Maxson, and Margaret A. Gordon. 1987. "Police Response to Street Gang Violence: Improving the Investigative Process." Center for Research on Crime and Social Control, Social Science Research Institute, University of Southern California, Los Angeles.

————, with Barbara G. Myerhoff (eds.), 1967). *Juvenile Gangs in Context: Theory, Research and Action*. Englewood Cliffs, NJ: Prentice-Hall.

Knapp, Elaine S. 1988. "Kids, Gangs, and Drugs." *Embattled Youth*. Lexington, KY: The Council of State Governments, pp. 10–15.

Knopf, Terry Ann. 1969. *Youth Patrols: An Experiment in Community Participation*. Waltham, MA: The Lemberg Center for the Study of Violence, Brandeis University.

Knox, George W. 1991. Personal communication. August 26.

————. 1991a. *An Introduction to Gangs*. Berrien Springs, MI: Vande Vere Publishing Ltd.

————. 1991b. "U.S. Gangs: An Analysis of Recent Data." Paper presented at the 43rd Annual Meeting of the American Society of Criminology. San Francisco. November 20.

————. 1991c. "Findings from the 1991 National Survey of Juvenile Corrections. A Preliminary Report." Gang Crime Research Center, Chicago State University, Department of Corrections and Criminal Justice.

————, Edward O. Tromanhauser, and David Laske. 1991. "Gangs in the Chicago School System. Preliminary Results from the Fall 1991 Safe School Survey." Gang Crime Research Center, Chicago State University, Department of Corrections and Criminal Justice.

Kobrin, Solomon. 1951. "The Conflict of Values in Delinquency Areas." *American Sociological Review* 16(1):653–661.

————. 1959. "The Chicago Area Project—A Twenty-Five Year Assessment." *Annals of the American Academy of Political and Social Science* 322 (March):1–29.

————, and Malcolm W. Klein. 1983. *Community Treatment of Juvenile Offenders*. Beverly Hills, CA: Sage Publications.

Kornblum, William S. 1974. *The Blue Collar Community*. Chicago: University of Chicago Press.

Kornhauser, Ruth R. 1978. *Social Sources of Delinquency*. Chicago: University of Chicago Press.

Kotlowitz, Alex. 1988. "Lords of the Slums." *The Wall Street Journal*, September 30, p. 1, 13.

Kotulak, Ronald. 1993. "How Brain's Chemistry Unleashes Violence." *Chicago Tribune*, December 13, Sec. 1, pp. 1, 8.

Kowski, Kim. 1988. "Cities Use Variety of Strategies to Wage War on Violence." *Los Angeles Herald*, May 13.

Koziol, Ronald. 1990. "Suburbs Trying to Nip Gang Activities in Bud." *Chicago Tribune*, August 12, Sec. 1, pp. 1, 20.

Krisberg, Barry. 1974. "Gang Youth and Hustling: The Psychology of Survival." *Issues in Criminology* 9 (Spring 1):115–131.

Kuczka, Susan. 1991. "Suburbs Form Team to Curb Gang Threat." *Chicago Tribune*, November 21, Sec. 3, p. 11.

Kyle, Charles L. 1984 (June). *"Los Preciosos" The Magnitude of and Reasons for the Hispanic Dropout Problem: A Case Study of Two Chicago Public Schools*. Ph.D. Dissertation, Sociology Department, Northwestern University.

Latimore, James. 1985. *Weeding Out the Target Population. The Law of Accountability in a Manpower Program*. Westport, CT: Greenwood Press.

Lauderback, David, Joy Hansen, and Dan Waldorf. 1992. "'Sisters Are Doin' It for Themselves': A Black Female Gang in San Francisco." *The Gang Journal* 1 (1):57–72.

Laurie, Bruce E. 1973. "Fire Companies and Gangs in Southwark: The 1840s." In *The Peoples of Philadelphia*, edited by Allen F. Davis and Mark Haller. Philadelphia: Temple University Press, pp. 71–87.

Lee, Felicia R. 1991. "For Gold Earrings and Protection, More Girls Take Violence." *The New York Times*, November 11, pp. A1, 16.

Lehmann, Daniel J. 1993. "Prosecution Blamed as Judge Orders 7 New Trials." *Chicago Sun-Times*, September 21, pp. 1, 6.

Levitan, Sar A., and Frank Gallo. 1990. "Uncle Sam's Helping Hand: Educating, Training, and Employing the Disadvantaged." In *New Developments in Worker Training: A Legacy for the 1990's*, edited by Louis A. Ferman, Michele Hoyman, Joel Cutcher-Gershenfeld, and Ernest J. Savoie. Madison, WI: University of Wisconsin, Industrial Relations Research Association.

Ley, David. 1975. "The Street Gang in Its Milieu." In *The Social Economy of Cities*, edited by Gary Gappert and Harold M. Rose. Beverly Hills, CA: Sage Publications, pp. 247–273.

Lieber, J. B. 1975. "Philadelphia's Brotherly Death." *The Nation* (January, 220):42–47.

Lo, T. Wing. 1986. *Outreaching Social Work in Focus*. Hong Kong: Cantos.

Lockwood, William. 1988. "Parole Services Branch." Department of the Youth Authority, Gang Information Services Unit, Sacramento, CA.

Long, Ray. 1993. "Secret Service Plan Targets Cabrini Green Gangs, Crime." *Chicago Sun-Times*, October 4, p. 5.

Los Angeles City News Service. 1988. "Police Chief Urges Declaration of National Drug Emergency." April 20.

Los Angeles County Office of Education. 1991 (July). *School Gang Survey*. Los Angeles County Office of Education.

Los Angeles County Probation Department. 1988. "Gang Community Reclamation Project." Application submitted to Office of Juvenile Justice and Delinquency Prevention, U.S. Department of Justice, Washington, DC. June 23.

Los Angeles County Sheriff's Department. 1985. "Testimony." California State Task Force on Youth Gang Violence.

————. 1991. "War Against Gangs Is Far from Over, Uno Leaders Say." *Los Angeles Times*, Sec. B, pp. 1, 8.

Los Angeles Unified School District. 1989. "Innovative Support Programs for At-Risk Youth and Their Families in Communities with High Incidence of Gangs Involved in Illicit Drug Use." 1988 Gang Task Force Parent-Community Recommendations.

Lyman, Michael D. 1989. *Gangland. Drug Trafficking by Organized Criminals*. Springfield, IL: Charles C. Thomas.

Manikas, Peter, John P. Heinz, Mindy S. Trossman, and Jack C. Doppelt. 1990 (November). *Criminal Justice Policy Making: Boundaries and Borderlands*. Final Report of the Criminal Justice Project. Evanston, IL: Center for Urban Affairs and Policy Research, Northwestern University.

Maxson, Cheryl L., Margaret A. Gordon, and Malcolm W. Klein. 1985. "Differences Between Gang and Nongang Homicides." *Criminology* 23:209–222.

————, and Malcolm W. Klein. 1990. "Street Gang Violence: Twice as Great or Half as Great?" In *Gangs in America*, edited by C. Ronald Huff. Newbury Park, CA: Sage Publications, pp. 71–102.

————, Malcolm W. Klein, and Lea Cunningham. 1992 (draft). "Defining Gang Crime: Revisited." Presented at the Western Society of Criminology Meetings, February. Center for the Study of Crime and Social Control Research Institute, University of Southern California.

Mayer, John A. 1983. "Notes Towards a Working Definition of Social Control in Historical Analysis." In *Social Control and the State*, edited by Stanley Cohen and Andrew Scull. New York: St. Martin's Press, pp. 17–38.

McBride, Wesley D. 1988. Personal communication. Los Angeles County Sheriff's Department, November 18..

————. 1994. Personal communication. Los Angeles County Sheriff's Department. February 4.

————. 1993. "Part II—Police Departments and Gang Intervention: The Operation Safe Streets Concept." In *The Gang Intervention Handbook*, edited by Arnold P. Goldstein and C. Ronald Huff. Champaign, IL: Research Press, pp. 411–415.

McConnell, William W., and William R. Bricker. 1987. *President's Child Safety Partnership*. Final Report. Washington, DC: U.S. Government Printing Office.

McGarry, T. W., and Steve Padilla. 1988. "Experts Warn Gang Sweeps May Have a Negative Effect." *Los Angeles Times*, April 24.

McKenna, George. 1990. "Lunch Speech." *Community Mobilization*, Conference Proceedings. Sacramento, CA: Office of Criminal Justice Planning, pp. 23–29.

McKinney, Kay C. 1988 (September). "Juvenile Gangs: Crime and Drug Trafficking." *Juvenile Justice Bulletin*. Office of Juvenile Justice and Delinquency Prevention, U.S. Department of Justice.

Merton, Robert K. 1957. *Social Theory and Social Structure*. Glencoe, IL: The Free Press.

Metropolitan Court Judges Committee. 1986 (August). "Deprived Children: A Judicial Response and Recommendation." National Council of Juvenile and Family Court Judges. Reno, NE: University of Nevada.

————. 1988 (June). "Drugs—The American Family in Crisis: A Judicial Response." National Council of Juvenile and Family Court Judges. Reno, NE: University of Nevada.

Miller, Benjamin. 1992. "Funding Issue Absent from Supreme Court Annual Report." *The Compiler*. Illinois Criminal Justice Information Authority, Spring, p. 6.

Miller, Jeffrey. 1988. "Councilman Calls for Sale of Gang Parks." *Los Angeles Times*, San Gabriel Zone, March 31, p. 1.

Miller, Ken. 1992. Personal Communication. Ethan Allan Boys School, Wales, Wisconsin, October 16.

Miller, Walter B. 1958. "Lower Class Culture as a Generating Milieu of Gang Delinquency." *The Journal of Social Issues* 14(3):5–19.

————. 1962. "The Impact of a 'Total-Community' Delinquency Control Project." *Social Problems* 19(2):168–191.

————. 1973. "Ideology and Criminal Justice Policy: Some Current Issues." *The Journal of Criminal Law and Criminology* 64(2):141–162.

————. 1975. *Violence by Youth Gangs and Youth Groups as a Crime Problem in Major American Cities*. National Institute for Juvenile Justice and Delinquency Prevention, Office of Juvenile Justice and Delinquency Prevention, U.S. Department of Justice. Washington, DC: U.S. Government Printing Office.

————. 1976a. "Violent Crimes in City Gangs." In *Juvenile Delinquency*, 3rd ed., edited by Rose Giallombardo. New York: John Wiley & Sons, pp. 349–364.

————. 1976b. "Youth Gangs in the Urban Crisis Era." In *Delinquency, Crime and Society*, edited by James F. Short, Jr. Chicago: University of Chicago Press, pp. 91–128.

————. 1977 (September). "Conceptions, Definitions, and Images of Youth Gangs." Center for Criminal Justice, Harvard Law School.

————. 1980. "Gangs, Groups, and Serious Youth Crime." In *Critical Issues in Juvenile Delinquency*, edited by David Schichor and Delos H. Kelly. Lexington, MA: D. C. Health and Company, pp. 115–138.

————. 1982. *Crime by Youth Gangs and Groups in the United States*. National Institute for Juvenile Justice and Delinquency Prevention, Office of Juvenile Justice and Delinquency Prevention, U.S. Department of Justice. Washington, DC: Office of Juvenile Justice and Delinquency Prevention.

————. 1990. "When the United States Has Failed to Solve Its Youth Gang Problem." In

Gangs in America, edited by C. Ronald Huff. Newbury Park, CA: Sage Publications, pp. 263–287.

Monroe, Sylvester. 1992 (June). "Life in the Hood." *Times Magazine*, pp. 37–38.

Moore, Joan W. 1978. *Homeboys*. Philadelphia, PA: Temple University Press.

————. 1988a. "Cooking Gang Statistics." *Los Angeles Herald Examiner*, April 17.

————. 1988b. "Introduction." In John Hagedorn, *People and Folks: Gangs, Crime and the Underclass in a Rust Belt City*. Chicago: Lake View Press.

————. 1990. "Gangs, Drugs, Violence." In *Drugs and Violence: Causes, Correlates and Consequences*, edited by Mario de la Rosa, Elizabeth Y. Lambert, and Bernard Gropper. NIDA Research Monograph 103. U.S. Department of Health and Human Services, Public Health Service, Alcohol, Drug Abuse and Mental Health Administration, National Institute on Drug Abuse, pp. 160–176.

————. 1991. *Going Down to the Barrio*. Philadelphia: Temple University Press.

————, Diego Vigil, and Robert Garcia. 1983. "Residence and Territoriality in Chicano Gangs." *Social Problems* 31(2):182–194.

Morales, Armando. 1982. "The Mexican American Gang Member: Evaluation and Treatment." In *Mental Health and Hispanic Americans*, edited by Rosina M. Becerra, Marvin Karno, and Javier I. Escobar. New York: Grune and Stratton, pp. 139–155.

————. 1989. "Urban Gang Violence: A Psychosocial Crisis." In *Social Work: A Profession of Many Faces*, edited by Armando Morales and Bradford W. Sheafer. Boston: Allyn and Bacon, Inc., pp. 413–450.

————, and Bradford W. Sheafer. 1989. "Gang Violence and Homicide Prevention." In *Social Work: A Profession of Many Faces*, edited by Armando Morales and Bradford W. Sheafor. Boston: Allyn and Bacon, Inc., pp. 605–613, 629–630.

Morash, Merry. 1983. "Gangs, Groups, and Delinquency." *The British Journal of Criminology* 23(4):309–335.

Morris, Noval, and Michael Tonry. 1990. *Between Prison and Probation*. New York: Oxford University Press.

Muehlbauer, Gene, and Laura Dodder. 1983. *The Losers. Gang Delinquency in an American Suburb*. New York: Praeger.

Mydans, Seth. 1990a. "Life in Girls' Gang: Colors and Bloody Noses." *The New York Times*, National, January 29, pp. A1, A12.

————. 1990b. "Trophies from the Gang Wars: Wheel Chairs." *The New York Times*, December 6, pp. A1, A12.

————. 1991. "As Cultures Meet, Gang War Paralyzes a City in California." *The New York Times*, May 6, pp. A1, A12.

————. 1992. "FBI Setting Sights on Street Gangs." *The New York Times*, May 24, Sec. 4, p. 8.

Myerhoff, Howard L., and Barbara G. Myerhoff. 1976. "Field Observations of Middle Class 'Gangs'." In *Juvenile Delinquency*, 3rd ed., edited by R. Giallombardo. New York: John Wiley & Sons, pp. 295–304.

National Advisory Committee on Criminal Justice Standards and Goals. 1976. *Report of the Task Force on Juvenile Justice and Delinquency Prevention*. Washington, DC: U.S. Government Printing Office.

National Center on Education and the Economy, Commission on the Skills of the American Workforce. 1990. *High Skills or Low Wages*. Washington, DC: William T. Grant Foundation.

National Crime Prevention Institute. 1988. *Habitual Juvenile Offenders: Guidelines*. Office of Juvenile Justice and Delinquency Prevention and the Serious Habitual Offender Information Clearinghouse, University of Louisville, KY.

National Institute of Corrections. 1991 (October). *Management Strategies in Disturbances and with Gangs/Disruptive Groups*. U.S. Department of Justice.

National Institute of Education. 1978 (January). *Violent Schools, Safe Schools: The Safe School Study Report to the Congress*. Vol 1. Washington, DC: U.S. Government Printing Office.

National Institute of Justice. 1992 (April). "Evaluation of Operation Weed and Seed." *Research and Evaluation Plan 1992*. Office of Justice Programs, U.S. Department of Justice, pp. 174–178.

———. 1994 (April). *1994–95 NIJ Program Plan*. Office of Justice Programs, U.S. Department of Justice.

National Law Enforcement Institute. 1990. "The CRIPS and Bloods—Black Street Gangs." Santa Rosa, CA.

Needle, Jerome A., and William Vaughan Stapleton. 1983 (September). *Police Handling of Youth Gangs*. Washington, DC: U.S. Department of Justice, Office of Juvenile Justice and Delinquency Prevention, National Institute for Juvenile Justice and Delinquency Prevention.

New York City Youth Board. 1957. *Teenage Gangs*. New York: New York City Youth Board.

New York City Youth Board. 1960. *Reaching the Fighting Gang*. New York: New York City Youth Board.

New York State Assembly, Subcommittee on the Family. 1974a (July). *The Resurgence of Youth Gangs in New York City*. Study Report No. 1.

———. 1974b (October). *Armies of the Streets. A Report on the Structure, Membership and Activities of Youth Gangs in the City of New York*. Study Report No. 2.

The New York Times. 1994. "Connecticut Monitors Inmate Phone Calls." *The New York Times*, April 24, p. 11.

Nidorf, Barry J. 1988. *Gang Alternative and Prevention Program. Program Policy and Procedure Handbook*. Los Angeles: County of Los Angeles Probation Department.

———. Undated. "Gang Member Supervision Program." Los Angeles: Los Angeles County Probation Department.

O'Connell, Richard J. 1988. "L.A. Gangs: Setting Up Shop All Over the U.S." *Crime Control Digest* 22(48):1, 7–9.

O'Connor, Matt. 1991a. "Noah Robinson Tied to Gang Drug Ring." *Chicago Tribune*, June 4, p. 7.

———. 1991b. "Robinson Hired Rukns, Court Is Told." *Chicago Tribune*, June 5, p. 7.

———. 1991c. "U.S.: Rukns Grew with Robinson's Help." *Chicago Tribune*, August 27, Sec. 2, p. 1.

———. 1992. "19 Indicted on Federal Drug Counts." *Chicago Tribune*, March 10, Sec. 2, pp. 1, 7.

———. 1993. "More Rukn Convictions Fall." *Chicago Tribune*, September 21, Sec. 1, pp. 1, 12.

———. 1994. "Rukn informant in botched trials gets 30 years." *Chicago Tribune*. June 14. Section 2, pp. 1, 6.

———, and Christine Haines. 1992. "ACLU Opposes Tougher CHA Security." *Chicago Tribune*, October 31, Sec. 1, pp. 1, 7.

O'Connor, Mike. 1994. "A New U.S. Import in El Salvador: Street Gangs." *The New York Times*. July 3, p. 3.

Office of Criminal Justice Planning Quarterly Newsletter. 1990. "Copycat Gangs: Phenomenon Among the Wealthy." *Newsline*, Vol. 5, No. 2 (Summer), p. 11.

Office of Justice Programs. 1990. "Weed and Seed." U.S. Justice Department, Washington, DC, October 30.

Office of Juvenile Justice and Delinquency Prevention. 1994. "A Comprehensive Response to America's Gang Problem." *FY 1994 Discretionary Competitive Program Announcements and Application Kit*. Office of Justice Programs, U.S. Department of Justice. NCJ #147529, pp. 38–51.

Oleisky, Walter. 1981. "The Inner City Battle Zone." *Police Product News* 5(7):26–29, 32–33.

Olen, Helaine, and Paul Lieberman. 1991. "National Tracking of Gangs Proposed." *Los Angeles Times*, February 1, pp. B1, B2.

Orange County, California Probation. 1989 (June). "A Youth Gang Drug Prevention, Social, School Program." Application submitted to the U.S. Department of Health and Human Services.

Oschlies, W. 1979. *Juvenile Delinquency in Eastern Europe: Interpretations, Dynamics, Facts*. Cologne, Germany: Boehlau Verlag.

Ostrow, Ronald J. 1992. "FBI Takes Aim at Car Jackers." *Chicago Sun-Times*, September 16, p. 28.

Overend, William. 1988. "New LAPD Tally May Cut Gang Killing Score." *Los Angeles Times*, October 20.

Papajohn, George, and John Kass. 1993. "Imprisoned Gang Leader's New Tool: Politics." *Chicago Tribune*, August 1, Sec. 1, pp. 1, 15.

Park, Robert E., and Ernest W. Burgess. 1921. *Introduction to the Science of Sociology*. Chicago: University of Chicago Press.

Patrick, James. 1973. *A Glasgow Gang Observed*. London: Eyre Methuen.

Pearl, Janet A. 1988. "Former Gang Members Earn Cash, Self-Respect." *Columbus Dispatch*, Columbus, OH.

Pearson, Geoffrey. 1983. *Hooligan. A History of Reportable Fears*. New York: Schocken Books.

Pérez-Peña, Richard. 1993. "Halfway Houses Being Misused, Jail Critics Say." *The New York Times*. November 1, p. A20.

Pennell, Susan. 1983 (December). *San Diego Street Youth Program. Final Evaluation*. San Diego: Association of Governments.

People [Illinois] v. M.A. [A Minor Appellee]. 1988. *Illinois Reports*. Illinois Supreme Court, No. 64476, September 22, pp. 135–147. Bloomington, IL, 1988, 1989.

Perkins, Useni Eugene. 1987. *Explosion of Chicago's Black Street Gangs: 1900 to Present*. Chicago: Third World Press.

Petersilia, Joan, and Susan Turner. 1993. "Intensive Probation and Parole." In *Crime and Justice: A Review of Research*, Vol. 17, edited by Michael Tonry. Chicago: University of Chicago Press, pp. 281–335.

Peterson, Paul E. 1991. "The Urban Underclass and the Poverty Paradox." In *The Urban Underclass*, edited by Christopher Jencks and Paul E. Peterson. Washington, DC: The Brookings Institution, pp. 3–27.

Philadelphia Police Department, Preventive Patrol Unit. 1987. *Policy and Procedure*, Vol 1. Philadelphia: Philadelphia Police Department Juvenile Aid Division.

Philibosian, Robert H. 1986 (January). *State Task Force on Youth Gang Violence. Final Report*. Sacramento, CA: California Council on Criminal Justice.

————. 1989. "Testimony before U.S. Senate Subcommittee on Juvenile Justice." *Gang Violence and Control*. Committee on the Judiciary, 98th Congress. 1st Session Hearings, February 7, 9. Sacramento, California.

Pillsbury, Samuel H. 1988. "Gang Sweeps Only Look Good." *Los Angeles Times*, April 17.

Pineda, Charles, Jr. 1974. "Chicano Gang—Barrios in East Los Angeles—Maravilla. Sacramento, CA: California Youth Authority.

Pitchess, Peter J. 1979 (May). "Street Gangs." Los Angeles County Sheriff's Department, Los Angeles County, Youth Services Bureau, Street Gang Detail.

Pleines, Edward. 1987. Personal communication. Chicago.

Poston, Richard W. 1971. *The Gang and the Establishment.* New York: Harper & Row.

President's Child Safety Partnership. 1987. *A Report to the President.* Washington, DC: U.S. Government Printing Office.

President's Commission on Organized Crime. 1985. *Organized Crime of Asian Origin.* Washington, DC: U.S. Government Printing Office.

Prophet, Matthew. 1988. "Youth Gangs." News Conference. Superintendent, Portland Public Schools, Portland, OR, February 4.

Puffer, J. Adams. 1912. *The Boy and His Gang.* Boston: Houghton Mifflin Company.

Quality Education for Minorities Project. 1990 (January). *Education that Works: An Action Plan for the Education of Minorities.* Cambridge, MA: Massachusetts Institute of Technology.

Quicker, John C. 1983. *Homegirls.* San Pedro, CA: International Universities Press.

Rand, Alice. 1987. "Transitional Life Events and Desistence from Delinquency and Crime." In *From Boy to Man, From Delinquency to Crime,* edited by Marvin E. Wolfgang, Terence P. Thornberry, and Robert M. Figlio. Chicago: University of Chicago Press.

Recktenwald, William. 1991a. "Farragut Closed by Gang Fights." *Chicago Tribune,* November 7, Sec. 3, pp. 1, 22.

————. 1991b. "L.A. Gang Moving In, Police Say." *Chicago Tribune,* November 8, Sec. 1, pp. 1, 15.

Reddick, Alonzo J. 1987 (October). *Issue Paper: Youth Gangs in Florida.* Committee on Youth, Florida House of Representatives.

Regulus, Thomas A. 1992 (January). "Corrections." Technical Assistance Manual. *National Youth Gang Suppression and Intervention Program.* Chicago: School of Social Service Administration, University of Chicago.

Reiner, Ira. 1992 (May). *Gangs, Crime and Violence in Los Angeles.* Los Angeles, CA: Office of the District Attorney of the County of Los Angeles.

Reiss, Albert J., Jr. 1987. "Co-offending and Criminal Careers." In *Crime and Justice: A Review of Research,* Vol. 10, edited by M. T. Tony and N. Morris. Chicago: University of Chicago Press, pp. 229–282.

————, and Jeffrey A. Roth (eds.). 1993. *Understanding and Preventing Violence.* Washington, DC: National Academy Press.

Riley, William E. Undated. "Prison Gangs: An Introduction." Washington State Penitentiary.

Robin, Gerald D. 1967. "Gang Member Delinquency in Philadelphia." In *Juvenile Gangs in Context: Theory, Research, and Action,* edited by M. W. Klein and B. G. Myerhoff. Englewood Cliffs, NJ: Prentice-Hall, pp. 15–24.

Roehl, Janice, and Royer F. Cook. 1984 (February). *Evaluation of the Urban Crime Prevention Program.* Washington, DC: U.S. Department of Justice, National Institute of Justice.

Roper, Clinton. 1988 (December). Personal communication. Chicago.

Rosenbaum, Dennis P. 1987. "The Theory and Research Behind Neighborhood Watch: Is It a Sound Fear and Crime Reduction Strategy?" *Crime and Delinquency* 33:103–134.

————, and Jane A. Grant. 1983. *Gangs and Youth Problems in Evanston: Research Findings and Policy Options.* Evanston, IL: Center for Urban Affairs and Policy Research, Northwestern University, July 22.

Rossi, Rosalind. 1991a. "Robinson Wanted Fort to Join City Colleges Deal, El Rukn Says." *Chicago Sun-Times,* July 18, p. 28.

————. 1991b. "Racketeering Trial Opens for Six El Rukns." *Chicago Sun-Times,* October 2, p. 7.

Royster, Eugene. 1974. "Final Report. Philadelphia Evaluation of the Youth Development Program." Philadelphia: Lincoln University Institute for Policy Analysis and Program Evaluation, March 1.

Rudel, David C. 1991. "School Votes Focus on Local Disputes." *Chicago Tribune*, October 9, Sec. 1, pp. 1, 18.

Rutter, Michael, and Henri Giller. 1983. *Juvenile Delinquency: Trends and Perspectives*. New York: The Guilford Press.

———, Barbara Maughan, Peter Mortimore, Janet Ouston, and Alan Smith. 1979. *Fifteen Thousand Hours*. Cambridge, MA: Harvard University Press.

Saavedia, M. E. 1991. "More than 50% in Poll Know Gang Members." *The Arizona Republic*, June 9, p. A7.

Sager, Mike. 1988. "Death in Venice." *Rolling Stone*, September, pp. 64–116.

Sahagun, Louis. 1990a. "Gang Crime Drops Sharply in South L.A." *Los Angeles Times*, May 4, p. 1.

———. 1990b. "Fight Against Gangs Turns to Social Solution." *Los Angeles Times*, November 11, pp. 1, A3.

Sample, Herbert A. 1988. "Brown Urges State Assault on Gangs." *Bee Capitol Bureau*, Sacramento, CA, April 20.

Sampson, Edwin H., III. 1985. *Final Report of the Grand Jury*. Circuit Court of the Eleventh Judicial Circuit of Florida in and for the County of Dade. Fall Term. May 14.

Sampson, Robert J. 1986. "Effects of Socioeconomic Context on Official Reaction to Juvenile Delinquency." *American Sociological Review* 5 (December):876–885.

Sampson, Robert J. 1993. "Linking Time and Place: Dynamic Contextualism and the Future of Criminological Inquiry." *Journal of Research in Crime and Delinquency*. Special issue: Symposium on the Future of Research in Crime and Delinquency, 30(4):426–444.

———, and W. Byron Groves. 1989. "Community Structure and Crime: Testing Social Disorganization Theory." *American Journal of Sociology* 94(4):774–802.

———, and John H. Laub. 1993. *Crime in the Making: Pathways and Turning Points Through Life*. Cambridge: Harvard University Press.

———, and William J. Wilson. 1991. "Race Crime and Urban Inequality." Paper presented at the 50th Annual Meeting of the American Society of Criminology, San Francisco, November 21.

San Diego Association of Governments. 1982 (June). *Juvenile Violence and Gang-Related Crime*. San Diego, CA: Association of State Governments.

Sanders, William B. 1994. *Gangbangs and Drive-Bys*. New York: Aldine De Gruyter.

Santa Clara County Probation Department. 1984. "Gang Crimes Investigation/Supervision Unit." Application to the California Department of the Youth Authority. San Jose, CA: Santa Clara Probation Department.

Sarnecki, Jerzy. 1986 (January). *Delinquent Networks*. Stockholm: Research Division, National Swedish Council for Crime Prevention, Report No. 1986:1.

Savitz, Leonard D., Lawrence Rosen, and Michael Lalli. 1980. "Delinquency and Gang Membership as Related to Victimization." *Victimology* 5(2–4):152–160.

Schiller, Steven. 1988 (June). Personal Communication. Cook County Criminal Court, Chicago, IL.

Schlossman, Steven, Gail Zellman, and Richard Shavelson. 1984 (May). *Delinquency Prevention in South Chicago. A Fifty-Year Assessment of the Chicago Area Project*. Santa Monica, CA: Rand.

Schwartz, Bob. 1988. "Santa Ana OKs School Anti-Gang Pilot Project." *Los Angeles Times*, March 8, p. 45.

Schwendinger, Herman, and Julia Siegel Schwendinger. 1985. *Adolescent Subcultures and Delinquency*. Research Edition. New York: Praeger.

Scott, Peter. 1956 (July). "Gangs and Delinquent Groups in London." *British Journal of Delinquency*, 7:4–26.

Shade, Oscar D. 1988 (May). "Ethan Allen School Program Descriptions." Wales, WI: State of Wisconsin/Department of Health and Social Services.

Shankar, Thom. 1993. "Neo-Nazi Attacks Call Turk Gangs To Arms." *Chicago Tribune*, August 30, Sec. 1, p. 3.

Shannon, Lyle W., Judith L. McKim, James P. Curry, and Lawrence J. Haffner. 1988. *Criminal Career Continuity: Its Social Context*. New York: Human Sciences Press.

Shaw, Clifford R., and Henry D. McKay. 1931. *Social Factors in Juvenile Delinquency. Report on the Causes of Crime*, Vol II. National Commission on Law Observance and Enforcement. Washington, DC: U.S. Government Printing Office.

———. 1943. *Juvenile Delinquency and Urban Areas*. Chicago: University of Chicago Press.

Sherman, Lawrence William. 1970 (November). "Youth Workers, Police and the Gangs: Chicago, 1956–1970." Master's thesis in the Division of Social Sciences, University of Chicago.

Short, James F., Jr. 1963. Introduction to *The Gang: A Study of One Thousand Three Hundred Thirteen Gangs in Chicago* by Frederic M. Thrasher. Chicago: University of Chicago Press.

———. 1976. "Gangs, Politics, and the Social Order." In *Delinquency, Crime and Society*, edited by James F. Short, Jr. Chicago: University of Chicago Press.

———. 1990. *Delinquency and Society*. Englewood Cliffs, NJ: Prentice-Hall.

———, and John Molland. 1976. "Politics and Youth Gangs: A Follow-up Study." *Sociological Quarterly* 17:162–179.

———, and Fred L. Strodtbeck. 1965. *Group Process and Gang Delinquency*. Chicago: University of Chicago Press.

Silbert, Jeffrey M., Leon Cristiano, and Gina Nunez-Cuenca. 1988 (April). "Proposal. Juvenile Gang Information and Coordination Project." Draft of a proposal prepared for the Dade-Miami Criminal Justice Council, Juvenile Justice Committee, by the Department of Justice Assistance.

Skolnick, Jerome H. 1969. *The Politics of Protest*. Washington, DC: National Commission on the Causes and Prevention of Violence.

———. 1988. "The Social Structure of Street Drug Dealing." *BCS Forum*. Bureau of Criminal Statistics. Sacramento: Office of the Attorney General.

———. 1992. "Gangs in the Post-Industrial Ghetto." *The American Prospect* (Winter) No. 8:109–120.

Smith, Cyril S., M. R. Farrant, and H. J. Marchant. 1972. *The Wincroft Youth Project*. London: Tavistock Publications.

Smith, Leslie Shacklady. 1978. "Sexist Assumptions and Female Delinquency." In *Women Sexuality and Social Control*, edited by Carol Smart and Barry Smart. London: Kegan Paul, pp. 74–88.

Smith, Wes. 1987. "4 Guards Are Injured at Pontiac." *Chicago Tribune*, September 17.

Specht, Walter. 1987 (February). Personal communication. Fachhochschule für Socialwesen. Esslingen, Germany.

Spergel, Irving A. 1964. *Slumtown, Racketville, Haulburg*. Chicago: University of Chicago Press.

———. 1966. *Street Gang Work: Theory and Practice*. Reading, MA: Addison-Wesley.

———. 1969. *Community Problem Solving: The Delinquency Example*. Chicago: University of Chicago Press.

―――. 1972. "Community Action Research as a Political Process." In *Community Organization: Studies in Constraint*, edited by Irving A. Spergel. Beverly Hills, CA: Sage Publications, pp. 231–262.

―――. 1976. "Interactions Between Community Structure, Delinquency, and Social Policy in the Inner City." In *The Juvenile Justice System*, edited by Malcolm W. Klein. Beverly Hills, CA: Sage Publications, pp. 55–99.

―――. 1983. *Violent Gangs in Chicago: Segmentation and Integration.* Chicago: University of Chicago, School of Social Service Administration.

―――. 1984. "Violent Gangs in Chicago: In Search of Social Policy." *Social Service Review* 58 (June).

―――. 1985. *Youth Gang Activity and the Chicago Public Schools.* Chicago: University of Chicago, School of Social Service Administration.

―――. 1986. "The Violent Gang in Chicago: A Local Community Approach." *Social Service Review* 60 (March).

―――. 1992a (January). *Community Mobilization.* Technical Assistance Manual. Chicago: University of Chicago, School of Social Service Administration.

―――. 1992b. "Youth Gangs: An Essay Review." *Social Service Review* 6(1):121–140.

―――, and Ron L. Chance. 1990 (January). *Community and Institutional Responses to the Youth Gang Problem.* Chicago: School of Social Service Administration, University of Chicago.

―――, and G. David Curry. 1988 (November). *Socialization to Gangs.* Baseline Preliminary Report. Chicago: University of Chicago School of Social Science Administration.

―――, and G. David Curry, with Ruth E. Ross and Ron L. Chance. 1990 (April). *Survey of Youth Gang Problems and Programs in 45 Cities and 6 Sites.* Chicago: University of Chicago, School of Social Service Administration.

―――, and Mary Ann Hartnett. 1990 (March). *Evaluation of the Illinois Department of Children and Family Services (DCFS) Comprehensive Community-Based Youth Service System (CCBYS).* Chicago: Chapin Hall for Children.

―――, with Castellano Turner, John Pleas, and Patricia Brown. 1969. *Youth Manpower: What Happened in Woodlawn.* Chicago: University of Chicago Press.

Spielman, Fran. 1993. "Police Ignore Gang Law Ruling." *Chicago Sun-Times*, October 1, p. 12.

Stark, Evan. 1981. "Gangs and Progress: The Contribution of Delinquency to Progressive Reform." In *Crime and Capitalism: Readings in Marxist Criminology*, edited by David F. Greenberg. New York: Mayfield Publishing Company, pp. 435–481.

Stein, Sharman. 1992. "No Surprises in Revamp for Police." *Chicago Tribune*, Sec. 2, p. 6.

Sullivan, Mercer L. 1983. "Youth Crime: New York's Two Varieties." *New York Affairs. Crime and Criminal Justice* 8(1):31–48.

―――. 1989. *"Getting Paid" Youth Crime and Work in the Inner City.* Ithaca, NY: Cornell University Press.

Summerhays, J. Jay, and Kenneth D. Lindbloom. 1989. "The Need for Better Police-School Relations." *The Police Chief*, November, pp. 69–70.

Sung, Betty Lee. 1977. *Gangs in New York's Chinatown.* New York: Department of Asian Studies, City College of New York, Monograph No. 6.

Sutherland, Edwin, and Donald R. Cressey. 1978. *Principles of Criminology.* 10th ed. New York: J.B. Lippincott.

Suttles, Gerald D. 1968. *The Social Order of the Slum.* Chicago: University of Chicago Press.

Taylor, Carl S. 1988. "Youth Gangs Organize for Power, Money." *School Safety*, Spring: 26–27.

————. 1990a. *Dangerous Society*. East Lansing, MI: Michigan State University Press.

————. 1990b. "Gang Imperialism." In *Gangs in America*, edited by C. Ronald Huff. Newbury Park, CA: Sage Publication, pp. 103–115.

————. 1993. *Girl Gangs, Women and Drugs*. East Lansing, MI: Michigan State University Press.

Tennyson, May A. 1967. "Family Structure and Delinquent Behavior." In *Juvenile Gangs in Context*, edited by M. W. Klein and B. G. Meyerhoff. Englewood Cliffs, NJ: Prentice-Hall.

Terhune, Clarence. 1988 (June). "Statement." Coordinating Council Meeting, Washington, DC: U.S. Department of Justice, Office of Juvenile Justice and Delinquency Prevention.

Testa, Mark. 1988 (August). Personal communication. University of Chicago, School of Social Service Administration.

Thomas, William Isaac, and Florian Znaniecki. 1918. *The Polish Peasant in Europe and America*. Chicago: University of Chicago Press.

Thornberry, Terence P., Alan J. Lizotte, Marvin D. Krohn, Margaret Farnworth, and Sung Joon Jang. 1994. "Delinquent Peers, Beliefs, and Delinquent Behavior: A Longitudinal Test of Interactional Theory." *Criminology* 32(1):47–83.

Thrasher, Frederic M. 1927, 1936. *The Gang*, 2d rev. ed. Chicago: University of Chicago Press.

Tijerina, Edmund S., and Rob Karwath. 1991. "Violence at Stateville Blamed on City Gang." *Chicago Tribune*, July 16, Sec. 2, p. 1.

Toby, J. 1983. "Violence in School." In *Crime and Justice: An Annual Review of Research*, Vol. 4, edited by Michael Tonry and Norval Morris. Chicago: University of Chicago Press.

Tocqueville, Alexis de. 1954. *Democracy in America*. Edited and abridged by Richard D. Heffner. New York: New American Library (Mentor).

Torres, Dorothy M. 1980. *Gang Violence Reduction Project Evaluation Report*. Sacramento: California Youth Authority.

————. 1985 (June). "Gang Violence Reduction Project Update." Sacramento: California Department of the Youth Authority Program Research and Review Division.

Tracy, Paul E. 1982. "Gang Membership and Violent Offenders: Preliminary Results from the 1958 Cohort Study." Philadelphia: Center for Studies in Criminology and Criminal Law, University of Pennsylvania.

————. 1987. "Race and Class Differences in Official and Self-reported Delinquency." In *From Boy to Man, From Delinquency to Crime*, edited by Marvin E. Wolfgang, Terrence F. Thornberry, and Robert M. Figlio. Chicago: University of Chicago Press.

————, Marvin E. Wolfgang, and Robert M. Figilo. 1990. *Delinquency Careers in Two Birth Cohorts*. New York: Plenum.

Trojanowicz, Robert C. 1990. "Community Policing Is not Police-Community Relations." *FBI Law Enforcement Bulletin*, October, pp. 6–11.

U.S. Department of Labor. 1990. "Youth Opportunities Unlimited Challenge Program." Request for proposal.

Utne, M. K., and McIntyre, L. J. 1982. *Violent Juvenile Offenders on Probation in Cook County*. Chicago: Public Affairs Research Practicum, University of Chicago Press.

Vigil, James Diego. 1988a. "Street Socialization, Locura Behavior, and Violence Among Chicano Gang Members." In *Violence and Homicide in Hispanic Communities*, edited by Jess Kraus and Armando Morales. Washington, DC: National Institute of Mental Health.

————. 1988b. *Barrio Gangs: Street Life and Identity in Southern California*. Austin: University of Texas Press.

————. 1990. "Cholos and Gangs: Culture Change and Street Youth in Los Angeles." In *Gangs in America*, edited by C. Ronald Huff. Newbury Park, CA: Sage Publications, pp. 116–128.

————. 1992. "Preface." In *Substance Abuse and Gang Violence*, edited by Richard C. Cervantes. Newbury Park, CA: Sage Publications.

————, and John M. Long. 1990. "Emic and Etic Perspectives on Gang Culture: The Chicano Case." In *Gangs in America*, edited by C. Ronald Huff. Newbury Park, CA: Sage Publications, pp. 55–70.

————, and Steve Chong Yun. 1990. "Vietnamese Youth Gangs in Southern California." In *Gangs in America*, edited by C. Ronald Huff. Newbury Park, CA: Sage Publications, pp. 146–162.

Vogel, Ed. 1991. "Experts Tell How to Curb Youth Gangs." *Las Vegas Review Journal*, October 8, p. 1B.

Waldorf, Dan. 1993. "When the CRIPS Invaded San Francisco—Gang Migration." *Home Boy* Study. Alameda, CA: Institute for Scientific Analysis, August 1.

Washington, Erwin. 1988. "Despite Violence Official Response to Drug Connection Was Slow." *Los Angeles Daily News*, April 24.

Westerman, Ted W., and James W. Burfeind. 1991. *Crime and Justice in Two Societies. Japan and the United States.* Pacific Grove, CA: Brooks/Cole Publishing Company.

Whyte, William F. 1943. *Street Gang Society.* Chicago: University of Chicago Press.

Whyte, William Foote, and Kathleen King Whyte. 1991. *Making Mondragon.* 2nd ed. rev. Ithaca, NY: ILR Press, Cornell International Industrial and Labor Relations Report, November 14.

Wilkerson, Isabel. 1991. "Crack Hits Chicago's Streets, Along with a Wave of Killing." *The New York Times*, September 24, pp. 1, A14.

Williams, Terry M. 1989. *The Cocaine Kids: The Inside Story of a Teenage Drug Ring.* Reading, MA: Addison-Wesley.

————, and William Kornblum. 1985. *Growing Up Poor.* Lexington, MA: Lexington Books.

Willman, Mark T., and John R. Snortum. 1982. "A Police Program for Employment of Youth Gang Members." *International Journal of Offender Therapy and Comparative Criminology* 26(3):207–214.

Wilson, James W., and Kelling, G. L. 1982. "Broken Windows: The Police and Neighborhood Safety." *Atlantic Monthly*, March, pp. 29–38.

Wilson, John J. 1993. "A National Agenda for Children: On The Front Lines with Attorney General Janet Reno." *Juvenile Justice* 1(2):pp. 2–8.

Wilson, Terry. 1992. "Court Told Details of Stabbing." *Chicago Tribune*, February 9, Sec. 2, p. 10.

Wilson, William J. 1987. *The Truly Disadvantaged: The Inner City, The Underclass, and Public Policy.* Chicago: University of Chicago Press.

————. 1991. "Public Policy Research and the Truly Disadvantaged." In *The Urban Underclass*, edited by Christopher Jencks and Paul E. Peterson. Washington, DC: The Brookings Institution, pp. 460–481.

Worthington, Rogers. 1991. "Minneapolis Enlists Gang Members' Help." *Chicago Tribune.* December 15. Sec. 1, pp. 29, 32.

Yablonsky, Lewis. 1962. *The Violent Gang.* New York: MacMillan.

Youth Today. 1992. "Youth Services Receive $63 Million Boost." *Youth Today* 1(7):22.

Zlobin, Nikolai. 1994. "The Mafiocracy Takes Over." *The New York Times*, July 26. Op Ed, p. A15.

Index

Administration on Children, Youth, and Families (ACYF), 294. *See also* Health and Human Services, Department of
African-American gangs. *See* Black gangs
Agency/community fragmentation. *See* Social disorganization
AmeriCorps, 277
American Civil Liberties Union, 198
American Correctional Association, 244
American Nazi Party, 66
Anderson, Elijah, 62, 95, 150, 273
Arellano drug lords, 132
Asbury, Herbert, 7, 8
Asian Advisory Committee on Crime, 201
Asian gangs, 10, 67–68, 153. *See also* Chinese gangs
   and behavioral differences with other non-Asian gangs, 68
   and criminal organization connections, 138–40
   distinctive ethnic patterns of, 68
   settlement patterns of, 67–68
Associated Press, 4
At-risk youth, 90

Balkans (gang), 85, 250
BATF, 190, 194
   and gang information systems, 195
Baugh, Dennis G., 22
Berkeley, Bill, 138
Berlin, Gordon, and Andrew Sum, 263, 264, 266, 273
Black gangs, vii, 10, 62–63, 73–74, 92, 93, 95, 106, 135–37, 153, 274. *See also* Corporate gangs
   and blocked legitimate opportunities, 62–63
   and corporate crime, 63, 74
   as drug entrepreneurs, 134–37
   rewards of membership in, 135
Black Gangster Disciples, 121, 122–23
Black Mafia, 133
Black Muslims, 282
Black P Stone Nation, 135
Blackstone Rangers, 123, 135, 136, 191
Blau, Robert, and John O'Brien, 135

Block, Alan A., 130
Block, Carolyn B., 37, 52
   and Richard Block, 53
Bloods, 81, 98
Bobrowski, Lawrence J., 33–34, 52, 57, 64, 80
Booz, Allen, and Hamilton study, 193–94
Boyle Heights, 155
Boys' Club of San Gabriel Valley, 278
Brother Modesto Leon, 284
Buhmann, Elizabeth T., 21
Bureau of Alcohol, Tobacco, and Firearms. *See* BATF
Bureau of Justice Assistance, 202, 293, 294
Burrell, Susan, 215, 227
Bursik, Robert J., Jr., and Harold G. Grasmick, 110, 154, 173, 253
Butterfield, Fox, 127

California Department of Corrections, 288
California Office of Criminal Justice Planning, 288
California Office of Justice Programs, 6
California Youth Authority, 288
   Gang Service Project, 243
   Gang Violence Reduction Project, 244, 251, 286
   Information Parole Coordinators, 245
California Youth Group Services (CYGS), 255
Calle Treinta street gang, 132
Camp, Camille Graham, and George M. Camp, 127, 238
Camp, George M., and Camille Graham Camp, 42, 127
Campbell, Anne, 93
Caplan, Nathan S., 278
CETA (Comprehensive Employment Training Act), 275
Chein, I., D. L. Gerard, R. S. Lee, and E. Rosenfeld, 44
Chicago Area Project, 172
Chicago Boys' Club, 249
Chicago Police Department Gang Intelligence Unit, 191, 193, 204
Chicago early intervention school project, 270–71

Chicago Sun-Times, 33
Chicago Youth Development Project (CYDP), 249
Chin, Ko-Lin, 73, 93, 101, 140, 157, 273
Chinese gangs, 67–68, 73, 92, 101. *See also* Asian gangs, Chinese
    behavior variation across cities, 139–40
    immigration of, 156
    and integration with Tongs, 140
Chinese-American gangs. *See* Chinese gangs
Chinn, Ignatius, 201
Choloization, 155
Citizen participation, 172, 175
Civilian Conservation Corps (CCC), 257, 277
Cloward, Richard A., and Lloyd E. Ohlin, 14, 44, 146–47
Cohen, Albert K., and James F. Short, Jr., 14
Cohen, Stanley, 20, 191
Coleman, James S., 160
Collins, H. Craig, 204
Comer, James
    School Development Program of, 265
Commission on National and Community Service, 257
Community mobilization, viii, 171, 172–74, 184. *See also* Community policy and program structure
    and coalitions of agencies, community groups, and gang members, 174, 281–87
    and community youth organizations, 285–87
    and current policy planning, 291–92, 295
    definition of, 262
    and East Los Angeles experience, 283–84
    and federal policy coordination, 293–95
    and "implant" hypothesis, 282
    integrated into provision of social opportunities, 262, 275–76
    limits of, 284–85
    a national comprehensive approach to, 290–95
    planning process summary (Appendix A), 297–98
    and specification of gang problem elements, 178–81
    state level, 287–90
    testing the model of, 187
Community organizing. *See* Community mobilization; Social disorganization
Community planning, 178–87. *See also* Community mobilization
Community policing, 200–6
    collaboration with local citizens, 201
    collaboration with other justice system elements, 201
    effectiveness, 205–6
    purpose, 201
    role of the officer in, 204–5
    strategy, 201–202
Community policy and program structure, 181–84. *See also* Community mobilization
    chronic problem context, 183–84

emerging problem context, 182–83
    and labeling, 186
    setting priorities for, 187
    strategies for, 184–86
    and targeting, viii, 171, 186–87
Concerned Parents Group of Los Angeles, 284
Conflict subculture
    and relation to criminal subculture, 132
Corporate gangs, 63. *See also* Black gangs
Corrections, 235–43. *See also* Prison gangs
    as a gang deviancy amplifying system, 235
    institutional responsibilities of, 236
Council of Social and Athletic Clubs, New York City Youth Board, 18
Court. *See also* Judges
    certification of juveniles to adult court, 221–22
    detaining gang youth, 222
    evidence against gang members, 223
    hearings, 222–23
    lack of resources, 221
    orders, 224–25
    placement of gang youth in institutions, 225–226
    placement on probation, 224–25
    review, 226–27
    sentencing, 223–24
    trial and appellate decisions, 227
"CRASH," 192–93
Crawford, Paul Z., Daniel I. Malamud, and James R. Dumpson, 173
Criminal justice definition(s) of gang
    California penal code, 21
    Chicago City Council, 21
    cross-city comparison of, 21
    Florida Street Terrorism Act, 21
    Texas legislature, 21
Criminal opportunities
    community location and, 129–31
    race and ethnic status of, 129
CRIPS, 53, 77, 81, 98, 103, 227
Crisis Intervention, 257. *See also* Social Intervention
Crisis Intervention Network. *See* Philadephia Crisis Intervention Network
Cummings, D. Brian, 201
Curry, C. David, and Irving A. Spergel, 23, 112

Daley, Richard J., Mayor, 251
DARE (Drug Awareness Resistance Education), 270, 272
Data limitations, 12–14, 15
    of federal policy, 12
    of law enforcement, 12
    of media reporting, 12, 13
Davidson, John L., 192
Davis, Robert, 131
DEA, 190, 194
    and gang information systems, 195
Decentralized local welfare councils, 172
De Concini federal gang tracking bill, 195, 291

Defense attorneys, 216–217
"discovery" of police records, 217
gang cases, 208
and gang member labeling, 216
use of evidence, 217
De La Rosa, Mario, Elizabeth Y. Lambert, and
Bernard Gropper, 50
Delfs, Robert, 5, 124
Delinquency. *See also* Organized crime;
Gang(s)
and gang development, 113
Dellios, Hugh, 132
Desegregation, vii, viii, 10
and gang development, 158–59
Dominican posse (gangs), 95, 138
Draper Hall Experiment, 241–42
effects of, 242–43
Drug Enforcement Administration. *See* DEA
Drug trafficking, vii, 10. *See also* Gang drug
use and trafficking; Gang homicide(s)
augmenting public aid, 133
capacity of youth gangs, 47, 48–49
and changes in economy, 45, 49–50
and criminal organization, 47–49, 50
increase, 45–46
Juvenile and Family Court judges'
perceptions of, 51
Drug Treatment Boot Camp (DTBC), 231
Drug use. *See* Gang drug use
Duane County Juvenile Court Prevention
Program, 278
Dunston, Leonard G., 20, 48, 161, 204, 258
Duxbury, Elaine B., 238

East Los Angeles, 155
East Los Angeles Skills Center, 271
Ecological theory, 110, 112
Eight Tray Gangsters, 103
El Monte Police Department, Community
relations unit, 278
El Monte "Project Return," 234
El Rukns. *See* Rukns
English, T. J., 134
Erikson, Erik, 169

Fagan, Jeffrey, 46, 71, 76–77, 283
Faison, Seth, 48
Family disorganization, 113–16, 159–63, 172
and gang development, 159
and gang member distress, 160
and inadequate youth supervision, 114, 115
as insufficient to explain gang problem, 113–
15
Family/Parent Programs, 258–59. *See also*
Social Intervention
Fattah, David, 253
Fattah, Sister Falaka, 17
FBI, 190, 194
and gang information systems, 195
Federal Bureau of Investigation. *See* FBI
Federacion de Barrios Unidos, 286

Female gang member, 38–40, 90, 96, 101. *See
also* Gang socio-demographic changes;
Leaving the gang; Gang structure
and next generation, 108
First Presbyterian Church, 136
Five Points district, 7
Folks (gang), 80
Ford Foundation, 176
Fort, Jeff, 135, 136
Free Puerto Rico Movement, 123
Friedman, C. Jack, Frederica Mann, and Alfred
S. Friedman, 41

Gallagher, James P., 4
Gang Alternative and Prevention Program
(GAPP), 231, 234
Gang(s). *See also* Youth gangs
as adaptive to social needs, 174
African-American. *See* Black gangs
Boryokudan, 5
Bowery Boys, 7
Cambodian, 68, 95
Chinese. *See* Chinese gangs
and community development, 123–24
concentration in certain neighborhoods, 112
Continentals, 92
contemporary, 9–11
Dead Rabbits, 7
distinct from delinquent group, viii, 13, 22
function, viii, 257–58
German, 4, 8
Hate, 62
Hispanic. *See* Hispanic gangs
Hmong, 68
Hong Kong, 68
and immigrants. *See* Immigration and gangs
as interstitial structures, 172
Japanese, 68
Juvenile, 55
Khmer, 68
Ku Klux Klan, 7
Laotian, 68
Latino. *See* Hispanic gangs
London, 3
Mafia, 8, 81
Moscow, 4
and neo-Nazi movement, 4
New Zealand, 6
and non-gang crime rate, 154
Pacific Island, 67–68
Papua, New Guinea, 6
perceptions of, 17–18
and politicians. *See* Politicians
providing social structure for you'
"Rascals," 6
and right wing activities, 4
Roach Guards, 7
Samoan, 68
size, 82–83
Skinheads. *See*
and social isolati

Gang(s) (*continued*)
  and social movements, 121, 123–24
  Spades, 75
  Taiwanese, 68, 138–39
  True Blue Americans, 7
  and urban development, 173
  undocumented Latin American, 10
  and union leaders, 8
  in the United States before 1900, 6–9
  and urban riots, 121
  and value transformation, 174
  Vietnamese, 68
  White. *See* White gangs
  Yakuza. *See* Yakuza
  Yamaguchi-gumi, 5
  Youth. *See* Youth gangs
Gang behavior
  and managing status, 99–100
  paradigm, 99
  and status threat, 99–100
  variability, 103–4
Gang cliques, 81–83
Gang cohesion, 98–113. *See also* Street-gang
    work
  and delinquency, 98, 100–3
  and social control, 101–102
  and status seeking, 98–99
  and violent behavior, 98–100
Gang conceptualization, 14–16
Gang definition(s). *See also* Criminal justice
    definition(s) of gang: Gang incident
    definition; Gang member definition;
    Glossary; Prison gang definition
  street, 25
  suggested, 22–23
  variations by city, 24
  variations by organizations, 24
  youth gang, 25. *See also* Youth gangs
Gang development and the local community,
    111–13
Gang/Drug-Pushers Project, 231
Gang drug use and trafficking, 8, 50–53
  distinctions, 46, 48
  function, 44–45
  historical perspectives, 43–45
  prevalence among gang and non-gang youths,
    45–46
  in prison population, 46
  race/ethnic differences, 53–54
Gang Event Response Team, 203
Gang files, 195–97
  expunging of, 196–97
  racism in, 197
Gang homicide(s). *See also* Gang problem;
    Violence
  age differences, 38–40
  Black victims, 37–39
  Chicago, 37–40
  d drug wars, 194
  res, 37, 38, 39
  nic victims, 38–39

  in Los Angeles, 39
  male-female differences, 38–40
  in prison, 36
  rates, 40
  table, 40
  trends, 37
  White victims, 38, 39
Gang incident definition, 12, 14. *See also* Gang
    definition
  changing, 20
  type of, 178, 179–80
Gang information systems, 13. *See also* Police
    data (systems); Data limitations
Gang initiations, 91
"Gangland," 111
Gang leader(s), 85–87, 134. *See also* Gang
    member(s), core
  and use in contract killing, 133
  in prison, as role models, 127
  titles, 86
Gang member(s)
  adaptation to social conditions, 165–67
  as aspiring politicians, 121–22
  associate, 85
  behavior, 20
  as both drug dealer and gang fighter, 133
  cognitive development of, 164
  as community leaders, 173
  core, 84, 85–87
  as data source, 115
  defiant character of, 91–92, 104, 163, 169
  definition, 12. *See the* Glossary
  and family drug connections, 133–34
  fidelity, 169
  floater, 85
  intellectual development, 163–65
  as maladjusted, 167–68, 169
  motivation of, 163
  need for social order, 168–69
  peripheral, 85
  personal disorganization, 163–69
  personality, 86–87, 165
  position and role, 75, 85
  protecting drug dealers, 133
  psychological liabilities of, 166
  as psychopath, 168
  as racketeer, 134
  recruitment, 97–98
  and social control perspective, 167–68
  street intelligence, 164
  types of, 83–85
  veteran, 85
  wannabe, 85
Gang organization. *See also* Gang cliques
  as alien to community, 112
  character, 70
  and classification schemes, 79
  coalition, 8
  and community, 70, 79
  and competitive advantage, 112
  corporate, 73, 74, 77–78

and criminal opportunities, 78–79
development, 70–74
and differential community structures, 72–73, 76, 77
as diffuse, 74–75, 80, 101
and female auxiliary, 82, 101
function of, 70, 72
horizontal, 25–76, 78
limits of idea of, 79–81
and member race/ethnicity, 78–79
as a network, 82
as rational, 77
and relation to delinquent patterns, 70
self-contained, 76
symbolism, 97–98
transformation of, 74, 88–89
types of, 75, 76–77, 79
vertical, 75, 78
Gang problem
and absence of father, 115
agency explanation of, 159
approach, 292
assessment, 171, 299
chronic, 24, 178, 180–81
decline of, 29
and defective families, 110, 112, 113–16. *See also* Family disorganization
and defective schools, 110, 112, 116–20. *See also* Schools
definition of, 12, 19–20, 171. *See also* Gang definition
denial of, 12
in different size cities, 26, 27
and distinctive cultural factors, 115
emerging, 24, 178, 180–81
explanation of, 116
exploitation of, 159. *See also* Gang symbolism
and family socialization, 115
growth in, 26, 27, 28, 29, 35
and gun control, 292
increase in youth gang violence, 33–36
increasing severity of, 10
law enforcement and other observer estimates of, 29–30
and media responsibility for, 291
and numbers of gang members, 27–30
and numbers of youth gangs, 27–30
in other countries, 3–6
and percentage of youth gang members, 30–33
and politics, 120–25. *See also* Politicians
and prevention, 292–93
in prisons and jails, 27, 30. *See also* Security Threat Groups
and racism, 31–32. *See also* Racism
in rural areas, 26
in schools, 27, 30. *See also* Schools; School gang approaches
solution to, 22–23
spread of, 8

Gang Risk Intervention Pilot Program (GRIPP), 272
Gangs and class. *See also* Gang socio-demographic changes
lower class, 60
middle class, 60–61
Gangs and drug dealers
symbiosis of, 135
Gang socio-demographic changes, 55–61, 75
Gang structure. *See* Gang organization; Gang cliques
Gang subcultures, 61–68
Gang summits, 252, 254, 286–87
Gang symbolism
exploited by business, 130–31
exploited by media, 130
and graffiti, 98
and search for honor, 97–98
Gang territory, 87–89
and competition over resources, 88–89
and competition over status, 88–89
warfare over, 87–88
Gang violence, 37–40, 103–4. *See also* Gang problem
California prison study of, 42
control of, 173
drug use and trafficking, related to, 50–54
gang–non-gang member patterns, 40–42
in Los Angeles, 41–42
Philadelphia studies of, 41
as preparation for drug trafficking career, 54
and socialization theory, 165–67
Gang Violence Reduction Program, vii, 203–4
Gang Violence Reduction Project. *See* California Youth Authority
Gang Violence Suppression Program, California, 288
Gangster Disciples, 77
Gates, Daryl, 190
Genelin, Michael, and Loren Naimen, 209
General Accounting Office, 49
"GET," 193
Glossary, 309–12
Goering, Lawrie, and Flynn McRoberts, 130
Gold, Martin, and Hans W. Mattick, 249
Goldberg, Danny, 227
Goldstein, Arnold P., Barry Glick, Wilam Carthon, and Douglas Blancero, 253
Goldstein, Henry, 200
Goldstein, Paul J., 50
Gonzalez, David, 65
Gordon, Robert A., 166
Gottfredson, Gary D., 256
and Denise Gottfredson, 265
Graffiti, 87, 98. *See also* Gang symbolism; Gang territory
Grant, William T., 264, 277
GRATS (Gang Related Active Trafficking System), 196
GREAT (Gang Reporting Evaluation and Tracking), 211

Group Guidance Project, 230, 250
Group processes, 20, 96–104
Guardian Angels, 282

Hagedorn, John, 45, 47, 158–59
Hahn, Andrew, and Jacqueline Danziger, with
    Bernard Lefkowitz, 264, 276
Hairston, Gene, 135
Hamilton Park, 274
Hard Core Gang Division of the Los Angeles
    County District Attorney's Office, 210,
    213. *See also* Prosecution; Vertical gang
    prosecution
Hargrove, Sergeant James, 191
Haskins, James, 6, 7, 8
Hawkins, Earl, 137, 258
Head Start, 176, 266
Health and Human Services (HHS), U. S.
    Department of, 257, 258, 293, 294–95
Hispanic gangs, vii, 10, 92, 93, 95, 103, 125,
    137, 153, 155, 274
    and Chicano gang tradition, 63–64
    and criminal organization connections, 137–
    38
    and drug organization recruitment, 137, 138
    and new waves of immigrants, 64
Hispanic Mafia, 133. *See also* Mexican drug
    lords; Mexican Mafia
Horowitz, Ruth, 19, 106
Humboldt Park gang program, 255
Hunt, Geoffrey, Stephanie Riegel, Tomas
    Morales, and Dan Waldorf, 235
Housing and Urban Development (HUD), 174,
    257, 293
Houston, Jack, 202
Hyman, Irwin A., 6

Ianni, Francis A. J., 129, 133, 169, 292–93
Illinois Department of Children and Family
    Services, 289–90
Illinois Department of Commerce and
    Community Affairs, 289
Illinois Department of State Police, 289–90
Illinois State Board of Education, 290
Immigration and gangs, viii, 6, 8, 73, 156, 172.
    See also Asian gangs; Chinese gangs;
    Gang(s); Hispanic gangs
Immigration and Naturalization Service (INS),
    194
Inner City Round Table on Youth (ICRY), 203,
    285
Innovative prosecution tactics. *See* Prosecution
Institute for Law and Justice, 22, 52, 211, 212,
    213
Integrated Criminal Apprehension Program, 202
Irish gangs, 123
    and organized crime, 134
    running guns to Catholics of Northern
    Ireland, 134
ISP (Intensively Supervised Probation
    Program), 231

Jacobs, James B., 101
Jankowski, Martin Sánchez, 20, 78, 91, 94, 97,
    134
Jansyn, Leon R., Jr., 102
Japanese Ministry of Justice, 5
JHERI Kurls, 138
Job Corps, 135, 176, 177, 275, 277
Joining the gang, 90–96
    for fun, 93–94
    individual motivations in, 91–96, 101
    for money making, 94
    for personal safety (protection), 92–93
    for psychological support, 101
    reasons for, 90–91
    risk factors for, 90–91
    for status (honor), 97, 98–99
    as a substitute family, 94–96
Jouzaitis, Carol, 277
JTPA (Job Training Partnership Act), 274, 275,
    277
Judges. *See also* Court
    attention to gang problem, 219–27
    use of a coordinated rehabilitation approach
    by, 220
Juvenile gangs, 55. *See also* Gang(s); Youth
    gangs

Kahn, Brian, and R. Neil Zinn, 252
Kass, John, and George Papajohn, 123
Kent, 221–22
Kifner, John K., 156
Kinzer, Stephen, 5
Klein, Malcolm W., 18, 22, 76, 102, 168, 230,
    248, 250
    and Lois Y. Crawford, 102
    and Cheryl L. Maxson, Lea C. Cunningham,
    49, 52
    and Cheryl L. Maxson, Margaret A. Gordon,
    199
Knopf, Terry Ann, 286
Knox, George W., 235
Korean gangs, 138
Kornblum, William S., 121
Kornhauser, Ruth R., 18
Krisberg, Barry, 151
Ku Klux Klan, 66

Labor, Department of, 176, 257
Ladino Hills, 102
La Raza Movement, 123
Latin Kings, 81
Latino gangs. *See* Hispanic gangs
Lauderback, David, Joy Hansen, and Dan
    Waldorf, 58
Laurie, Bruce E., 120
Law enforcement task forces, 177
Leaving the gang, 104–8
    and availability of legitimate opportunities,
    106–7
    and battle fatigue, 105
    females, 107–8

influence of female on male in, 108
and "maturing out," 104–5
and position of gang member, 105–6. See *also* Gang organization
and religious conversion, 107
Levitan, Sar A., and Frank Gallo, 274, 275, 276
Lieber, J. B., 190
Local community mobilization. *See* Community mobilization
Local school programs. *See* Social Opportunities Provision, at school micro level
Lockwood, William, 243–44
Locura, 103–4, 168
Los Angeles City Police Department, 190, 192–3, 194, 196, 197. *See also* Police
Los Angeles County Probation Department, 229–32
Los Angeles County Probation Group Guidance Project. *See* Group Guidance Project
Los Angeles County Sheriff's Department, 192, 193, 195, 284. *See also* Police
Los Angeles Reclamation Project (CRP), 284
Los Angeles Riot, 256
Los Angeles Unified School District, 270, 271
Lower class theory, 148–49

Machismo, 103, 104, 168
MacLaren School, 243, 244
Mafia, 136, 138, 156
"Mains 21," 136
Mainstreaming, 239, 263
Maxson, Cheryl L., and Malcolm W. Klein, 21
and Margaret A. Gordon, Malcolm W. Klein, 41–42
McBride, Wesley D., 195, 205
McGarry, T. W., and Steve Padilla, 198
McKenna, George, 270
Merton, Robert K., 146, 147
Metropolitan Court Judges Committee, 51, 219–20
Mexican drug lords. *See also* Organized crime
and U.S. youth gangs, 132
Mexican gangs. *See* Hispanic gangs
Mexican-American gangs. *See* Hispanic gangs
Mexican Mafia, 125, 252
Miller, Benjamin, 227
Miller, Jeffrey, 285
Miller, Walter, 9, 13, 18, 23, 88, 148, 163, 249, 290, 291
Moore, Joan W., 14, 44, 51, 72, 74, 95, 103, 106, 107, 108, 113, 114, 148, 152
Moorish Science Temple, 135
Morales, Armando, and Bradford W. Sheafer, 257, 260
Morningside Heights project, 250
Morris, Norval, and Michael Tonry, 224
Mothers Against Gangs
Chicago, 283
Los Angeles, 283
"Multiple marginality," 151

"Nation" (gang), 80
National Advisory Committee on Criminal Justice Standards and Goals, 9
National Center on Education and the Economy, 263
NCCC (National Civilian Community Corps), 277
National Council of Juvenile and Family Court Judges. *See* Metropolitan Judges Committee
National Data Center, 13. *See also* Data limitations
National Institute of Corrections, 125, 236–37, 240
"National Socialist White Workers Party," 66
National Youth Gang Suppression and Intervention Program, 293
"Near-group," 74
Needle, Jerome A., and William Vaughan Stapleton, 193
Neighborhood Watch, 282
Neighborhood Youth Corps, 277
Neighbors Against Gang Violence, 283
Neo-Nazi, 62
New York City Youth Board, 18, 75, 76, 173, 248, 249
New York Civil War draft riots, 7
"New York State Task Force on Juvenile Gangs," 20

O'Connor, Mike, 6, 134, 136, 137
Office of Economic Opportunity, 173, 176, 251–52
Office of Human Development Services, 174, 294
Office of Juvenile Justice and Delinquency Prevention (OJJDP), vii, 202, 231, 293, 294
Office of National Drug Control Policy, 293
OJJDP News Notes, 277
Opportunity theory, vii, 146–48. *See also* Social opportunities provision
Orange County Probation Department, 233–34
Organizational change strategy, 171, 185
Organized crime
alienation of unemployed males, 132
definitions of, 129. *See also* Criminal justice definition of gang(s)
distinguished from youth gang activity, 130
and youth gang connection, 131–34
Outreach social services, 172–73. *See also* Social intervention

Paramount's "Alternative to Gangs Program," 271–72
Parents Against Gangs, 283, 284
Parents Against Murdered Children, 283
Park, Robert E., and Ernest W. Burgess, 110
Parole—After Care, 243–45
and evaluation of programs of intensive supervision, 245
and problems of coordination, 245

Peace Corps, 277
Pearson, Geoffrey, 3
Peer Group Intervention
    a structural approach, 259. *See also* Social
    Intervention
Pennell, Susan, 255
People (gang), 81
Petersilia, Joan, and Susan Turner, 245
Peterson, Paul E., 148
Philadephia Crisis Intervention Network, 234,
    252, 253–55
Philadelphia Preventive Patrol Unit, 202
Philadelphia Youth Service Corps, 277
Philibosian, Robert H., 194
Pineda, Charles, Jr., 286
Pitchess, Peter J., 155
Police. *See also* Suppression
    acting like another gang, 191
    community approach, 199–200. *See also*
        Community policing
    and communication with gang youth, 204–5
    community mobilization, 203–4
    constitutionality of tactics, 198
    data (systems), 13, 195–97
    educational strategy, 203
    emerging approach, 199–206
    gang job development strategy, 203
    gang unit, 193, 203
    new structures and programs, 202–6
    officer role, 204–5
    organizational arrangement, 192–94
    policy toward gang violence, 190–92
    problem-solving approach, 199–200, 201
    response to gangs, 177
    sharing information across units, 196
    social activities strategy, 203, 204
    sweeps, 197–98
    tactics, 194, 197–98
    traditional strategy, 195
Politicians
    and gang relationships, 8, 120–21, 122–23
Portland school system, 269
Poston, Richard W., 252
Poverty, 281
    "belt," iii
    and high rates of gang crime, 154
    and limited access to opportunities, 61
    -related theories, vii, 145–52
President's Commission on Organized Crime,
    129, 136
President's Committee on Juvenile Delinquency
    and Youth Crime, 147
President's Committee on Juvenile Delinquency
    and Youth Development, 176
Preventive counseling approaches, 247, 255–56
    limitations of, 255–56
Prisons. *See* Corrections; Prison gang(s)
Prison gang(s), 101
    and control of inmates, 126
    collaboration by prison officials with, 126
    definition of, 125. *See also* Gang definition(s)

and deterrence, 127
    in Illinois, 125–26
    and relation to street gangs, 125, 126, 235
Prison gang problem, 42
    approaches to, 236, 237–43
    causes of, 237
    and maintaining social order, 240–41
    reasons for, 236, 237
    screening for, 238–39
    and suppression of, 237–38
Probation
    community based programs, 232–34
    conflicting missions of, 232
    coordination with other agencies, 230, 232,
        233–34
    effects of, 232, 234
    entrepreneurship, 229
    and police "ride alongs," 230
    prevention strategy, 229, 234
    suppression emphasis, 229
Prosecution. *See also* Vertical gang prosecution
    code of responsibility, 209
    and early intervention, 212–13
    gang cases as special problems for, 209–10
    and innovative tactics, 213–16
    and interagency gang task force, 211
    need for a broad approach to, 218–19
    specialized gang strategy, 208, 209–16
Puerto-Rican gangs. *See* Hispanic gangs
"Punks," 61, 62

Quality Education for Minorities Project, 263,
    265

Racism, vii, 161–63
    in black community, 161
    charge and exploitation of gang problem,
        163
    decline of, and increase in gang problem, 162
    definition of, 161
    in Mexican-American community, 161–62
Rand Corporation, 245
Recktenwald, William, 118
Reddick, Alonzo J., 66–67
Regulus, Thomas A., 236, 237, 239
Reiner, Ira, 46, 63, 103, 196, 212, 229, 235,
    260, 278, 279
Reno, Attorney General, 219
Research method, 12, 14–16, 172
RICO (Racketeer Influenced Corrupt
    Organizations), 208, 287
    California, 287–89
    Illinois, 289–90
Robinson, Noah, 136, 137
Rollin' 60's, 103
Roper, Clinton, 6
Rosenbaum, Dennis P., 282
Rossi, Rosalind, 136
Roxbury Project, 248, 249
Royster, Eugene, 252
Rukns, 121, 122, 132, 135–37, 191

Sampson, Robert J., 70–71
and William J. Wilson, 116
SANE (Substance Abuse Narcotics Education), 270
San Jose Youth Conservation Corps, 279
Santa Clara Probation Department, 232–33
Sarnecki, Jerzy, 41
"Satanics," 61, 62
SCAN teams, 260
"Scavenger" groups, 63
Schiller, Steven, Judge, 225
Schools. *See also* School dropout
control of violence in, 173
defects of, and gang problem, viii, 116–20
and gang crime surveys, 116–17
School Crime Suppression Program (SCSP), 231
School dropout
and gangs, 118–20
and later return to school, 119
and school defects, 119–20
School gang approaches. *See also* Social opportunities provision
Chicago's comprehensive proposal for, 271
coordinated, 270
evolving, 270–72
police, 268
preventive, 175, 269–70
security, 269–70
traditional, 268–70
Secret Service, 190, 194
Security Threat Groups, 22
Segmented labor market theory, 147–48
Segregation. *See* Racism
Sentence enhancement, 177
Serious Habitual Offender Comprehension Action Program, 202
Shaw, Clifford R., and Henry D. McKay, 111, 172
Short, James F., Jr., 19, 100, 101, 111, 156
and Fred L. Strodtbeck, 99, 249
Simon City Royals, 81
Skinheads, 5, 23, 62, 123
"SMASH," 193
Smith, Cyril S., M. R. Farrant, and H. J. Marchant, 250
Smith, Leslie, 19
Social disorganization, vii, 3, 110, 281
as agency/community fragmentation, 157–59
and citizen groups, 154
class and, 153–54
and conflict subculture, 111
cultural, 156–57
definition of, 152
degrees of, 111
and gang violence, 112
and "interstitial areas," 111
and lack of integration of institutions, 16
political aspects of, 156–57
population change and, 157
and population movement, 154–57

structural, 156–57
theory, 152–61
Social intervention, 171, 174–76, 185. *See also* Street-gang work
definition of, 247
innovative approaches to, 256–61
new organizational contexts for, 259–62
and problems of coordination, 260
tradition of dealing with gangs, 247
Social opportunities provision, viii, 171, 172, 176–77, 184
definition of, 262
and employment and training strategies, 274–77
and failure of legitimate economy, 273–74
and job placement, 272–73
and remedial education, 275
and lack of jobs, viii
and local employment, 277–79
at macro level employment, 272–77
restructuring schools and, 263–65
at school macro level, 262, 263–67
at school micro level, 262, 267–72
and school models for adolescent gang youths, 266–67
and school models for gang-prone children, 265–66
and school-work linkage, 266–67
and social intervention, 262
and subsidizing employers, 276–77
Soledad Enrichment Action, 284
SPECDA (School Program to Educate Drug Abusers), 268
Spielman, Fran, 198
Spergel, Irving A., 58, 173, 175, 248, 252
and Ron L. Chance, 284
and G. David Curry, 78–79, 271
with Castellano Turner, John Pleas, and Patricia Brown, 252
Stark, Evan, 120
Status seeking
and "rep," 97–99
STEP (The California Street Terrorism Enforcement and Prevention Act), 211, 287
constitutionality of, 217
and deterrent effect, 212
STEP (Summer Training and Education Program), 266
"Stoners," 61, 62
Strain theories, 146–48
Strategic Activities/Structures framework (Appendix C), 301–7
Strategies for dealing with gang problem
historical, 171–78
Street gang. *See* Gang(s); Youth gangs
Street-gang work, 174–76. *See also* Social intervention
and coordinated community approaches, 253–55
critique of, 248, 258
and gang cohesion, 250–51

Street-gang work (*continued*)
  and use of gang structure, 251–53
  values of, 248–49, 249–50, 253, 253–55, 256
Sullivan, Mercer L., 14, 62, 147, 274
Sung, Betty Lee, 161
"Supergang," 80
Suppression, 171, 177, 185
  based on war model, 190, 191, 191–92, 194
  and development of specialized information
    systems, 194–97
  effectiveness of, 198–99
  politics of, 198
  role of judge, 208
  role of prosecution, 208
  traditional approaches to, 189–99
"Supreme White Pride," 66

Targeting. *See* Community policy and program
  structure
Taylor, Carl S., 63, 73, 77–78, 93, 151
Theoretical framework. *See also* Poverty,
  related theories; Social disorganization
  theory
  figure, 145–46
32nd Street gangs, 106
Thrasher, Frederic M., 14, 71–72, 111, 120–21
Tijerina, Edmund S., and Rob Karwath, 126
Tocqueville, Alexis de, 282
Tongs, 68, 139, 140, 167
Torres, Dorothy M., 251
Tracy, Paul E., 41
Triad, 68, 81, 139, 140, 156, 167
Trojanowicz, Robert C., 200
Tweed Ring, 120

UMOJA (House of UMOJA), 253–54
Uncoordinated agency programs. *See* Agency/
  community fragmentation
Underclass theory, vii, 149–52. *See also*
  Poverty, related theories
  critique of, 150, 152
"United in Peace," 286
UNO (United Neighborhood Organization in
  Los Angeles), 283–84
Urban Youth Corps, 177
U. S. Department of Education, 293
U. S. Department of Health and Human
  Services. *See* Health and Human Services
U. S. Department of Labor
  Youth Opportunities Unlimited Challenge
    Program, 276
U. S. Justice Department, 174, 257, 293

Value transformation approach, 250–51
Vertical gang prosecution, 209–13. *See also*
  Prosecution
  efficiency of, 217–18
Vice Lords, 77, 81, 123
Vietnamese gangs, 138–39, 151, 156
Vigil, James Diego, 20, 43, 44–45, 94, 151,
  155, 156, 162, 167, 274
  and Steve Chong Yun, 139, 151

Violence, vii. *See also* Gang(s); Gang cohesion,
  and violent behavior; Gang homicide(s);
  Gang problem
  gang and non-gang comparison, 23
"Violence by Youth Gangs and Youth Groups
  as a Crime Problem in Major American
  Cities," 9
"The Violent Crime and Law Enforcement Act
  of 1994," 189
V.O.T.E., 122–23

Wah Ching, 73, 92
Waldorf, Dan, 54
War on Poverty, 147
Weaponry, vii, 292
"Weed and Seed," 189–90
Westerman, Ted W., and James W. Burfeind, 5
White gang(s), 10, 64–67, 92, 153, 274
  Albanian Boys, 65–66
  changing patterns of, 65
  and disorganized families, 66
  lower middle class origin of, 66, 67
  motorcycle, 67
  skinheads, 66–67
  stoners, 66
  taggers, 66
"White Supremacists," 61
Williams, Terry M., 95, 137, 138, 151–52
Willman, Mark T., and John R. Snortum, 205
Wilson, John, 219
Wilson, William J., 149
Wincroft Youth Project, 250
"Win saik," 273–74
The Woodlawn Organization, 251–52
WPA (Works Progress Administration), 277

Yablonsky, Lewis, 74, 250
Yakuza (gang), 5, 81, 124, 136, 139
  and Liberal Democratic Party (LDP), 124
YMCA, 277–78
YMCA-detached workers, 249
"Young Grassroots Independent Voters," 121–
  22
Young Lords
"The Young Voters of Illinois," 121
Youth agencies, 175. *See also* Social
  intervention
Youth Conservation Corps, 278, 279
Youth gangs. *See also* Gang(s)
  assumption about elimination of, 202
  and increased rationalization of, 132
  as substitutes for employment market, 273–74
Youth Gang Drug Prevention Program, 294
Youth gang problem assessment (Appendix B),
  299
Youth Manpower Project, 251–52
Youth Organizations United, 252
Youth Outreach, 174–76. *See also* Social
  Intervention

Zlobin, Nikolai, 4
Zoot Suit Riots, 230